MUSIC IN THE AGE
OF ANXIETY

MUSIC IN AMERICAN LIFE

*A list of books in the series appears
at the end of this book.*

MUSIC IN THE AGE OF ANXIETY

American Music in the Fifties

JAMES WIERZBICKI

UNIVERSITY OF ILLINOIS PRESS

Urbana, Chicago, and Springfield

1 2 3 4 5 C P 5 4 3 2 1
♾ This book is printed on acid-free paper.
Printed and bound in Great Britain by
Marston Book Services Ltd, Oxfordshire

Library of Congress Cataloging-in-Publication Data
Wierzbicki, James Eugene.
Music in the age of anxiety : American music in the fifties / James
Wierzbicki.
     pages cm
Includes bibliographical references and index.
ISBN 978-0-252-04007-8 (hardcover : alk. paper) —
ISBN 978-0-252-08156-9 (pbk. : alk. paper) —
ISBN 978-0-252-09827-7 (e-book)
1. Music—United States—20th century—History and criticism.
2. Popular music—United States—1951–1960 —History and
criticism. I. Title.
ML3477.W58   2016
781.64097309'045—dc23   2015035754

To my father, Eugene V. Wierzbicki, who suffered through
the Fifties more than he ever let on

Contents

Acknowledgments

Books are hard to write, and surely no book results from its author alone. In the case of this particular book, which was long in the making and whose progress was often interrupted by the exigencies of career and life, the number of facilitators is enormous.

Officially I owe thanks to the University of Sydney and the Sydney Conservatorium of Music for granting me, in the first half of 2014, the SSP (special studies programme) leave that enabled me to finish the damned thing. Officially too, but in a less officious way, I owe thanks to the late Judith McCulloh, who when she was an editor at the University of Illinois Press listened with interest to my original plan and asked exactly the right questions to get me started; to the several anonymous readers who perused the first draft and made valuable comments thereon; to University of Illinois Press editor in chief Laurie Matheson, who convinced me to trim the originally bulky manuscript down to manageable size; and to all the other people at UIP—production managers, art directors, copyeditors—who helped me turn what was once just an idea into an actual book.

Unofficially, but no less importantly, I am indebted to my daughters, Helene and Eva, who over the course of numerous summer vacations endured my endless babbling about the long-ago Fifties and who, in spite of that, helped me build my small but inspirational collection of Elvis impersonators (not mere statues of Elvis, which are ubiquitous in American gift shops and a dime a dozen no matter what their price, but those rare and thus invaluable figurines of rubber chickens, zombies, etc., made up to somehow "look" like Elvis); to my many students and former students at both the University of

Michigan and the University of Sydney who found the concept of a book on the whole of American music in the anxious Fifties to be, at the very least, intriguing; and to my colleagues at these same institutions who, whenever the going got tough, commiserated. The students and former students at Michigan and Sydney to whom I owe real thanks include Dan Blim, Rebecca Fülöp, Sarah Gerk, Jessica Getman, Iain Hart, Anthony Linden Jones, Natalie Matias, Craig Morgan, Nathan Platte, Steven Reale, Colin Roust, and Evan Ware. The supportive colleagues certainly include Christopher Coady, Richard Cohn, Jason Geary, David Larkin, Cynthia Marin, and Joseph Toltz, but most special among them—because of her rare combination of strength and wisdom—is the incomparable Helen Mitchell.

MUSIC IN THE AGE
OF ANXIETY

Prologue

Having enlisted in the Navy during his sophomore year at
a Mid-Western university, he suffered from that anxiety
about himself and his future which haunts, like a bad
smell, the minds of most young men, though most of
them are under the illusion that their lack of confidence
is a unique and shameful fear which, if confessed,
would make them an object of derision to their normal
contemporaries.

—W. H. Auden, *The Age of Anxiety: A Baroque Eclogue*

It was a time when the American nation, ostensibly united through its war-time concerns and efforts, found itself riven by conflict. In the self-proclaimed "land of the free" the march toward racial integration was inexorable, yet on numerous fronts the civil rights movement triggered battles as bitter as any fought during World War II. Married couples achieved the "American dream" of life in the suburbs, but many of them suffered nightmares triggered by rampant consumerism, mind-dulling conformity, and psychologically erosive feelings of sexual inadequacy. Although the economy roared in a way that had not been witnessed since the 1920s, the nation's prosperity was clouded over by mortal fear of nuclear holocaust. For many reasons, Americans were decidedly uneasy during the "long" decade of the Fifties, by which is meant not simply the ten years between 1950 and 1959 but, rather, the bomb-focused postwar period that began, obviously, with atomic explosions over Hiroshima and Nagasaki in August 1945 and ended, supposedly, when the United States and the Soviet Union, along with England, in July 1963 signed the first limited nuclear test-ban treaty. And what bothered Americans during this painfully protracted time for the most part went unspoken.

In 1946, seven years after he took up residence in the United States and one year before he became an American citizen, W. H. Auden wrote a book-length prose poem titled *The Age of Anxiety: A Baroque Eclogue*. In this work

Auden reflected on World War I, the global economic depression of the 1930s, and the horrific devastations that wracked Europe and Asia during World War II; the symbol-laden stories told by the four main characters in his poem summarize what for the entire Western world amounted to thirty or so extremely difficult years. For his inspiration Auden of course looked to the past, yet the emotions he explored were poignantly relevant to the present and, although Auden would not have known this, to the future.

Not surprisingly, many American intellectuals gravitated toward Auden's effort. A year after its publication in 1947, Auden's *Age of Anxiety* was awarded the Pulitzer Prize for Poetry. In 1949 composer Leonard Bernstein not only borrowed the poem's title but also used it as a structural model for his Symphony No. 2. In 1950, on commission from George Balanchine, choreographer Jerome Robbins used Bernstein's music for an *Age of Anxiety* ballet. And in 1951 the philosopher/poet Alan Watts, born in England but a resident of the United States since 1938, used "The Age of Anxiety" as the title of the first essay in his *The Wisdom of Insecurity*. Auden's poem, Bernstein's symphony, Robbins's ballet, Watts's essay . . . these are prescient works, for throughout the Fifties, anxiety—deep-rooted yet seldom articulated—was endemic among Americans young and old, regardless of gender or ethnicity, in all parts of the country, on every level of society.

Some of this anxiety was forced upon America from abroad. In a flash the United States became the world's first-ever superpower when it dropped atomic bombs on Japan, but politicians and military commanders alike knew that America's victory in "an unwanted war had not brought a true peace,"[1] and that the end of the heated struggle marked the onset of what would soon be known as the Cold War.[2] The atomic bomb was a frightening weapon, but at least it "did not carry us outside the scope of human control or manageable events."[3] With five hundred times as much explosive power, the hydrogen bomb that the United States exploded over the tiny Bikini atoll in the South Pacific in May 1956 was destructive beyond belief, something that one of its developers confessionally called "the most terrible weapon in human history."[4] American research on this photogenic yet horrific device began partly because the United States suspected that the Soviets, following up on their own research into atomic bombs, would soon be working on their own version of the dreaded H-bomb. When it was eventually learned that the Soviet Union had indeed been testing hydrogen weapons at least since November 1955, the effect on the American public was greatly unsettling.

American consciousness during the Fifties was powered by nuclear-related thoughts, and surely the most frightening of these had to do with the idea that weapons of mass destruction were in the hands of an enemy. But disturbances to peace of mind did not come entirely from the other side of what Winston Churchill in 1946 dubbed the Iron Curtain. Indeed, much of what bothered America during the Fifties came from within.

For some Americans, fear of air raids by wild-eyed Russians was matched, perhaps even surpassed, by fear of infiltration by communists who for all intents and purposes "looked" just like us. Hearings conducted by the House Committee on Un-American Activities (HUAC), intended primarily to ferret out communist sympathizers in Hollywood, had begun as early as 1947,[5] and seven years later the "Red Scare" erupted spectacularly when Senator Joseph McCarthy initiated investigations into alleged communist infiltration of the United States armed forces. In September 1957 the same newborn medium of network television that carried gavel-to-gavel coverage of the McCarthy circus brought into American living rooms the sounds and images, night after night, live, of white mobs reacting violently to the court-ordered desegregation of public schools in Little Rock, Arkansas. Television in the Fifties also offered American viewers *The Adventures of Ozzie and Harriet* and *Leave It to Beaver*,[6] sitcoms that portrayed utopian family life in a suburbia whose real-life equivalent was often anything but blissful. For novelist Sloan Wilson, the typical suburban home of the Fifties was "a trap" whose residents "no more enjoyed refurbishing . . . than a prisoner would delight in shining up the bars of his cell,"[7] and for social critic Lewis Mumford, "the ultimate effect of the suburban escape" was "a low-grade uniform environment from which escape [was] impossible."[8]

Not surprisingly, considering the ebullience of young men just released from the armed forces, the marriage rate in the United States in 1945 was the highest since the National Center for Health Statistics began keeping track of such things more than a half century earlier, but that same year also went on record with the nation's highest-ever divorce rate.[9] In a classic sociological study published at the start of the 1950s, David Riesman and his colleagues attributed the high divorce rate and "the so-called disintegration of the family" at least in part to rigid gender roles demanded by suburban life.[10] These gender roles were publicly reinforced not just by television and cinematic fiction but also by such popular women's magazines as *Redbook* and *Ladies' Home Journal* and by men's magazines such as *Playboy*. *Playboy* did not create "the masculine fetishization of breasts" that in the Fifties "clashed with body phobias and asexual dreams of romance,"[11] but it certainly capitalized on the period's "mammary madness."[12] At the same time, with articles and advertisements focused on a hedonistic lifestyle available only to financially comfortable bachelors, the magazine month after month reminded Fifties husbands of the independence they had sacrificed for the sake of pursuing the highly touted middle-class lifestyle.

Along with the birth of rocket science, the racial integration of major league baseball, the G.I. Bill of Rights, and prefabricated suburban tract houses, Americans witnessed the introduction into the culture of such marvels as interstate highways, the push-up bra, franchised fast-food restaurants, television soap operas, the hula hoop, transistor radios, the "Dear Abby" and "Dear Ann Landers" newspaper columns, a pill originally designed to help women with menstrual disorders but soon discovered to be an effective contraceptive, the Corvette, 3-D and Cinerama movies, Cheez Whiz, *Playboy* and *Mad* magazines, disposable diapers, the electric guitar, Holiday Inn motels, the automatic telephone answering machine, and Disneyland.

Americans during the long decade of the Fifties also experienced the entirety of the Korean War, violent responses to the civil rights movement, the initial rumblings of what would eventually become militant feminism, a consumer culture characterized by an obsessive need to keep up with the Joneses, the establishment of the Hollywood blacklist and the pogroms of the so-called McCarthy era, and, perhaps most tellingly, the acceleration of an arms race that on both sides of the Iron Curtain necessitated development of potentially earth-shattering weapons.

For America, the years following World War II were comparable to those "best of times, . . . worst of times" described by Charles Dickens on the opening page of *A Tale of Two Cities*. On the one hand, the nation at mid-century rejoiced in its victory, celebrated its prosperity, boasted of its scientific progress, and relished the opportunity—stymied first by the Great Depression and then by the war—to at last live a "normal" life. On the other hand, America trembled at the thought of not only losing all that it had gained but also of having everything go up, literally, in flames.

About This Book

Music is consistently the object of study here, but it is considered less as a phenomenon unto itself than as a manifestation of the conditions under which it emerged or receded, thrived or withered. The music under consideration represents a wide range of styles that attracted the attention of a wide range of audiences, and in their sounds alone they have little in common. What these various types of music do have in common is the fact that all of them sprang up in a particular cultural environment, an environment identified by a set of attitudes and conditions that in American history seems to have been quite unique. All of this music, I suggest, was somehow affected by the anxious spirit of the times; the period's zeitgeist thus haunts this book.

A great many forces—technology; the economy; politics domestic as well as international; relationships between black and white people, between men and women, between young and old—animated American society during the Fifties. Too much attention paid to any one of these would likely distort the picture, for the origins of these forces long predate World War II, and in most cases these forces in one way or another are still very much active. Moreover, the boundaries of the Fifties' various "force fields" were porous, and the energies of any one of them spilled often, but in irregular ways, into the territory of others. For example, the widespread fear that communist infiltrators lurked everywhere helped fuel America's urgent development of aerospace technology and nuclear weapons, and fear of nuclear weapons in the hands of the Soviet Union in turn fueled paranoia about communists. The sexual tension that fairly dominated the Fifties—visual and verbal references to sex almost everywhere, overt acknowledgments of sex almost nowhere—bothered not just adults of the period but also their postpubescent children, who constituted the newly defined social class known as "teenagers." The friction between black and white America during the Fifties was as much colored by the imbalances of a generally prosperous postwar economy as by legislation having to do with the integration of public schools and by ideologies that for some made the very idea of "blackness" a cause célèbre.

With all that in mind, this book concentrates on societal forces that warrant the adjective "postwar" for reasons not just chronological but etiological as well. In other words, the lenses through which the whole of American music in the Fifties is examined here represent forces whose interconnected and often mutually influential dynamics between 1945 and 1963 are linked to the fact that, for America, the war ended the way it did.

The book's nine chapters deal in turn with mainstream popular music, rock 'n' roll, jazz, the music and musical imagery of Hollywood, Broadway, opera, the classical music mainstream, modernistic music both serial and otherwise, and the difficult-to-categorize music that sometimes goes under the rubrics "experimental" or "avant-garde" but that I choose to identify as the work of American "maverick" composers. Each of these chapters is offered as a self-standing piece of writing, with cross-references kept to a minimum. Nevertheless, the book's content flows in a single direction, with the subject matter progressing from the most easily accessible music to what is perhaps the most puzzlingly abstruse, and its overall thrust is intended to be cumulative, with the anxiety-tipped "points" of each chapter sharpened, I hope, by all that has come before.

None of the chapters delivers a simple survey of a particular type of American music within a particular period of time, and certainly none of them attempts an interpretive history with suggested reasons for the occurrence of *all* of any genre's arguably momentous developments. Full accounts of momentous developments are easily found elsewhere, so these chapters deal only with those developments—some of them not really momentous at all—that pertain to this book's theme.

Readers should not expect to find in this book any sort of "through line," any sort of narrative thread that extends unbroken from the beginning of the Fifties to the period's putative end. In fact, there *is* no single, unidirectional thread; there is only an "anxiety fabric" woven from a great many threads, a fabric with spots thin as well as thick, that shrouds the entirety of the Fifties. To indulge in just one more metaphor, again and again these nine chapters look at the same long decade that stretches from Hiroshima to the test-ban treaty; from chapter to chapter, however, the focal points of the looking differ, and so do the filters through which the looking is done.

Christopher Small reminded us at the turn of the century that "there is no such *thing* as music. Music is not a thing at all, but an activity, something that people *do*."[13] Subscribing wholeheartedly to that idea, in this deliberately selective study I explore some of the reasons why Americans in the Fifties "did" their music. The book's primary goal is to regard American music from the Fifties in the context of the culture in which it was produced and thus to shed at least a bit of light on how this music, at the time of its creation and initial consumption, related in one way or another to the period's prevailing moods.

The book's secondary goal, addressed in the epilogue, is to prod readers to reflect on how American music from the Fifties is received today. We now stand at a distance of more than a half century from the troubled long decade identified in this book's title, but perhaps the present era has more in common with the anxious Fifties than we care to admit. If readers think at least for a moment about what the long-ago Fifties might have in common with the here-and-now second decade of the twenty-first century, then *Music in the Age of Anxiety* will have done its job.

A Personal Note

This book springs in part from a historical musicologist's scholarly interest in what is arguably one of the most volatile periods of American music. It also springs in part—perhaps in very large part—from a curiosity about personal memories.

I lived through the entirety of the Fifties, but I was just a child, and as a grown-up I know full well that what I "think" I remember about those years is likely colored by a great deal of what I have since read. Certain memories, however, seem clear enough even today, and certain others seem perhaps not altogether clear but nonetheless strong.

Technology, I know, made a deep impression on me. I distinctly recall being fascinated, at age five, by the television set that my father brought into the flat that we (my parents and three kids) occupied on the second floor of my grandmother's house; I asked him why the dial below the ten-inch screen had numbers on it, and he explained that although "there's just one channel now, soon there'll be others."[14] I distinctly recall, at age nine, standing with my older brother in the backyard of the first home of our own, in the early evening, not really seeing yet very much wanting to see the flash of light that the teacher at school said would be reflected at a certain time off the just-launched Sputnik satellite.[15] I recall the afternoon, a few months later, when Dad installed in our living room the main console and bulky remote speaker of a stereo phonograph. As a kid who had already been taking clarinet lessons for a few years, I was certainly interested in the recording of Gershwin's *Rhapsody in Blue* that was part of the purchase package, but I was far more intrigued by the "demo" album that featured the three-dimensional sounds of a ping-pong match, a railway station, and a thunderstorm.[16] And I recall, but only in a general sort of way, the kitchen radio that played almost constantly and whose cheery broadcast fare seemed to enliven the mother of what by the late 1950s had become the four of us.

In fact I possess *many* happy memories of life in the Fifties. But as I ponder them now, it seems that more than a few of these memories are clouded over—in ways that I find difficult to articulate—with puzzlement.

I remember, for example, that once a month throughout my first several years of elementary school, the wail of a very loud siren triggered our regular air-raid drill, during which all the kids marched in orderly fashion to the school's basement and then huddled against the walls. When I politely asked the nun in charge of us second-graders what an air raid actually was, she never gave me an answer. I remember, too, getting not much of an answer when, as our burgeoning family piled into a station wagon and headed off for a summertime vacation in northern Wisconsin, I asked my father why certain of Milwaukee's streets were marked with big blue circles that bore directional arrows and the words "Evacuation Route."

I remember being much impressed, because the displays of emotion were so uncharacteristically strong and overt, but also confused, because no one would offer an explanation to just a kid like me, when at a family Christmas party my uncle Bill actually used "bad" language to excoriate a Wisconsin senator named Joe McCarthy, and when my father flew into a moralistic rage after witnessing the performance of Elvis Presley on our beloved Sunday-night *Ed Sullivan Show*.[17] I also remember being much impressed, albeit in a thoroughly negative way, when, after my older brother hinted that I was starting to express an interest in sexual matters, my parents, instead of having a chat with me, simply handed me a pamphlet they'd picked up from the local church.

On a lighter note, from the later 1950s I remember cockily taking the bus almost every Saturday—in the company of just my older brother and a cousin—and participating in the wonderful educational program that the Milwaukee County Museum called its "Explorers' Club." Always there was an after-lunch free movie, and almost always it was a low-budget science fiction flick in which the good guys (i.e., the American military) prevailed against whatever mutant insects or invading aliens formed a threat. We exited such films the way high school students exit a pep rally, and as the three of us wandered boldly through the alleys and backstreets of downtown Milwaukee I took heart in noting the many signs that indicated—in brightly patriotic red, white, and blue—that this or that basement had been designated a civil defense shelter.

Our family moved from the crowded south side of Milwaukee to the spacious suburb of Hales Corners in the summer of 1961, and I remember—with pangs of guilt, I admit—chiding my father about the fact that whereas the recently built homes of many of my new friends were equipped with spiffy bomb shelters, our new custom-built house, alas, was not. And I remember barely keeping my obnoxious adolescent mouth shut when during the early autumn of 1962, as tensions built toward what would eventually be known as the Cuban Missile Crisis, my very Catholic family night after night got down on its knees and prayed a pope-sanctioned rosary for the sake of fending off global destruction.

Richard Taruskin tells the poignant story of how, as a precocious seventeen-year-old sophomore at Columbia University, he

> wander[ed] aimlessly all day, . . . from movie theater to movie theater (and they were all full of wanderers like me, even at noon), on Thursday, October 25, 1962, when the Strategic Air Command was in the air in a state of full readiness for the only time in its history, when Soviet freighters bearing military hardware were approaching the quarantine line John F. Kennedy had

declared around Cuba, and when millions like me were convinced it would be the last day of their lives.[18]

I, too, remember that day, but I was younger, in my first year at a college-prep Jesuit high school, and I readily admit that my understanding of global politics was not especially sophisticated. Nevertheless, I had the sense, as doubtless did all of my classmates at Marquette High, that something big was about to happen. I recall that, as we discussed the matter in what was billed as a "religion" class but what in essence was a freshman philosophy seminar, none of us actually *acted* as though he were afraid. But I can only speak for myself. I recall that I—a supposedly talented fourteen-year-old boy who often had been told that the whole world awaited him—felt very, very disappointed.

1

The Pop Music Mainstream

In 1950 the two most successful commodities in the field of popular music were "The Tennessee Waltz" and "Goodnight, Irene." "The Tennessee Waltz" was a cover by Patti Page of a country-western song first recorded three years earlier by Pee Wee King and His Golden West Cowboys. The version by Page was released on the Mercury label in November 1950 as the flip side of a holiday-oriented product titled "Boogie Woogie Santa Claus." Before the year was out Page's version had reached the very top of *Billboard* magazine's "Most Played by [Disc] Jockeys" chart; although other recordings of the song were suddenly abundant,[1] Page's treatment remained on the *Billboard* chart for twenty-six weeks, and for thirteen weeks it held the number one position. Compared to its rivals, the treatment by the twenty-three-year-old Page and a studio orchestra led by Jack Rael was a marvel of postwar sophistication, for it had its star performer singing in four-part harmony that could only have been realized by means of the magnetic tape recorders that had been developed by German scientists and that, after being appropriated by the Allies, had first come on the American market in 1948. In the bargain, it gave Mercury a marketplace foothold for one of the music industry's new formats: Mercury simultaneously issued Page's version of "The Tennessee Waltz" on 78 and 45 rpm discs, but it was as a 45 that the recording eventually sold more than six million copies, and with its commercial success it likely "established the 45 rpm format."[2]

"Goodnight, Irene" had total sales of only two million, but in the short run it made just as strong an impact as "The Tennessee Waltz." Released in the summer of 1950, it stayed on the *Billboard* chart for twenty-five weeks and occupied the number one position for more than three months. Like "The Tennessee Waltz," "Goodnight, Irene" was a recycling of older material, but in this case the song's provenance is more complicated. The lyrics for "Goodnight, Irene" apparently belong to Huddie Ledbetter, aka Leadbelly, an itinerant folksinger (and convicted murderer) who committed the words to paper as early as 1943. The tune, however, is one that Woody Guthrie concocted in 1941 when he was employed by the U.S. Department of the Interior to write songs that somehow commented on the dam projects that were then being constructed by the Bonneville Power Administration on the Columbia River. In their heydays both Ledbetter and Guthrie had been symbols of populism, and presumably this made them attractive to the left-leaning folk group called the Weavers that in 1948 began to hold forth in Greenwich Village bistros.[3] Curiously, the song's political resonances seem to have gone unnoticed by the record-buying public in the early years of the Cold War. Along with Gordon Jenkins, the bandleader/arranger for the Decca label who recruited the Weavers and produced "Goodnight, Irene," the public apparently was interested only in the Weavers' cheerful sound.

As is obvious from its title, "The Tennessee Waltz" is a composition in 3/4 time, and so is "Goodnight, Irene." In terms of meter alone, these two extraordinarily successful songs from 1950 stand as much in contrast to the rock 'n' roll music that captured the attention of American teenagers later in the decade as to the swing music that appealed to Americans of diverse age groups in the years leading up to and including World War II. But meter is not the main thing that distinguishes "The Tennessee Waltz," "Goodnight, Irene," and contemporaneous hits from their swing and rock 'n' roll counterparts. To be sure, other waltzes topped the charts during the late 1940s and early 1950s, but most of the period's songs were cast in 4/4. Rather than meter, or tempo, or even rhythm, what most distinguishes these songs from earlier and later efforts is their *treatment* of rhythm.

A few hit songs from early in the Fifties, most of them novelty numbers or dance tunes based on newly fashionable Latin styles, were indeed highly energetic. These exceptions, however, only prove the rule. The very terms "swing" and "rock 'n' roll" suggest a powerful relationship between the music itself and physical responses on the part of its audiences; more than a half century after the fact, there is still no kinetic-based nickname for the stylistically homogeneous American popular music that won the attention of large numbers of record buyers in the 1946–1954 period. Compared with so much American popular music that came before and after, the postwar pop music mainstream was remarkably sedate.

A New Era in American Popular Music

The number one spot on *Billboard* magazine's Top 100 chart for 1943 was held, for a dozen weeks beginning in early November, by the Mills Brothers' recording of "Paper Doll." "Paper Doll" is perhaps not so memorable as "In the Mood," "Chattanooga Choo Choo," and other recordings that today serve as aural icons of the World War II years. Yet it is a historically important recording, and not just because with eventual sales of more than six million copies it became "the biggest hit of the decade"; "Paper Doll" is historically important because its success arguably heralded "the demise of big-band swing music."[4]

The Mills Brothers were African Americans, but there is nothing in their vocal stylizations that even remotely resembles the "race music" recordings that had been in circulation since the 1920s. After its slow introduction "Paper Doll" indeed sets a listener's toes a-tapping, but compared with the products of the mostly white big bands its "swing" elements seem quite tame. One of the things that makes "Paper Doll" stand strikingly apart from big band recordings is its sound: "four smoothly harmonizing voices accompanied only by acoustic guitar, keyboard, and bass."[5] Another thing that sets it apart—something more significant, in terms of how it foreshadowed the immediate future of American popular music—is the fact that both on the charts and in the popular press "Paper Doll" was linked not to a band but to a quartet of singers.

Bing Crosby's phenomenally successful 1942 recording of "White Christmas" focused attention on a single vocalist. However, this was an anomaly, due in large part to Crosby's well-established status not just as a soloist but also as a movie star. While many of the hit recordings of the late 1930s and early 1940s indeed involved lyrics, the singers of these lyrics were typically regarded as members of an ensemble whose main attraction clearly was the bandleader. With few exceptions, the hits of the swing era are attributed to "So-and-So and His Orchestra." Between 1939 and 1943, when *Billboard* magazine polled college students to determine the "most popular" of the big band male and female vocalists, favorite singers were indeed identified, but for the most part they figured no more importantly in the hierarchy than did favorite drummers or saxophone players.

An important exception was Frank Sinatra, who as featured vocalist with Tommy Dorsey's band ranked high on the *Billboard* collegiate polls of 1941 and 1942. Even during his short stint with the Harry James band in 1939, Sinatra was starting to become "the center of a cult of teenaged girls" who were popularly known, because of their preferred footwear, as "bobby-soxers."[6] Affirmation by the *Billboard* polls was incentive enough for Sinatra, aided by press agent George Evans, to strike out on his own. On December 20, 1942, Sinatra began a four-week engagement, as guest artist, with the Benny Goodman band at the same Paramount Theater in New York where six years earlier a horde of dancing teenagers had assured Goodman's place in the pantheon of swing music. Although by this time Goodman was accustomed to the adulation of young fans, he was nonetheless "astonished by [the] wall of screaming" that greeted Sinatra's onstage entrance.[7] Donald Clarke perhaps exaggerates when he writes that, with this, "modern pop hysteria was born."[8] Clearly, though, the popularity of Sinatra—coincident with the recording of "Paper Doll" by the Mills Brothers, for whom there was no hysteria at all— marks the start of a new era in American popular music.

Not until September 1943, a month and a half before the release of "Paper Doll," would Sinatra have a hit record whose packaging identified him as featured performer,[9] and not until 1946 would he again reach *Billboard*'s Top 100 chart.[10] The seeds of Sinatra's success had been planted in his recordings with the Harry James and Tommy Dorsey bands, and the dramatic sprouting of his fame can be directly linked to the extraordinary interactions between performer and audience that transpired during his appearances with Goodman's and other bands. Sinatra's stardom in the mid-1940s, however, owes less to his recording and concert activity than to his radio broadcasts.[11] To a large extent, it owes as well to Sinatra's developing persona.

Early in 1945 Sinatra starred in *The House I Live In*, an eleven-minute film during which he sang the poignantly egalitarian title song and admonished a group of boys for their anti-Semitism. Later that year he authored an article for *Scholastic*, a magazine for schoolchildren, in which he advocated abandonment of discrimination not just toward Jews but also toward Italian and African Americans, Catholics, Asians, and representatives of any other non-WASP minority.[12] Over the course of the Fifties Sinatra would gain notoriety aplenty for, among other things, his temper, his sexual proclivities, and his alleged involvement with underworld characters. But at the dawn of the postwar period his musical popularity was enhanced primarily by his swaggering stance as an outspoken individual who defied prevailing norms.

* * *

By the end of 1945 Sinatra was much more than a singer. He was a personality, and like Bing Crosby he was marketed as such. The public images of Sinatra and Crosby had little in common; whereas the forty-two-year-old

Crosby was being presented as a suave yet desexualized avuncular character, the thirty-year-old Sinatra was still "a skinny kid with big ears" who served as a "softly crooning, teen-female-identified heartthrob" while perhaps appealing as well to young women's "maternal urge."[13] Other singers of the time were arguably less charismatic than Sinatra and Crosby, but they were nonetheless individualistic in what they projected to their audiences, and they, too, were emerging as personalities.

The postwar displacement of bandleaders by singers (or groups of singers who, like the Andrews Sisters, the Mills Brothers, and the Ink Spots, had strong collective identities) can be attributed at least in part to the American Federation of Musicians' (AFM) 1942–1944 ban on recordings.[14] It is likely, however, that the shift would have occurred even without the ban. Doubtless inspired by Sinatra's 1942 decision to pursue a career as a soloist, in that same year band singers Dinah Shore, Jo Stafford, and Perry Como also decided to set out on their own. Although hardly stars, these singers nevertheless ambitiously detached themselves from the successful bands for which previously they had been mere employees. In order to survive as soloists, of course, they needed to call attention to themselves. Thus their interpretations, regardless of how their performances on recordings or radio might have been accompanied, of commercial necessity grew more and more individualistic.

Audiences at the end of World War II had not lost their taste for swing rhythm or for the big band sound. But with solo singers competing for their attention, and with country-western music steadily making inroads into the marketplace via both radio and films, audiences were acquiring new tastes as well. Once Sinatra and other vocal soloists had endeared themselves with the public, what mattered to fans was not so much the type of music that these singers delivered as the fact that music of whatever sort was being delivered by *these* particular singers. While some of what the soloists offered was bouncy and in other ways comparable with what they had done with the swing bands, much of it was relatively subdued. Reminded by press agents and the record labels' artist-and-repertoire (A & R) men that their most valuable assets were not so much their voices as their personalities, the solo singers naturally gravitated toward material that allowed them to highlight their interpretative idiosyncrasies. In most cases, this meant songs whose lyrics were somehow more "intimate" than those that typified the big band hits of the late 1930s and early '40s.

Like the ascendance of the solo singer, American popular music's move toward more "heartfelt" songs likely would have happened with or without the AFM's ban on recordings. Certainly not everything served up by the big bands during the war years had the powerful rhythmic energy that, back in the mid-1930s, prompted concertgoers to break into spontaneous dancing. According to one bandleader who reflected bitterly on the end of swing era, the big bands brought about their own demise because during the war years they "neglected the dancers" who had fueled their initial success and concentrated instead on "flag-wavers and slow smoochers."[15] Some of the big band appeals to "flag-wavers," of course, had as much rhythmic energy as anything served up earlier.[16] But other patriotic offerings by the big bands were indeed appropriate accompaniments for slow smooching.[17] As victory for the Allies seemed more and more inevitable, and as the solo singers endeavored to stake their claims on listeners' affections, songs of this same basic type (more relaxed in rhythm, and with lyrics clearly focused on one-to-one romance) came increasingly to the fore.

Pop Music's "Sentimental" Journey

The flow of America's pop music mainstream in the immediate aftermath of World War II is conveniently summarized by the title of the recording that just before V-J Day for nine weeks held the number one position on *Billboard*'s Top 100 chart: from the end of the war until rock 'n' roll exploded in the middle of the 1950s, the course of American popular music would indeed for the most part be a "Sentimental Journey."[18]

This is not to suggest that all of the music was in the same style. Early in the period such postwar technologies as the magnetic tape recorder, more sensitive microphones, and vinyl discs made it easier than ever before for small record companies to make and distribute commercially viable products. At the same time, the massive expansion of radio outlets that began in 1947 made it at least possible to bring new products—some of them in quite atypical musical styles—quickly to the attention of potential buyers.

The decentralization of the music industry coincided not just with the growth of audiences whose musical tastes, for reasons of social class and ethnicity, were narrowly focused but also with an obvious broadening of tastes within the "general" audience. Whereas just five years earlier the *Billboard* Top 100 chart had been inundated by big band swing, the number one hits of 1947 included such items as Tex Williams's country-flavored "Smoke! Smoke! Smoke! (That Cigarette)," two versions (by the Count Basie band and by a vocal group called the Three Flames) of the boisterous "Open the Door, Richard!" and no less than three versions (by Buddy Clark, the Three Suns, and the Harmonicats) of the 1913 song "Peg o' My Heart." Among the more outré chart-toppers from 1948 were a bit of vintage ragtime (Pee Wee Hunt's "Twelfth Street Rag"), the theme music for a popular animated cartoon series (Kay Kyser's big band treatment of "The Woody Woodpecker Song"), and a boldly comic novelty number (Spike Jones's "All I Want for Christmas Is My Two Front Teeth"). And 1949, with Vaughn Monroe's "Ghost Riders in the Sky" and two offerings from Frankie Laine ("That Lucky Old Sun" and "Mule Train") leading the pack of top-ranked hits, seemed to be the year of the cowboy song.

Notwithstanding this diversity, it remains that between 1946 and 1954 the American pop music mainstream was dominated by recordings that featured solo vocalists who had already achieved or were in the process of achieving (by means of exposure first on radio and then, after 1948, on television) some measure of stardom. It remains, too, that most of the material with which these singers came to be identified was of the sort that is easily described as "sentimental."

Granted, the term is problematic, and possibly offensive to readers whose first reaction is to take "sentimental" to mean "mawkish" or "maudlin." But *Webster's New World Dictionary* gives as its first definition "having or showing tender or delicate feelings," and the *American Heritage Dictionary*, after a primary definition that suggests extravagant emotional display, reminds us that the word "sentimental" can mean simply "appealing to the sentiments, especially to romantic feelings."

Surely it was in this more restrained sense that the adjective figured into the titles of Les Brown's 1945 "Sentimental Journey," Nat "King" Cole's 1946 "(I Love You) For Sentimental Reasons," and the Ames Brothers' 1950 "Sentimental Me." It is in this restrained sense, too, that the adjective seems applicable to both the lyrics and the overall musical qualities of the many hit songs with which solo singers in the postwar years established their fan bases.

Along with singers whose names posterity seems to remember only slightly, the first wave of "star" vocalists included Frank Sinatra, Nat "King" Cole, Dinah Shore, Perry Como, and Vaughan Monroe; the second wave, beginning around 1948–1949, included Jo Stafford, Vic Damone, Peggy Lee, Mel Tormé, Mary Ford, Teresa Brewer, Rosemary Clooney, Tony Bennett, Eddie Fisher, Doris Day, Al Martino, Joni James, and Patti Page. All of these singers topped the *Billboard* chart with at least one recording whose lyrics were overtly romantic and whose interpretation—typically supported by an arrangement that de-emphasized rhythm instruments and cushioned the vocal line in the soft textures of a string orchestra—allowed the soloist to indulge freely in the expression of tender, or delicate, feelings. Most of the singers had numerous such hits, each one different enough in surface details from its predecessor to make it seem fresh while similar enough in substance and treatment so that it could readily be identified as yet another offering from a performer in whom fans had invested a certain amount of loyalty. The most prolific of the recording artists had to "change their tune" from time to time so as not to bore their audiences. But even when they momentarily jumped the stylistic fence, the established singers still delivered material that in a fairly innocent way was "appealing to the sentiments."

In terms of innocence, a mainstream hit that stands peculiarly apart from the crowd is Rosemary Clooney's 1951 recording of "Come On-a My House."[19] Vocal soloists in the postwar years trafficked in songs that fairly wallowed in matters of romance, but almost always the songs' lyrics and interpretations—no matter how heartfelt—adhered to a strict sense of propriety (when Jo Stafford scored a number one hit in March 1954 with "Make Love to Me," the song's title phrase clearly did not mean what it means today). Contrasting sharply with the norm of the typical postwar sentimental song, the lyrics of "Come On-a My House" resonate like an advertising jingle from a prostitute. Raucous barrelhouse rhythms in the accompaniment seem to place the communication at the entrance of a brothel; an archly affected yet not readily identifiable accent on the part of the singer suggests that the enticement comes from some "cultural Other"; the much-repeated title phrase becomes an increasingly heated invitation, acceptance of which apparently will result in a smorgasbord of physical delights that, doubtless metaphorically, include such things as candy, an apple, a plum, an apricot, figs and dates, grapes and cakes, a pomegranate, a peach, a pear, a Christmas tree, and an Easter egg.

Clooney's recording of "Come On-a My House" topped the *Billboard* chart on July 28, 1951, and held the number one position for eight weeks. It was the first hit for Clooney, who during the war years had worked as a singer with the Tony Pastor band, and it remains the song with which she is most strongly identified today. Clooney's memorable interpretation perhaps had precedents in some of the race music recordings that had circulated since the 1920s, but certainly nothing like it had ever before been presented to America's predominantly white general audience for popular music. Indeed, not even in the heyday of rock 'n' roll, when straitlaced critics regularly lambasted the new genre for its morally corruptive influences on American youth, would a hit song be in both verbal content and musical expression so blatantly sexual.

Sexuality was a potent force in American culture of the Fifties, and its linkage with the chilly climate of the Cold War has often been explored. As Joanne Meyerowitz notes,

Various scholars have argued that the Cold War assault on communism reinforced the subordination of women and the suppression of sexuality. In the most common variant of this argument, the fear of communism pushed middle-class Americans to look to masculine strength and the patriarchal home as protective forces in a dangerous world. In this anxious context, independent women, gay men, lesbians, "domineering moms," and "matriarchs," among others, seemed to threaten masculinity, the nuclear family, and the nation, just as communism seemed to threaten the international order.[20]

Alfred Kinsey's 1947 report on sexual behavior in males and its 1953 follow-up study on females made it perfectly, albeit uncomfortably, clear that in the postwar years Americans' public attitudes toward sex were at odds with what Americans did or thought about in private. Hugh Hefner's *Playboy* magazine, launched late in 1953 and obviously geared toward males, was a pioneering effort to confront the hypocrisy head-on. The mainstream media, on the other hand, preferred to capitalize on the tensions that went unspoken. Hollywood offered products that "were all *about* sex, yet *without* sex," writes film critic Molly Haskell; the Fifties were "a box of Cracker Jack without a prize; or with the prize distorted into a forty-inch bust [on a] forty-year-old virgin."[21] In her introduction to a retrospective novel about the Fifties, Sara Davidson observes: "The entire country seemed fixated on sex. Young women beckoned suggestively from billboards, movies, magazines; young men were in a state of near constant arousal, but there was no outlet."[22]

In terms of sexuality, popular metaphors for the Fifties range from the proverbial calm before the storm, to a volcano just before eruption, to a body of water under whose still surface roil dangerous currents. The aquatic image invites consideration of what role the pop music mainstream might have played in all this. While at the time "The Tennessee Waltz" and most of its *Billboard* chart-mates were likely regarded as comforting, in retrospect it seems that they contributed hugely to the pervasive discontent of the Fifties. Indeed, one could argue that the pop music mainstream in general and the sentimental style in particular—because of such a wide gap between, on the one hand, the songs' innocent lyric content and, on the other hand, the often steamy nature of the music itself—are symbolic of the period's sexual hang-ups.

Sex Symbols and Role Models

Established female vocalists appeared regularly on the television shows that early in the Fifties, at the behest of corporate sponsors, offered "a relatively homogeneous image of American life, dominated by middle-class lifestyles and middle-class values,"[23] and over the course of the long decade Doris Day, Debbie Reynolds, June Allyson, and Judy Garland became hugely popular not just as singers but also as movie stars. None of these female singers *ever* appeared in the stiletto heels or conical bra that, according to Hollywood's prevailing semiotic code, identified a female who was both sexually desirable and, importantly, available. The fictional characters portrayed in films by Day, Reynolds, and other female singers, like the "real life" image projected on television by Dinah Shore, were, of course, attractive. But the visual focus was always on the female singer's cuteness or prettiness, not on her sexuality, and the narratives into which the singers were cast invariably emphasized personal charm over physical allure.

"She looks lovely before the electronic cameras," *New York Times* radio/television columnist Jack Gould wrote after the December 1951 premiere of *The Dinah Shore Show*, which NBC would telecast twice weekly for the next five years. "She was the picture of poise and naturalness and conducted her show with a disarming combination of authority and humility."[24] Most of the adjectives apply just as well to Perry Como, who made his television debut with a 1948 Christmas Eve special for NBC and then hosted weekly programs for the next two decades. Como, who liked to remind audiences that before the launch of his singing career he was simply a barber in Canonsburg, Pennsylvania, soon acquired the nickname "Mr. Casual." Relaxed and clean-cut, confident yet humble, Como's persona was every bit as "nice" as Shore's. Indeed, in a 1953 review Gould decried "the baleful moanings . . . of juvenile baritones and tearful soubrettes" and identified Shore and Como as "the two individuals who regularly abjure the butchery of modern tunes and subscribe to the sensible if old-fashioned notion that their assignment is to please an audience, not exhaust it."[25]

Gould's tirade against what he termed "muscle singers" likely was prompted by performers such as Johnnie Ray, who for eleven weeks in 1951–1952 topped the *Billboard* chart with his recording of "Cry" and then for several years based a career on "the excruciating formula of virtually breaking into tears while singing a song."[26] But even Ray, who was nicknamed the "Nabob of Sob" and the "Million Dollar Teardrop," seems to have known the value of moderation; his 1952 recording of "Walking My Baby Back Home" is hardly something in which he "flaunted his neuroses."[27] Notwithstanding Gould's complaints, most of the star singers of the early 1950s emulated the altogether wholesome images projected by Shore and Como in their appearance as well as in their vocal stylings.

In terms of projected imagery, an important exception to the norm was that offered by Frank Sinatra. Largely because of his charismatic performances on radio, as early as 1947 Sinatra was famous enough to be the subject of a book titled *The Voice: The Story of an American Phenomenon.*[28] Shortly after the book's publication, however, his career hit the skids. Along with suffering damage to his vocal cords, Sinatra ended a long marriage to his childhood sweetheart and famously took up with Ava Gardner, a movie star who (quite unlike June Allyson and Doris Day) wore conical brassieres to spectacular effect. His marriage to Gardner was brief, but it resulted in connections with Hollywood that likely led to his eventual comeback. Sinatra had successfully co-starred, with Gene Kelly and Jules Munshin, in the 1949 MGM musical *On the Town.* In 1953 he was given a non-singing part in Columbia's *From Here to Eternity*, and his efforts won him an Academy Award for best supporting actor. Other screen roles—some musical, some not—quickly came his way. In most of these, Sinatra was cast as a likeable ne'er-do-well, and he applied this same persona to many of the songs on the thematically related albums he started to make for Capitol Records in 1952. In the early 1950s Sinatra's former image of a "fragile, boyish crooner who caused countless bobby-soxers to dampen the seats of the Paramount Theater" was replaced by that of "the tough, worldly, swinging lover with hat cocked, cigarette dangling, and coat thrown over his shoulder."[29] Remarkably, the transformation from boyish crooner to "tender/tough, swinging playboy" marked "an unprecedented shift from a predominantly female to a predominantly male audience."[30]

Postwar Hollywood was spangled with stars that the industry, both in films and in the publicity that surrounded them, deliberately presented as objects of heterosexual desire. The typical female sex symbol of early 1950s Hollywood was ravishingly beautiful and mammarily well-endowed, and her male counterpart was typically gifted with a strong physique and handsome facial features. The two actors most often mentioned as examples of the male sex symbol are Rock Hudson and Tab Hunter,[31] in comparison with whom the still skinny and big-eared Sinatra could hardly have seemed to be much of a "hunk."

Whether triggered by dramatic performances in films or by musical per-formances on recordings, Sinatra's appeal in the early 1950s was not so much to women who desired him as to men who somehow wished to emulate him. "For the youth of the early 1950s," writes T. H. Adamowski, Sinatra "repre-sented the urban, East Coast swagger of the older brother, with flickerings of Cagney and Bogart shading into the Brando who followed them,"[32] and in this respect the dynamic anticipates the relationship between male fans and certain rock 'n' roll stars later in the decade. More complex is Sinatra's relationship with men who were no longer teenagers. Adamowski claims that "for consensus-era people Sinatra represented the triumphalism of their early middle age."[33] But this would apply only to those relatively few "consensus-era" men who bucked the tide and remained unmarried. For the large number of adult American men who immediately upon release from military service had taken on the obligations not just of marriage but of fatherhood as well, Sinatra's persona symbolized the independence they might have enjoyed had circumstances been different.

Like the pictorial, editorial, and advertising content of Hefner's aptly named *Playboy* magazine, Sinatra's "playboy" image simply fueled a fantasy. That the fantasy was widespread is evidenced by the immediate (and enduring) success of *The Seven Year Itch*, a 1955 comedy in which Tom Ewell plays an otherwise subdued husband/father who indulges in innocent "swagger" while his wife and children are away. This fantasy was fair game for the popular media, but the frustrated reality confronted daily by adult men—and women, too—went largely unspoken.[34]

The revitalized Sinatra in the early 1950s was not so much a sex magnet for women as a role model for men, and Sinatra stands importantly apart from the crowd in that the role he modeled was in marked opposition to the behavioral-attitudinal norm. Indicative of the "double standard" that was famously endemic to the Fifties, Sinatra had a few male imitators but virtually no female counterparts.[35] Most of the male pop music singers, and all of the females, held strictly to a code of propriety that by the early 1950s—thanks in large part to the corporate sponsorship of television programs—had in effect become institutionalized.

Like Sinatra, Perry Como and Dinah Shore were role models. But whereas the distinctive Sinatra was a model for what men *might* be, Como, Shore, and all the others were models for what Cold War culture determined men and women *ought to* be. And, clearly, what adult men and women ought to be, if they aspired to membership in the burgeoning middle class, was married.

Some observers in the late 1940s worried that traditional family structures might be jeopardized by the independence in the workplace that women had acquired during the war, by the social mobility that resulted from postwar prosperity, and by abundant new opportunities for tertiary education. But these fears came to naught. As early as 1960 Eric F. Goldman observed that "the tug toward the traditional [had been] powerful in American thinking. Every area of living showed the trend. Most of the college girls were telling the pollsters they wanted babies, not careers," and "the vogue among men was to stay home at night and do-it-yourself."[36] Writing from a more distant perspective, and after sorting through mountains of demographic data, historian Elaine Tyler May noted: "The evidence overwhelmingly indicates that postwar American society experienced a surge in family life and a reaffirmation of domesticity that rested on distinct roles for men and women."[37] More to the point, May concluded, "postwar Americans believed wholeheartedly that the happiness of men and women depended on marriage. According to one study, only 9 percent believed that a single person could be happy."[38] According to another study, one that involved more than four thousand adult subjects, "the majority believed that people who did not marry were sick, immoral, selfish, or neurotic."[39]

The fact that Sinatra's success as a recording artist in the early 1950s owes not to 45 rpm singles but, rather, to 33⅓ rpm albums that featured a sort of "music noir" reinforces the idea that the pop music mainstream had a homogeneous agenda.[40] Increasingly visible through their appearances on network television, the solo singers showed middle-class Americans how they should look, and with the lyrics of their songs they informed postwar Americans as to how they should think. Patti Page's 1953 "Doggie in the Window" and other novelty songs invited innocent lapses into childlike playfulness. Obviously more mature in content, the sentimental songs that dominated the charts tended to be either passionate statements that affirmed the bliss of monogamous love or wistful soliloquies that explored the pain of failed romance.

Even Sinatra, despite his swagger, helped deliver this message. In 1955 he co-starred with Debbie Reynolds in *The Tender Trap*, a romantic comedy from MGM whose title suggests that matrimony, for all its sweet rewards, is nevertheless confining. In the same year, the album-oriented singer reached the number five spot on *Billboard*'s Top 100 chart—and stayed on the chart for seventeen weeks—with one of his relatively rare singles. Vis-à-vis the "general" audience for American popular music, Sinatra made his comeback with a song that Sammy Cahn and Jimmy Van Heusen penned for a 1955 television production of Thornton Wilder's vintage *Our Town*. The song's lyrics, credibly sung by a major star whose popular image was that of a playboy, attest that

> Love and marriage, love and marriage,
> Go together like a horse and carriage.
> This I tell you, brother,
> You can't have one without the other.

The "Mating Ritual"

The lyrics of the typical postwar sentimental song reinforced the prevailing ideas that monogamous love was a wonderful thing, that such love would lead naturally to marriage, and that men and women truly needed to be married not just in order to be happy but in order to be full-fledged members of the American middle class. Day after day this litany was repeated, and when the songs were performed on television their persistent textual message was usually linked with visual representations of how men and women should deport themselves throughout their relationships. Corporations that invested in sponsorship of network television programs clearly were in favor of a homogeneous public, and so was a government that in the midst of the Cold War looked with suspicion on all deviations from the norm. With their romantic lyrics and chaste presentations, sentimental songs did their patriotic duty in supporting those elements of the norm that were marriage-oriented yet devoid of sexuality. With their music, however, many of those songs fueled the fires that beneath the desexualized surface of postwar culture burned with what must have been frustrating intensity.

Only twice in the course of America's twentieth century, notes James Lincoln Collier in his book on swing music, were there gaps in the continuum that links young people with "some sort of strongly rhythmic, usually fairly simple kind of music which they not only danced to but simply listened to for the sheer pleasure in it."[41] The first of these occurred in the early 1930s and stems from the fact that in the darkest days of the Great Depression the market for commodities that hitherto had propelled social dancing—that is, recordings—had drastically shrunk. The second gap, which began with the end of the swing era around 1946–1947 and sustained until the advent of rock 'n' roll in the middle of the 1950s, can hardly be attributed to economic pressures. Especially in the prosperous early years of the postwar period, before independent labels encroached on its turf, the consolidated music industry could pretty much have done anything it wanted to do.

Had there been a market for it, swing music surely could have endured. But in the postwar years the market, clearly, had changed. Entirely for commercial reasons, the industry chose to cut back on swing-style recordings and instead offer its postwar customers a smattering of novelty recordings mixed with a huge amount of sentimental material that featured emergent solo vocalists. Notwithstanding the extent to which sentimental music played conveniently into the eventual consolidation of the Cold War cultural norm, there seems to have been no attempt to manipulate, for ideological reasons, the public's tastes; it was simply a matter of the industry giving the public what the public seemed to want.

This marked shift in the nature of American popular music can be attributed largely to the simple fact that a great many young Americans who had enthusiastically danced to the swing music of the big bands opted, in the aftermath of World War II, to enter into marriages that resulted quickly not just in mortgages for suburban houses but also in the spawning of children. A comparative survey of the *Billboard* charts for the war years and the early postwar period reveals that recordings of swing music, formerly the staple of the music industry, went out of fashion just at the time when erstwhile swing dancers were beginning to settle down. And common sense dictates that newly married couples determined to procreate would have had little interest in vigorous social dancing. For youths whose wartime experiences suddenly transformed them into adults, sedate sentimental music provided an apt underscore for their urgent movement toward the altar.

But what of the young Americans who in the postwar years did *not* marry and start families? Some of the bobby-soxers who in 1942 established Sinatra as a "heartthrob" were still in high school in 1946, and so were their potential boyfriends. The first children born during the baby boom would not become teenagers until late in the 1950s, but obviously there were teenagers before them, and as the postwar period rolled along their numbers would annually be replenished. Teenagers in the late 1940s and early 1950s were too young for marriage. They were not too young, however, to be interested in members of the opposite sex.

It seems that from time immemorial dance-based popular music in Western culture has served not just as aural entertainment but also as accompaniment for a culturally approved "mating ritual." This generalization applies to genres like clog dancing, in which solo dancers in effect "strut their stuff" before an audience that includes members of the opposite sex; it applies as well to genres like the English contra dance and the American square dance, in which males and females are only occasionally brought into physical contact with one another. But it applies especially to genres in which the dancing is performed by male-female dyads who identify themselves as couples. Although hardly related in terms of music, in terms of social function the rustic Bohemian polka has much in common with the seventeenth-century French minuet, the nineteenth-century Viennese waltz, and the Lindy Hop, which was all the rage in the late 1920s. Such dances of course provided young males and females with a chance to demonstrate individual skill and grace; perhaps more important, such dances provided young persons with an opportunity to make exploratory physical contact with potential marriage partners.

Thanks to the proliferation of small record labels and independent radio stations, the postwar years witnessed a blossoming of country-western, Latin, and what eventually came to be known as "rhythm and blues" music.

Within the minority cultures that supported these genres there were many small-scale hit recordings, and with these rivulets of hits the minority cultures always had fresh, fashionable music to the tune of which postpubescent boys and girls could easily sustain their cultures' traditions of social dancing. American teenagers of the overwhelmingly white middle class—in other words, the pre-adult members of the group whose patronage supported mainstream pop music and that, indeed, represented the mainstream of American society—were not so fortunate.

This is not to say that white middle-class teenagers, and white middle-class adults, suddenly stopped dancing. As is evidenced aplenty by advertisements for cruise ships, country clubs, and summer camps, social dancing was hugely popular in the late 1940s and early 1950s. Many advertisements touted social dancing as a way to, in effect, "share a delightful experience with your favorite partner,"[42] and their testimonials declared how learning to dance allowed persons to overcome their shyness. As late as 1955 an article in the *Ladies' Home Journal* advised that the ability to participate in social dancing should be cultivated by young women who thought themselves unattractive to men.[43]

Like mainstream popular music of the late 1940s and early 1950s, mainstream social dancing aimed for generational inclusiveness. "Fun for All . . . Regardless of Age!" reads the caption under a photograph included in a full-page 1954 advertisement for the well-established Arthur Murray dance studios. "Age makes no difference when it comes to dancing. . . . Our Student/ Teacher Parties are so gay and the ages vary from grandparents to teenagers!"[44] Ads from the late 1940s offered lessons in the staid foxtrot and waltz. Beginning in the 1950s, concurrent with the penetration into the *Billboard* charts by Latin-flavored songs, advertisements began to mention lessons in the rumba, the mambo, and the cha-cha, and usually these advertisements were cast in language that equated the new Latin dance styles with adult sophistication. Only once in a while did an advertisement for a dance studio pay special attention to youth by making reference to the jitterbug.

The jitterbug, not so much a dance per se as a mode of dancing, was a holdover from the swing era, and in many respects it was the precursor of the vigorous couple dancing that would be triggered by rock 'n' roll music. Because it was freewheeling and exhibitionistic, it was largely the property of middle-class teenagers, who early in the postwar period were in the process of discovering not just their individual identities but also their collective cultural autonomy. Reflecting on several decades' worth of social dancing, choreographer Jerome Robbins in 1954 observed: "In the bold, frenzied steps of jitterbugging, young people may be asserting themselves, may be saying to the world, 'Look at me.'"[45] In large part because it was so showy in nature, the jitterbug was almost by definition a very public form of dancing, and thus it had societal approval even if grown-ups sometimes claimed not to understand it.

Despite the widespread popularity of jitterbugging among postwar middle-class white teenagers, the music that supported this kind of dancing was considerably distanced from the pop music mainstream. Although in instrumentation they resembled the touring ensembles of the swing era, dance bands in the early 1950s were usually made up of local musicians, and their repertoire relied heavily on foxtrots and waltzes geared to a multigenerational audience. Most jitterbugging, therefore, was done to recordings. And this meant that, in order to jitterbug, teens either had to dust off swing-style 78s collected by their older siblings or purchase the new dance-oriented LPs—typically featuring upbeat versions of whatever songs had recently led the Hit Parade—featuring Ray Anthony and other veterans of the big band era.[46]

Most of the recordings that topped the *Billboard* charts in the early 1950s were not at all conducive to jitterbugging. Postwar teenagers doubtless had fun tapping their toes or collectively rocking their shoulders to the rhythms of such novelty hits as "Rag Mop" (the Ames Brothers, 1950), "The Thing" (Phil Harris, 1950), "Glow-Worm" (the Mills Brothers, 1952), and "Doggie in the Window" (Patti Page, 1953). Doubtless, too, teens responded as their parents did to such rhythmically infectious chart-toppers as Clooney's "Come On-a My House," "How High the Moon" (Les Paul and Mary Ford, 1951), "Blue Tango" (Leroy Anderson, 1952), and "Delicado" (Percy Faith, 1952). But most of the chart-toppers were not of the sort that would prompt teenagers, in public situations, to work up a terpsichorean sweat. On the other hand, quite a few of the mainstream hits might well have led teenagers, in relatively private situations, to work up sweat of a rather different sort.

In the "Sexual Puzzles" chapter of her *Young, White, and Miserable: Growing Up Female in the Fifties*, sociologist Wini Breines offers abundant evidence that middle-class teenagers in the early 1950s were far more sexually active than is suggested by their "prim and proper" representation in films and television shows.[47] On a scale whose precisely denotative terminology was coined by the teens themselves, activity ranged from "necking" and "petting" to "going all the way." According to the so-called double standard, it was expected that boys would attempt to progress as far as possible along this scale and that it was the responsibility of girls to hold the progression in check.[48] It was generally acknowledged that moving too fast would result, at least for girls, in social ostracism, but it was also acknowledged that no movement at all would result in the stigma of being unpopular. For a girl to be "popular" in the 1920s and 1930s meant to be well-liked and to be invited on dates by a large number of boys; to be "popular" in the postwar years meant to be well along the way toward "going steady," and the shift in dating practice, Breines writes, "had its sources in a need for security that paralleled the adult celebration of domesticity."[49] In order to remain socially on track, teenage girls in the Fifties had to give a little in terms of sexual favors but not too much. One of the ways they could engage in more or less intimate physical contact with boys yet still control the situation was to participate in what was generally known as "slow dancing."

Inspired by movie stars, girls in the Fifties regularly used padded and conical brassieres to flaunt their breasts, yet boys in public situations were obliged to keep their distance. The excruciating tension that throughout the postwar years resulted from slow dancing under the watchful eyes of chaperones has often been represented, usually with a touch of comedy, in retrospective movies.[50] Less amusingly, the more heightened and sometimes more dangerous tension that occurred when chaperones were not around is documented in numerous autobiographical novels.[51] Free of adult scrutiny, couples who engaged in slow dancing pressed close, and often their hands explored regions other than the smalls of their partners' backs. Considering that the choreography of unsupervised slow dancing consisted of little more than embracing and then swaying back and forth, it is hardly surprising that one thing often led to another.

Teenage or otherwise, dancers for whom postwar sentimental hits served as accompaniments to vertical make-out sessions to a certain extent were simply doing what came naturally. But one could also argue, with a fair amount of positivistic evidence, that such dancers were not just following their instincts but were responding to the songs' numerous textual, harmonic, timbral, and rhythmic cues.

As mentioned, the lyrics of sentimental songs consistently focused on monogamous romance that, if requited, would lead to connubial bliss. Although the melodies and formal structures of the sentimental repertoire were in keeping with the relatively simple models established by Tin Pan Alley songsmiths and then sustained in the 1920s by composers for the Broadway stage, the accompaniments for the postwar songs tended to be quite sophisticated. The small coterie of arrangers employed by the major labels to support their star vocalists were especially attracted to the enriched tonal vocabulary of fin-de-siècle impressionism, a repertoire that, as Rebecca Leydon points out, was "long associated with intoxicating sensuality" and was "saturated with an array of . . . sensualistic codes."[52] Pressing her point on sensuality, Leydon writes illuminatingly about the plush orchestral sound that in the early 1950s permeated LPs by Annunzio Paolo Mantovani and such numerous "Mantovani-wannabees" as the Melachrino Strings, the 101 Strings, the Mystic Moods Orchestra, and the Living Strings.[53] Like the teen-oriented dance albums issued by Ray Anthony and others, the LPs featuring "mood music" were somewhat removed from the pop music mainstream; they were pitched not to the general audience but to adults who presumably used them to accompany candlelit dinners for two, and their "highly reverberant soft-focus sound was supposed to magically inspire physical intimacy."[54] But this same sound—smooth, warm, sensuous—was applied endemically to recordings targeted for the Hit Parade.

The lyrics, harmonies, and timbres of sentimental songs were richly suggestive of sexual activity. But even more suggestive was the songs' rhythmic nature. Compared with swing and rock 'n' roll, the music was indeed sedate. This is not to say, however, that it lacked energy; on the contrary, many of the songs—albeit in a slow-moving way—were almost irresistibly propulsive. Typical of the chart-topping sentimental songs were "Mona Lisa" (Nat "King" Cole, 1950), "Too Young" (Nat "King" Cole, 1951), "Cry" (Johnnie Ray, 1951), "Kiss of Fire" (Georgia Gibbs, 1952), "Wheel of Fortune" (Kay Starr, 1952), "You Belong to Me" (Jo Stafford, 1952), "No Other Love" (Perry Como, 1953), "Rags to Riches" (Tony Bennett, 1953), "Make Love to Me" (Jo Stafford, 1954), and "Secret Love" (Doris Day, 1954). Almost always these duple-meter songs had tempos that, at approximately sixty pulses per minute, were much too slow for a proper foxtrot or anything else that involved even a modicum of footwork patterning. For reasons related to balance and human physiology, the *only* way couples could possibly have danced to this music would have been to embrace and then move—gently, to and fro, this way and that—at a tempo approximating that of "tender" sexual intercourse.

Toward Release

Seriously competing with the Soviet Union in a space race and an arms race, America in the 1950s placed high value on the opinions of professionals. "Whether or not all Americans read or believed the professionals," Elaine Tyler May writes, "there can be little doubt that postwar America was the era of the expert."[55] As suggested above, so-called experts in the social sciences publicly opined that marriage was essential for the stabilization of American society, and their numerous studies showed that most Americans believed that marriage was not only desirable but, indeed, the *only* male-female relational situation that could be considered normal. In the wake of World War II, young adults married as soon as they could, and middle-class teenagers rehearsed for marriage through their dating practices.

Something the experts of the 1950s never seemed to address was the extraordinary tension that resulted from the official encouragement of conjugal bliss amid a culture whose popular media for the most part treated sex as nonexistent. Nor did experts of the 1950s see a relationship between purely sexual anxieties and anxieties of a more general sort triggered by widespread fear of nuclear holocaust and America's infiltration by communists. Not until the mid-1960s—after the rise of militant feminism, the start of the so-called sexual revolution, and the marked escalation of the United States' involvement in the Vietnam conflict—did critics start to make the connection. It may well be, as May suggests, that Stanley Kubrick's 1964 film, *Dr. Strangelove; or, How I Learned to Stop Worrying and Love the Bomb,* was the first serious essay that "equated the madness of the cold war with Americans' unresolved sexual neuroses."[56]

But the neuroses existed whether they were acknowledged by experts or not, and surely they were exacerbated by the pop music mainstream. Notwithstanding the overt suggestiveness of "Come On-a My House," the hits of the early 1950s were overwhelmingly in keeping with a culture that valorized both marriage and premarital chastity. At the same time, the many hits whose rhythmic elements made them so conducive to slow dancing were very, very sexy.

In a bitter assessment of the generally "sweet" music of the early 1950s, Douglas T. Miller and Marion Nowak write:

> The music was, for the most part, very carefully made: mild, artificial, emotionless, cute. Any real feelings seemed to have been rendered out in a long and deliberate process. Pop records had the final passionate impact of marshmallow whip. . . . The songs spoke of yearning, longing, caring—of emotions reduced to cliché as substitutes for actual feelings. Similarly, they spoke in such euphemisms for sexual passion as the embrace of the one kiss that quenches desire. These phrases were certainly code words for sexual intercourse. But the code was so repressed, so deeply buried in the cultural subconscious, that most people could pretend it was not a code at all.[57]

However wracked with tension their private psyches might have been, married adults who were determined either to gain or maintain a secure place in postwar society readily accepted this repressive cultural code. Middle-class teenagers were conditioned to accept the code as well, and likely an influence far more powerful than their parents' admonitions was simply the prevalence in the pop music mainstream of Dinah Shore, Perry Como, and other icons of normalcy. Teenagers were encouraged to go with the flow, yet as a group they were sensitized—in large part because of their recent emergence as an economically, and thus ideologically, empowered social class—to the disturbing contradictions that lurked beneath the cultural mainstream's apparently tranquil surface.

Although the appropriate music had been marginalized by the major labels and broadcast networks, middle-class teenagers in the Fifties had a socially acceptable outlet for their physical energies in the form of jitterbug dancing. There was no vent, however, for the arguably far more potent hormonal energies that were constantly stirred by sentimental pop songs and at the same time squelched by prevailing societal norms. And then, midway through the 1950s, there occurred an explosion.

The musical genre that radically altered America's music industry—indeed, perhaps America's entire culture—did not appear out of thin air. Its incursion into the pop music mainstream was nonetheless sudden, and its nationwide impact was enormous. While adults in the mid-1950s continued to favor music of the sort that had prevailed since the end of World War II, their children gravitated en masse toward a new kind of music that seemed custom-made for their adolescent needs. To be sure, sexual tensions plagued Americans of all ages throughout the Fifties. But frustrated teenagers found at least something of a release in rock 'n' roll.

2

Rock 'n' Roll

The romantic genealogy of rock 'n' roll has it that the style resulted from the happy integration, in the early years of the civil rights movement, of decidedly white "hillbilly" music with decidedly black "race music" or, as it came to be known in the 1950s, "rhythm and blues." Supported by recent scholarship that has delved into the files of record companies, crasser analyses affirm that rock 'n' roll represents a blatant appropriation, even an "unconscionable exploitation,"[1] of black music by white entrepreneurs. And a postmodern view might regard rock 'n' roll not even as music, but as simply "a marketing concept that evolved into a lifestyle."[2] The truth, if it exists, doubtless involves all of this.

Bill Haley, whose recording of "Rock Around the Clock" upon its reissue late in 1955 turned the tide of American popular music, attested that his motivations had been purely musical. "Around the early 1950s the musical world was starved for something new," he told an interviewer for his self-published promotional newsletter.

> About the only thing in fact that was making any noise was progressive jazz, but this was above the heads of the average listener. . . . I felt that if I could take, say, a Dixieland tune and drop the first and third beats, and accentuate the second and fourth, and add a beat the listeners could clap to as well as dance this would be what they were after. From that the rest was easy . . . take everyday sayings like "Crazy Man Crazy," "See You Later Alligator," "Shake, Rattle and Roll," and apply what I have just said.[3]

But there is reason to doubt Haley's proclamation of innocence. Born in 1925 in Michigan and raised in Pennsylvania, Haley made his show business debut as a radio performer known as the Ramblin' Yodeler. He made his first recording in 1944 with a cowboy-style group called the Four Aces of Western Swing, and later he fronted the Down Homers and the Saddlemen. Significantly, with the Saddlemen in 1951 he achieved moderate success with recordings of "Rocket 88" and "Rock the Joint." Both of these indeed accentuated the second and fourth beats of a 4/4 meter; at the same time, both of them were "covers" of songs that had already climbed high on *Billboard*'s rhythm-and-blues chart.[4]

Apparently hoping for more than a just meteoric career, in 1952 Haley changed the name of his group to the Comets. The next year, for the small Essex label, Bill Haley and His Comets recorded Haley's own "Crazy Man Crazy." Although the song only briefly held the number twelve spot on the *Billboard* pop chart, it was enough of a hit to prompt Decca to purchase Haley's contract and team him up with veteran producer Milt Gabler.

"Rock Around the Clock" figured into Haley's debut recording on this major label, but the now legendary song was merely the B-side of a 45 rpm single whose main attraction was supposed to be "Thirteen Women (and Only One Man in Town)," a song whose lyrics lightheartedly describe the predicament—only dreamed—of the sole male survivor of an atom bomb attack. The disc's marketability owed more to its ebullient B-side than to its dystopian and sexually suggestive A-side, but in any case the recording "barely made the top twenty-five" on the *Billboard* chart upon its release in the summer of 1954.[5] A more impressive product, for three months holding a place on *Billboard*'s Top 10 list, was Haley's September 1954 recording of "Shake, Rattle, and Roll." "Crazy Man Crazy" had been an original creation arguably based, apropos of Haley's later comments, on the rhythmic properties of a common phrase. "Rock Around the Clock" possibly had similar roots, although in most history books Haley's version is described as a cover of a rhythm-and-blues song recorded in 1953 by Sonny Dae and the Knights. "Shake, Rattle, and Roll" was definitely an adaptation of proven rhythm-and-blues material recorded by Big Joe Turner earlier in 1954. As far as Haley was concerned, its originality had to do primarily with the facts that the song was performed by a white group and was offered, by a major label, to the mostly white audience for mainstream pop music.

The turning point for Bill Haley and His Comets—indeed, the turning point for rock 'n' roll—was the use of "Rock Around the Clock" as the main title music for the 1955 film *Blackboard Jungle*. Based on a novel by Evan Hunter that had been published the previous year, this black-and-white MGM production centers on an idealistic young English literature teacher (played by Glenn Ford) who literally risks his life in his efforts to connect with students at a vocational high school in the Bronx. Like the novel, the film features a scene that reveals much about youth's shifting attitudes toward music. In both cases a secondary character, a math teacher, attempts a lesson in symmetry by playing jazz recordings. Whereas in the novel the students reject jazz for not having the emotional immediacy of Perry Como and Tony Bennett, in the film the students react adversely to "adult" music in general. The screenplay never articulates precisely what it is that the teenagers want in lieu of adult music. Yet it is clear from *Blackboard Jungle*'s opening moments—during which the title sequence's forceful underscore transforms into "source music," apparently sounded via a portable radio, accompanying carefree schoolyard dancing—that the teenagers' appetites run along the lines of "Rock Around the Clock."

Precisely how "Rock Around the Clock" came to be connected with a gritty film about inner-city juvenile delinquents remains a matter for speculation. A rumor has it that the film's music director—that is, the person in charge of selecting and licensing preexisting music for use within the soundtrack— had a financial interest in the song.[6] More credible is the account of Glenn Ford's son, Peter, who recalls that the "Thirteen Women" / "Rock Around the Clock" disc was simply one among several that his father borrowed from his collection and brought in for perusal by the film's director.[7] In any case, a connection was made between the song and the film's subject matter, and this triggered a variety of intense responses.

Alan Freed, the Cleveland disc jockey whose promotion of recordings by rhythm-and-blues artists in the early 1950s blazed the trail for the urban white audience's acceptance of what eventually became known as rock 'n' roll, protested that the linkage was a figment of Hollywood's imagination. No more than 5 percent of teenagers were delinquents, Freed said, yet this small minority had lately been glamorized by Hollywood, and "it was unfortunate that that hoodlum-infested movie [*Blackboard Jungle*] . . . seemed to associate rock 'n' rollers with hoodlums." For conservative parents who feared that rock 'n' roll might somehow be subverting the morals of their children, however, *Blackboard Jungle* was graphic evidence of a problem they felt should be nipped in the bud.

For the record industry, the evidence offered by *Blackboard Jungle* suggested not a problem but an opportunity. Attuned to the aftershocks of *Blackboard Jungle*'s first public screenings in March 1955, Decca quickly rereleased Haley's rendition of "Rock Around the Clock." By early July the recording had reached the number one spot on the *Billboard* pop chart, and it held that position for a full eight weeks; according to a report in the trade magazine *Cashbox*, by year's end the song had proved to be 1955's biggest hit. Quite apart from whatever social critics had to say about the relationship between the music and the film, the recording's commercial success, as Charles Hamm has noted, simply "confirmed what the music industry already knew—that a revolution of major proportions was sweeping the field of popular music. At no other point in the two-hundred-year history of popular song in America had there been such a drastic and dramatic change in such a brief period of time. And it was an all-encompassing revolution, affecting not only musical style but also the entire music industry and the audience for such music."[8]

The revolution affected more than the music industry. For teenagers in general, most of whom were far removed from overt delinquency, "Rock Around the Clock" was a potent reminder of their status in America's new societal structure. Never before had teenagers possessed as much buying power, physical mobility, or leisure time as they had in the economically flush postwar years; more important, never before had they been recognized as a social class unto themselves. The controversy over *Blackboard Jungle* was much publicized, and doubtless this helped make the song an emblem for teenagers' increasing distance from the norms of their parents. Played over cinema loudspeakers far more aggressively than it ever could be on radios or phonographs, "Rock Around the Clock" for teenagers all across the country in effect became an anthem of solidarity.

Black 'n' White

"Rock 'n' roll" is a loaded phrase. On the one hand, its key words imply a sort of dancing, and in this sense it is as innocent as such other kinetically flavored genre labels as "swing," "jitterbug," or, more recently, "hip-hop." On the other hand, the idiom is notoriously sexual.

Long before the dawn of the so-called rock 'n' roll era, Harlem Renaissance poet Langston Hughes traced the phrase to a 1920s blues song whose lyrics had a female asking an intimate to "rock me all night long, Daddy, with a steady roll."[9] What is simply implied here is made explicit in a 1939 song whose protagonist says: "Take me, pretty mama / Chunk me in your big brass bed / And rock me, mama / Till my face turns cherry red."[10] The meaning of "rock and roll" is explicit, too, in a 1950 rhythm-and-blues hit in which the singer boasts: "Listen here, girls, I'm telling you now / They call me lovin' Dan. / I'll rock 'em and roll 'em all night long / 'cause I'm a sixty-minute man."[11]

Alan Freed doubtless was aware that "rock 'n' roll" in rough African American parlance was a euphemism for sexual intercourse. But he also knew that in both black and white polite society the phrase since the late 1930s had suggested simply swing-style dancing and the carefree atmosphere in which such dancing might occur.[12] Surely it was with the latter definition in mind that Freed included "rock 'n' roll" in the titles of radio programs that began in 1951 on Cleveland's WJW and then moved, in 1954, to New York's WINS. Until the reemergence of Bill Haley's recording in the soundtrack of *Blackboard Jungle*, Freed tended to use "rock 'n' roll" and its variants in reference only to dancing; at least while he remained in Cleveland, he invariably described the music itself as rhythm and blues.

Like most industrial cities built on the shores of the Great Lakes, Cleveland in the postwar years had a relatively large black population. Whereas at the turn of the century only about 2 percent of the city's residents were African Americans, the waves of migration from the rural South that followed both world wars shifted the balance considerably. In the early 1950s Cleveland had about one million residents, and approximately an eighth of those were black. But those demographics were of little concern to the city's WJW radio, which in the wake of World War II had blossomed into a prosperous media outlet whose listeners, like those of most powerful big-city radio stations, were presumed to represent postwar America's homogenized general audience.

WJW apparently was not thinking of catering to black youth when it hired Freed as a disc jockey in February 1951. Freed was expected to do in Cleveland what for the previous six years he had done for station WAKR in nearby Akron—that is, host a program that entertained late-night listeners with eclectic music and lively banter. Early in his WJW stint Freed made the acquaintance of Leo Mintz, who operated a record shop near the edge of the area where Cleveland's black population was concentrated. And from Freed's relationship with Mintz was born a long-enduring fiction.

John A. Jackson, whose research for his 1991 *Big Beat Heat: Alan Freed and the Early Years of Rock & Roll* seems impressively thorough, writes:

> The myth enshrouding Freed's introduction to rhythm-and-blues holds that in April 1951 Leo Mintz noticed a growing number of white teenagers frequenting his store, browsing through the rhythm-and-blues record section, and listening to such black stars as Charles Brown, Fats Domino, Amos Milburn, and Ruth Brown. Taken aback by the "unusual" sight of white youths perusing the heretofore all-black section of his music store, Mintz allegedly summoned his disc-jockey friend, Alan Freed, to see the sight himself.

The myth took shape with Freed saying he was "amazed" at the sight before his eyes, a sight the deejay described as "a picture of excitement," with (presumably white) teenagers "enthusiastically listening to a type of music I presumed alien to their culture." As a result of this observation, concludes the myth, Freed went on the air playing rhythm-and-blues records for white teenagers, and rock & roll was born. This romanticized version of Freed's discovery of young white America's affinity for rhythm-and-blues music has become gospel over the years, embellished upon by Freed himself, but the facts simply do not support the myth.[13]

Among the facts, Jackson says, are that in 1951 white teenagers in Cleveland or anywhere else paid almost no attention at all to rhythm-and-blues recordings; that when Freed began to feature rhythm-and-blues recordings on his radio program, he "at first attracted an audience that was nearly all Negro";[14] and that Freed claimed it was not until early in 1955—after a New York concert whose audience was estimated to be 70 percent Caucasian—that he had his "first inkling . . . that white people enjoyed rhythm-and-blues."[15]

"Moondog's Rock 'n' Roll Party," as Freed labeled his rhythm-and-blues program, debuted in July 1951.[16] Listener response was hugely supportive, and the next year Freed decided to try his hand at entrepreneurship. In partnership with Mintz and veteran booking agent Lew Platt, he rented the Cleveland Arena for the presentation, on March 21, 1952, of Moondog's Coronation Ball, a dance featuring popular rhythm-and-blues recording artists Varetta Dillard, the Dominoes, and Paul Williams. The venue accommodated approximately ten thousand, but more than twice that many people attempted to get in, and the result was a dangerous pandemonium that required police intervention and cancellation of the in-progress event. The next day Cleveland's two major newspapers, the *Plain Dealer* and the *Press*, dutifully reported on what for all intents and purposes had been a riot. Curiously, neither newspaper noted that the crowd both inside and outside the arena was almost all black. But the crowd's makeup did not escape the attention of the city's black newspaper, one of whose editors—apparently referring not just to the event but also to the radio show on which it had been promoted—wrote: "The shame of the situation lies not in the frustrated crowd that rushed to the Arena, but in a community which allows a program like this to continue and to exploit the Negro youngsters!"[17]

Probably intimidated by the city's threat of criminal charges for overselling Moondog's Coronation Ball,[18] Freed wisely proceeded to present events only on a reserved-seat basis. Most of these events—primarily in northern Ohio, but at least on one occasion in New Jersey—somehow incorporated the "Moondog" pseudonym in their titles. Most of them, too, featured black performers who had lately been given considerable airplay on Freed's radio program.[19] Long before payola was declared to be illegal,[20] Freed likely enjoyed a cozy relationship with independent labels that specialized in rhythm and blues. Yet his championing of rhythm and blues, for musical reasons alone, seemed genuine.

Its "almost unique acceptance by Negro audiences" was responsible for rhythm and blues' strong sales, declared a writer for *Variety* magazine early in 1953.[21] By the middle of the next year it was clear that the taste for rhythm and blues—or rock 'n' roll, as it was soon to be known[22]—was not at all unique to the black community, and the music's more general acceptance was due at least in part to the fact that much of it was being repackaged by white performers. Bill Haley was certainly not the only Caucasian rock 'n' roll performer who scored major hits with songs originally recorded by blacks. Elvis Presley's July 1954 debut on the Sun Records label featured Arthur "Big Boy" Crudup's "That's All Right (Mama)"; his 1955 hit "Mystery Train" was a cover of a 1953 song by "Little Junior" Parker and His Blue Flames; and his trademark 1956 "Hound Dog" was based on material recorded three years earlier by blues singer Big Mama Thornton. Pat Boone, like Presley, began his recording career in 1954, but his breakthrough did not occur until 1956, when he released cover versions of songs originally recorded by Fats Domino ("Ain't That a Shame") and Little Richard ("Tutti Frutti" and "Long Tall Sally"). Jerry Lee Lewis, merely a session piano player from 1954 to 1956, emerged as a star in 1957 with his covers of "Whole Lotta Shakin' Goin' On" and "Great Balls of Fire."

Eventually signed to major labels, Bill Haley, Elvis Presley, Pat Boone, and Jerry Lee Lewis all attracted extensive media attention and benefited from new marketing techniques that only the major labels could afford.[23] While their onstage personae represented polar opposites (Haley and Boone were "clean-cut," Presley and Lewis were "wild"), each of them was clearly a star. But many lesser lights in the firmament of white performers, especially in the formative days of rock 'n' roll, also benefited from material first recorded by blacks.[24] Until the end of 1954, writes Charlie Gillett in his *The Sound of the City: The Rise of Rock and Roll*, the white covers "invariably outsold the originals. Whether this was because of the assistance of much greater exposure from disc jockeys and the easier distribution to the retailers in white areas available to the major companies is impossible to say with certainty. But it seemed that the major companies expected, or hoped, that the audience would be satisfied by having the 'black' songs, and would not worry too much about not getting the black singers."[25]

In a context wherein white disc jockeys much preferred to play recordings by white performers, Alan Freed stands out. The son of a Jewish immigrant from Lithuania, during his Cleveland years Freed was often accused of being a "nigger lover."[26] Even as disc jockeys around the country leaned more and more toward covers, and even as his own audience—albeit more so for his radio broadcasts than for his live events—grew ever whiter, Freed persisted in programming authentically black material. Indeed, at least until the rerelease of "Rock Around the Clock" effectively homogenized the audience for rock 'n' roll, Freed remained a rhythm-and-blues purist. He protested that white covers of rhythm-and-blues songs were "anti-Negro,"[27] and on occasion he accused fellow DJs, in their preference for these covers, of racial prejudice.[28]

For black adults aspiring in the postwar years to membership in America's middle class, rhythm-and-blues music of the sort that Freed promoted was dismissed as "vulgar" entertainment. The music was held in even lower regard by middle-class adult whites, many of whom doubtless would have agreed wholeheartedly with the *Cleveland Press*'s description of both rhythm and blues and rock 'n' roll as "caterwauling" that in its listeners aroused "jungle instincts."[29]

Allusion to "the jungle" is common in criticism of rock 'n' roll as reported in the press during the 1955–1956 period. Explicit reference to blacks, however, seems to have been confined to statements issuing from America's Deep South. Asa E. Carter, the leader of the White Citizens Council of Alabama, famously argued that rock 'n' roll "appeals to the base in man, [and] brings out animalism and vulgarity," because it features the "heavy beat of Negroes."[30] Carter went so far as to claim that rock 'n' roll was part of a plot concocted by the National Association for the Advancement of Colored People for the purpose of dragging Caucasians "down to the level of the Negro" and, alternately, a kind of "psychological warfare" fought by "Communist-infiltrated groups . . . for the minds of the children and teenagers of the United States by attempting to integrate the white with the Negro."[31]

This was the exception, not the rule. As Linda Martin and Kerry Segrave point out in the quote-filled early chapters of their *Anti-Rock: The Opposition to Rock 'n' Roll*, "most anti-rock hysteria contained little that was openly racist."[32] But covert racism certainly figured into attacks on rock 'n' roll, especially after the genre established itself not just in the United States but internationally following the release of a film titled after Bill Haley's hit song.

Rock Around the Clock, made by Columbia Pictures and released in April 1956, was not the first feature-length film that attempted to capitalize on the rock 'n' roll revolution that had been sparked by MGM's *Blackboard Jungle*. Even before Decca rereleased the Haley recording, the small Studio Films company brought out *Rock and Roll Revue* and *Harlem Variety Revue*. Both of these were compilations of live-performance footage shot during the summer of 1954 at New York's Apollo Theater; both failed at the box office, but this doubtless owes as much to Studio Films' poor distribution system as to the fact that the films lacked plot and featured only black performers. In contrast, *Rock Around the Clock* (directed by Fred Sears, produced by Sam Katzman) featured "mixed" performers and at least the semblance of a plot. More important, it was a commodity issued by a major studio, and thus it had worldwide distribution.

Responding to the excitement that *Rock Around the Clock* seemed to trigger in young people all across the United Kingdom, a prominent British conductor dismissed the film's music as amounting to little more than "primitive tom-tom thumping."[33] Similarly, a Canadian clergyman, prompted by boisterous reaction to the film, said that the music called to mind "the heathen rhythms of Africa."[34] In the United States, a Baptist minister preached that teenagers' response to rock 'n' roll shows that "morally we are not far removed from the Kenya tribesman."[35] Arguing that probably much ado was being made about nothing, a writer for a major American newspaper nevertheless granted that rock 'n' roll might be described as "hillbilly music" recast into the rhythms of "the festive chorus of a tribe of Amazonian[s]" or "a Mau Mau war dance."[36] Even before *Rock Around the Clock* in effect internationalized rock 'n' roll, an American psychiatrist declared the genre as a whole to be "cannibalistic and tribalistic."[37] It is difficult to read such comments without thinking that their well-bred white authors did not somehow associate the new music with what in the mid-1950s was a very particular cultural Other.

"All Worked Up"

Racist or not, the much-publicized criticism that helped fuel the excitement in rock 'n' roll's early years fell into two main categories. One of these was essentialist and had to do with the music's aesthetic qualities and lyric content. The other—on the surface responsive to reactions from teenagers, and on a deeper level more tightly intertwined with the root system of Cold War anxiety—was sociological in nature.

Criticism of rock 'n' roll for artistic reasons alone was perhaps innocent of racism, but, considering its prime sources, it was probably guilty of jealousy. By the middle of the decade, the relatively new Broadcast Music, Inc. (BMI) was proving to be a serious thorn in the side of the royalty-collection organization (the American Society of Composers, Authors and Publishers, or ASCAP) that had prevailed since early in the century. Testifying in 1956 before the Anti-Trust Subcommittee of the House Judiciary Committee, songwriter and longtime ASCAP member Billy Rose pointed out that 74 percent of the current top-selling songs were BMI properties. "Not only are most of the BMI songs junk, but in many cases they are obscene junk, pretty much on a level with dirty comic magazines," Rose said.[38] Waxing even more confrontational, Rose argued: "I don't see how [BMI] can escape the charge that it is responsible for rock-and-roll and the other musical monstrosities which are muddying up the airwaves."[39] Three years later, *Variety* magazine reported that it was a letter from ASCAP president Burton Lane, a Broadway composer, that triggered the hearings by the House Subcommittee on Legislative Oversight into the so-called payola scandal. Although it was not publicized at the time, Lane supposedly informed the subcommittee that BMI existed "to suppress genuine talent and to foist mediocre music upon the public."[40]

To be sure, journalists who presumably had no stake in the commercial fracas issued plenty of statements that condemned rock 'n' roll in purely musical terms. But dismissals of rock 'n' roll also came from such prominent recording artists as singers Tony Bennett and Perry Como, bandleaders Bob Crosby and Paul Whiteman, and jazz musicians Milt Hinton and Billy Taylor.[41] This teenage-oriented music was popular, they granted, but it was just a passing fad, and so utterly simplistic that it was of no consequence. Later, after it seemed that wave upon wave of rock 'n' roll might indeed be eroding traditional musical values, at least a few established musicians were less polite in their criticism. Classical cellist Pablo Casals called it "an abomination" and "a disgrace," "the raucous distillation of the ugliness of our times"; veteran pop/jazz singer Mel Tormé said that rock 'n' roll is simply "rubbish"; and, not putting too fine a point on it, Broadway composer Meredith Wilson opined that rock 'n' roll was "utter garbage" that "should not be confused with anything related to music or verse."[42]

Of condemnations by mainstream artists, one of the most forceful came from Frank Sinatra, who lambasted rock 'n' roll on grounds not just musical but moral. "Rock 'n' roll smells phony and false," Sinatra declared. "It is sung, played and written for the most part by cretinous goons and by means of its almost imbecilic reiteration, and sly, lewd—in plain fact, *dirty*—lyrics . . . it manages to be the martial music of every sideburned delinquent on the face of the earth."[43]

Swaggering and forthright, Sinatra's statement articulates the criticism that a great many parents and civic leaders in the mid to late 1950s directed against rock 'n' roll. For people who grew up to the accompaniment of rock 'n' roll, or who nowadays hear in rock 'n' roll the musical symbol of a carefree bygone era, Sinatra's screed perhaps seems misinformed and mean-spirited. Read in the context in which it was delivered, however, the argument makes perfect sense.

In itself, dance-driven popular music that to postwar adults might have seemed childish would hardly have been objectionable. No one raised a fuss, for example, when Ray Anthony's supremely puerile "Bunny Hop" and "Hokey Pokey" proved to be hits among teenagers in 1953. Indeed, such music was seen as having societal benefits, because it gave teenagers an opportunity to let off steam in ways that amounted to good, clean fun. Besides, the type of dancing that rock 'n' roll inspired was not far removed from the jitterbugging that had occupied teenagers earlier in the decade and the vigorous swing-style dancing in which '50s adults had participated during the war years. To certain listeners the music may indeed have been "rubbish," but this was only part of the problem.

Another part of the problem was rock 'n' roll's lyrics, or as some of them were dubbed by *Variety* early in 1955, "leer-ics."[44] An apologist for rock 'n' roll could easily argue that the songs' words in most cases amounted to little more than doggerel verse that favored kinetic language and nonsense syllables. But an etymologically informed moralist could trace to the brothel the origins of the genre's name, and a prude could point to phrases—albeit found more often in the original black versions of certain songs than in their white covers—that indeed suggested sex. (Neither prudes nor moralists, interestingly, objected to the powerful undercurrents of eroticism that throughout the Fifties powered pop music's mainstream.)

In any case, "leer-ics" and rock 'n' roll's allegedly trashy artistic quality were merely components of what was perceived to be the real problem. The real problem had nothing to do with literary or musical aesthetics. It had to do, rather, with the way young people seemed to react to the apparently toxic blend of music and lyrics that, "dirty" or not, seemed quite mindless.

Sinatra argued that rock 'n' roll appealed to juvenile delinquents of the sort portrayed in 1955's *Blackboard Jungle*. If this were as far as it went, the rock 'n' roll problem would have been limited to members of a self-defined minority group—that is, it would have been simply a matter of young people who were already "bad" being drawn to music that was likewise "bad." But parents and civic leaders nervously took a broader view than did Sinatra.

They realized that the appeal of rock 'n' roll was endemic, not confined to a societal ghetto. And they feared that this music was triggering delinquent behavior in teenagers who, before the advent of rock 'n' roll, seemed perfectly law-abiding.

Notwithstanding the fact that the only real trouble at Moondog's Coronation Ball ensued outside the Cleveland Arena as a large crowd competed for a small number of available tickets, by the middle of the decade many adults assumed that music of the sort that Freed promoted was capable of inciting riots. Proof of this music's negative influence, even when the music was "cleaned up" by the likes of Pat Boone and other white artists, seemed to be plentiful. In May 1955 the simple blaring of a recording of "Rock Around the Clock" through a dormitory window reportedly sparked otherwise "staid Princetonians" to "set fire to a can of trash" and parade about the campus "until an assistant dean dampened their hilarity by pointing out the advantages of a more sedate mode of life."[45] In March 1956 students at the Massachusetts Institute of Technology caused a ruckus when three thousand of them packed a concert venue that allowed them no opportunity for dancing.[46] Six months later a concert featuring rhythm-and-blues singer/pianist Fats Domino at the enlisted men's club of a naval station in Newport, Rhode Island, had to be aborted, according to the investigating officer, not because of interbranch rivalry or interracial tension, but simply because of "the excitement accompanying the fever-pitched rock 'n' roll."[47]

In 1956 rock 'n' roll concerts were scheduled and then canceled, for fear of disturbances, in states as widespread as New Hampshire (Portsmouth), Texas (San Antonio), New Jersey (Jersey City and Asbury Park), and California (Santa Cruz and Burbank).[48] Entrepreneurs faced a dilemma. As *Variety* observed, rock 'n' roll was clearly "the most explosive showbiz phenomenon of the decade," yet it seemed that the music's "Svengali grip on teenagers has produced a staggering wave of juvenile violence and mayhem."[49] Echoing the theme that it was the music itself that sparked the trouble, *Newsweek* offered graphic details and an off-the-cuff analysis of an event featuring Bill Haley that took place at the National Guard Armory in Washington, DC, in June 1956. "As 5,000 people, mostly teen-agers, poured in for some rock 'n' roll, knives flashed and one young man was cut in the arm," the magazine reported. "Some of the kids danced, some scuffled, fights broke out, a chair flew. . . . The Armory manager commented, 'It's that jungle strain that gets 'em all worked up.'"[50]

Reference to "that jungle strain" is arguably an example of veiled racism. The key element of the armory manager's statement, however, is not his quasi-ethnomusicological analysis but, rather, his observation that it was the music itself, regardless of its origins, that provoked the violence. This, it seems, is at the heart of rock 'n' roll's negative reception. As voiced by spokespersons who represented the mainstream of American society, criticism directed toward rock 'n' roll had to do only to a limited extent with the music's simplistic aesthetics and the perceived obscenity demonstrated by the songs' lyrics and the onstage personae of certain performers. To a large extent, it had to do with the music's apparently causal relationship with antisocial behavior.

Those still struggling to understand what all the fuss was about would do well to remember that most adults who in the postwar years gained entry to the middle class had spent their childhoods in the darkness of the Great Depression. They were thankful for their good fortune, and they were deeply committed to the "American" values—defended during World War II at the cost of life and limb—that had made possible their upward mobility. Regardless of their race, religion, or national origin, they believed in self-discipline, hard work, and respectful conformity to societal norms. Because as children they had tasted poverty and later suffered in one way or another through a global conflict, these Americans knew better than to take their postwar situation for granted. Having paid their dues, they regarded as precious a lifestyle that was ostensibly placid. For them, music or anything else that got their children "all worked up" was far from acceptable.

Rock 'n' roll was irksome at the very least because it threatened to upset middle-class America's status quo. To some analysts, however, rock 'n' roll was pernicious on a much deeper level.

"One Step from Fascism"

Despite their European roots, the values cited above were as "American" as motherhood and apple pie, and thus almost by definition they stood in opposition to the ideologies of the United States' fearsome Cold War enemy. To argue overtly against these values was to argue against American-ness, but even subtle challenges were cause for suspicion. The infamous McCarthy hearings represent an extreme reaction to perceived anti-Americanism as articulated or implied by adults, and at the same time there was official concern over perceived anti-Americanism as expressed, however tacitly, by unruly teenagers.

Juvenile delinquency in the American '50s was not a figment of paranoid imaginations. According to the Federal Bureau of Investigation, 42.3 percent of the people arrested in 1955 for major crimes (murder, rape, grand larceny, extortion) were under the age of eighteen, and the rate of juvenile arrests in 1955 represented an increase of 11 percent compared with the previous year.[51] Naturally, government officials were concerned that seriously offensive delinquents were being portrayed in such well-financed and widely distributed films as *The Wild One*, *Rebel Without a Cause*, and *Blackboard Jungle*; indeed, Clare Booth Luce, the American ambassador to Italy, successfully campaigned to have *Blackboard Jungle* removed from the proposed slate of the 1955 Venice Film Festival for fear that the film would project "a negative image of the United States at a time when it was trying to exercise world leadership."[52]

Objections to 1955's *Blackboard Jungle* centered on the activities of the film's antagonistic secondary characters, a motley crew of high school thugs depicted as habitual practitioners of robbery, mayhem, and rape. In contrast, the brouhaha stirred by 1956's *Rock Around the Clock* had to do not with anything in the feeble plot, but with the allegedly cause-and-effect relationship between the film's abundant rock 'n' roll music and the behavior of members of the film's audience. Although the word "riot" appeared often in the headlines of newspaper accounts, in fact the worst that happened after American screenings of *Rock Around the Clock* was an incident of window-smashing in Minneapolis.[53] Fiction and reality were separated by a great distance, yet they shared a common ground of concern over what in the postwar years was regarded as a dangerous rift in the fabric of American society.

In April 1953 the United States government established a Senate Subcommittee to Investigate Juvenile Delinquency, headed initially by Robert Hendrickson of New Jersey and then, more famously, by Estes Kefauver of Tennessee. The subcommittee's first public hearings took place in New York in April and June 1954; the next year hearings took place in Chicago, Nashville, and Pittsburgh. Using psychiatrist Frederic Wertham's recently published *Seduction of the Innocent* as its prime intellectual ammunition, the subcommittee in 1954 concerned itself mostly with certain comic books that had debuted earlier in the decade.[54] The Chicago hearings (June 15–18, 1955) focused specifically on the possible relationship between juvenile delinquency and motion pictures. They involved testimony from MGM executive Dore Schary, who acknowledged that in his experience with screenings of *Blackboard Jungle* there were indeed "the usual demonstrations on the part of the kids towards the exciting music at the beginning, which now has that of a vogue, the rock-and-roll music," and that early in the film the young members of audiences indeed laughed at the character of the teacher. On the whole, though, *Blackboard Jungle* taught a positive message, Schary said, and he noted that teenagers "always applaud[ed] the end of the picture where the teacher triumphs over bad."[55]

The Nashville hearings (August 10–12, 1955), which focused on problems relating to youth unemployment, dealt not at all with music. The transcripts of the more or less general Pittsburgh hearing (December 7, 1955), on the other hand, dealt quite a bit with music, but the music-related comments had to do not so much with the malicious effect of "bad" music on American youth as with the apparently documented positive effect that "good" music, especially in the form of "good" music performed by well-disciplined and uniform-wearing members of community-supported bands, had had in numerous American cities and towns. The testimony included a lengthy statement from University of Michigan band director William Revelli that anticipates the pitch that con man Harold Hill would make to the citizens of fictional River City, Iowa, in Meredith Wilson's 1957 Broadway show *The Music Man*:

> Someday in the very near future I should like to see a survey made of juvenile delinquency as it relates to members from school bands. I am confident that our young bandsman would not be among those who are included in that vast army of present-day delinquents.
>
> Put a boy in a band uniform and his spine straightens out, his shoulders snap back, and he ceases to slouch. His carriage, which means so much to him in life, and his health are vastly improved. He realizes too that he belongs to a respected organization. He feels that he "is somebody" and the manner in which he performs not only as a member of the band, but as an individual as well will have [an effect] on both himself and his organization.[56]

For American adults who cared not to consider the possibility that the problem of juvenile delinquency might be at least in part of their own making, all that came under the subcommittee's purview coalesced into a convenient target. Once it had been identified and demonized, youth-oriented entertainment in effect "solved the mystery of delinquency," wrote historian James Gilbert in his landmark study of postwar censorship. It represented "an outside force from media centers in New York and Hollywood. It affected all classes of children. It penetrated the home." The threat to America posed by comic books and rock 'n' roll was perhaps not so grave as that posed by nuclear weapons or enemy infiltrators, but it was nonetheless serious, and it seemed that it could not be quelled by law enforcement alone. "Thus as the movement to control delinquency grew in the early 1950s," Gilbert wrote, "one of the most important corollary developments was the impulse to investigate, control and censor mass culture" in general.[57]

Suspicion of a connection between juvenile delinquency and mass culture was hardly limited to concerned parents, religious leaders, and paternalistic government agencies such as the U.S. Children's Bureau and the FBI. Whereas earlier in the century Western intellectuals tended to regard popular culture as undeserving of serious consideration, in the postwar years—informed by fresh memories of Hitler's virtuosic manipulation of the German media— they paid it considerable attention. In 1952 the magazine *Partisan Review* published "Our Country and Our Culture," a symposium to which two dozen prominent thinkers contributed opinions as to whether intellectuals should or should not serve as "inspector[s] of the nation's cultural health."[58] Most of the contributors felt that intellectuals were indeed obligated to engage with popular culture,[59] and five years later Bernard Rosenberg observed that "academicians and detached intellectuals [were] being drawn into the vortex by a suction force none can resist."[60] As Rosenberg noted in his introduction to one of the first entries in the still-burgeoning field of pop culture studies, while some critics regarded popular culture as harmless, "many more [were] alarmed by its destructive force."[61]

Contrary to values that were perceived not just as "American" characteristics but as moral absolutes, popular culture's "destructive force" was patently manifest in the arguably pornographic comic books and the violence-filled movies that came under the Senate subcommittee's scrutiny. Rock 'n' roll— because its essence was to a large extent abstract—was harder to pillory. Yet simply by its ubiquity rock 'n' roll "helped define a youth culture" that to fearful conservatives must have "seemed criminally different" and that for confirmed pessimists apparently formed "teenagers' link to the nihilism of our time."[62] Thus "critics were quick to connect the music" not just with "juvenile delinquency [and] moral decay" but also with "Communist subversion."[63] (Ironically, critics in at least a few communist countries were just as quick to connect rock 'n' roll with attempts at subversion on the part of the West.[64]) Relative to its lyrics and the onstage mannerisms of certain of its performers, the suddenly popular new music could easily be vilified for its "immoral undertones, tasteless posturings, and uncivilized character," but it took special effort to articulate precisely how the genre as a whole might somehow represent "a totalitarian phenomenon or radical plot."[65]

At a time when American intellectuals preferred to dance around the question of rock 'n' roll's political dangers, one of the relatively few direct statements came from Mitch Miller, the Columbia Records A & R executive who at the start of the decade cannily paired Patti Page with "The Tennessee Waltz" and later engineered the mid-1950s comeback of Frank Sinatra.

Miller's 1957 political interpretation of rock 'n' roll is remarkable for its bold-
ness, but it is also remarkable for the fact that it represents a reversal of an
earlier attitude. Invited to pontificate on American popular music, in April
1955 Miller had likened the whole of it, including the "rhythm-and-blues
songs" currently fashionable with "millions of white teen-agers,"[66] to a parade
of youth-oriented passing fancies, each of them novel enough to be irritating to older listeners but all of them in essence perfectly innocent. Two and
a half years later, after rock 'n' roll had radically altered the structure of the
American music industry, Miller sang a very different tune.

The aesthetic failings of rock 'n' roll were insignificant compared with its
dire societal implications, he argued. At around the time that Frank Sinatra
was claiming that rock 'n' roll songs were the products of "cretinous goons,"
Mitch Miller declared such songs to be a "glorification of monotony."[67] Echoing Sinatra's opinion that rock 'n' roll is the "martial music" of "sideburned
delinquent[s]," Miller, too, waxed patriotic. Teenagers "accept almost any
form of it, even the lowest and most distasteful," he wrote. "It seems to en-
courage sloppy clothes that become the accepted uniform. The kids take it
all without discrimination. It's one step from fascism."[68]

Fitting In

There was indeed an "accepted uniform" among fans of rock 'n' roll. In the
same 1958 article that put into general circulation Sinatra's blistering attack
on the genre, *New York Times* writer Gertrude Samuels reported her observations of young people who attended rock 'n' roll events. After commenting
briefly on rock 'n' roll's musical characteristics, its roots in African American culture, and its rise to prominence via the promotional efforts of Alan
Freed, she focused on the music's audience. She observed that the girls for the
most part wore "tight, revealing sweaters with colorful kerchiefs, skin-tight
toreador pants, white woolen socks and loafers," and that the boys generally
opted for "leather or sports jackets" and "blue jeans." "Their clothes and mannerisms speak a kind of conformism," Samuels wrote. "Physically, it would
seem as though the children feared to look different from one another, or
lacked confidence in individuality. Inside, many admit to this cheerfully: 'All
the kids have this jacket,' said one boy, 'and I don't want to be different.'"[69]

Young people in the mid-1950s of course sought to avoid being different
from one another. As will likely be admitted by anyone who has survived
adolescence, the desire to fit in sartorially with one's peers is as much a part of
the teenage condition as is the desire to rebel, somehow, against one's elders.

Conformity of dress was no more unusual for rock 'n' roll fans as it earlier had been for bobby-soxers during the World War II years or as it has lately been for American youth who have espoused the music-related "grunge," "goth," "hip-hop," "emo," or "hipster" looks. And as natural as it is for adolescents to want to dress in a way that identifies them with their cohort and at the same time sets them apart from adults, so is it natural for members of the "older generation" to abhor adolescent styles.

Miller's and Sinatra's diatribes point to specific elements of adolescent fashion that they, and doubtless many other adults, understandably found distasteful. Mixed with their attacks on sideburns and sloppy clothes, however, is an expression of genuine fear. The heartfelt eruptions by these leaders of the music industry brought to the surface a strain of gut-level criticism that was implied in the highfalutin writings of most American intellectuals who regarded rock 'n' roll as something potentially dangerous. Rooted firmly rooted in ideology, this criticism by comparison made the other complaints—that rock 'n' roll promoted racial integration, that it featured "dirty" lyrics, that it inspired unruly behavior, that as music it was just crap—seem like expressions of mere annoyance. The ideological criticism sprang from concern over the music's apparent ability to unite a relatively new, and thus not much understood, societal class.

Collectively known as "teenagers," this new societal class was very much a product of the Fifties. During World War II a handful of American psychologists and sociologists had begun to take note of a demographic group that hovered uncomfortably between childhood and adulthood.[70] It was not until a decade later, however, that older adolescents became a force with which to be reckoned.

The evolution of teenage culture and its vital link with rock 'n' roll owes hugely to fortuitous timing. Postwar sociological thinking gave the new group an official label; postwar shifts in the structure of the broadcast media provided outlets for music with which members of this new group, if they so chose, could affiliate; and along with contributing to the characteristic sound of rock 'n' roll, postwar technology allowed for rock 'n' roll commodities to be inexpensively manufactured and widely distributed. America's postwar prosperity afforded teenagers economic independence from their parents; this same postwar prosperity—hard-won, cherished, and closely guarded— invested heads of households with a sense of authority that echoed the stance of the national government. Fearful of anything that might threaten a status quo that involved repressed sexuality and racial segregation, the conservative parental authority that was endemic to the Fifties gave teenagers something against which they could easily test their newfound emancipation. Especially for middle-class white teenagers who sought to be rebellious, rock 'n' roll music—exuberant and sensual, demonstrably black in origins, so simplistic that it was guaranteed to annoy grown-ups—seemed made to order.

As fictionalized in such family-oriented television programs as *Leave It to Beaver* and *The Ozzie and Harriet Show*, and as represented by the carefully screened participants in Dick Clark's *American Bandstand* telecasts, teenagers of a certain type represented all that was officially "good" about postwar American society. The TV sitcoms dealt exclusively with white teenagers; the *American Bandstand* shows indeed included African American teenagers, but they represented an appropriately small minority of the onscreen participants, and they never, ever, engaged in interracial dancing. For his *American Bandstand* shows, Clark enforced not just strict rules of behavior but also a strict dress code that forbade girls to wear shorts, slacks, or tight sweaters and required boys to wear ties with either a sweater or a jacket. ("Nobody dressed that way in real life," Clark acknowledged, "but it made the show acceptable to adults who were frightened by the teen-age world and their music."[71]) Whether fictional or actual, and whether black or white, what all the mid-1950s televised teenagers had in common was their apparent middle-class backgrounds and, much more significant, a demeanor that was obviously respectful of authority.

Persons of intelligence, of course, realized that what was represented on television was not necessarily the same as what transpired in their own neighborhoods. Membership in the class of "teenagers," they knew, was determined only by age, not by such tried-and-true caste limiters as race, gender, education, geography, and economic status. As Samuels observed in her *New York Times* article, teenagers' enthusiasm for rock 'n' roll fairly erased traditional class distinctions. And thus, for postwar American ideologues haunted by fears of Axis fascism and burgeoning Soviet socialism, the sudden emergence of an economically empowered yet largely uncontrollable new class must have been downright scary.

There is rich irony in mid-'50s adult trepidation over codified teenage dress and the nondiscriminating behavior that, for some, it seemed to imply. In the midst of the Cold War, anxiety over fascism and socialism is certainly understandable. Especially for veterans of World War II, the garb of motorcycle gangs doubtless called to mind distasteful images of officers in the recently defeated German army, and it is true that in postwar America the black leather jacket served as an identifier for determined young rebels. But for most American teens the rock 'n' roll look was just an innocent fashion statement.

Curiously, the "accepted uniform" of teenagers that Mitch Miller found so threatening began to take shape at about the same time that Sloan Wilson and Betty Friedan were exploring, in fiction and essays, the negative effects on postwar adults of pressures to hold rigidly to societal norms. The "kid in the leather jacket," in other words, was contemporaneous with *The Man in the Gray Flannel Suit* and also with the fictionalized suburban housewife who every afternoon dutifully greeted her home-from-work husband in apron and high heels. Apparently unaware of the toll it might be exacting on their own psyches, most adults in the Fifties at least acted as though they took comfort in conformity. That so many of them tended to dress alike—and to behave alike, no matter what the emotional cost—seemed to matter little. For postwar American adults who knew better than to rock their own boats, the only "herd instinct" that caused concern was that demonstrated by their teenage children.

Straddling the Lines

Rock 'n' roll was archly gender-biased. The "race" records that helped provide the new genre with its material had female performers aplenty, and so did the pop music mainstream into which rock 'n' roll so suddenly intruded. Rock 'n' roll, in marked contrast, was almost devoid of women. As Steve Chapple and Reebee Garafalo have noted, before 1955 "female artists accounted for one-third of the positions on the year-end singles charts," but by 1956 "the proportion of women on the singles charts had declined to 8 percent."[72]

Some critics might interpret the gender shift as reflective of postwar male hegemony. Leerom Medovici, for example, argues: "Most rock music from the fifties until the end of the sixties shared the misogynist narrative politics of male modernism in its construction of a villainous feminine Other (mass culture/society) against which it rebels. Like modernism, early (and some later) rock provided a male preserve of masculine heroes whose story is the struggle for authenticity against the ever-present danger of selling out to the feminizing horror of pop."[73]

But this is an extremist view. It seems more likely that the gender imbalance of rock 'n' roll resulted fairly innocently from the savvy awareness on the part of major record labels that the largely white audience toward which they aimed their products was just not ready for uninhibited, possibly sexually suggestive, performances by women. Apropos of the volatile mix of mid-'50s conservatism and its concomitant breakthroughs in musical expression, Glenn Altschuler writes: "Women were the subjects of songs, and the objects of affection, jealousy, or betrayal. They did not *sing* rock 'n' roll songs; men sang *about* them."[74]

Females, of course, contributed enormously to the success of rock 'n' roll. It is unthinkable that Elvis Presley, for example, could have shot to stardom as quickly as he did had his live performances not been accompanied by the screams of very "worked up" young women. Frank Sinatra in the early 1940s and the Beatles in the early 1960s likewise benefited from the attention of young women, but the fact remains that the hits of Sinatra and the Beatles shared space at the top of the charts with recordings by numerous female artists. Executives of record companies in the mid-1950s recognized, and capitalized on, the explosive nature of rock 'n' roll, yet as adults surely they were aware of Fifties norms. The music they marketed could be plenty sexy, but only if packaged in a certain way, and thus rock 'n' roll in its formative years was exclusively male territory. Not until the advent of "girl groups" toward the end of the decade would the role of females in rock 'n' roll move beyond that of dancing partner and adulating fan.

Although rock 'n' roll was restricted in terms of gender, it was remarkably open—considering Fifties norms—in terms of race. Many white artists rose to national prominence with reinterpretations of material first recorded by blacks, and critics with chips on their shoulders cite the "cover phenomenon" as evidence that "prejudice, plagiarism, and financial exploitation were central factors in American recording industry practices between 1953 and 1957."[75] In the context of the Fifties, however, covers that deliberately smoothed over the "rough" sound of the original versions—for the sake of appealing to a white audience—make perfect socioeconomic sense. What makes less sense, from a Fifties perspective, is the racial vagueness of certain of rock 'n' roll's key players. Just by hearing their recordings (more specifically, by attending to their vocal inflections), anyone in the 1950s would have known instantly that Bill Haley and Pat Boone were white and that Fats Domino and Little Richard were black. But Elvis Presley, as his many biographies attest, took listeners by storm in large part because he was a white guy who "sounded black," and Chuck Berry likely scored his early successes because he was a black guy who "sounded white."

A decade after Presley, Berry, and other racially "liminal" performers rose to fame, civil rights leader Martin Luther King Jr. observed that "social integration is much easier now that [young people both black and white] share a common music . . . that sweeps across race, class and nation."[76] Whereas the idea of "a common music" perhaps seemed obvious in the open-minded late 1960s, in the Fifties this idea scarcely existed. As will be explored in the next chapter, a small yet vociferous group indeed insisted that "black" and "white" musics were fundamentally different. But the argued distinctions came mostly from adults who had distanced themselves from mainstream society yet still represented, even as they resented, Fifties norms. Teenagers in the Fifties by and large seemed not to give a hoot about the racial politics of most grown-ups. Considering how invested white America in general was in keeping the races separate, that rock 'n' roll straddled the lines as effectively as it did counts almost as a minor miracle.

3

Jazz

If Fifties teenagers thought at all in large-scale societal terms, probably they regarded rock 'n' roll as a sort of musical badge, the wearing of which identified members of a widespread new class that was defined not by race or economic status but only by age. Most teenagers in the Fifties, however, were not budding social theorists, and likely they heard in rock 'n' roll nothing more than encouragement to follow their ebullient adolescent instincts. If they puzzled over anything, it would have been the question of why so many adults, their own parents included, raised such strong objections to music that innocently prompted teenagers to enjoy themselves. Why, kids must have asked, were grown-ups making such a fuss over good-time music? Wasn't having fun, they must have wondered, what teenagers were supposed to do?

A sixteen-year-old in 1955 would have been born in 1939 and by the end of World War II would have been in either kindergarten or the first grade. In 1951 he or she would have been much exposed to the Federal Civil Defense Administration's educational cartoons in which a character named Bert the Turtle melodiously taught children that to protect themselves in the event of an atomic attack they should simply "duck and cover,"[1] and as the decade wore on he or she would have heard countless tests of air-raid sirens. Any teenager in 1955 likely would have had at least a vague idea of what the family's father—and perhaps the mother, as well—had done during the war. But, given the reticence that characterized America's postwar culture, it is highly unlikely that a teenager at the dawn of the rock 'n' roll era would have had even an inkling of the emotional trauma that adults in general had recently endured.

"Probably, we will never be able to determine the psychic havoc of the concentration camps and the atom bomb upon the unconscious mind of almost everyone alive [during the war] years," wrote Norman Mailer at the start of a retrospective essay from 1957. The essay's breathless second sentence argues:

> For the first time in civilized history, perhaps for the first time in all of history, we have been forced to live with the suppressed knowledge that the smallest facets of our personality or the most minor projection of our ideas, or indeed the absence of ideas and the absence of personality could mean equally well that we might still be doomed to die as a cipher in some vast statistical operation in which our teeth would be counted, and our hair would be saved, but our death itself would be unknown, unhonored, and unremarked, a death which could not follow with dignity as a possible consequence to serious actions we had chosen, but rather a death by *deus ex machina* in a gas chamber or a radioactive city; and so if in the midst of civilization—that civilization founded upon the Faustian urge to dominate nature by mastering time, mastering the links of social cause and effect—in the middle of an economic civilization founded upon the confidence that time could indeed be subjected to our will, our psyche was subjected itself to the intolerable anxiety that death being causeless, life was causeless as well, and time deprived of cause and effect had come to a stop.[2]

The title of the essay is "The White Negro,"[3] its deliberately provocative point being that during America's postwar years at least some Caucasian adults began to feel an alienation from mainstream society comparable to what had traditionally been the lot of black people. Mailer's essay is hardly a disciplined sociological study; it is a literary flight of fancy, a "hybrid" experiment by a "Romantic visionary" novelist,[4] "an act of myth-making, a work of fiction."[5] Personal rant though it may be, and by the author's own assessment "difficult to read,"[6] the essay is nonetheless potent, not the least because of the vocabulary with which Mailer spurs himself—and perhaps sympathetic readers—to vent frustration. The appropriate parlance, Mailer writes, includes such terms as "man, go, put down, make, beat, cool, swing, with it, crazy, dig, flip, creep, hip, square."[7]

This is the language of a new social class that came to be defined, by its detractors as well as by its members, in the wake of the construction of the "teenager." Because the two groups emerged in the mid-1950s almost simultaneously, and because middle-class Americans saw them as equally threatening to the status quo, in the popular media they were sometimes conflated. The teenage characters in the films *The Wild One* (1954), *Rebel Without a Cause* (1955), and *Blackboard Jungle* (1955) all sling the lingo that Mailer catalogs, but they do not represent the caste with which Mailer affiliates. Indeed, a flaw that all three of these films share is the inappropriateness of so much of their dialogue. Teenagers, of course, did not pen the scripts; adult screenwriters did, and they erred by assigning to juvenile characters an argot that was fast becoming fashionable among members of their own age group. In these films the jargon spewed by teenagers is actually the jargon of the adult hipster.

The term "hipster" was not unique to the Fifties. Nine years before "The White Negro," literary critic Anatole Broyard, a light-skinned African American who in effect "passed" for white, had described certain denizens of New York's Greenwich Village in an essay titled "Portrait of the Hipster."[8] But Mailer's bitter hipster differed markedly from Broyard's effete prototype. Although magnified into an archetype by Mailer's panegyric, the late-Fifties hipster was not a social fiction; he—for he was always male—was not an invented character of the sort who serve as dual protagonists in Jack Kerouac's 1957 novel *On the Road*. Kerouac's novel and Mailer's essay are autobiographical to the extent that they communicate a worldview taken by the authors themselves, not to mention many others in their circles of acquaintance. The outlook of the hipster as described by Kerouac and Mailer was far removed from quotidian anxiety over America's postwar comfort being disrupted by communist infiltrators, and it was only tangentially related to postwar fears that the arms race might escalate into a global holocaust. The late-Fifties hipster did not worry that the end was near; he *knew* it, and his prime concern was how to live in a world that had no future.

Seeking models for life in such a bleak milieu, hipsters gravitated toward a minority group that in their eyes had endured an existence without hope or promise for centuries. Hipsters—as white as they were male—looked for guidance to the black community. Most often born into middle-class environments and relatively well educated, hipsters chose to ignore the optimism expressed by the many African Americans who regarded secure employment in postwar factories as their families' point of entry into the societal mainstream. Instead, the disenchanted white hipsters gravitated toward the nether regions of black society and therein found a coping mechanism that struck them as more sensible than anything being demonstrated by their peers.

"Knowing in the cells of his existence that life was war, nothing but war," Mailer wrote, the Negro (all exceptions admitted) could rarely afford the sophisticated inhibitions of civilization, and so he kept for his survival the art of the primitive, he lived in the enormous present, he subsisted for his Saturday night kicks, relinquishing the pleasures of the mind for the more obligatory pleasures of the body, and in his music he gave voice to the character and quality of his existence, to his rage and the infinite variations of joy, lust, languor, growl, cramp, pinch, scream and despair of his orgasm.[9]

From the perspective of the twenty-first century, Mailer's idea that the prototypical Negro "gave voice" to his existence primarily through his music seems as much myopic as racist. In America's postwar years, however, the idea of Negro music as a somehow natural response to centuries of official oppression had currency not just with self-defined hipsters but also with intellectuals who in most ways swam with the cultural-political mainstream. The Negro music in question, of course, was jazz.

White Man's Music

Whether praising the music or decrying it, white authors during the so-called Jazz Age of the 1920s tended to regard the period's eponymous music as something that once upon a time perhaps originated in the African American community but that, by the time of their writing, had been fully integrated into the American cultural mainstream. Jazz during the 1920s, in other words, was a phenomenon not "black," but simply "American." Notwithstanding George Gershwin's efforts to incorporate elements of jazz into music for the concert hall, jazz was in essence the product of a music industry made up of not just performers and composers but also publishers and record labels, an industry whose prime objective was to make a profit by catering to audience tastes. At the same time, jazz was generally accepted as the natural accompaniment for young (or young at heart) people who amid the booming economy of the Roaring Twenties were bent on having a good time.

This echoes the previous chapter's assessment of rock 'n' roll as youth-oriented music born in an apparently carefree period of prosperity but disliked—because of its newness, its associations with black culture, and its allegedly corruptive influences—by conservative members of an older generation. Yet the parallels run even deeper. Contemplating the jazz phenomenon from the perspective of 1929, just before the stock market crash that plunged the United States and the rest of the world into the Great Depression, Paul Fritz Laubenstein attributed the music's enormous popularity at least in part to the "frenetic" spirit that infected America during its first twentieth-century postwar period, a period marked "by disorder, by hectic speed and high-pressure methods, by profiteering, by the passion for pilfering and for destruction, by revolt against conventions of all sorts—artistic, religious, moral, social, political—and by hurried experience in all these fields."[10] A few pages later Laubenstein acknowledged the roots of jazz and explained how jazz's seminal impulse had been absorbed by modern society as a whole. The music in effect was a "revolt against the machine domination," he wrote, an expression of the feigned "optimism of the pessimist who says, 'Eat, drink and be merry, etc.'"[11]

Laubenstein's analysis is fascinating not only because it eloquently distances 1920s jazz from jazz's ethnic origins but also because, in contrast to the accounts of most jazz historians, it links the enthusiasm for jazz to widespread anxieties triggered by culture-rocking shifts in technology, politics, the economy, and ethics. And it confirms the widely expressed idea that, by the time of the Jazz Age, the music clearly had evolved from spontaneous expressions of "Negro primitivism" into carefully crafted commodities whose reigning exponent in the marketplace was the aptly named Paul Whiteman. Jazz Age jazz did not just flow along with the cultural mainstream; so far as American popular music was concerned, Whiteman's white man's form of jazz *was* the mainstream.

* * *

The commercial vitality of Whiteman-style jazz took a hard hit with the onset of the Great Depression. Widespread closings of venues for live performance meant that many jazz musicians were suddenly unemployed, and the bankruptcies of small record companies seriously limited the public's exposure to new manifestations of music in the jazz vein. The economic crash, however, did not dampen the appetite for music that still seemed to be the ideal accompaniment for vigorous, care-relieving dancing. Jazz scholars, of course, can point out stylistic differences between music from one decade and the other. But in a general sense—that is, in terms of the music's societal function—the swing era that began in the mid-1930s simply picked up where the Jazz Age had left off. As had been the case during the Jazz Age, "jazz" during the swing era was synonymous with dance-oriented popular music.

To say that jazz as popular music lost its momentum with the last oscillations of the swing era would be a gross misstatement. This music did *not* stop; jitterbug-style dancing remained fashionable well into the 1950s, and until rock 'n' roll came along only jazz of the sort produced by the big bands was propulsive enough to suit the needs of energetic dancers. In the postwar years, however, jitterbuggers formed a rather small minority of free spirits, and music suitable for their carefree style of dancing perforce emanated mostly from vintage recordings. For a complex of reasons, after World War II America's collective musical taste (expressed especially by young adults who were newly affluent and newly married, or at least wishing to be so) shifted markedly from "hot" to "sentimental" music. Still dominated by just a handful of record labels and radio networks that together sought to distribute a limited amount of material to the largest possible audience, the music industry responded in the commercially sensible way. The effect on the marketplace was sweeping: energetic and dance-oriented jazz, for the previous quarter century the dominant strain of American popular music, was suddenly shooed out the door.

And then a strange thing happened. "Like the mythological phoenix," as one critic has eloquently put it, "[jazz] died as popular entertainment only to be reborn as serious art."[12]

Bebop/Rebop

There was no precise moment when an apparently moribund genre of popular music was resuscitated as art or when it gave up the ghost and ascended to an aesthetic/philosophical heaven. As will be readily apparent to anyone who partakes of recent jazz historiography,[13] the evolution of jazz-as-art was a gradual thing that began in the early 1940s, when jazz-as-entertainment was still in its heyday. To complicate the matter, by the dawn of the Fifties there had developed two strains of music that laid equal claim to the name "jazz" but had little in common except their self-conscious distance from the pop music mainstream.

On the one hand, typified by the suites that Duke Ellington and his band offered at such prestigious places as Carnegie Hall and the Metropolitan Opera, was jazz-flavored or jazz-influenced concert music for large ensembles whose material was for the most part fully composed and fully notated.[14] On the other hand was a new style of music, almost entirely improvised, that was delivered by small groups in relatively small venues. Because in structure, content, and mode of presentation they had much in common with the classical repertoire, the well-publicized examples of the former sort attracted attention, and sometimes won accolades, from music critics for mainstream newspapers. Music of the latter sort during its formative years was known only to its practitioners and the patrons of the smoky bars in which it was most often performed. Word spread quickly, however, and within a few years this new style—as different from jazz-based "classical" music as it was from commercial products in the still-popular swing genre—attained something of a cult status.

Allegedly born in the early 1940s in clubs in Harlem, by 1944 the new music had migrated south to New York's Midtown.[15] Before long it was being celebrated by at least a few adventurous journalists, and soon it found its way onto radio broadcasts and recordings. By the end of the 1940s the new style had even acquired a name. "Bebop" is the label by which the music was known throughout the Fifties and by which it is still known today, but early documentation as often as not identifies it as "rebop."

Clearly favoring "rebop" over "bebop," one early jazz historian suggests that the term derives from the Spanish "*arriba*," which by the twentieth century had evolved from an adverb into an exhortative.[16] This seems unlikely, however, since few of the founders of the new musical style spoke Spanish. More plausible is the idea that, as a journalist observed in 1947, "the name bebop (sometimes called rebop) came onomatopoetically, from a two-note 'BEEbop' tag that recurrently ends many of the music's phrases."[17] In 1948 another journalist took a historical view and suggested "the name probably derives from scat-singing, the nonsense phrases of Cab Calloway's heyday [in the 1930s] such as 'skee-bop.' From there the transition was easy to 're-bop' and 'be-bop,' which the music was called a year or so ago when it moved into the spotlight."[18] Looking back even further, the author of the "bop" entry in the 1986 *New Grove Dictionary of American Music* traced the term to a pair of scat syllables sung by Louis Armstrong in a recorded performance from 1927.[19]

A precise etymology of "bebop/rebop," or simply "bop," remains as elusive as one for "jazz." In any case, in January 1945 a sextet led by trumpeter Dizzy Gillespie recorded the instrumental piece "Be-Bop," and later in the same year vibraphonist Lionel Hampton scored something of a hit with a song titled "Hey! Ba-Ba-Re-Bop." By the middle of 1946, journalists in Chicago were identifying Gillespie as both the "creator of bebop music" and "its outstanding exponent."[20] An advertisement from October 1946 noted that Larry Wulfing's Los Angeles Club Royale would feature entertainment by Howard McGhee, "The Be Bop Sensation of the Nation";[21] six months later an ad in New York announced a Festival of African Dance and Music starring "Dizzy Gillespie, Be-Bop Trumpeter."[22] Nevertheless, the older label persisted. Late in 1948 the *Los Angeles Times* reported that for the past three years the University of California at Berkeley had been offering a pop music survey course that covered "the development of jazz, blues, swing, boogie-woogie and the rebop."[23] And in January of that year a feature article in the same newspaper had mentioned that bandleader Charlie Barnet owned two pet monkeys, named Xavier Cugat and Rebop, the latter name referring to "a type of jive music which both the monkey and Barnet seem to enjoy."[24]

* * *

In contrast to their often hopelessly vague accounts of "jazz," music dictionaries, when they discuss "bebop/rebop," typically at least aspire to come to grips with the actual music. The *Grove* entry, for example, states:

> [The style's] most significant characteristic was the highly diversified texture created by the rhythm section, compared with the insistent four-beat approach of the swing era. In the newer style, the basic beat was stated by the double bass player and elaborated by the drummer on ride cymbal and hi-hat, while a variety of on- and off-beat punctuations were added on the piano, bass drum, and snare drum. These punctuations sometimes reinforced and sometimes complemented the melody, causing much rhythmic interplay during improvised solos; the best bop soloists were adept at improvising rapid melodies filled with asymmetrical phrases and accent patterns.[25]

Less clinically specific, but still pointed in their descriptions, are dictionary entries that define the music as a type of jazz "characterized by improvised solo performances in a dissonant idiom with complex rhythmic patterns and continuous, highly florid melodic lines,"[26] or "distinguished by solos using dissonant chords, complex rhythms, and a continuous, mainly improvised melodic line,"[27] or "characterized by rapid, complex improvised melodies, unusual chord changes, and energetic drumming."[28]

These dictionary entries were penned well after bebop had made its mark on postwar America's musical landscape. But even when bebop was bursting upon the scene there was a rush to define it, or at least to explain how it differed, in purely musical terms, from swing-style jazz. Leonard Feather, host of a nightly jazz program on New York radio station WHN, launched a weekly series in August 1948 titled "The History of Bebop" that was devoted, according to a promotional announcement, "to tracing the evolution of the new jazz movement."[29] A few months later Sidney Finkelstein brought out his *Jazz: A People's Music*, advertised as "the authentic story of America's own music, and the people who created it, from New Orleans to bebop."[30] And the next year Feather published his *Inside Bebop*, in which he noted how the music was influenced not only by "Dixieland jazz" but also by "Debussy, Schoenberg and Stravinsky."[31]

Finkelstein's and Feather's books are notable for their efforts to put bebop into an historical perspective. Just as notable, though, are the journalistic accounts that examine not bebop's roots but simply its musical essence. In January 1947 Will Davidson, entertainment reporter and record critic for the *Chicago Tribune*, attempted to provide readers with potentially useful information. "Just in case you want a definition of rebop or bebop music," he wrote, "here is Leonard Feather's: 'It features two eighth notes, staccato, on the first beat of the bar. Its main characteristics are long, intricate improvised threads of music which go way off the original harmonic patterns of the tune, make extensive use of augmented chords, whole tone scales, and flatted fifths, and depend upon extraordinary technical facilities.'"[32] Davidson was not yet a fan of the new music. "A lot of people have had other things to say about rebop," he quipped, "but it's better not to repeat them."[33] And he observed that while the several sides of a new multidisc album that feature "the great panjandrum of rebop, Dizzy Gillespie," are indeed worth a listen, much more satisfying to his ears are the sides that showcase the playing of saxophonist Coleman Hawkins. "This isn't rebop at all—just good modern jazz."[34]

Clearly more sympathetic, eight months later the *Washington Post*'s Bill Gottlieb listed as the music's characteristics "the use of dissonant chords, the avoidance of simple oom-cha rhythmic backgrounds, the extensive use of flatted fifths and ninths, the constant shifting of basic chords within a measure (rather than the customary repetition of a chord four times in a measure), the unison playing of rapid figures and other progressive extensions into musical expression."[35]

An even more detailed description was delivered in December 1948 by *New York Times* critic Carter Harman:

> It is called "bop." Its exponents will tell you it is nothing more than a liberated style of playing jazz. Its semicontrolled frenzy, however, epitomizes a strong new tendency toward popular music for listening rather than dancing. . . .
>
> [B]op makes more "advanced" use of harmonic materials including dissonance. It is moving away from atonality, its exponents claim, although one would hate to have to determine the key from the last chord.
>
> Melodically, the music develops more like Stravinsky than Tchaikovsky. The brasses and saxophones play flying melodies of virtuoso complexity in unison, and the augmented fourth (once known as "the devil's interval") is strongly in evidence.
>
> There is freer use of uneven meters than one could hear two years ago in dance music, for the younger performers are more flexible with rhythms. They delve into the hitherto sacrilegious waltz time and even five-four bars—changes which arrangers believe would "throw a curve" to older play-

ers. Rhythms are "more legitimate" than formerly, as eighth notes are now played as written—evenly instead of "dotted."[36]

Harman's account is interesting for several reasons, not the least of which is his identification of bebop as "popular music for *listening* rather than dancing." Along with the new style's musical characteristics, the focus of Harman's attention is not on the small ensembles that gave birth to bebop and that in the 1950s would be the genre's prime source but, rather, on bebop's effect on the big bands that in the postwar years were struggling to survive. Jazz in the aftermath of World War II may indeed have been on the verge of being reborn as "serious art," but this is not reflected in Harman's otherwise astute observations. Jazz had gained enormously in sophistication under bebop's influence, but for Harman it was still a form of popular—that is, commercial—music.

Also interesting in Harman's account—and in the coverage of the new music by Gottlieb, Davidson, and most other columnists for the mainstream press—is the "colorblind" nature of the writing. Harman refers to the "bop-influenced" music of Woody Herman and the "progressive jazz" of Stan Kenton, which, "while not bop, [nevertheless] makes equal use of the modern . . . idiom." He notes that bands led by Boyd Raeburn and Ray McKinley have similarly experimented with the "progressive kick," and he concludes that "the style has influenced nearly every band in the land," including that of Duke Ellington, who seems to "have come to it in [his] own creative development."[37] Although his main concern is big bands, Harman acknowledges that the instigators of instrumental bebop were the small-group leaders Thelonious Monk, Dizzy Gillespie, Charlie Parker, and Charlie Ventura, and that bebop's vocal champions include Ella Fitzgerald, Mel Tormé, and Billy Eckstein. Significantly, nowhere in the article does he so much as hint at these artists' skin color or ethnicity.[38] To Harman and most of bebop's other early witnesses, all that mattered was the music itself.

The "Blackness" of Jazz?

Soon other things also mattered, and before long bebop would become enduringly linked with America's black culture. But the forging of this link—as a matter of perception in the mind of the general public—took place not when bebop was most vital but when the style was well on the wane.

Insistence on the black "ownership" of bebop would, of course, eventually be voiced by commentators who perhaps sought to further a particular sociopolitical agenda. One strain of the argument, introduced in hushed tones during the early days of the civil rights movement and then given strong voice in the writings of LeRoi Jones,[39] sprouted most obviously during the so-called Black Power movement of the late 1960s, when "almost overnight," according to one historian, "African-American music acquired political significance."[40] Another strain, as much neo-Marxist as the Black Power movement was Maoist, developed around the same time at universities in France and England, and this line of thought, whether coming from sources black or white, continues today.[41] In its logic and tone of voice, the politically flavored second strain stands in marked contrast to the heated claims that bebop is black music by reason of birthright and, indeed, genetics. For champions of the neo-Marxist view—that is, for members of America's late-Fifties mostly white intelligentsia—the essence of bebop's blackness was its decidedly "cool" attitude.

Although polemics have often complicated the discourse, arguments for an intimate connection between bebop and black culture are not without foundation. In recent years a rather large amount of scholarship has concentrated on interpreting the relationship between what Krin Gabbard calls "jazz mythology and jazz culture."[42] This interpretive effort has involved not just clearheaded thinking but, importantly, citation of documentary evidence. With regard to bebop, the consensus of research-based opinion seems to be that the music's wellspring was likely not at all a font of "pure" artistic impulse but, rather, a mire of resentment and bitterness that had long festered within the community of black musicians.

Steering clear of dogmatic statement, Eric Porter writes in a 1999 article that while bebop was indeed "a product of a 1940s African-American social, cultural, and intellectual milieu," it was nevertheless one that manifested itself in "varying musical expressions" and thus resulted less from "a cohesive movement" than from "a collective orientation."[43] Exercising less caution, Preston Whaley Jr. reminds readers that it is simply "well known that bebop was an artistic counter-punch to commercial pressures in the music industry that seemed to privilege white jazz players and stifle improvisation and innovation. Bebop also coincided with and mirrored disruptive social responses of African Americans being asked to support a war in behalf of a country that did not reciprocate that support."[44] And in an attempt to locate the new style within the context of the larger genre's history, Scott DeVeaux in his *The Birth of Bebop* states boldly: "If any movement in jazz can be said to reflect and embody the political tensions of its time, the aspirations, frustrations, and subversive sensibilities of an elite group of African-American musicians, it is bebop."[45]

Later in his study of bebop's origins, after detailed examination of the music itself, DeVeaux returns to this theme. Relative not just to the nation's demographics in general but especially to the demographic distribution of well-paying jobs, he explains, the number of black musicians in the ranks of wartime swing bands was disproportionately high. "By virtue of their special skills and their unique access to the broader white market," these musicians "constituted a tiny and privileged professional elite" who "lived and worked in a world apart" from most members of their ethnic minority. Indeed, while during and immediately after the war American blacks in general experienced "an enormous and often painful economic transformation," the big band musicians among them "preserved, and even strengthened, a status they had earned years before."[46]

DeVeaux notes that "the vast changes in the [American] economy and . . . social fabric" that came in the wake of World War II impacted the lives of black big-band musicians, of course, but at first the impact was little different from that felt by their white counterparts. As was the case for white band members, the sudden postwar shift in musical taste affected black players "mainly insofar as it changed the nature of their audiences and the conditions of their work."[47] But at the same time—a time that in American history stands out infamously, like the years following World War I, for the brutality of its white-on-black violence—black musicians no matter what their style occupied a special sort of spotlight:

> Their very visibility, prosperity, and social freedom made [them] lightning rods for social change. During a time when the status of black men and women was threatening to change more rapidly than at any time since Reconstruction, successful black musicians became volatile symbols: rallying points of pride for the black community (and its white supporters) or targets for abuse and violence by those desperately trying to preserve the old order.[48]

And by the mid-1950s at least a few black musicians had become "rallying points of pride" not just for the black community and its white supporters but also for the United States government.

Anxious to counter charges from the Soviet Union that American treatment of blacks was somehow repressive, in 1952 the State Department under President Harry S Truman launched a production of Gershwin's opera *Porgy and Bess* on what would end up being a four-year international tour. Impressed by the "fabulous success" that the all-black *Porgy and Bess* seemed to be having in "the free countries of Europe,"[49] in the summer of 1954 the recently inaugurated president, Dwight D. Eisenhower, asked Congress to

fund an International Program for Cultural Presentations designed to facili-
tate appearances by American manufacturers at international trade fairs and
to sponsor international tours by American sports teams and performing
groups. Along with the *Porgy and Bess* production, the first cohort of funded
traveling performers included the New York Philharmonic, the José Limón
Dance Company, the American Ballet Theater, organist E. Power Biggs, and
(when free of obligations to the *Porgy and Bess* production) baritone William
Warfield. But not until November 1955, six months after the Supreme Court
issued its volatile order for prompt integration of public schools throughout the country, and just a few weeks after the much-publicized lynching of
fourteen-year-old Emmett Till in rural Mississippi, was it suggested that the
International Program for Cultural Presentations get involved with jazz.

Addressing a crowd that had gathered in front of the House Office Building in Washington, DC, Congressman Adam Clayton Powell (D-New York)
declared: "Instead of talking about a cold war we can call it a 'cool war' from
now on."[50] And then he introduced bebop star Dizzy Gillespie, who before
tooting a few notes on his trumpet offered that, yes, "the weapon we'll use is
the cool line."[51] "Before long," Powell reportedly said, "jazz will become an
arm of this country's foreign policy in such places as the Far East, Middle East
and Africa." Along with Gillespie, Powell's plan included Louis Armstrong
and Count Basie, all of whom would lead bands "into countries where communism has a foothold."[52] Announced in early February 1956, the Gillespie
itinerary called for stops in India, Pakistan, Iran, Lebanon, Syria, Turkey,
Yugoslavia, and Greece,[53] all of them countries where communism indeed
had a foothold but also countries with which, as Gillespie later recalled, the
United States had "some sort of 'security' agreement."[54]

It was hardly a secret that the Gillespie tour had an extra-musical agenda.
By and large this was not a problem for the countries slated to host the free
entertainment, but India's prime minister Jawaharlal Nehru apparently "saw
through the cultural game that the Americans were playing."[55] Just a few
weeks before the tour was to open in Bombay, Nehru canceled the concert
and simultaneously affirmed a policy of nonalignment with the United States.
Thus "before the tour even started, Gillespie [had] a good feel for what he
later called [his trip's] 'political implications.'"[56]

These political implications may have been blatant, yet the American
media—the entertainment-focused journals as well as the mainstream
press—perceived them as not just benign but, indeed, as altogether positive. After Congress voted to support Powell's idea of making Gillespie
an ambassador of jazz, *DownBeat* magazine described the decision as "a

Utopian dream come true."[57] A few years later, in the wake of apparently successful international tours not just by Gillespie but also by Louis Armstrong, Count Basie, and Benny Goodman, jazz critic Burt Korall wrote in *Billboard*: "Jazz has succeeded where American diplomats have floundered. It has created a meeting ground, been something that made for a deeper understanding of the American way of life, for to be interested in jazz is to be interested in things American."[58] Around the same time, more or less simultaneous with television's nightly reports of Southern white mobs attacking black children as they tried to do nothing more than go to school, Willis Conover, an on-air host for the government-sponsored Voice of America radio broadcasts, claimed proudly that jazz programming "corrects the fiction that America is racist."[59]

According to Scott DeVeaux's account, "The growing acceptability of jazz as an 'indigenous American art' represented [a] first possibility" for black musicians in the Fifties, a possibility by which "black achievement could gain the attention, if not the wholehearted embrace, of the establishment." But a second and much grimmer possibility, DeVeaux notes, was illustrated by "innumerable instances of repression." As DeVeaux tells the story, it was "this explosive combination—the relatively successful and isolated world of the black musician, and the vulnerability of any black American to the slings of racial hatred—[that] provided the unique and potent social subtext for bebop."[60]

To dispute the idea that bebop's unique "social subtext" is indeed the "explosive combination" of pressures that bothered American blacks in general and American black musicians in particular in the years following World War II is to invite a fight. Ronald Radano has courageously extended just such an invitation, first in a 2000 essay and then in a landmark 2003 book whose premise is that what is alleged to be "the whole, authentic truth of black music" is really just "a lie, a social narrative that ascribes differences in order to repress subtexts fundamentally resonant in [both] black and white." Radano writes:

> The resonances of black music not only reveal the social construction of race but serve to voice and ultimately to shape and advance them. As the key cultural expression of race since the early nineteenth century, "black music," in its various articulations, has projected racial notions into the public sphere, displaying incomparable potential to travel across the social landscape. As a form easily recognized by anyone who can hear patterns in sound, black music infects white bodies with a difference that they themselves have constructed.[61]

Anyone wishing to challenge the idea that the "blackness" of bebop or any other kind of music is a socially constructed fiction can deal directly with Radano. For the purposes of this discussion, the legitimacy of Radano's archly iconoclastic views—or, for that matter, the legitimacy of the conventional views of DeVeaux and other white scholars who regard bebop as a fundamentally "black" music—is beside the point. The point to be made here is simply that during bebop's genesis and heyday in the 1940s, the opinion that the style had a racial undercurrent was voiced neither by its mostly black performers nor by its mostly white chroniclers. That opinion came later, and it was a product of the anxious period we call the Fifties.

The Beat Generation

Two years before Mailer published his "White Negro" essay, Allen Ginsberg produced a free-verse poem that begins:

> I saw the best minds of my generation destroyed by madness, starving hysterical naked,
> Dragging themselves through the Negro streets at dawn looking for an angry fix,
> Angelheaded hipsters burning for the ancient heavenly connection to the starry dynamo in the machinery of night,
> Who poverty and tatters and hollow-eyed and high sat up smoking in the supernatural darkness of cold-water flats floating across the tops of cities contemplating jazz.[62]

Ginsberg was born in 1926 in Newark, New Jersey, and in 1948 earned a bachelor of arts degree from Columbia University. Because of drug use, open homosexuality, and a history of arrests for petty crimes and hospitalization for mental illness, he was not invited—as were most other men his age—to participate in the Korean War. Many of his friends, however, were veterans, and it is tempting to think that Ginsberg saw stressful combat duty in Korea, or duty on the European or Pacific fronts during World War II, as a prime trigger of unrest among his contemporaries. But the destructive "madness" to which Ginsberg refers, like the "psychic havoc" that Mailer identifies at the very start of his essay, seems to be primarily domestic in origin.

For Ginsberg in his 1955 "Howl" as much for Mailer in his 1957 "The White Negro," the alienation experienced by certain members of their largely white, largely well-educated peer group resulted not from wartime trauma but from peacetime frustration. While most American adults at least acted as though they enjoyed the prosperity and security of the Fifties, some found the situation hard to bear. The postwar years yielded not just bountiful fruits but also endemic complacency and ever-pressing demands to conform. Along with America's new status as a superpower came the government's harsh response to perceived internal threats and the citizenry's awareness of the dreaded weapons that supposedly kept at bay the external enemies. Those who cared to think about this took on a heavy yoke, for they knew that trying to change the flow of American society was impossible and that their best-intentioned acts of rebellion were hopeless. Increasingly as the postwar years wore on, the deep thinkers felt defeated and spent.

According to a 1952 article that novelist John Clellon Holmes contributed to the *New York Times*, the term "beat generation" had been first used several years earlier, in casual conversation, by fellow novelist Jack Kerouac. Holmes wisely cautioned that "any attempt to label an entire generation is unrewarding." Nevertheless, he wrote, "the generation which went through the last war, or at least could get a drink easily once it was over, seems to possess a uniform, general quality which demands an adjective."[63] And the appropriate adjective, he suggested, is "beat."

"More than mere weariness," Holmes explained, the word "beat" suggests the feeling of "having been used, of being raw," the feeling of being "reduced to the bedrock of consciousness," of being "undramatically pushed up against the wall of oneself." "A man is beat whenever he goes for broke and wagers the sum of his resources on a single number."[64] And the young American adults of the early 1950s, he claimed, had been doing precisely that—going for broke—since their early youth.

By the end of the decade, thanks largely to Holmes's article, the phrase "beat generation" was in common usage. Its popularization had nothing to do with the fact that in 1957 Kerouac wrote a play called *Beat Generation*, for the play went unstaged and has only recently come to light.[65] But in 1958 the term figured in the title of a widely reviewed literary anthology,[66] and a year later there was actually an attempt to copyright it in conjunction with the making of a low-budget Hollywood film.

Independently produced yet distributed by MGM, 1959's *The Beat Generation* was a murder mystery that reflected little of the utter seriousness intended by Holmes and Kerouac when they first used the adjective "beat" to describe themselves and certain of their contemporaries. Nor was there anything serious, or complimentary, conveyed in the coinage, by *San Francisco Chronicle* columnist Herb Caen in April 1958, of the term "beatnik." Writing shortly after the Soviet Union's much-publicized launch of the Sputnik satellite, Caen wrote: "*Look* magazine, preparing a picture spread on S.F.'s Beat Generation (oh, no, not AGAIN!), hosted a party in a No[rth] Beach house for 50 Beatniks, and by the time word got around the sour grapevine, over 250 bearded cats and kits were on hand, slopping up Mike Cowles' free booze. They're only Beat, y'know, when it comes to work."[67] Despite Caen's claim that he never meant the term to be derogatory,[68] soon enough "beatnik" was being used by mainstream publications around the country as a synonym for people who perhaps shared certain tastes in fashion and music but whose most significant attribute was their fundamental laziness.[69]

As portrayed in the media, beatniks of the male sort were indeed bearded "cats" who typically wore berets, sandals, and, even at night, dark glasses, and whose philosophical ramblings were richly spiced with hipster talk of the sort that Mailer cataloged in his essay. Their female counterparts favored "black wool stockings, dark green or black skirts, black sweaters and flat-heel walking shoes" and often sported "long straight hair and severe eye make-up."[70] For all their dark clothing, the beatniks as stereotypes were nonetheless plenty colorful, and, thanks first to abundant newspaper and magazine coverage and then to theatrical fictionalizations that invariably featured jazz-flavored accompaniments, by the end of the decade beatniks had become solidly established cultural icons.

Whether caricatured or not, those who were affiliated with the beat lifestyle served as convenient scapegoats for mainstream American adults who, while perhaps reluctantly tolerant of overt misbehavior on the part of teenagers, had little use for brooding dissent among members of their own age group. For a Fifties teenager, to be "hip" was simply to be "with it," to join with his or her peers in a sweeping cultural trend whose apparent acts of rebellion—for the most part directed against parental authority—were correctly regarded by psychologists of the time as just so many innocent manifestations of adolescence. Irritating as they must have been for many parents, the shenanigans of the average would-be hip teenager could easily be forgiven; after all, the parents of Fifties teenagers had themselves suffered through the hormonal and emotional throes of adolescence, and doubtless even the most tightly wound of them remembered what it had been, once upon a time, to be young and foolish. All things considered, most Fifties teenagers acted out in ways that were arguably quite normal; beatniks, on the other hand, pursued a lifestyle that, in comparison to what seemed to be expected of Fifties adults, was decidedly—and perhaps dangerously—abnormal.

Articulating significant differences between the stereotypical rebellious teenager and his beat generation counterpart, in 1958 the *Chicago Tribune*'s William Leonard wrote of the latter:

He is beyond the teen-ager's leather jacket uniform, the motorcycle, Elvis Presley, switchblade knives, or rock 'n' roll. He is a more complicated neurotic, a
highly dedicated rebel several years or more past his teens, who loathes all of
modern western society, including Christianity, comfort, respectability—and
even teen-agers themselves!

He hates the thought of the 40-hour working week, of suburbia and its television antennae, of supermarkets and bowling leagues, of commuter trains
and dry cleaning, of conformity and respectability.[71]

The so-called Beats, in other words, were against almost all that postwar
America was for. Instead of acting their age, which in the postwar years
meant holding a steady job, heading a family, and in all other ways playing
by societal rules, these older rebels chose "to opt out of the System altogether
and to try to remain permanently within the youth culture."[72] At a time when
many American husbands were at least attempting to respond to their wives'
first stirrings of gender liberation, the Beats remained defiantly masculinist,
favoring "non-binding commitments" over marriage and linking themselves
only with women who fell easily into "the 'chick' category of the attractive,
young, sexually available and 'dumb' female."[73]

The Beats were colorful, indeed. Were they merely immature ne'er-do-
wells, however—were they just "eternal children, divine fools, pure-hearted
simpletons detached from the world and innocent of its machinations"[74]—
they likely would have been ignored. But for the most part they were people of
conscience whose disavowal of mainstream society resulted not from inertia
but from acts of will; their location on society's edge resulted from choice,
not circumstance. They tended to come from privileged backgrounds; by
and large they were well educated, and thus many of them—doubtless to
the chagrin of those who served as guardians of America's "official" postwar
values—were quite articulate. Typically the literary output of the Beats involved not just grim portrayals of Fifties consumerism and conformity but
also pointed criticism of the frightful situation into which the United States,
through its participation in the Cold War and the arms race, had gotten itself. As one literary critic recently observed, during the 1950s "virtually no
mainstream theater and very little mainstream American fiction directly
addressed the possibility of nuclear annihilation," yet "of the writers who
did take on the subject, the Beat poets were the most vocal."[75]

The reverberations of his "Howl" still ringing, Ginsberg followed up with
a poem in which he expressed a sentiment that was doubtless shared by all
his fellow Beats. One suspects that in subtle forms the basic sentiment was

also shared by a great many other Americans—teenagers as well as adults—
who in the Fifties seemed to have little choice but to accept the status quo
and who felt compelled, for various reasons, to toe society's line. Addressing
not so much the U.S. government as the society that the government in the
postwar years had created, Ginsberg wrote:

> America I've given you all and now I'm nothing.
> America two dollars and twenty-seven cents January 17, 1956.
> I can't stand my own mind.
> America when will we end the human war?
> Go fuck yourself with your atom bomb.[76]

A "Bunker Mentality"

From a Parisian perspective that had little to do with postwar American-style
supermarkets, bowling leagues, fast-food outlets, or dry cleaning establish-
ments, André Hodeir in 1954 noted that "jazz fans live in a world apart."[77] It
was a difference that Hodeir not so much observed as presumed, a social strati-
fication that was perhaps largely imagined by Hodeir and other French jazz
aficionados who regarded themselves, by virtue of their ability to appreciate
"difficult" music, as members of an intellectual elite. But jazz-related "isolation and self-segregation" had been documented by the American sociologist
Howard S. Becker as early as 1949.[78] Serious ethnographic research into the jazz
crowd's distance from mainstream American society continued through the
postwar years.[79] And all of it supports the conclusion drawn decades later by
jazz historian Ted Gioia, to the effect that jazz, ever since the demise of swing,
has been "an underground movement" whose stars have been "cult figures from
beyond the fringe," a movement whose self-conscious resistance to trends in
commercial music reinforced, as much among its devotees as among its practitioners, a "bunker mentality."[80]

"Bunker mentality" seems an apt term for the attitude harbored not just
by those who truly belonged to the beat generation but also by those who
merely sojourned, at their convenience, in the hip demimonde. There is no
telling, of course, how participants in the beat/hip culture truly felt about art
of any sort. It makes perfect sense, though, that those who deliberately and
often ostentatiously positioned themselves outside American society would
have chosen, as the accompaniment for their lifestyle, a music that was officially beyond the fringe. The narrator of Jack Kerouac's *On the Road* recalls:
"At lilac evening I walked with every muscle aching [through] the Denver

colored section wishing I were a Negro, feeling that the best the white world has offered me was not enough ecstasy, not enough life, joy, kicks, darkness, music, not enough night."[81] Kerouac's fellow travelers apparently agreed; most of them, keenly aware of appearances, rather liked to see themselves "reflected darkly in the dangerous, uneven surfaces of contemporary avant-garde" music.[82]

In postwar America "contemporary avant-garde" music took many forms. But for the hipster, the description applied only to bebop and its offshoots; the "blacker" the better, jazz served as the perfect aural unifier for the small but articulate minority of adult white Americans who in the Fifties boldly opted to distance themselves from the societal mainstream. It certainly seemed that way to writers like Kerouac, Ginsberg, and Mailer, whose prose and poetry fairly drips—sometimes almost in an obscene way—with celebrations of jazz's primordial qualities. But it seemed that way, too, for Fifties psychologists and psychiatrists whose involvement with jazz and its subculture was purely clinical.

One of these clinical professionals observed that jazz, in and of itself, was an irritant to the general public, a form of music that right from the start was in conflict with America's "Puritan tradition" and thus caused for the majority of Americans "uncertainty, bewilderment, confusion and ultimately anxiety." Because of this, he concluded, jazz, with its "unspoken protest, [its] kinesthetic release, [and its] stimulation of repressed erotic drives," has an "irresistible appeal" and "strike[s] a responsive chord in the spirits of those members of society who regard themselves as at once its outcasts and its prisoners."[83] Clearly influenced by the Freudian theory that held sway in the mid-'50s, another clinical professional attested:

> Jazz as the music of the Negro represented a protest against an existing oppressive culture; that it therefore became the music attractive to those social elements in protest; that through its resultant associations in [the New Orleans brothel district of] Storyville, jazz came to symbolize the repressed Id drives; that because of this symbolization and its role as a cultural protest, jazz is continually rejected by the mass representation of the Superego, the culture; that each change of jazz style resulted from an attempt to weaken or intensify its symbolization of the Id drives; that the psychology of jazz represents an ambivalent conflict between the forces of the Id and Superego.[84]

Offered such heady explanations of his fondness for jazz, a beatnik in the late 1950s likely would have snapped his fingers in offbeat accompaniment to some imagined melody and then responded with something along the lines of "Yeah. Cool, man. And, like, I really dig those symbolizations of my crazy id drives." But were he sober, and were he far enough away from other cats and chicks so that he could safely step back from his hipster façade, the beatnik might well have agreed with the psychologist's assessment.

Especially late in the Fifties, bebop was as potent an emblem for the self-consciously sophisticated adult hipster as rock 'n' roll was for the admittedly confused teenager. Today's readers should not be misled by the fact that Hollywood screenwriters, most of whom might be counted as clueless "squares," often erred egregiously in their attempts to link teenagers or hipsters with their presumably iconic music. In fact, bebop and rock 'n' roll, like the cultural subgroups with which they are affiliated, have very little in common.

The apparently open-minded protagonist of Chuck Berry's 1957 song "Rock 'n' Roll Music" in the first verse declares:

> I have no kick against modern jazz
> Unless they try to play it too darn fast
> And change the beauty of the melody
> Until it sounds just like a symphony.

Modern jazz may not have sounded "*just* like a symphony," but clearly it contained more complexity than the average Fifties teenager was willing to confront. At least some modern jazz shared with rock 'n' roll the important "backbeat" that Berry mentions in his song's chorus.[85] And perhaps modern jazz and rock 'n' roll also shared a concept of blackness that had both negative and positive connotations. But what the two genres most had in common was their deep and fundamental contrast—in the music itself, in what it stood for—with the still pervasive popular music mainstream.

4

Hollywood

One of the ironies that color the history of the American film industry is the fact that its most glorious years, in terms of profitability, were those during which the entire nation struggled desperately to pull itself out of the abysmal depths of the Great Depression, and its darkest period, measured by the same criterion, were the postwar years that found "the American people . . . in the pleasant predicament of having to learn to live 50 percent better than they [had] ever lived before."[1]

Hollywood was as hard hit as any other industry by the stock market crash of 1929. Between 1930 and 1932 weekly attendance at the movies plummeted by 40 percent, and the number of movie theaters that managed to stay in business fell from around 22,000 to 12,480.[2] But the captains of the film industry cannily took advantage of several of the "New Deal" offers extended in 1933 by President Franklin D. Roosevelt. Older cinemas were refurbished and new ones were built, and almost all of them were equipped with air-conditioning systems. After 1933 "movie houses across the country opened at a rate of about 1000 yearly"; over the course of the decade, weekly attendance increased from 45.1 million to 54.6 million, and "the upward spiral continued through the war years."[3] Owing in part to smart business practices and in large part to an audience desperately in need of inexpensive escapist entertainment, the American film industry after 1933 "thrived on a felicitous circle of economic dependence on attendance, exhibition, and production," and "only after World War II did the circle of dependence reverse itself and turn vicious."[4]

Hollywood's reversal of fortune was so dramatic that by 1949 a prominent producer was telling his assembled colleagues not only that "the economics of the business [had] gone very sour" but also, and without exaggeration, that many of the nation's film studios were "struggling desperately to make ends meet."[5] The decline had been precipitous since 1946, when the industry's domestic box office receipts reached an all-time high of $1.7 billion.[6] This was not due to mismanagement on the part of generally savvy movie moguls; rather, it was due to a "perfect storm" of problems that were all quite beyond the moguls' control.

A "Perfect Storm"

Some of the problems came from overseas. Hollywood in physical terms was bothered not at all by World War II, and its export business profited hugely from the fact that hitherto productive film industries elsewhere in the world were seriously disrupted—in some cases literally devastated—by the conflict. In the war's dusty aftermath these industries put themselves together again as quickly as they could, and many of them, in willful acts of self-resuscitation, declared a restrictive limit on the number of American films that could be shown in their cinemas. The result, as the New York Times reported, was "a sharp decline in [Hollywood's] overseas markets."[7]

Most of the problems that beset postwar Hollywood, however, were home-grown, and at least some of them were directly related to America's postwar anxiety. For example, the mood of Hollywood throughout the Fifties was severely darkened by a cloud of suspicion emanating from hearings conducted by the House Committee on Un-American Activities.[8] Commonly known as HUAC, the committee in 1947 was determined to ferret out communists and communist sympathizers in the film industry. One of its first targets was Hanns Eisler, a German composer who had settled in Hollywood in the early 1940s and who had the misfortune not just of associating with left-leaning Hollywood figures but also of being the brother of the leader of America's Communist Party. Although neither the HUAC hearings nor a six-year investigation by the FBI revealed evidence that Eisler was in any way a threat to the American way of life, a deportation order was nonetheless issued. Eisler's harsh treatment by HUAC in May and September 1947 attracted the attention of members of America's relatively small classical music community; the HUAC events that began in October of that year—in large part because they were spectacularly protested against by such popular movie stars as Humphrey Bogart, Lauren Bacall, and Danny Kaye—captured the attention of the entire American public.

Taking its cue from a series of finger-pointing articles authored by William R. Wilkerson and published in the Hollywood Reporter in the summer of 1946, for its second round of hearings HUAC first elicited testimony from such Hollywood stalwarts as Walt Disney and Ronald Reagan to the effect that there indeed were "commies" in Hollywood and then subpoenaed the forty-three individuals named in Wilkerson's articles. The ten of these who absolutely refused to answer questions—the famous "Hollywood Ten"—served prison sentences for contempt of Congress.[9] Most of the other subpoenaed witnesses cooperated, more or less, and some of them identified colleagues that they knew to have, or suspected of having, communist tendencies. The result was an unofficial but nonetheless real "blacklist" that over the course of the next several years, and especially after yet another round of HUAC hearings in 1951, grew to contain more than three hundred names.[10]

Around the same time that individual members of the film industry started to come under attack for political reasons, Hollywood in general came in for an onslaught of criticism on grounds not political but moral. Moralistic criticism of American motion pictures was certainly not unique to the postwar years, but throughout the long decade of the Fifties filmmakers found that they needed to respond not just to their own Production Code Administration but also to increasingly loud complaints both from autonomous censorship boards in various states and cities and from such high-minded national organizations as the American Legion, the Council of Churches of Christ, and, most powerful of all, the Roman Catholic Church's Legion of Decency.

According to the watchdogs, censorship was entirely benevolent, a form of oversight designed primarily for "the protection of our youth," enacted only for the sake of "improving their moral fiber" and giving them "a lift along the right road to life."[11] But according to film producer Samuel Goldwyn, censorship was "an intolerable invasion of our rights as free people in a free nation."[12] In 1948 the Catholic archbishop of Chicago suggested to the Theater Owners of America that the *absence* of proper censorship was in large part responsible for the film industry's financial problems.[13] Contrarily, in 1949 Goldwyn told the same group that "censorship of films is the reason that people in adult age brackets stay out of movie houses in droves."[14]

But there was another reason, easier to quantify than the effects of censorship or the lack thereof, that led people on the eve of the 1950s to stay away "in droves" from movie theaters. In 1942, just before the Federal Communications Commission (FCC) temporarily halted the production of broadcasting equipment for civilian purposes, approximately 7,000 television sets were in operation within the borders of the United States, most of them in the vicinity of New York City.[15] With wartime restrictions relaxed, by 1947 the number of television sets had grown to 44,000; by 1949 the number was estimated at 950,000, with sets "being produced at the rate of 161,000 per month";[16] and in 1950, the FCC reported that that year's sales of television sets amounted to 7.3 million.[17] Just as there was a staggeringly huge increase in the number of television sets in the early postwar years, so there was an exponential increase in the number of broadcast facilities that attempted to provide owners of television sets with what they apparently wanted.

It is understandable that when commercial television in the United States was still in its infancy, Hollywood executives would think of television as an "enigmatic shadow" that caused them "apprehensive bewilderment."[18] But it is a wonder as to why the trade magazine *Variety* as late as 1951 would publish an article that bore the headline "TV's Impact a Puzzler."[19] Even in 1951 a great many Americans were opting to forgo the movies and, instead, sit in front of their television sets and enjoy such fare as *The Ed Sullivan Show, Texaco Star Theater, Fireside Theatre, What's My Line?, The Trouble with Father, The Jack Benny Program,* and *The Honeymooners.* For the movie industry, television posed serious competition. To use a cliché doubtless born during the space age, one did not need to be a rocket scientist to see that there was a real problem.

*   *   *

As hard a blow to its box office as television surely was, as much as censorship seemed to be an "awful millstone around the neck of the motion-picture industry,"[20] and as much as the blacklist polluted the entire business with an "atmosphere of uncertainty and, later, downright fear,"[21] the thing that hurt Hollywood the most during the Fifties—and the one that ultimately had the largest effect on film music—was a decision by the U.S. Supreme Court.

For Hollywood, World War II had perhaps been "a blessing in disguise . . . , what with the artificially stimulated movie market, the vigorous economy, and the government's suspension of its anti-trust efforts" that dated back to 1938.[22] But in 1948 the Office of the U.S. Attorney General revived what a decade earlier had been described as "one of the largest anti-trust suits ever filed by the government against an industry."[23] The original suit targeted eight of the leading film studios—Paramount, MGM, RKO, Warner Bros., Twentieth Century-Fox, Columbia, Universal, and United Artists—and charged them with "monopolistic practices" that would, "unless checked, drive all the independent exhibitors out of business";[24] the 1948 suit was directed primarily against Paramount, but the other studios were listed as co-defendants.

The Supreme Court's ruling of May 1948 ordered that the major studios divest themselves of the hundreds of movie theaters they owned nationwide. This "dealt staggering blows to the motion picture industry,"[25] because in effect it mandated a "complete divorcement" of the studios' production facilities from their guaranteed distribution outlets. It took several years before the details of divestiture were worked out, but all the studios eventually complied with the ruling. And with this, Hollywood's once glorious studio system—which involved veritable armies of full-time employees who ranged from high-profile movie stars and directors to anonymous seamstresses, set painters, and animal wranglers to ticket takers and popcorn vendors in cities around the country—came to a bitter end.[26]

"The biggest, richest studios were hit the hardest," writes film historian Gerald Mast, because two of their hitherto most valuable assets—physical property and a large stable of very talented people—"suddenly became liabilities."[27] "In 1949, MGM declared wage cutbacks and immense layoffs. The giant studio's rows of sound stages and acres of outdoor sets became increasingly empty; the huge film factories now owned vast expanses of expensive and barren land. Even more costly than land were the contracts with people—technicians, featured players, and stars—that required the studio to pay their salaries despite the fact that it had no pictures for them to make."[28] Among the hundreds of rank-and-file employees laid off at MGM and at the other studios, and among the dozens of high-profile employees whose multiyear contracts were simply allowed to expire, were the composers, orchestrators, copyists, conductors, and orchestra members who over the previous decade and a half had contributed so much to the golden age of film music.

Scores for large orchestras certainly continued to accompany films through the 1950s and beyond; also continuing, because they worked so well in escapist entertainments with clear-cut plots, were the musical conventions of the so-called classical-style film.[29] But big orchestral scores would now be written and performed by freelancers, not by composers and orchestral musicians employed full-time by one studio or another. And the tried-and-true musical conventions of the past would now be challenged by up-to-date filmmakers whose work was intended to be not so much escapist as thought-provoking.

The postatomic world inspired filmic stories that in various ways reflected the period's zeitgeist. Because of both their emotional tone and their subject matter, these stories encouraged filmmakers to experiment with types of music whose sounds and styles would have been simply unthinkable in earlier days. As Hollywood hunkered down for its prolonged "winter of extreme discontent,"[30] American film music in effect reinvented itself.

A Crash of Symbols

Changes in the industry around 1950 allowed such outré genres as modern jazz and rock 'n' roll to find their way into film soundtracks, but on the whole the spirit of the times was represented less by Hollywood's music than by its narratives and images. "Whatever their genre," writes Peter Biskind, films from the Fifties "share a preoccupation with the pressing issues of the day—conformity, dissent, minorities, delinquency, and sex roles. All reflect the particular constraints of the Fifties' cultural and political climate."[31] To claim that *all* of Hollywood's postwar output was preoccupied with pressing societal issues, or reflective of "particular constraints," is surely an exaggeration. One need not search very hard, however, to find films that indeed articulate one or another of the period's conflicting ideologies.

Symbols of sex roles are perhaps the easiest to spot. The idea that married women should be pretty but essentially sexless wives and mothers, devoted completely to their husbands and children, was projected powerfully by characters such as those played by June Allyson in *The Glenn Miller Story* (1954) and by Doris Day in *The Man Who Knew Too Much* (1956). The idea that physically attractive yet still unmarried women aspired to the same status of self-sacrificing wifehood, no matter what their talents or career interests, was just as powerfully projected by, for example, Grace Kelly in *Rear Window* (1954), Dana Wynter in *Invasion of the Body Snatchers* (1956), Audrey Hepburn in *Funny Face* (1957), and Eva Marie Saint in *North by Northwest* (1959). And the idea that at least *some* women were for morally upstanding men dangerous temptresses was stunningly illustrated by the likes of Marilyn Monroe in *The Seven Year Itch* (1955) and Jane Russell in *The Las Vegas Story* (1952). One need only glance at the bosoms of these actresses to understand the characterizations: the soft voluptuousness of Monroe and Russell contrasts as much with the perky "pointiness" of Wynter and Saint as it does with the buttoned-up chasteness of Allyson and Day.

Juvenile delinquency was conveniently depicted by dramas involving characters who sported ducktail haircuts and leather jackets or, worse, rode motorcycles. But in this case one has to follow the plot with a modicum of attention to distinguish films that state the obvious message from films that suggest delinquency might be caused by some fixable social problem. Virtually all the teenage characters who populate *Blackboard Jungle* (1955) and such low-budget drive-in films as *Girls in the Night* (1953), *The Green-Eyed Blonde* (1957), and *Young and Wild* (1958), for example, are stark illustrations of all that seemed to be wrong, or could go wrong, with the youth of the 1950s. In contrast, the gang leader played by Marlon Brando in *The Wild One* (1953) is a young man turned bad simply because of lack of love and understanding, the loner played by James Dean in *Rebel Without a Cause* (1955) is the product of aloof and self-absorbed parents, and the violence-prone character played by Michael Landon in *I Was a Teenage Werewolf* (1957) is the victim not just of a faulty scientific experiment but also, and primarily, of unchecked adolescent hormones.

I Was a Teenage Werewolf is of course a science fiction film—that is, a film whose fiction depends at least in part on something arguably having to do with science. Science fiction had been a part of the American film tradition since as early as 1910, when the Edison Company released a sixteen-minute silent treatment of Mary Shelley's *Frankenstein*, and prewar Hollywood produced such enduring sci-fi classics as *Frankenstein* (1931), *Dr. Jekyll and Mr. Hyde* (1931), *The Bride of Frankenstein* (1935), and *The Invisible Man* (1933). But science fiction, generally speaking, remained a marginal Hollywood genre until the start of the 1950s. Then, and suddenly, it became all the rage. Indeed, the production of hundreds of science fiction films within the span of a decade represents something of a cinematic landmark, for "never in the history of motion pictures has any other genre developed and multiplied so rapidly in so brief a period."[32]

The proliferation of American sci-fi films around 1950 is symptomatic of an explosive fusion of postwar concerns that became increasingly public after the first round of HUAC hearings in 1947; the numerous accounts of developments in Soviet as well as American rocketry in 1948; and the especially frightening news, in September 1949, that the Soviets, too, had an atomic bomb. Some science fiction films, of course, were simply adventure stories that involved the exploration of outer space. But most of them had to do with invaders from other planets, monstrous by-products of radiation, or some sort of cataclysmic end of the world. Most of them, too, were low-budget affairs aimed at teenagers and their younger siblings. Regardless of their target audience, as a whole these films served as "an important vehicle for articulating cultural anxieties and for commenting . . . on those concerns."[33] Even children in the Fifties had to learn to live with the possibility of a Soviet takeover or, worse, the concept, "almost insupportable psychologically," of "collective incineration and extinction which could come at any time."[34] Perhaps they learned their lessons more easily from cinematic exposure to Martians and giant mutant ants than from anything that might have been said to them by their nervous parents.

A science fiction film that doubtless entertained plenty of kids but nevertheless has a disturbingly adult theme is *Invasion of the Body Snatchers*.[35] It is only coincidence that the film's male star (Kevin McCarthy) shared a surname with Joseph McCarthy, the senator from Wisconsin who distinguished himself in February 1950 by declaring that he knew the names of communists who worked in the U.S. State Department and then later, from his position as chairman of both the Senate Committee on Government Operations and the Senate Permanent Subcommittee on Investigations, in 1953 and 1954 led the most notorious witch hunts the American political system has ever known. It is hardly a coincidence, though, that the film presses hard on a sore spot that likely bothered most grown-up Americans during the Fifties. Whether one regards the cold-blooded fruits of the body-snatching "pods" as representing communism or militant anticommunism, it remains that the horrific theme of *Invasion of the Body Snatchers* is "neither death nor destruction but dehumanization, a state in which emotional life is suspended, in which the individual is deprived of individual feelings, free will, and moral judgment."[36] In other words, the film is a nightmare vision of enforced conformity.

There were, of course, other films from the Fifties—serious films, not at all for kids, in genres other than science fiction—that dealt with individuals struggling against societal pressures to conform. One thinks, for example, of *12 Angry Men* (1957), a courtroom drama in which a lone juror stands up to his prejudiced peers; or *The Man in the Gray Flannel Suit* (1956), in which an executive for a television network has to choose between loyalty to his family and very lucrative loyalty to the company; or *Paths of Glory* (1957), a World War I picture that depicts a unit commander defying the orders of his megalomaniacal general.

There were films that dealt with the typically high cost of outspoken dissent against a prevailing norm; these famously include *On the Waterfront* (1954), in which a stevedore is beaten to within an inch of his life for defying the criminals who control the dockworkers' union, and *Spartacus* (1960), a sword-and-sandals epic that in its final scene shows the title character gruesomely crucified for leading a slave rebellion. And, to finish off Biskind's list of "pressing issues of the day," there were films that dealt seriously with the uncomfortable relationships between America's WASP majority and its various minorities. These range from westerns such as *Broken Arrow* (1950) and *The Searchers* (1956), whose plots center on the role in society of "halfbreeds," to "contemporary" films such as *Gentlemen's Agreement* (1947), about a journalist's pained efforts to write about American anti-Semitism, and *Imitation of Life* (1959), at least in part about the equally pained efforts of a young light-skinned African American woman to pass for white.

At the same time, the Fifties produced plenty of films whose narratives suggested that the foundations of postwar American society were bothered by no problems whatsoever. For every film that sympathized with an abused member of a racial or ethnic minority, a dozen more portrayed everyone happily in his or her "proper" place. For every film that purported to explore the psyches of juvenile delinquents, a dozen more presented such types as inconsequential outsiders in a society whose "normal" teenagers were well-adjusted, law-abiding, and respectful of parental authority. Titillating females figured in a great many films, but usually they were depicted either as temptations to be avoided or, more often, as "wildcats" who, at heart, longed to be domesticated. Although a few Fifties science fiction films—for example, *The Day the Earth Stood Still* (1951) and *It Came from Outer Space* (1953)—communicated the liberal idea that strange-looking aliens were not necessarily malevolent, the vast majority of the period's sci-fi films promoted the ultraconservative idea that "the problem," whatever it was, and no matter what its cause, could best be solved by forceful exercise of American military/scientific might. Although in a few Fifties films the central characters indeed worried seriously about pressures to conform, in most of them the characters, without thinking about it even for a moment, simply conformed.

There is likely a difference, of course, between how films of the Fifties are regarded today and how they were regarded back then. Cultural historian Thomas Doherty makes the telling points that the troubled characters from Fifties films who are so "indelible for the modern viewer . . . may not have had that preeminent stature for their contemporary audience," that the "luster" of these characters "derives from a historical hindsight in which the 1950s rebel without a cause and housewives on the verge of revolt become certified precursors to the 1960s counterculture, hence closer to the sensibilities of the generation that came to write most of the canonical film criticism."[37] It is true that most post-Fifties writers on the sociological implications of Fifties films have concentrated—as I have certainly done in at least a few of the preceding paragraphs—on a relatively small handful of films that exemplify what might be seen in retrospect as various of the period's essential conflicts. But as Doherty reminds us, the memorable "special" films that have perennially attracted the attention of scholars need to be considered in the broad context in which they were created, distributed, and consumed.

Along ideological lines, the modern view of the Fifties remains sharply divided. On the one side are the still left-leaning intellectuals who view the Fifties as "a dismal decade, contemplated with the distaste usually reserved for [such] other bugaboos of American history [as] the antebellum South or the Vietnam War."[38] On the other side are the right-leaning romantics who remember the Fifties "with nostalgic yearning for a simpler, happier time when cars had fins, gas was almost free, women were home and men were on the range."[39] But there is another way—less biased, and probably more accurate—in which the films of the Fifties might be regarded. This approach, writes Biskind, sheds light on "an era of conflict and contradiction, an era in which a complex set of ideologies contended for public allegiance," an era during which the "warring ideologies . . . slugged it out frame by frame across a battlefield of sounds and images that stretched from one end of the country to the other, from Times Square to Hollywood and Vine—without explicit political allusions."[40]

The big picture of the Fifties, thus, is revealed in myriad little pictures. And when they took the form of *moving* pictures, representations of the conflicted Fifties were almost always supported by music. A good deal of any film's music came in the form of its "underscore"—that is, the accompanying music that illustrated action, defined locations, set moods, and so forth, and that was heard only by the film's audience. But some of the music came in the form of "source music," music whose often visible source supposedly belonged to the film's fictional world and was heard not just by the audience but also by the fictional characters. And in a period when "warring ideologies . . . slugged it out frame by frame" in the movies, Hollywood's source music was typically as rich in symbolism as were its brassieres and flying saucers.

Broken Records, the Blues, and Biopics

The 1955 MGM film *Blackboard Jungle* has been mentioned in each of the previous two chapters: in the chapter on jazz for its screenplay that put adult hipster language in the mouths of inner-city teenagers, and in the chapter on rock 'n' roll both for its use and resultant popularization of Bill Haley's "Rock Around the Clock" and for its inclusion of a scene in which a high school math teacher unsuccessfully tries to make a point about symmetry by means of jazz.

For people who care deeply about music of any sort, but especially for those who take a broadly historical view of music and focus their tastes on particular treasures from the past, *Blackboard Jungle*'s math lesson scene is surely horrific. The film offers a graphic depiction of an attempted rape, and it features several sequences in which the central character is brutally beaten by the young hoodlums he hopes, perhaps naively, to help. While these scenes are doubtless shocking aplenty for the average movie watcher, it is hard to imagine that for the music-loving movie watcher anything could be more fundamentally disturbing than the segment during which hooligans not only laugh derisively at an earnest attempt to explain traditional values but then go on to smash—with gleeful, sadistic pleasure—the precious discs on which the teacher's valued music had been preserved. It may well be that with regard to contemporary music the film's math teacher is "out of touch, stuffy, and elitist,"[41] but he is punished with such cruelty mostly because he is "old-fashioned."

Jazz as a symbol of values and lifestyle fairly permeates the films of the Fifties. In the cryptic scheme of Fifties semiotics, however, the meaning of this easily recognizable aural symbol varies widely from situation to situation. In early sound films, jazz as an actual plot element typically represents a break from tradition that first strikes its onscreen observers as shocking but soon enough is accepted as a form of innocent self-expression and—as its fictional proponents always knew it to be—a means to a psychologically healthy life. In *The Jazz Singer* (1927), for example, the titular character, played by Al Jolson, flees the restrictions of the synagogue to find his "true voice" in nightclubs and the vaudeville theater, and in the long run this proves to be not at all so blasphemous as it first seemed; in *Every Sunday* (1936) a pair of teenage girl singers, played by Deanna Durbin and Judy Garland, whose musical proclivities lean diametrically toward opera and jazz learn that, all things considered, their goals are really not much different; and as a terpsichorean variation, in *Shall We Dance?* (1937) a tight-laced ballet master played by Fred Astaire and a loose-legged hoofer played by Ginger Rogers eventually reconcile and find not just musical but also romantic harmony.

In contrast to these earlier films, jazz-based films from the Fifties rarely dealt with the happy resolution of apparent differences between old and new musical styles that represented old and new ways of looking at the world. In most of the Fifties films in which jazz figured into the plot, and therefore into the soundtrack, the music was not so much an element in a polarity as a stand-alone image that typically signified one or another of several quite different things. If one can accept Kathryn Kalinak's premise that "for white audiences . . . jazz represented the urban, the sexual, and the decadent in a musical idiom perceived in the culture at large as an indigenous black form," then it seems that early in the postwar period at least the "slinkier" type of jazz was indeed "a musical trope for otherness, whether sexual or racial."[42] Later in the period, when emotional exhaustion was felt by a population that extended far beyond the small group of self-proclaimed beatniks, fictional dramas with musicians as their central characters tended to use "modern jazz" as a symbol of "contemporary urban disaffection and turbulence."[43] Yet throughout the postwar period, so-called biopics—that is, pictures based on biographies of actual persons—often used jazz of a more vintage sort as a symbol of what some moviegoers might well have regarded as "the good old days."

Some of these postwar biopics looked deep into jazz's past: *Young Man with a Horn* (1950), for example, was a melodrama based loosely on the life of Jazz Age cornetist Bix Beiderbecke, and *St. Louis Blues* (1958) was a portrait of W. C. Handy. But the most successful of the jazz-based postwar biopics were romantic celebrations of heroes of the recently ended big band era. Along with *The Fabulous Dorseys* (1947), *With a Song in My Heart* (1952), and *The Five Pennies* (1959), the box office hits included films with such remarkably uninventive titles as *The Glenn Miller Story* (1954), *The Benny Goodman Story* (1954), *The Eddy Duchin Story* (1956), *The Helen Morgan Story* (1957), and *The Gene Krupa Story* (1959).

With the notable exception of *St. Louis Blues*, which had an almost entirely African American cast headed by Nat "King" Cole and Eartha Kitt, the jazz-based biopics express a racially flavored subtext. In the biopics, "white and black achievement of the same standards are viewed differently: black musicians can do it by nature, automatically, while the skill of the white hero is a mark of individual merit."[44] Put another way, in the jazz biopics "Hollywood suggests that it takes a white person to bring substance to something that anyone—black or white—can do simply by instinct."[45]

*   *   *

Probably as much to demonstrate its patriotism as to appeal to a wide audience, Hollywood in the blacklist years offered biopics focused on composers whose music was sure to stir the hearts of flag-waving Americans. One thinks most readily of *I Dream of Jeanie* (1953), a sentimental portrayal of the nineteenth-century songwriter Stephen Foster, and *Stars and Stripes Forever* (1953), a sonically spectacular film that glorified the career of military band leader John Philip Sousa. But Hollywood's blacklist-era output also included tributes to such contributors to iconic American music as Tin Pan Alley songsmith Fred Fisher (*Oh, You Beautiful Doll*, 1949); Broadway operetta composer Sigmund Romberg (*Deep in My Heart*, 1954); lyricist Sammy Kahn (*I'll See You in My Dreams*, 1951); and the songwriting teams of Lorenz Hart and Richard Rodgers (*Words and Music*, 1948), Bert Kalmar and Harry Ruby (*Three Little Words*, 1950), and Buddy de Sylva and Lew Brown (*The Best Things in Life Are Free*, 1956).

Like the standards of popular music, the familiar repertoire of classical music provided financially beleaguered postwar Hollywood with ready-made, and thus inexpensive, material for soundtracks. Quite unlike popular music, however, the arena of classical music by this time had produced no American idols worth putting on a filmic pedestal, so the subjects of Hollywood's postwar classical-music biopics were all—and not surprisingly, considering America's still xenophilous attitude toward high culture—in one way or another "foreign."

With *A Song to Remember*, a 1945 film about the life of Chopin, director Charles Vidor began a series of composer-based Hollywood biopics whose titles feature the word "song." The life of Robert Schumann, especially his romance with Clara Wieck, was presented in *Song of Love* (1947); the life of Franz Liszt was the subject of *Song without End* (1960). Even though the Soviet Union gave postwar Americans plenty to worry about, the Russian composers Rimsky-Korsakov and Tchaikovsky nevertheless were featured, respectively, in *Song of Scheherazade* (1947) and *Song of My Heart* (1948).[46]

*   *   *

In addition to *The Great Caruso* (1951), between 1949 and 1959 Philadelphia-born tenor Mario Lanza starred in five entirely fictional films whose central male character was an opera singer.[47] These fictional films, like most of the biopics mentioned above, were melodramas or romances in which a person of talent works hard to establish himself or herself, encounters obstacles of more or less severity, triumphs over all adversity, finds true love, and in effect lives happily ever after.[48] The stereotypical Hollywood ending—that is, one in which all of a plot's major issues are pleasantly resolved—also characterized the occasional music-based comedy. On the classical side of the fence, for example, there were such sentimental bonbons as *Unfaithfully Yours* (1948), about a conductor who while performing staples of the standard orchestral repertoire frets over his wife's supposed infidelities, and *Once More, with Feeling* (1960), about an egocentric maestro who learns to appreciate his hitherto neglected wife. On the jazz side there were such fast-paced "screwball" comedies as *A Song Is Born* (1948), about a team of musicologists who only at the last minute realize that their soon-to-be-published music encyclopedia lacks an entry on jazz, and *Some Like It Hot* (1959), about a pair of Jazz Age musicians who, in an effort to escape pursuing mobsters, disguise themselves and take jobs in an all-girl band.

Along with romances and comedies, of course, Hollywood during the Fifties produced music-centered films whose endings are anything but cheery. Because they lack the flawed antihero and the dangerous femme fatale, some of these perhaps do not "officially" qualify as films noir.[49] But these are dark films nonetheless, with plots that involve marital infidelity, mayhem both physical and psychological, and—often—murder.

The dark films whose fictions revolve around classical music include *Hangover Square* (1945), in which a very serious composer happens to be a murderous psychopath;[50] *Humoresque* (1946), in which a struggling violinist becomes dependent on the patronage of a severely neurotic woman; *Deception* (1947), in which a young female musician's love for a cellist her own age is so thwarted by the jealous older composer who pays her bills that she ends up shooting the composer dead at the very moment that the cellist is premiering the composer's new concerto; *September Affair* (1950), in which a female concert pianist finds passionate love, but also emotional pain, with a married businessman; *Rhapsody* (1954), in which a young woman follows her violinist boyfriend to a conservatory in Switzerland and then falls in love with another music student; and *Interlude* (1957), in which a young American woman working as a clerk in Munich falls tragically in love with a married and megalomaniac German conductor.

The dark films involving jazz include *Pete Kelley's Blues* (1955), in which a Jazz Age trumpet player in Kansas City has a deadly run-in with gangsters; *The Man with the Golden Arm* (1955), in which a man who aspires to be a drummer in a jazz band is absorbed instead into the underworld of gambling and narcotics; *The Wrong Man* (1956), in which a bass player is severely prosecuted for crimes he did not commit; *Sweet Smell of Success* (1957), in which a jazz guitarist is framed for various offenses by a ruthless newspaper columnist and his lackey; *All the Fine Young Cannibals* (1960), in which a trumpet player from rural Texas finds not only musical success but also a load of trouble in New York; and *Paris Blues* (1961), in which a white trombonist and a black tenor sax player working in Paris fall in love with a pair of female American tourists and then, sadly, abandon them for the sake of their music.

One cannot help but notice that in these jazz-based fictional films, all of which date from relatively late in the Fifties, the central characters are usually presented neither as heroes nor as villains but, rather, as victims.

*   *   *

In his book on the lore of what modern society calls "musical genius," philosopher Peter Kivy explains that popular thinking for centuries has distinguished between the artist who possesses a superb talent and one who in effect is possessed *by* his or her art.[51] But John C. Tibbetts, in a gloss on Kivy, points out that neither of these types of genius suited the agenda of postwar Hollywood, because neither of them was "responsive to popular responsibilities." Especially in the Fifties, when Americans of all ages were being pressured to conform to behavioral norms, the "possessed" genius would have been seen to be "too detached from worldly affairs" and the "possessor" genius would have been regarded as "too arrogant and overriding to respect societal and artistic conventions."[52] Instead, Tibbetts suggests, postwar Hollywood opted for a third category that Kivy deals with only toward the end of his book. It was in this third category of "the hard-working craftsperson," Tibbetts writes, that both types of musical genius could be set in balance and thus "impressed into the service of popular entertainment."[53]

The obvious villains in the fictional music-based films—the composers in *Hangover Square* and *Deception*, the conductor in *Interlude*—are so possessed by their art that they cannot relate in any sort of normal way to the people around them. In marked contrast, most of the characters who are the actual centerpieces of Hollywood's music-based films—whether those films are biopics or exercises in pure fiction—indeed represent the balance that Tibbetts proposes. These characters are blessed with talent, but they have to work hard to gain mastery of their art, and in the long run they are rewarded not so much for their genius as for their industriousness and perseverance. Glenn Miller, Benny Goodman, and the other eponymous figures in the jazz biopics were portrayed, above all, as red-blooded Americans. In a way, so were Schumann and Liszt.

Miller and Goodman, like Schumann and Liszt—and like most of the music-based films' other male characters, including the villains and the protagonists of the dark jazz fictions—had something else in common. The female characters who happen to be musicians are loved, or desired, not so much because they are musicians but because they are women. With the male characters, in contrast, musicianship typically has very much to do with their appeal. Her book on cinematic musician characters focuses on the melodramatic "woman's film" from the 1940s in both the United States and England, yet Heather Laing's generalizations on gender roles in music-based films apply easily enough to the products of Hollywood in the Fifties:

> The male musician, whether in the biopic or fictional narrative, is often positioned as the object of a kind of female adoration marked by such devotion that, in certain contexts, it can easily transform into love or even obsession. . . . Following a particularly Romantic ethos of the emotional constitution of the musician, the man's musical "voice" in performance signifies much more to the woman than merely a talent or profession, and the perception of an unusual depth of feeling and sensitivity combined with the potent masculine strength of artistic expression proves, perhaps unsurprisingly, his most powerful and fascinating attraction.[54]

The female saloon singer, like the female character who displays cleavage, in Fifties films is most often an easily read symbol of temptation. But even the "serious" female musician, on the rare occasions when she makes an appearance, is likely a cautionary sign. She is almost never "the equivalent of a Romantic male artist," Laing writes. Instead, she "only serves to realize the nineteenth-century warnings to women of the perils of elite artistic endeavour."[55]

Changing the Score

Writing bitterly in 1972, in a magazine article titled "What Ever Happened to Great Movie Music?" veteran Hollywood composer Elmer Bernstein argued that "the beginning of the end of the golden age of film music" was signaled by "two innocent events in the early and middle Fifties." One of these events, Bernstein claimed, was the "extraordinary commercial success of the title song by Dimitri Tiomkin for the 1951 motion picture *High Noon*"; the other was "the success of [his] own *The Man with the Golden Arm* in 1955."[56]

The *Golden Arm* music "was not a jazz score," Bernstein rightly noted, "but a score in which jazz elements were incorporated toward the end of creating a specific atmosphere for that particular film." Similarly, Tiomkin's faux cowboy song for *High Noon*, which featured lyrics by Ned Washington, was concocted deliberately to suit the needs of a particular western. Both the jazzy music for *The Man with the Golden Arm* and the folksy *High Noon* song admirably served their filmic purposes, Bernstein granted, and it was only their recycling—as recordings independent of the cinema—that caused the trouble. "With the commercial bonanza of these 'pop' sounds in two perfectly *legitimate* situations," Bernstein wrote, "producers quickly began to transform film composing from a serious art into a pop art and more recently into pop garbage."[57]

Hollywood in fact had been making use of potential hit songs, and in the process enjoying a "cozy" relationship with the songs' publishers, since the earliest years of the sound-film era. It is true, however, that both Tiomkin's song and the main title theme from *The Man with the Golden Arm* did extremely well on the radio and in the shops that sold records,[58] and it seems that from their success Hollywood indeed took a cue. For more than a decade after *High Noon*, an impressively large number of films offered by the major studios included potentially marketable songs, most often heard in the title sequences but sometimes only embedded, as source music, into the plot. And for at least a few years after *The Man with the Golden Arm*—until around 1960, by which time "jazz had ceased to be a popular music and the nostalgia for swing had played itself out"—jazz-influenced scores flourished, especially in examples of film noir.[59]

The term "film noir" was coined in 1946, in an appreciative essay by the French critic Nino Frank on recent developments in Hollywood. Along with characteristic plots and protagonists, the accompanying music of film noir, no matter what its vintage, arguably has a characteristic sound that emphasizes a "sense of displacement by defying the tonal tradition of classical Hollywood film scoring,"[60] that features "a wavering sonority" that is "unnatural and disturbing,"[61] and that is loaded with "clichéd deviance triggers."[62] These descriptions of noir soundtracks are, to be sure, frustratingly vague. It remains, though, that before the mid-1950s the characteristic sound of film noir was produced by a standard symphonic orchestra, not by a jazz ensemble.

The change in the sound of noir, and the sound of much else that Hollywood produced after the late 1950s, had to do not just with new tastes on the part of audiences and a growing hunger for commercially viable spin-off products on the part of studio executives. Those things mattered, of course, but what mattered more in the long run was a seismic shift in the relationship between the Hollywood studios and the musicians' union.

Since the start of the sound-film era, the small as well as the large Hollywood studios had had various agreements with the American Federation of Musicians (AFM). For the smaller studios, however, the agreements had always been much more relaxed. The two-year contract with the major studios that was signed in 1946, for example, specified that each of these eight studios maintain full-time orchestras of between thirty-six and fifty players.[63] In contrast, the contract with the independent filmmakers that covered the same period of time specified that, between them, these seventy or so companies keep only one hundred players on year-round salaries.[64] The numbers were always in contention, with the AFM perennially demanding that more musicians be under contract and the studios countering that they could get by with less. Nevertheless, the numbers held steady until certain landmark events of 1958.

Simple arithmetic explains the considerable sonic difference, until 1958, between the scores for films produced by the major studios and films produced by the independents: with a mere one hundred musicians shared by seventy companies, the accompaniments for the independent films tended to be, at least in terms of instrumentation, relatively sparse; with each of the eight major studios employing its own orchestra, accompaniments for their films tended to be, in terms of instrumentation, relatively rich.

In the case of the independent studios, intermittent access to a small number of musicians sometimes resulted in wonderfully creative scores. In the case of the major studios, constant access to large orchestras whose members needed to be paid regardless of whether or not they actually played resulted in fairly homogeneous scores. Of course, no union contract ever mandated that a composer assigned to a particular film *had* to use all the musicians available to him, but using the entire orchestra again and again resulted in an efficiency that was consistent with the overall smooth workings of the studio system. Experienced staff composers knew how to conceive theatrically effective music for the ensembles that were always at their disposal, and staff orchestrators knew how to arrange for such ensembles whatever the composers wrote into their "short scores." Staff conductors knew precisely how to get the desired sounds out of these fleshed-out full scores, and veteran staff musicians knew exactly how to give the conductors what they wanted. At the independent studios, necessity was often the quite fruitful mother of invention; at the major studios, "reinventing the wheel" for each new project was simply not an option.

Beset by its perfect storm of troubles, after 1948 Hollywood in general sought to rein in its expenses. After they expired in 1948, the union contracts were not replaced, but simply extended, a year at a time, for six more years. New contracts were finally signed in 1954, by which time all the major studios had disbanded their music departments and all the Hollywood musicians—estimated at between five hundred and seven hundred players—worked on a freelance basis.[65] When these new contracts expired in January 1958, the major studios resisted the AFM's demands much more vigorously than they ever had before; negotiations hit an impasse, and the Hollywood musicians—by this time estimated to number approximately twelve hundred—called a strike. Because the major studios simply would not budge on their tight-pursed demands, the strike was in effect a lockout. Resolution came in July 1958, when the major studios as well as the independents signed an agreement not with the AFM but with a recently formed splinter organization called the Musicians Guild of America (MGA).

The 1958 contract with the MGA specified payments of $55.00 for three-hour recording sessions involving thirty-five or more players, $57.74 for sessions involving between thirty and thirty-four players, $60.50 for sessions involving between twenty-four and twenty-nine players, and $63.25 for sessions involving fewer than twenty-four players.[66] This agreement brought an end to the AFM's "thirty-year monopoly in the film industry."[67] Also ended with this agreement was the long-standing tradition of having films produced by the major studios accompanied, as a matter of course, by full orchestral scores. So long as they were willing to pay premium wages, the major studios from this moment on could score their films—just as the independent filmmakers had long been doing—however they chose.

* * *

Sometimes the major studios, or what was left of them by the time the 1958 musicians' strike ended, chose to take the modern route and use jazz-influenced scores composed by Hollywood regulars such as Elmer Bernstein and Henry Mancini or, perhaps for the sake of prestige, by such prominent jazz musicians as John Lewis and Duke Ellington. And sometimes the major studios opted for the pop music route that was later so vilified by Bernstein. Before the settlement of the 1958 strike, rock 'n' roll star Elvis Presley had already starred in Twentieth Century-Fox's *Love Me Tender* (1956), MGM's *Jailhouse Rock* (1957), and Paramount's *King Creole* (1958). After the strike, and after his service in the U.S. Army, Presley would go on to star in *G.I. Blues* (1960), *Blue Hawaii* (1961), and a dozen more films produced, or at least distributed, by Paramount or Fox. Fox also competed for the "clean teen" music audience by having Pat Boone act and sing a few songs in *Journey to the Center of the Earth* (1959) and *All Hands on Deck* (1961); Columbia offered *Gidget* (1959) and *Gidget Goes Hawaiian* (1961); and MGM offered *Where the Boys Are* (1960).

With such films, Hollywood indeed concentrated on potential hit songs. But during the 1950s Hollywood also concentrated, for the sake of competing with television, on various cinematic novelties. Hollywood's efforts included wide-screen formats such as CinemaScope, Panavision, Todd-AO, and Vistavision, three-dimensional (3-D) imagery, and stereophonic sound. All of these technological experiments, along with the use of potential hit songs and pop- or jazz-flavored soundtracks, counted among the American film industry's many efforts to survive an economic climate that—for Hollywood, if not for the rest of the country—was dangerously hostile. The main thrust of Hollywood's effort to survive, however, involved trying to lure audiences away from their black-and-white television sets by offering films in full color.

Whereas up until around 1950 color photography had been reserved for films deemed to be somehow "special," after 1950 for the major studios color photography became the norm. Some of the full-color films made by the major studios during the 1950s were contemporary dramas, romances, or comedies. Significantly, a large proportion of them featured plots on an arguably epic scale. These visually spectacular offerings included such westerns as *The Searchers, The Alamo* (1960), and *The Magnificent Seven* (1960); such war movies as *The Bridge on the River Kwai* (1957) and *The Guns of Navarone* (1961); such biblical films as *The Robe* (1953), *The Ten Commandments* (1956), *Ben-Hur* (1959), and *King of Kings* (1961); and such battle-centered swashbucklers as *Knights of the Round Table* (1953), *The Vikings* (1958), *Spartacus* (1960), and *El Cid* (1961). That most of these cinematically ambitious efforts were indeed successful at the box office doubtless owes as much to their sweeping orchestral scores as to the fact that both their plots and their cinematography were impressively larger than life.[68]

Also larger than life were films of yet another type that Hollywood, in its postwar doldrums, hoped would woo audiences. These, too, depended on music for their success, but it was music of a sort altogether different from everything discussed above. The so-called musical, a staged fiction in which characters not necessarily identified as musicians periodically break into song, had been a part of Hollywood tradition since the start of the sound-film era in the late 1920s. Never before or after, however, did the genre flourish to the extent that it did in the Fifties. Some of the period's best-loved film musicals—*On the Town* (1950), *An American in Paris* (1951), *Singin' in the Rain* (1952), *Seven Brides for Seven Brothers* (1954), *Funny Face* (1957), *Gigi* (1958)—were created especially for the screen. But most of the filmic musicals that entertained audiences of the Fifties were adaptations of shows that had played more or less recently on Broadway.

5

Broadway

Writing several years after the long decade of the Fifties had at last given way to the compact yet eventful decade of the Sixties, veteran Broadway factotum Lehman Engel—in one of the first solid books that dealt with the substance of American musical theater as well as its history—delineated the distinguishing traits of what he called "the contemporary musical." Engel's time frame is only slightly different from that of this book; his chapter on "contemporary" musicals starts with Richard Rodgers and Lorenz Hart's *Pal Joey* (1940) and extends through Jerry Bock and Sheldon Harnick's *Fiddler on the Roof* (1964).[1] But most of the representative works that Engel discusses fall squarely within the limits of the postwar period we call the Fifties, and almost all of the plot-related characteristics he mentions are things of the sort that indeed come into focus when we regard the material at hand through such Fifties-specific lenses as American foreign policy, race relations, the burgeoning youth culture, and sexual politics.

Had the Viennese psychiatrist Sigmund Freud still been around, and had he been at all interested in American popular culture, doubtless he would have noticed that in the contemporary musical, leading men were no longer necessarily young; "more important," Engel notes, "in middle age they are still romantically attractive."[2] Freud died in 1939, so he missed out on all of this. He missed out, too, on his posthumous heyday of popularity in the United States, a heyday that coincides precisely with America's anxious postwar period. But surely Freud's numerous American disciples would have been intrigued, even titillated, by postwar Broadway's—and Hollywood's—representations of nubile women who fall in love with men old enough to be their fathers.

Not so sexy, perhaps, but nonetheless relevant to the profound societal changes that America experienced during the Fifties, are Engel's observations on the moral qualities of many of Broadway's principal males. When *Pal Joey* premiered in December 1940, Engel writes, the time was not yet right for "the odiousness of its leading character," something that "repelled critics and audiences alike," and thus "the initial run was not long." By the time of the show's 1952 revival, however, "the public had accommodated itself to the new antihero, and *Pal Joey* had a run commensurate with its quality."[3]

Engel points out that the title character of *Pal Joey* is hardly an isolated example. Not mincing words, he describes *Carousel*'s Billy Bigelow as "a libertine, a hustler, and a bum." Continuing the litany, he notes that *Guys and Dolls*' Sky Masterson is a ne'er-do-well professional gambler, that the male lead of *The King and I* is a sadist, that *My Fair Lady*'s Professor Higgins is a self-centered egotist, and that *The Music Man*'s Harold Hill is a swindling con man.[4] Like the central male characters in the films noir that Hollywood cultivated during precisely this same period, Broadway's "bad boys" were in most ways despicable yet in at least some ways likeable, and surely that gave audiences—male as well as female—something to think about.

Broadway's women, perhaps more so than the women of Hollywood, also gave audiences something to think about. Summarizing, Engel writes that the leading ladies of the contemporary Broadway musical, in obvious contrast to their stage forebears, and in arguable contrast to most of their screen contemporaries, exhibit "a lifelike dimension." These women are, at least in the best that postwar Broadway had to offer, not mere figurines but "motivated human beings." The worlds inhabited by the heroines of *Annie Get Your Gun*, *South Pacific*, *Brigadoon*, *My Fair Lady*, *The King and I*, *Guys and Dolls*, and *West Side Story*, Engel writes, are "concretely defined and plausible," and "the problems [these heroines] confront, like those of the heroes, are universal."[5]

"I Think She's Got It!"

Broadway shows from the Fifties involve male-female romance, "the fuel that ignite[s] the music and lyrics," the element without which "no musical . . . has [ever] worked."[6] But the romance in these and other Broadway shows from the Fifties stands in sharp contrast to the romance in earlier musicals and turn-of-the-century operettas, almost all of them entertainments whose feeble plots amounted to little more than boy meets girl, boy loses girl, and boy eventually—as everyone knows he must—gets girl. Broadway romance in the Fifties also stands in sharp contrast to the romance depicted in most

Hollywood films of the period, because often its principal agent is not "the boy" but, rather, "the girl."

Actually, in many musicals from the Fifties the principal female character is not a girl at all. No matter what her chronological age, typically she is a fully formed adult, equipped not just with a feisty personality but also with a solid set of ethics and prejudices. And often, in one way or another, she breaks quite free of leading lady stereotypes. As theater historian Stacy Wolf reminds us:

> Representations of women in the [golden age] musical differ in kind from those in mass culture and nonmusical theater. While many musicals do feature the ingénue/girl-next-door in the soprano romantic lead, such as Laurie in *Oklahoma!* and Julie in *Carousel*, and a few musicals offer temptresses, such as Lola in *Damn Yankees*, just as many contain strong, dominating women like Anna in *The King and I*, Auntie Mame in *Mame* [1966], and Dolly Levi in *Hello, Dolly!* [1964]. Even women coupled with men emerge as powerful and singular.[7]

Significantly, the "powerful and singular" females of Fifties Broadway differ from their theatrical predecessors, and from most of their cinematic contemporaries, in that most of them hold full-time jobs. Their employment is gainful, and often it is also meaningful. *South Pacific*'s Nelly Forbush, for example, is a professional military nurse. *The Sound of Music*'s Maria is an aspiring nun who, after her polite expulsion from the convent, takes a position as governess for the seven children of a widowed former naval officer. Anna Leonowens, whose name is the antecedent of the first-person pronoun in the title of *The King and I*, is a widowed schoolmarm hired to teach Western culture to the children of the king of Siam. *The Music Man*'s Marian Paroo is a part-time piano teacher and a full-time librarian. *Carousel*'s Julie Jordan works in a mill; *West Side Story*'s Maria works in a bridal shop. *Kiss Me, Kate*'s Lilli Vanessi is an actress; *Flower Drum Song*'s Linda Low is a nightclub showgirl. *My Fair Lady*'s Eliza Doolittle, before signing on as a human lab rat for a professor of phonetics, humbly yet happily plies the trade of a Covent Garden flower vendor.

That so many of Broadway's fictional women with apparent contentment worked for a living made them, in a curiously provocative way, both like and unlike their real-life counterparts. On the one hand, throughout the Fifties a great many American women in fact did work outside the home. On the other hand, many women who held a job felt uncomfortable about it.

With men being called to military service, during World War II the number of females in the American workforce increased: whereas before the war's onset approximately 25 percent of adult American women held full-time jobs, by the war's end "the figure had soared to 36 percent—an increase greater than that of the previous forty years combined."[8] Although popular mythology has it that the large number of women who entered the American workforce during the war years (approximately 6.5 million of them) did so primarily out of patriotic duty, and that after the war they readily yielded their positions to returning servicemen, statistics gathered by the U.S. Department of Labor's Women's Bureau paint quite a different picture. According to various Women's Bureau surveys, the large majority of female workers who entered the labor force between 1941 and 1945 were not middle-class housewives volunteering to help out with the war effort but "working-class wives, widows, divorcées, and students who needed the money to achieve a reasonable standard of living."[9] At war's end, according to a Women's Bureau survey, 75 percent of these female workers expressed a strong desire to retain their full-time jobs.[10] Most of them did not get their wish, largely because of long-entrenched workplace attitudes—conveniently suspended during the war—that favored men over women. After a precipitous drop in the immediate aftermath of the war, however, "female employment figures showed a sharp upturn beginning in 1947, and by 1950 [they] had once again reached wartime peaks."[11]

At the same time, American women during this period were fairly bombarded with messages informing them that a woman's place was in the home. These messages came via cinema and television, articles in a host of magazines aimed specifically at female readers, advertising wherever it was found, and even speeches from high-ranking officials. In 1956 no less a figure than J. Edgar Hoover, head of the FBI, advised American women that they could best combat "the twin enemies of freedom, crime and communism," by serving as "homemakers and mothers."[12] But for at least a decade publications both academic and popular had been making the case that the true calling of the American woman was a combination of childbearing and dutiful service to a husband. Indeed, early in the baby boom an article in the *American Journal of Sociology* suggested that women's employment outside the home "has probably been a substantial contributing factor" to "the decrease in fertility,"[13] and in the same year, 1946, an article in *Newsweek* went so far as to suggest that fertility might also be negatively impacted by a woman's having too much education.[14] Both ideas were echoed in 1947 by economist Ferdinand Lundberg and psychiatrist Marynia Farnham in their *Modern Woman: The Lost Sex*, a book whose "brilliant pastiche of Freudianism, functionalism, and distorted history achieved an astonishing amount of intellectual influence," and whose content was "paraphrased in innumerable places."[15]

Most adult Americans, the opinion polls tell us, at least pretended to agree with these archly sexist views. Whether male or female, they indicated that they truly believed it was the job of the husband to "wear the pants in the family"—that is, not just to support the family financially but also to make all the "big" decisions—and that it was the job of the wife to ensure that within the confines of the home everything was "nice."[16] So long as married women worked outside the home for the sake of helping their families keep pace with both inflation and their neighbors in the accelerating "race for affluence," their efforts likely "receive[d] social sanction as a fulfillment of their traditional family role."[17] But if married women who took jobs were motivated by "a desire to prove their equality with men," "their employment would probably have encountered bitter resistance."[18] Far more bitter would have been the resistance experienced by single women who pursued careers, for the Fifties was a period during which the majority of Americans apparently "believed that people who did not marry," regardless of their gender, "were sick, immoral, selfish, or neurotic."[19]

The typical leading female character in Broadway shows of the Fifties was hardly neurotic, selfish, immoral, or sick. Nor was she lonely; she accepted romance when it came her way, but she did not actively seek it, and she did not wistfully believe—as many real-life American women had been taught since childhood—that "someday [her] prince will come."[20] She was often a nurturing person, professionally as well as personally, but almost never did she have children of her own.[21] No matter how she earned her living, the typical Broadway woman went about her business comfortably oblivious to pollsters' declarations that although "to make a woman completely content it takes a man, . . . the chief purpose of her life is motherhood."[22]

Midway through the first act of *My Fair Lady*, the professor gloats over his apparent success in at last teaching Eliza how to give proper upper-class resonance to the diphthongs in such words as "rain," "Spain," "mainly," and "plain." "I think she's got it!" he shouts to his colleague; "by George, she's got it!" The "it" to which the egotistical professor refers is, of course, the pronunciation for which he takes full credit. But there was an "it" of quite a different sort that Eliza possessed from the very start of the show, a highly attractive "it" that was shared by many members of her Broadway cohort. This had little to do with the supremely attractive combination of innocent charm and raw sex appeal exhibited by Clara Bow's character in the 1927 silent film *It*. Rather, the "it" that Eliza Doolittle had all along— a quality that the professor barely noticed but was likely envied by many female members of her audience—was an independence of mind, body, and spirit.

"Stick to Your Own Kind"

In 1954, the year when *South Pacific* finally ended its extraordinary initial run of 1,925 performances, and three years before *West Side Story* had its opening night, twenty-seven American states still enforced laws that made it a felony for adults to engage in miscegenation.[23] Simply stated, antimiscegenation laws made it illegal for a person of "the white race" to marry (and, by implication, to engage in sex with) a person of "a nonwhite race"; in most cases "nonwhite" meant blacks or Native Americans, and in some cases—usually in states in the western half of the country—it also included Asians. But some laws were more finely tuned in their discrimination. Oregon's law, for example, outlawed marriage between whites and native Hawaiians. Oklahoma's law outlawed marriage between "a person of African descent" and "any person *not* of African descent." Maryland's often revised law eventually banned not just white–Filipino marriages but also black–Filipino marriages. Arizona's original 1865 law did not proscribe marriage between whites and Native Americans, but its 1931 update put "Malays" (Filipinos) and "Hindus" (East Indians) on the "forbidden" list, and its 1942 update prevented a person of "mixed" blood from marrying *anyone*.[24]

In fact, American servicemen had been hooking up with, and often marrying, Filipino women since the dawn of the twentieth century, when during the Spanish-American War the United States military established large naval bases on the island of Luzon. In fact, a great many American servicemen engaged not just casually with "pan pan girls" (i.e., prostitutes) but also romantically and then matrimonially with perfectly respectable Japanese women during the occupation that followed World War II. In fact, more than six thousand American servicemen married Korean women during and immediately after the 1950–1953 Korean War. Throughout the long decade of the Fifties, in many American states such unions were considered illegal, and thus repatriated servicemen, with their Asian wives, needed to be very careful about where they might settle. Even in states that had abolished or had never enacted antimiscegenation laws, however, the sexual coupling of whites with nonwhites was generally considered, at least by white observers, to be somehow "icky."

Audiences of the Fifties were not sheltered from theatrical depictions of this troublesome topic. Opera lovers among them, of course, would have known Puccini's *Madama Butterfly*, about an American naval officer who during a shore leave at Nagasaki for a lark "marries" (and impregnates) a young Japanese woman. And fans of Broadway surely would have been fa-

miliar with the perennially popular *Show Boat*, a bold yet ultimately inconsequential subplot of which—exposed, developed, and resolved before the
curtain falls on act 1—has to do with the illegal marital status of the obviously white male star and the not at all obviously "mulatto" female star of
the titular vessel's performing troupe. Along with these "canonic" treatments
of miscegenation there were, especially after 1950, various Hollywood efforts. Relationships between white American men and Asian women were
dealt with, for example, in such films as *Japanese War Bride* (1952), *Love Is a
Many-Splendored Thing* (1955), *Sayonara* (1957), and *Diamond Head* (1963);
troublesome relationships between white men and black or mulatto women
were the focus of *Band of Angels* (1957), *Island in the Sun* (1957), *Kings Go
Forth* (1958), and *Night of the Quarter Moon* (1959); negatively viewed relationships between white Americans and dark-skinned Mexicans figured
into *High Noon* (1952), *Giant* (1956), and *Touch of Evil* (1959). Perhaps using a
long-ago concern as a metaphor for various contemporary frictions, marital/
sexual relationships between whites and Native Americans were explored in
such westerns as *Duel in the Sun* (1946), *Broken Arrow* (1950), *Distant Drums*
(1951), *White Feather* (1955), and, most disturbingly, *The Searchers* (1956).

Almost all of these theatrical works deal with relationships between white
men and nonwhite women, a combination that, although certainly problematic, was tolerated so long as true love, or true passion, was at the heart of it.
"Casting logic," as Frances Negrón-Muntaner notes, dictated that it was "acceptable for leading white men in Hollywood to seduce a nonwhite woman,
an option rarely offered to actresses of color in relationship to unhyphenated
American men."[25] Logic of a different sort, stemming not from the brains but
from the viscera of white Americans, dictated that it was quite *un*acceptable
to depict, or even to suggest, romance-flavored miscegenation between a
white woman and a nonwhite man. Throughout the Fifties, for most white
Americans the very idea of sexual penetration of a white woman by a "colored" man was so repulsive that such a union, it was generally thought, could
only result from rape.

* * *

There is nothing suggestive of rape in *South Pacific* or *West Side Story*. All
three of the miscegenation plots are of the "acceptable" type, which is to say
that they involve white men engaging with nonwhite women, for reasons of
love. The narratives that form the contexts of these relationships, however, are
fraught with emotional pain on the part of the participants and disapproval
on the part of onlookers. Like the makers of most of the films named above,

the makers of *South Pacific* and *West Side Story* discomfortingly reminded audiences of the Fifties, by means of dialogue and action, not that interracial romances *were* distasteful but also that they were *thought* to be so by a large majority of Americans. Quite unlike the Hollywood filmmakers, the Broadway maestros were also able to remind audiences, through enduringly glorious music, that love, no matter what its palette, can indeed be beautiful.

Rodgers and Hammerstein's 1949 *South Pacific* gives center-stage treatment to two intertwining subplots having to do with miscegenation. One of these concerns a well-bred, well-educated American naval officer who falls head-over-heels for a young Tonkinese woman. He breaks off with her, alas, because he knows he could never bring a woman "of color" home to his upper-class Philadelphia family. The other subplot concerns an American military nurse, not exactly a "spring chicken" but in many ways unsophisticated, who after numerous misgivings enters into a romantic relationship with a Frenchman twice her age. All is well until the nurse, raised in America's famously racist South, to her horror learns that the man she loves had years before fathered a pair of children by a female islander.

Compared to their source materials—several of the nineteen short stories that make up James A. Michener's 1947 Pulitzer Prize–winning *Tales of the South Pacific*—the subplots of the musical perhaps seem sugarcoated. In Michener's "Our Heroine," for example, nurse Nellie Forbush finds out that the French-born plantation owner had fathered not just two children, but eight of them, and by three different nonwhite women. As Michener tells it: "Emile De Becque, not satisfied with Javanese and Tonkinese women, had also lived with a Polynesian. A nigger! To Nellie's tutored mind any person living or dead who was not white or yellow was a nigger."[26] In "Fo' Dolla," the Princeton-polished lieutenant Joseph Cable in effect purchases, for one U.S. dollar, the deliciously nubile daughter of an entrepreneurial island woman. He has his way with her, and then he simply abandons her when he is shipped off to another naval base. Not until "A Cemetery at Hoga Point," the last of Michener's tales, are readers casually informed that Cable was killed in action on some distant beachhead.

Sugarcoated or not, *South Pacific*'s story lines were troublesome to many Americans. The controversy had little to do with the relationship between the widowed French plantation owner and his Polynesian wife; this miscegenation, after all, had happened in the past, and eventually Nellie—in the Broadway show as in the Michener book—overcomes her prejudice and agrees to serve as adoptive mother of the mixed-race children. Rather, the controversy centered on the relationship between Lieutenant Cable and the island girl Liat, which transpires very much in the show's "real time" and is celebrated in the perennially popular act 1 song "Younger Than Springtime." In the second act Cable delivers another song, one that—perhaps because it is short and not very tuneful, perhaps for other reasons—has never managed to enter the standard "show tune" repertoire. Cable sings this song after he comes to the pained conclusion that the society to which he has been born and bred would never allow him to actually marry a woman of color, and after the plantation owner asks him why Nellie is so appalled by the fact that his household includes mixed-race children. Addressing De Becque, Cable bitterly explains that fear, or even hatred, of racial "others" is not something with which human beings are born; apprehension about persons whose skins are differently colored or whose eyes are differently shaped, he says, is something that young children have to learn from their parents.

"You've Got to Be Carefully Taught" is a song that Rodgers and Hammerstein, during rehearsals and tryouts, were often advised to cut from the show. Outspokenly liberal in their political views, "the authors replied that this number represented why they had wanted to do this play, and that even if it meant the failure of the production, it was going to stay in."[27] The song indeed stayed in, but when a touring production of South Pacific visited Atlanta in 1953 it so offended certain Georgia lawmakers that they "introduced a bill to outlaw entertainment having, as they stated, 'an underlying philosophy inspired by Moscow.'"[28]

The obviously sexual relationship between Cable and Liat was controversial when South Pacific was fresh. It remains controversial today, not because of the problematic miscegenation that it portrays but because of how its situation is resolved. Near the end of South Pacific, Cable and De Becque—downhearted because their love lives have turned sour—volunteer to go together on a dangerous reconnaissance mission, but only De Beque returns. "This has the effect," writes John Bush Jones, "of making Cable more of a romantic hero than the cad he seems to be in Michener, [but] it raises questions."[29]

One of the questions has to do with whether or not Cable's death might be simply "an attempt to placate potential ticket-buyers of the 'I don't care if they live next door, but they're not going to marry my daughter' mindset, who otherwise might have stayed away in droves."[30] Another question has to do with the possibility that the killing off of Cable might have been an attempt "to satisfy censors who might object to the liaison as fostering miscegenation."[31] Philip D. Beidler suggests that an almost mathematical formula is at play, that, "as if in expiation" for De Becque's miscegenation, Cable's miscegenation "must be allowed to find its eventuation in tragedy.

. . . All that is required additionally for moral punctuation is that the lieutenant, for his sins, undertake a secret mission and be killed. And thus the
racial calculus is complete. "[32] Similarly, Andrea Most suggests that the ill-
fated relationship between Cable and Liat balances with the "complex [yet]
successful love story between two white people," in the process amplifying
a long-standing "formulaic and stereotypical" structure.[33] "Joe is killed off
as soon as he realizes the problematic nature of his own behavior. Death is
the neatest and easiest solution."[34]

South Pacific's Liat is hardly a femme fatale of the sort that populated so
many films noir of the Fifties. Desirable as she surely is, she is not at all a
temptress, and nothing in the plots of either Michener or of Rodgers and
Hammerstein suggests that she is in any way luring Cable toward a bitter
end. It remains, though, that Liat is not just an attractive woman but also a
woman of color, and that after his physical involvement with her Lieutenant Cable ends up quite dead. Also quite dead in the final scenes of their
respective stories are the white male practitioners of miscegenation in the
Hollywood films *Love Is a Many-Splendored Thing*, *Kings Go Forth*, and *Duel
in the Sun*. And likewise dead—spectacularly shot down in full view of the
audience and most of the cast—is *West Side Story*'s Tony.

*   *   *

As is well known, the 1957 *West Side Story* is loosely based on Shakespeare's
Romeo and Juliet, a tale of "star-cross'd lovers" whose relationship, it seems
in retrospect, had been doomed from the very start. But whereas Shakespeare's *Romeo and Juliet* involves the sexual coupling of members of two
long-feuding but otherwise equal Veronese families, *West Side Story* involves
the attempted coming together of a man and a woman from either side of a
line marked not just by differences of race and ethnicity but also by degrees
of "American-ness."

The show was conceived in 1949—by composer Leonard Bernstein, choreographer Jerome Robbins, and writer Arthur Laurents—as something ten-
tatively titled *East Side Story*, and it was originally to have involved conflict
not between whites and Puerto Ricans, but between Catholics and Jews.[35]
This idea, however, was quickly abandoned. Laurents felt that its essential
premise bore too close a resemblance to Anne Nichols's *Abie's Irish Rose*, a
romantic comedy that played on Broadway from 1922 until 1927. And Bernstein, himself a Jew, realized soon enough that "World War II had created
a new context for Jews in America," a context in which "anti-Semitism was
at an all-time low" and in which "many first-generation Jews and Irish [had

in fact been] integrated" into America society.[36] The idea was resurrected in 1954 when Bernstein was in Hollywood working on the score for Elia Kazan's film *On the Waterfront*. As Bernstein tells the story, he and Laurents were relaxing alongside a swimming pool in Beverly Hills, "talking ruefully about what a shame" it was that the original idea "didn't work out." Bernstein recalled: "Then, lying next to us on somebody's abandoned chair was a newspaper headline, 'GANG FIGHTS.' We stared at it and then at each other and realized that *this*—in New York—was it. The Puerto Rican 'thing' had just begun to explode, and we called Jerry [Robbins], and that's the way *West Side Story*—as opposed to *East Side Story*—was born."[37]

In *Show Boat* and *South Pacific*, lavish film versions of which were released in 1951 and 1958, respectively, and in most of the Hollywood films mentioned earlier, objection to mixed-race relationships comes entirely from white characters. In *West Side Story*, interestingly, the most heated protests against the romance between Tony and Maria come from the "colored" side of the divide. Before her immigration, Maria apparently had been promised to Chino, a lieutenant in the Puerto Rican gang, and Chino's negative reaction is thus attributable in large part to jealousy. On the other hand, the fierce reaction of Bernardo—Maria's brother and the leader of the Puerto Rican gang—seems to be based on something that cuts much deeper: his sister has betrayed him in numerous ways, perhaps most hurtfully by pledging allegiance to someone whose group acts superior to Bernardo's own group, mostly because of the color of their skin.

As in *Romeo and Juliet*, in *West Side Story* the plot is simple but the action that leads to its various climaxes is complicated. The first act ends with Bernardo killing the leader of Tony's gang and Tony, in enraged response, killing Bernardo. The second act is a long dénouement: with murderous intent, a pistol-armed Chino searches for Tony; Tony and Maria remain rapturously in love despite what happened earlier; Tony is maliciously misinformed that Chino has killed Maria; despondent, Tony begs Chino to kill him, too; just a moment after Tony realizes that Maria is in fact still alive, Chino indeed shoots Tony dead.

One of the most glorious moments in *West Side Story* is the act 1 "Tonight Quintet" that combines musical expressions of the two gangs' mutual animosity with the at this point largely platonic love between Tony and Maria and the obviously erotic feelings that Maria's friend Anita has for Bernardo. One of the show's most bitter moments is the act 2 duet "A Boy Like That / I Have a Love," during which first Anita in punchy phrases berates Maria for engaging with "the enemy" and then Maria, singing over Anita's ongoing diatribe, lyrically attests that although she, too, grieves for Bernardo, her feelings for Tony nevertheless remain undiminished. With its "pungent ferocity," Wilfred Mellers opined, this duet is "potent enough to serve as musical climax to the whole play. Were the music not so forceful, the effect of Maria's delayed entry would be less moving: for she, despite everything—even death—counters Anita's negation with affirmation."[38]

Love conquers all, as much in *West Side Story* as in *South Pacific* and *Show Boat*. But the "all" that love apparently conquers in these influential Broadway shows includes an element of racism that was not to be easily swept under the rug. Anita's repeated admonition, in *West Side Story*'s poignant act 2 duet, that Maria should "stick to your *own* kind, one of your *own* kind," is advice that most Americans—regardless of their color—likely would have shared with their friends and, especially, with their children. With regard to relationships between whites and variously colored "others," Broadway in the Fifties, like its counterpart in Hollywood, did not offer solutions to the problem of racism. Like Hollywood, Broadway simply illustrated the problem, perhaps in the hope that someday the problem might be solved.

"Getting to Know You"

The big hope in *West Side Story* is expressed early in act 2 by Tony and Maria when they reconnect after the deaths of Bernardo and the leader of the white gang. Meditating on the violence born of intolerance, they sing: "Somewhere, we'll find a new way of living, we'll find a way of forgiving." This utopian message was apparently not powerful enough for government cultural officers to allow a production of the show to be mounted at the 1958 Brussels World's Fair; originally scheduled as part of the United States' panoply of offerings, *West Side Story* was removed from the agenda "on the ground that," with its depictions of juvenile delinquency and interracial gang warfare, "it was bad publicity for America."[39]

This negative treatment of *West Side Story* is unusual. Intentionally or not, most Broadway shows of the Fifties quite adequately served the needs of American policy both foreign and domestic. Indeed, some scholars of Broadway have suggested that the very genre of the musical seemed almost custom-made for the expression of a particular aspect of the official Cold War agenda. In this respect, the musical has something in common with two of the period's most popular film genres.

As noted in the previous chapter, the long decade of the Fifties was the heyday of the science fiction film, a good many representatives of which are built around the idea of Earth being somehow invaded by creatures from other planets and the alien invaders being eventually defeated by the combined efforts of American science and American military strength. The Fifties was also the heyday of the Hollywood western, most examples of which depict in their final scenes the good guy(s) battling and defeating, often against the odds, the bad guy(s). With few exceptions, the invader-based sci-fi films are easily read as metaphors both for the nation's vague yet widespread anxiety about infiltration by mystery-shrouded communists and for the fundamental trust that, should infiltration actually occur, America's postwar might would make things right.[40] Likewise with few exceptions, the typical Fifties western is easily read as a metaphor for the nation's willingness and proven ability to confront, if necessary with blazing guns, not just communism but all evils that go against the American way of life. As metaphors, both the sci-fi invader film and the western deal with action against threats—covert or overt—to America and American values, and they count among the "images of containment [that] circulated in many areas of American culture during the Cold War."[41]

The word "containment" figures often in the writings of historians of the Cold War. It stems from an article titled "The Sources of Soviet Conduct" that George F. Kennan, writing under the pseudonym "X," published in July 1947 in the journal *Foreign Affairs*.[42] Kennan, a professional diplomat who from 1944 until 1946 had been the U.S. deputy chief of mission in Moscow, originally wrote up his thoughts in a private letter to U.S. Secretary of Defense James Forrestal, and it was only through the machinations of *Foreign Affairs* editor Hamilton Fish Armstrong that the text was made public. Hardly an official statement of American foreign policy, Kennan's anonymously published 1947 letter simply recommended that the United States would do well to engage in a "long-term, patient but firm and vigilant containment of Russian expansion tendencies."[43] Since then, "containment" has evolved into a term that, for scholars of Cold War politics, in a single word encapsulates America's dominant postwar policy on communism.

Containment was certainly the dominant, and most pressing, of America's Cold War policies, but it shared space on the agenda with a policy generally known as "integration." Driven not by racial but by economic concerns, this "other fundamental goal of postwar U.S. policymakers" was closely related to the policy of containment; indeed, the concepts of "the containment of the Soviet Union and the integration of the capitalist 'free world' are best understood as two sides of the same coin."[44]

Focusing on one particular Rodgers and Hammerstein show but addressing Fifties musicals in general, Christina Klein suggests that "a close reading of *The King and I* in relation to postwar modernization theory allows us to see the musical as an ideological genre on par with, but radically different from, the more familiarly ideological genre of the western."[45] Whereas the western, like the sci-fi invader film, metaphorically expressed the idea of stopping the spread of communism by means of military or intellectual force, the Broadway musical metaphorically expressed the idea of stemming communism by means of inviting various at-risk nations into the single family of nations that share American values. "*The King and I* is an exemplary instance of [the] postwar culture of integration," Klein writes; "it imagines that differences could be transcended rather than policed, and [that] Others could be transformed through an intimate embrace rather than exterminated through violence."[46]

Along with *The King and I*, perhaps the most obvious examples of the musical as expression of American integration policy are Rodgers and Hammerstein's *South Pacific* and *Flower Drum Song*. Writing a decade before Klein, Broadway historian Bruce A. McConachie stated that these three "oriental" musicals were "metaphors of containment," not of integration, and he argued that their popularity "helped to establish a legitimate basis for the American war against the people of Southeast Asia in the 1960s."[47] He did not mean that these shows in any way instigated hostility toward their Asian characters; rather, the shows suggested that at least *some* Asian peoples were indeed friendly and thus deserving of protection from Asians who were perhaps not so friendly. *The King and I* in particular, McConachie wrote, "prepared its spectators to accept U.S. intervention into Southeast Asia as responsible, benevolent, and necessary."[48] But all three of these musicals, he noted, express an integration-based "plea for tolerance" that "rests on the conviction that all people are fundamentally the same."[49]

That statement feels all warm and cuddly, and it provides a comforting context for the moment when Anna, midway through the first act of *The King and I*, lyrically informs the Siamese monarch's many children and their various mothers that she delights not only in "getting to know you, getting to know all about you" but also in the fact that she is "getting to *like* you" and "getting to hope *you'll* like me." Underlying this sweet sentiment, however, are hard-edged qualifications directly related to prevailing postwar attitudes.

Yes, Asians were just like "us," but only if at heart they were "good people, yearning to free themselves from external oppression."[50] Yes, Asians deserved all the best that the world has to offer, but only if they "believe[d] in the fundamental American values of romantic love, marriage, freedom, and equality."[51] In the wake of World War II, these seemingly gentle provisos mattered a great deal. Regardless of how much the Nazis' anti-Semitic attitudes figured into the hostilities, it remains that the battles in Europe involved one largely "white" force fighting another; in marked contrast, the battles in the Pacific involved a largely "white" force fighting an enemy of an obviously different color. For most Americans, "the war in the Far Eastern/Pacific front—unlike the one against Nazi Fascism in Europe—had explicitly racial undertones."[52] Although on neither front was the war explicitly racist in its motivations, "in the Pacific it became for most American soldiers a racially coded conflict."[53]

Regarded from that perspective, Rodgers and Hammerstein's three oriental musicals indeed come across as efforts to express the policy of integration that went hand in hand with the United States' Cold War policy, when it came to communism, of containment. But a good case has been made, by Klein and others, that the Fifties musical in general—in contrast to pre-Fifties and post-Fifties musicals—is a metaphor for integration. Much attention, for example, has been called to Rodgers and Hammerstein's 1943 *Oklahoma!*, a decidedly pre–Cold War show that nevertheless "dramatically produces and enacts" a "realisation of the American dream" and that "celebrates the ideology and politics of liberal democracy, where differences of political interest can be reconciled through cooperation and coexistence rather than resolved through conflict."[54] Attention has been called, too, to *West Side Story*, not just because in act 1 Maria's friend Anita exuberantly "sing[s] the praises for cultural assimilation"[55] (in the song "América") but also because at the very end of act 2, after Tony has been killed, the Sharks and the Jets temporarily set aside their mutual hatred and together carry away Tony's body.

To call the last bit of *West Side Story* a happy ending is surely to stretch the meaning of the word "happy." Yet even this scene, tear-provoking though it is, symbolizes the coming together of cultures that hitherto had been divided, and in so doing it taps directly into Cold War integration policy. Most Broadway musicals before the Fifties told simple, even simplistic, stories of male-female romance. Likewise, they centered on male-female relationships, but most often their plots took the one-on-one hook-up merely as a starting point for an exploration of deeper, more complex human relationships.

"The romantic couple of a [Fifties] musical represents more than simply two people falling in love," writes Stacy Wolf in the first of her two books that examine Broadway's sociological implications through a lens of gender studies. In the typical Fifties musical, she writes, "the entire cast reassembles at the end . . . to celebrate the uniting of the [romantic] couple, which serves as the synecdoche for the unification of the community, of the world at large. The celebration that attends the finale of [Fifties] musicals symbolically resolves

U.S. social conflicts of class and labor."[56] In her second book, Wolf is more specific about the "larger and cultural divisions" that are represented by the romantic couple's "divergent personalities" and often "overdetermined . . . differences in gender." By the end of the typical Fifties musical, she writes, the audience witnesses not just the couple's linkage but also the bridging of gaps "between high and low class in *My Fair Lady*, between law and freedom in *Guys and Dolls*, between discipline and impulse in *The Music Man*, between nature and the city in *The Sound of Music*. . . . Gender difference, then, signifies *all* difference, and heterosexual union . . . performs the unification of the entire community."[57]

The typical Broadway musical of the Fifties, in other words, was a metaphor of integration of one sort or another. Rodgers and Hammerstein's *South Pacific*, *The King and I*, and *Flower Drum Song* in obvious ways promoted the official Cold War foreign policy of making friends with distant peoples before those peoples could be wooed by communism. But in variously subtle ways most of the other Fifties shows promoted the implied but seldom stated domestic policy of postwar nation-building. "This most innocent of cultural forms," Wolf reminds us, was "distinctly and powerfully political."[58]

Giving America What It Needed

On March 28, 1954, a year after Senator Joseph McCarthy began his "television-friendly investigations" into the roles that communists purportedly played in various American institutions, less than a month before the Senate Subcommittee on Investigations launched its famously televised investigation into McCarthy himself,[59] all four of the American television networks simultaneously aired a show titled *A Tribute to Rodgers and Hammerstein*. The show was the brainchild of NBC's president and chairman, Sylvester L. Weaver Jr., who throughout the early 1950s argued that the new medium of television, if it were to capture the public's attention, needed to provide its audience not just with a generous supply of regular material but also with a limited amount of tantalizingly "special" material. In September 1954 NBC launched a series of what Weaver aptly called "spectaculars," expensively produced one-off events that every three or four weeks competed directly against the other networks' most successful regular shows. For this, the *General Foods 50th Anniversary Tribute to Rodgers and Hammerstein*—also known as the *Rodgers and Hammerstein Cavalcade*—was in effect just a warm-up, but it was a warm-up so intense that nothing like it was ever again attempted.

Produced and directed by NBC's Ralph Levy, with scripted banter penned by Sam Perrin, George Balzer, and Samuel Taylor, the ninety-minute live show was aired not just by NBC but also by the ABC, CBS, and DuMont networks. Its host was Mary Martin, who had starred in the 1947 touring production of Irving Berlin's *Annie Get Your Gun* and who, more significantly, had created the role of nurse Nellie Forbush in Rodgers and Hammerstein's 1949 *South Pacific* and was slated for the title role in Mark Charlap and Carolyn Leigh's soon-to-open and thus much-publicized *Peter Pan*.[60] The non-singing guests included television personalities Ed Sullivan, Jack Benny, Groucho Marx, and, with his dummy Charlie McCarthy, ventriloquist Edgar Bergen. In addition to Mary Martin, the singers—almost all of whom had a close relationship either with Rodgers and Hammerstein or with NBC—were Yul Brynner, Jan Clayton, Rosemary Clooney, Bill Hayes, Florence Henderson, Gordon MacRae, Tony Martin, Patricia Morison, Ezio Pinza, John Raitt, and Janice Rule. Repertoire for the *Rodgers and Hammerstein Cavalcade* consisted of "Oh, What a Beautiful Morning," "People Will Say We're in Love," and, at the show's end, the finale from *Oklahoma!*; "It Might as Well Be Spring" and "It's a Grand Night for Singing" from the 1945 film musical *State Fair*; "If I Loved You" from *Carousel*; "You Are Never Away" from the relatively unsuccessful 1947 *Allegro*;[61] "Some Enchanted Evening," "I'm Gonna Wash That Man Right Out of My Hair," and "I'm in Love with a Wonderful Guy" from *South Pacific*; "Getting to Know You" and "A Puzzlement" from *The King and I*; and "No Other Love" from the 1953, also relatively unsuccessful, *Me and Juliet*.[62] The show's viewing audience was estimated at seventy million, "the largest entertainment audience in history."[63]

NBC's telecast of *Peter Pan* attracted an audience of only sixty-five million, but in a sense it was an even bigger success. The network had purchased the show before its October 1954 opening on Broadway, and its limited run of just 152 performances was planned from the outset as a "setup" for the March 7, 1955, telecast—live and in color—that was part of a new NBC series titled *Producers' Showcase*. NBC certainly got its money's worth out of the investment: not only did it draw "the largest audience ever" for a program aired not by a consortium but by a single network;[64] the telecast also easily "overwhelmed CBS's extremely popular *I Love Lucy* in the ratings" and, according to an NBC producer, "got more newspaper coverage than the invasion of Poland."[65] The network restaged *Peter Pan* twice more, in January 1956 and, with videotape cameras rolling, in December 1960.[66]

The 1954 *Rodgers and Hammerstein Cavalcade* and NBC's various telecasts of *Peter Pan* were significant events both in the history of television and the history of the Broadway musical. But they were hardly the only means by which the music of Broadway during the Fifties was shared with Americans who had never had the opportunity to experience a show in New York or even a touring production of the sort that went on the road almost as soon as it was determined that a Broadway show was indeed a success. The songs of Broadway, and with them Broadway's political ethos, were also disseminated through radio and television variety shows, through adaptations of Broadway shows into Hollywood films, and, perhaps most significantly, through original cast recordings.

*   *   *

Although the idea for recordings featuring members of the original casts of Broadway shows was born in the late years of the Great Depression,[67] the original cast recording as it is known today was most definitely a product of postwar technology. Before 1948, all of the more or less successful efforts were in the shellac-based 78-rpm format that had been the norm almost since the recording industry's inception,[68] and most of them consisted of six double-sided discs. Momentously, in 1948 Columbia introduced the new vinyl-based "long play" (LP) 33⅓-rpm format,[69] and the next year it had top sellers with its original cast recordings of *Kiss Me, Kate; Pal Joey;* and *South Pacific.* The *South Pacific* album was especially significant: just as Mercury's 1950 recording of Patti Page singing "The Tennessee Waltz" helped establish the new vinyl-based 45-rpm format for singles, so Columbia's 1949 recording of *South Pacific* in effect established the 33⅓ format for LPs.

Exaggerating only slightly, Philip D. Beidler writes that it was "almost by divine conjunction of technological accident with promotional opportunity" that this new medium—the original cast LP—appeared, and its "blend of popular appeal with minor cultural cachet" seemed to capitalize on "the marriage of its audience demographics with [the] demographics of the soon-to-be-eclipsed Broadway form, elevated but not highbrow, popular but not plebian."[70] In any case, original cast LPs proved to be highly successful, and their success differed markedly from that of LPs built around hit singles: whereas "albums sired by singles hits" had an "average life of 6.7 weeks" on the charts, "original cast albums [had] an average chart tenure of about 69 weeks."[71] Indeed, "the reliable 'continuing turnover' as back catalogue" made original cast LPs, "in essence, the backbone of the U.S. record industry.... By the 1960s, it was not uncommon to see 'Original Cast and Soundtrack' LPs like *Oklahoma!, South Pacific, The King and I, My Fair Lady* or *The Sound of Music* remaining on the bestseller charts for five or more years."[72]

As its name suggests, the soundtrack LP is an LP whose contents are gleaned from a film soundtrack, and such a product did not exist until the 1950s. But Hollywood had gravitated toward the Broadway musical almost since the very start of the sound-film era. Of the thousand or so films issued by Hollywood between 1929 and 1930, a fifth of them could be accurately described as musicals, and most of these were fairly direct translations to the sound stage of shows that had recently played on Broadway. Apparently having sated its audience, in 1931 and 1932 Hollywood in effect abandoned the musical, but it seems that by the mid-1930s the right balance had been found. This balance shifted in the postwar years, not so much because the Fifties coincided with Broadway's golden age but because both the independent film producers and the beleaguered major Hollywood studios realized that colorful big-screen versions of musicals offered viable competition to the fare that audiences were seeing for free on their mostly black-and-white small-screen television sets.

Of the shows included in Geoffrey Block's list of "The Canonic Twelve: The Broadway Canon from *Show Boat* to *West Side Story*,"[73] all but two were made into films during the long decade of the Fifties; of the shows included in Block's list of "The Thirty Longest Running Musicals on Broadway, from *Show Boat* to *West Side Story*,"[74] only six were *not* made into films or television productions during that same period. The shift in balance that saw Hollywood once again favoring musicals had to do with quality as well as quantity. There were indeed more film musicals in the Fifties than in the previous decade and a half. More significant, Fifties film musicals, whether original productions or adaptations from Broadway, were spectacular in ways that were both unprecedented and never again matched. That films such as *Annie Get Your Gun* (1950), *Brigadoon* (1954), *Oklahoma!* (1955), *Guys and Dolls* (1955), *The King and I* (1956), *Pajama Game* (1957), *South Pacific* (1958), *Bells Are Ringing* (1960), and *West Side Story* (1961) remain popular today is testament to their content and production values; that in their day these films collectively ranked among the most successful products that Hollywood until that time had made bears witness to Broadway's enormous popularity and, by extrapolation, its impact.

Mary Martin's shampoo routine in *South Pacific*'s "I'm Gonna Wash That Man Right Out of My Hair"—enacted not just on stage but also in the film and on television—triggered not just the rapid development of "once-a-day home care products" but also "a highly manageable, easily dryable, cropped hairstyle that became instantly fashionable" among independent-minded women.[75] At the same time, "the Broadway cast album on the 'hi-fi' in the suburban living room [developed into] a new and important cultural artifact for the emerging middle class,"[76] a sort of electronic hearth around which entire families could comfortably gather. In the postwar Age of Anxiety, Broadway in all of its manifestations gave Americans not just what they obviously wanted but also what, deep down, they apparently needed.

6

Opera

From a distance of more than a half century, it seems safe to say that during the Fifties the two most celebrated American composers of "serious" music—and the two composers of that period whose music today is still most regularly programmed not just in the United States but around the world—were Aaron Copland and Leonard Bernstein. Not widely known during the homophobic Fifties is the now well-documented fact that Copland and Bernstein were closeted gays. Much publicized at the time, on the other hand, was the non-secret that Copland and Bernstein, along with numerous less-stellar composers, held decidedly left-leaning political views. And for both composers this had consequences.

In April 1949 *Life* magazine included Copland and Bernstein in a list of fifty "dupes and fellow travelers" who had participated in, or at least supported, the previous month's Cultural and Scientific Conference for World Peace—a three-day event that brought together thinkers from east and west for the sake of establishing "a spirit of peace in a time when there is heavy noise of great armaments and war"—held at New York's Waldorf Astoria hotel.[1] In June 1950 a special issue of the right-wing journal *Counterattack* named Copland and Bernstein—along with 149 other individuals involved in journalism, the arts, and entertainment—as suspected "subversives."[2] Copland was surprised (although it seems hardly surprising from a modern perspective) that in May 1953, after he had attracted attention when on very short notice his *Lincoln Portrait* was removed from the program scheduled to support the inauguration of President Dwight D. Eisenhower, he was called to testify before a closed-door session of Senator Joseph McCarthy's increasingly powerful Subcommittee on Investigations.[3] Bernstein was spared this inconvenience and humiliation, but his curriculum vitae was nonetheless scrutinized by the FBI, and in 1953 the renewal of his passport was delayed until he delivered to the U.S. State Department an affidavit in which he swore that he was not, and had never been, a communist.[4]

Likely not just by coincidence, then, both Copland and Bernstein in the mid-1950s produced operas that in a general way "comment—quite critically—on anticommunist red-baiting and the Cold War culture of fear" and that specifically, in certain of their key scenes, "take square aim at McCarthy and his methods."[5] These operas are Copland's 1954 *The Tender Land* and Bernstein's 1956 *Candide*.

* * *

The Tender Land was commissioned in 1952 by the New York–based League of Composers, and even in its conceptual stages it was determined that the work should be premiered on television, not in a theater. The producers of NBC's adventurous *Opera Workshop*, alas, decided that the effort was not "telegenic" enough for their tastes, so *The Tender Land* had its first performances, in April 1954, at the New York City Center. Notwithstanding its potentially appealing blend of folk song and the composer's characteristic "homespun" harmonies,[6] the ninety-minute two-act opera fell flat with its audience and with most of its critics. The prime reason for this, most modern commentators agree, is the libretto by Copland's then-lover Erik Johns.[7] The problem is not that the libretto is flawed but rather that it quite deliberately lacks the dynamic of conflict and climax that makes most non-comic opera, as Bernstein put it to a 1958 television audience, "bigger than spoken theater, bigger than life."[8] Not only was *The Tender Land* conceived, musically as well as dramatically, with television's capacity for close-ups in mind; it was also conceived, according to Johns, not as "a big dramatic number" but as something "in the nature of an operatic tone poem."[9]

Inspired by the Depression-era fortitude celebrated in James Agee and Walker Evans's 1941 *Let Us Now Praise Famous Men*, the opera indeed tells a story, but it is not a terribly gripping one: As a farm girl prepares for her graduation from high school, two drifters arrive on the scene. The jubilant mood is clouded by news that a neighbor girl had earlier that day been sexually assaulted, yet the drifters are nevertheless happily welcomed, and one of them catches the amorous fancy of the farm girl. In act 2, when the graduation party is in full swing, and after the farm girl's inebriated grandfather catches her smooching with one of the drifters, the two strangers are openly suspected of the previous day's crime. Word comes that the actual assaulters have been caught, yet still the party disintegrates into a miasma of barely suppressed hostility. The next day, at the strong urging of the grandfather, the drifters quietly depart. To the chagrin of her family, the farm girl, who had seriously planned to elope with her drifter friend, decides that her best option now is simply to go off on her own.

The entirety of *The Tender Land* is shrouded with feelings of "suspicion, ill-will and dread" that Copland said, five years in advance of the opera's premiere, permeated America's postwar period.[10] These feelings shroud the opera, perhaps, but as Vivian Perlis observes in one of her oral history volumes devoted to Copland, "except for one moment in the plot, there is no trace of the bitter taste of the McCarthy hearing and its aftermath."[11] That "one moment" comes at the end of the accusation scene, when, even after the two drifters' innocence has been made obvious, the grandfather says, in effect under his breath but nonetheless loud and clear: "They're guilty all the same."

This potent line, it is interesting to note, was added at Copland's suggestion only after the opera had had its brief run of just two performances.[12] The composer might have been inclined to include an "apparently . . . conscious reference to McCarthy" in the version that was presented twice at the City Center, but it is likely that only after the second performance did he feel it was safe to do so.[13] On the very day of that second performance the ABC and Dumont television networks had begun their gavel-to-gavel live coverage of the so-called Army-McCarthy hearings that eventually brought about McCarthy's downfall.

* * *

As was doubtless intended by their organizers, the open- and closed-door hearings that McCarthy himself conducted, and before them the largely Hollywood-focused hearings conducted by HUAC, instilled fear in both those who actually came under scrutiny and those who, from a distance, were simply aware of what was going on in Washington. In marked contrast, the Army-McCarthy hearings that ran for seven weeks generated, at least for some Americans, feelings of immense satisfaction. It is hard to imagine that Leonard Bernstein did not have this in mind when he wrote the wickedly gleeful "Auto-da-Fé" chorus that resounds early in his 1956 *Candide*.

In *Candide's* second scene the merchants of Lisbon are delighted to learn of the Inquisition-ordered public executions of the title character and his teacher, Dr. Pangloss, because such events, they know from experience, are good for business. Primed by increasingly favorable reactions to the McCarthy exposés that had been offered since March 9, 1954, by journalist Edward R. Murrow on the CBS network's *See It Now* program,[14] the ABC and Dumont networks knew that it would likewise be good for business to telecast evidence-rich proceedings that inevitably would lead to McCarthy's demise. Even as those hearings began, on April 22, 1954, it was clear to many Americans that McCarthy was "toast." Still, for Bernstein the *Candide* project was not without risks.

The resolution of his problems with the U.S. Passport Office in 1953 had gotten Bernstein off the unofficial but nonetheless effective blacklist. But in March 1956, eight months before *Candide* was set to open, Bernstein was informed that he was soon to be interrogated by the House Committee on Appropriations because the Symphony of the Air with which Bernstein was affiliated had a "supposed but unnamed communist" in its midst.[15] The interrogation never took place, but only because Massachusetts senator John F. Kennedy, a personal friend of Bernstein, intervened.[16]

In any case, the idea for a politically relevant update of the satiric Voltaire novella came from Lillian Hellman, a playwright who had been named along with Bernstein and Copland in both the 1949 "Dupes and Fellow Travelers" article in *Life* magazine and the 1950 *Counterattack* publication. Upon reengaging with a thought she first had in 1950, Hellman planned to write simply a play with incidental music similar to her 1955 *The Lark*, an adaptation of Jean Anouilh's 1952 *L'Alouette*, about the trial and execution of Joan of Arc. Bernstein, who had provided the modest score for *The Lark*, saw greater possibilities in Hellman's *Candide* proposal. He suggested something along the lines of an operetta—that is, a show leavened aplenty with tart interludes of spoken dialogue but nonetheless heavily loaded with music.

Whether or not the Bernstein-Hellman effort actually *is* an operetta, or even an opera, or whether or not it somehow became an operetta or opera due to the various cultural contexts into which it has been placed, are questions best left for another forum.[17] But no matter how *Candide* might be regarded today, it remains that at the time of its creation it was treated like a Broadway show. In contrast to Copland and Johns's *The Tender Land* and most other operas, it had an out-of-town tryout. Again in contrast to most operas, it featured contributions by people other than its nominal author and composer: although the "book" was indeed by Hellman, the lyrics were for the most part by Richard Wilbur, with contributions by a group that included Dorothy Parker, John La Touche, and Stephen Sondheim; although the music was entirely by Bernstein, the orchestration was crafted jointly by Hershy

Kay and Maurice Peress. Still again in contrast to most operas, in the weeks before its premiere *Candide* was subject to extensive executive-mandated revisions.

Hellman's original text included "pointed references to HUAC" and "specific allusions to McCarthyism,"[18] but these were all removed during the Boston tryout, likely because of fears on the parts of producer Ethel Linder Reiner or, as Hellman surely thought, director Tyrone Guthrie.[19] What remains is still very much anti-McCarthy, albeit only in a general, metaphoric way. Especially in the *auto-da-fé* scene, it is hard not to notice that "conspiracy is seen anywhere," that "scapegoats are used to explain the inexplicable," that "Pangloss and Candide are the quintessential aliens to be gotten rid of."[20] And one indeed gets the impression that the butts of most of *Candide's* jokes, as Bernstein wrote a few weeks before the premiere, are "puritanical snobbery, phony moralism, inquisitorial attacks on the individual, brave-new-world optimism, [and] essential superiority," and that, like Voltaire's model, the show "throws light on all the dark places."[21]

Bernstein published those words in a newspaper article cast as a dialogue between himself and his intellectual conscience, "a friendly enemy of long standing" that he identified as his "irrepressible demon."[22] The topic of discussion was not so much *Candide's* content as its form. Pointedly, the demon reminds Bernstein of how, on his *Omnibus* television program just a month earlier, he had attempted to pigeonhole the so-called musical comedy. Caught up now in his own contradictory thoughts on the eve of *Candide's* premiere, Bernstein articulately admits to struggling with definitions of such genres as musical comedy, comic opera, operetta, and opera.

Because it arguably falls into all of those categories—not because of its political allusions or the complexity of its plot, and certainly not because of the quality of its music—is doubtless the reason why *Candide* failed in its initial run. It may well have been right from the start an opera or an operetta, but it was presented to the public as if it were just another Broadway musical. Its targeted audience did not know what to make of it, and so, after opening on December 1, 1956, at Broadway's Martin Beck Theatre, it closed after seventy-three performances. By Broadway standards of the day, *Candide* was a flop.

Politics Cuts Both Ways

Hardly flops at the times of their premieres—but then again, hardly works whose composers have entered the pantheon of twentieth-century American music, or who, like Copland and Bernstein, have become legendary because of their personal involvement with and resistance to McCarthy and HUAC—were Carlisle Floyd's 1955 *Susannah* and Robert Ward's 1961 *The Crucible*. Both of them, by two of America's most prolific producers of opera, have been almost continuously on the boards, somewhere, since their creations. And both of them take aim, more directly than do *The Tender Land* and *Candide*, at the culture of McCarthyism.

Arthur Miller, author of the same-titled 1953 play on which Ward's *The Crucible* is based, recalled that in the early 1950s he was fascinated by the "surreal spiritual transaction" that occurred in so many of the hearings conducted by McCarthy and HUAC. "In effect," Miller wrote in an autobiography, "it came down to a governmental decree of *moral* guilt that could easily be made to disappear by ritual speech: intoning names of fellow sinners and recanting former beliefs. . . . The rituals of guilt and confession followed all the forms of a religious inquisition, except, of course, that the offended parties were not God and his ministers but a congressional committee."[23]

Whereas religion plays no part whatsoever in *The Tender Land*'s scene of false accusation, it fairly dominates at least the *auto-da-fé* scene in *Candide*. But *Candide* deals with religion-based persecution in a joke-filled way. Audiences laughed—and continue to laugh, albeit likely with their consciences pricked—at the Lisbon citizens' complaints that not enough of them will be able to "see the bones" of the victims and their relief upon being reminded that most of them, nevertheless, will still be able to "hear their moans." In contrast, religious persecution in Floyd's *Susannah* and Ward's *The Crucible* is not at all a laughing matter.

Set in rural Tennessee but based on an episode in the Bible's book of Daniel, *Susannah* tells the story of a young woman who is falsely accused of lewd behavior and then ordered by the new church minister to repent in front of the entire congregation. She refuses, and the ensuing trouble includes her being raped by the minister, her brother killing the minister, and, in the final scene, her chasing off vigilantes with a shotgun and then leaving the community of her own accord. Ward's *The Crucible*, like Miller's play, is based on the so-called Salem witch trials, a famously inglorious moment of American history during which, in a small Massachusetts town in 1692, more than a thousand people were interrogated and nineteen of them, along with two dogs, were put to death by hanging. In both operas the key elements are false accusations, public events during which the accused are given opportunities for forgiveness so long as they confess, and the consequences of not confessing. And in the dramatic arc of both operas the accusation/trial scene—"voyeuristic, dramatic, trance-like, orgiastic"[24]—is central.

Miller's three-act *The Crucible* opened at New York's Martin Beck Theatre on January 22, 1953, and ran for 197 performances. The playwright immediately recognized the musical potential in what won not only Broadway's Tony Award for 1953's best play but also a central place in the canon of great American drama. Indeed, when the play was still fresh, Miller asked his literary agent to discuss the possibility of an operatic *Crucible* with both Copland and Floyd. Copland was busy with *The Tender Land* at the time, and Floyd had just started work on both the music and the libretto for *Susannah*. Ward and his librettist, Bernard Stambler, came across *The Crucible* via an off-Broadway production in 1959; they immediately invited Miller to the next performance of their *He Who Gets Slapped*, then in production at the New York City Opera. Miller liked what he saw and heard but granted the rights to *The Crucible* only after Ward and Stambler provided him with two sample scenes.[25]

Floyd's two-act *Susannah* was premiered in Tallahassee at Florida State University, where since 1947 the composer had been on the music faculty. It was quickly taken up by the New York City Opera and won the New York Music Critics' Circle Award for best new opera of 1956. Two years later it was presented, as a representative of American opera, at the Brussels World's Fair. Ward's four-act *The Crucible* fared even better; written on commission for the New York City Opera, it won not only the Critics' Circle award but also the 1962 Pulitzer Prize for Music. That these two operas should be so lauded at the times of their premieres, and so often performed over subsequent decades, perhaps says something about more than just their musical/dramatic effectiveness.

When Ward first presented his operatic version of *The Crucible*, on October 26, 1961, McCarthyism was all but dead and buried. That was not the case, however, when Floyd was working on *Susannah* and when Miller was working on his play. Reflecting on the first half of the 1950s in a liner note essay for a 1994 recording of *Susannah*, Floyd wrote that McCarthy-inspired fear "permeated everything at that time. . . . It took all kinds of forms, [including] suspicion, and the idea that accusation was all that was needed as proof of guilt. It terrified and enraged me."[26] Two years later, reflecting on the impetus for *The Crucible*, Miller wrote: "I was motivated in some great part by the paralysis that had set in among many liberals who, despite their discomfort with the inquisitors' violations of civil rights, were fearful, and with good reason, of being identified as covert Communists if they should protest too strongly."[27]

It was indeed a fearful time, a nasty time. And so one wonders if both the immediate success and the enduring popularity of Floyd's and Ward's operas, and of Miller's play, might possibly involve the genuine *need* of Americans—Americans with consciences who lived through it, but also Americans with consciences who were born long after the Fifties—for cathartic theater that would somehow cleanse them of the residue left over from one of the darkest periods in their nation's history.

* * *

Politics, in the Fifties as now, of course cuts both ways. It may well be that most scholarly writing on politically influenced American operas from the postwar years focuses on works that in one way or another criticized the likes of McCarthy and HUAC, but it remains that at least a few operas approached the issue from the right. German musicologist Klaus-Dieter Gross, at any rate, has identified two operas in which "an aggressive anti-Communism seems to be at work."[28]

Nicolas Nabokov is today better known for being the cousin of the author of the scandalous 1955 novel *Lolita* than for being, from 1951 until 1967, the secretary-general of the influential CIA-funded propaganda organization called the Congress for Cultural Freedom,[29] and probably he is better known for his politics than for his music. But the Russian-born Nabokov identified himself as a composer throughout his entire life. Likely because of his time-consuming work as "impresario of the cultural Cold War,"[30] his output is limited, and thus his two-act opera *The Holy Devil*—commissioned in 1954 by the Louisville Orchestra and premiered in 1958 by the Kentucky Opera Association—represents, for Nabokov, something of a high-water mark. Musically, this telling of the story of the last days of the "mad monk" Rasputin is not without interest; indeed, Richard Taruskin calls it "an effective study in Musorgskian dialogue set against a background of traditional and popular musics of the period, including that of the Orthodox liturgy."[31] But the music is by any standard conventional, and the libretto, by the right-wing British poet Stephen Spender, is feeble. For sure, Nabokov's *The Holy Devil* advocates ridding a nation of evil influences. But "without the political context" of McCarthyism, the opera today seems "irrelevant."[32]

Perhaps even more irrelevant, not just to the world of today but also to the world of the Fifties, is William Grant Still's *Troubled Island*. Yet although its creation predates the McCarthy era, this opera did manage to raise a political stink during the postwar years. Based on a 1928 Langston Hughes play about the Haitian revolution, *Troubled Island* was completed in 1939 but had to wait until ten years later for its premiere, by which time leftist nuances had been removed from its libretto and Still had personally distanced himself from the blacklisted Hughes. That the performances by the New York City Opera were limited to three, and that the reviews were middling, was ascribed by Still and his aggressively careerist wife to "conspiratorial actions" against "the colored boy" on the part of the New York music critics.[33] That the U.S. State Department's recording of one of the performances was withdrawn in August 1950 after only two broadcasts in Europe was ascribed both to racist prejudice and to "the influence of Communists who will advance any colored man who plays their game, and will persecute those who do not."[34] Evidence of a genuine conspiracy has never surfaced, and *Troubled Island* remains best known for Still's, but mostly his wife's, loud expressions of "hysterical anti-Communism."[35]

Three-Dimensional Action on a Two-Dimensional Screen

Copland's *The Tender Land* had the misfortune of being conceived for television but performed in a large opera house. It also had the misfortune of being paired at its premiere with Gian Carlo Menotti's *Amahl and the Night Visitors*, another opera conceived for television but one for which the transfer from one medium to the other was not at all a problem.

Menotti's *Amahl* was the first opera commissioned especially for American television, but it was hardly the first operatic property to be televised in the United States. Following examples set in England and Germany, as early as 1940 NBC served up a truncated version of *Pagliacci*, but only via its outlet in Schenectady, New York. The first postwar American effort at televised opera was a much bigger deal; aired on the ABC network on November 29, 1948, it involved no less than curtain-to-curtain coverage of the Metropolitan Opera's opening night production of *Otello*, the results of which were witnessed by almost two million viewers.[36] The response was positive enough that the Texaco Company, which had sponsored the Met's radio broadcasts since 1940 and sponsored the telecast as well, committed to supporting the opening nights of the 1949–1950 and 1950–1951 seasons (productions of *Der Rosenkavalier* and *Don Carlo*, respectively).

There were great hopes for opera on television. Network television was still in its infancy in 1948, and programmers really had no idea what would appeal to their hoped-for audiences. "So opera," notes media historian Richard C. Burke, "had its chance along with roller skating, wrestling matches, and countless variety shows."[37] But then it began to be noticed—by audiences, by producers, and, importantly, by critics—that the small screen of television and the expansive performance style of grand opera perhaps formed a less than ideal coupling. After an expensive round of efforts that included not just productions of "grand opera" shown on network television but also productions broadcast via closed-circuit television to more than thirty cinemas around the country, New York Times film critic Bosley Crowther finally stated what many opera lovers had doubtless long been thinking: "It is hard to imagine any system—even wide screen—that will be able to overcome the feeling of confinement and monotony that is induced by the straight pickup of a production on a stage."[38]

The Met's productions were "on a stage," of course, and the general failure of their well-intentioned telecasts by ABC and a short-lived company called Theater Network Television centered on the simple fact that they attempted to present, on a two-dimensional screen, three-dimensional action that had clearly been designed for a very large opera house. But two of America's other television networks, CBS and NBC, took care early on to avoid this mistake.

* * *

CBS made its first foray into televised opera on December 12, 1948, just two weeks after ABC had telecast the Met's opening-night performance of Otello. In the case of CBS, the material at hand was Menotti's The Medium, a work that, like Bernstein's Candide, has been identified over the years as both an opera and a Broadway musical.

The Medium was written for the stage, commissioned by Columbia University and premiered there, with student performers, on May 8, 1946. In February of the next year the darkly tragic two-act opera had its first performance by professionals, and in May 1947—with the same professional cast, and now prefaced by a one-act comedy titled The Telephone that Menotti created especially for the occasion—it moved to Broadway to begin a run of 211 performances at the Ethel Barrymore Theatre. The "medium" named in the title of Menotti's work is a woman who conducts séances. Reading that word a different way, it seems fitting that in November 1948 a studio performance of The Medium was aired live by NBC Radio and that in 1951 the opera was translated into a moderately successful Hollywood film; it seems fitting, too, that on December 12, 1948, The Medium was included in a CBS television series called Studio One.

Studio One was the brainchild of Canadian director Fletcher Markle, who early in 1947 launched a CBS radio series whose serious dramatic content was intended to compete with the other networks' lightweight fare. In 1948 the series moved to television, where it lasted ten seasons and delivered a total of 466 one-hour dramas. *The Medium* was the third offering of the debut season and the only opera the series ever attempted.

By the time of the 1948 telecast the Italian-born Menotti was already an established figure in American opera. After its premiere in Philadelphia, his 1937 *Amelia Goes to the Ball* was performed the next season at the Met, and the work was so well received that NBC promptly commissioned his 1939 radio opera *The Old Maid and the Thief*. Menotti's 1942 one-act opera *The Island God*, which premiered at the Met, was a failure even in the composer's eyes, but Menotti felt that the problem was in large part the fault of the staging, and from that point on he served not just as composer and librettist for his operas but also, at least at their premieres, as director.

The lasting success of *The Medium* can be attributed to the dramatic strength of the libretto and the overall quality of its sometimes eerily dissonant, sometimes memorably melodic, and always dramatically effective music. But the success of its early manifestations—in all of their various formats—also stems in large part from the fact that Menotti himself managed the staging. Because of union regulations, he could not get official credit for directing the *Studio One* presentation of *The Medium*,[39] but he certainly had a hand in how his work was treated by the cameras. Unlike the carefully edited 1951 film over which Menotti had total control, the 1948 live telecast did not feature special filters on the camera lenses, bizarre angles, or intense close-ups in quick succession. Nevertheless, in the CBS telecast *The Medium* was effective not just as opera but also, significantly, as television.

* * *

That their product be effective as television, not just as opera, was right from the start the primary goal of the founders of the NBC Opera Theatre: television producer Charles Polachek, director Kirk Browning, conductor Peter Herman Adler, and, most potently, Samuel Chotzinoff, the longtime NBC music executive who in 1939 had had the good sense to commission Menotti's *The Old Maid and the Thief* for the network's radio division. The various criteria established by Chotzinoff, Adler, and Polachek—criteria that would be emulated by the many regional opera companies that sprang up in the United States over the next several decades, but criteria very different from those which governed the Metropolitan Opera—all centered on the idea of credibility.

In terms of casting, these criteria meant that the performers had to look their parts, had to be convincing as actors as well as singers, and had to be equipped with clear diction. In terms of production values, the criteria meant an emphasis on camera work that showcased acting and a downplaying of the spectacle that thrived in the large opera house but simply would not fit into the small screen of black-and-white television. In terms of repertoire, the criteria meant that the selected operas had to have plots that were at least somewhat believable and also, importantly, that they be performed in English. "It would seem to be altogether obvious," Chotzinoff said after his brainchild had been alive and well for a few years, "that Americans who go to listen to opera should be able to *understand* the words that are being sung."[40]

In order to achieve their goal, Chotzinoff and his colleagues first had to convince NBC chief executive David Sarnoff of their project's viability. Reportedly they did this by surprising Sarnoff, after a dinner at his home, with a piano-accompanied bit from the last act of *La bohème*.[41] Impressed by what he experienced, he gave the go-ahead not for an actual program but simply for a few experiments. The first of these, on February 2, 1949—just weeks after ABC's curtain-to-curtain telecast of the Metropolitan Opera's *Otello* and CBS's hour-long presentation of *The Medium*—involved a mere fifteen minutes' worth of *La bohème*. Three more similarly brief telecasts featured excerpts from *The Barber of Seville*, *The Bartered Bride*, and *The Old Maid and the Thief*. Perhaps won over more by Chotzinoff's enthusiasm than by the operas themselves, eventually Sarnoff agreed to a half-hour time slot on occasional Saturday nights. Momentously, the NBC Opera Theatre debuted on January 14, 1950, with a presentation of Kurt Weill's *Down in the Valley*.[42]

That initial presentation, one critic recalled years later, "swept through the musico-entertainment world like a fresh breeze,"[43] and this encouraged Sarnoff to allot at least an hour for ensuing telecasts. Before the end of the debut season there were three more productions—of *Madame Butterfly*, *Die Fledermaus*, and *Tales of Hoffmann*, each of them with their material truncated but nonetheless edited so that they told complete stories. The 1950–1951 season offered productions of *Carmen*, *Hansel and Gretel*, and *Gianni Schicchi*, the last of these needing no truncation, since it was only fifty minutes long. Along with *Pagliacci* and a confection billed as *R.S.V.P.* (drawn from Offenbach's 1861 operetta *M. Choufleuri restera chez lui le . . .*), the historically significant 1951–1952 season featured the world premiere of the first-ever opera commissioned especially for television.

A lightweight Christmas story inspired by Hieronymus Bosch's painting *The Adoration of the Magi*, Menotti's *Amahl and the Night Visitors* was acclaimed as "the best production of opera yet seen on TV,"[44] held up as "living proof that television can accommodate itself to greatness if it wishes,"[45] and heralded as a demonstration that "television, operatically speaking, has come of age."[46] And yet, for all the genuine hope that it inspired, in retrospect *Amahl* seems to have been not the vital seed from which American television opera was expected to grow but, rather, a brilliant flash in the pan after which, throughout the rest of the Fifties, "the affair between opera and television was little more than a flirtation."[47]

In the case of the NBC Opera Theatre, at least, the flirtation was earnest and sustained. ABC abandoned its relationship with opera in 1950, after just three attempts at telecasting the Metropolitan Opera's opening nights. CBS, which with its 1948 telecast of *The Medium* in effect pioneered the idea of studio-produced television opera, announced a new program called Opera Television Theater in December 1949, but after only two shows (a trimmed-down version of *Carmen*, delivered in French, and an English-language *La Traviata*) the Opera Television Theater was discontinued. CBS's only other involvements with opera during the Fifties came in the form of the occasional presentation of scenes on the *Omnibus* program that it launched in 1952 and then, four years later, handed over to ABC. In remarkable contrast to the arguably halfhearted efforts of ABC and CBS, the NBC Opera Theatre lasted for fifteen seasons.

After the sensational premiere of Menotti's *Amahl and the Night Visitors*, the NBC Opera Theatre went on to present, in part or in whole, no less than thirty-nine other operas, all performed in English.[48] Works from the standard repertoire were usually shortened, but not always: a complete *Der Rosenkavalier* was delivered in two installments in the spring of 1953, and in February 1954 *The Marriage of Figaro* was given similar treatment. Works not at all standard were sought out: along with the above-mentioned Offenbach *R.S.V.P.*, the offerings from off the beaten track included Richard Strauss's 1912 play with music, *Le Bourgeois Gentilhomme*; the 1953 ten-scene version of Prokofiev's *War and Peace*; Poulenc's 1956 *Dialogue of the Carmelites*; and Italo Montemezzi's 1913 *L'amore dei tre re*. Perhaps most significant, the NBC Opera Theatre championed new works, especially new works by American composers.[49]

Viewed from a distance, the NBC Opera Theatre's fifteen-year track record seems heroically impressive. In its time, however, the effort won mostly a *succès d'estime*. Writing sympathetically in the wake of the November 8, 1959, telecast of *Fidelio*, music critic Paul Henry Lang extolled the apparent fact that "millions of Americans who cannot hope [ever] to see live opera" benefit tremendously from the NBC telecasts. But he wondered about how the NBC Opera Theatre would survive; surely, Lang concluded, "there must be some enlightened souls in the general staff of NBC who make [the Opera Theatre's] existence possible."[50]

The NBC Opera Theatre indeed had patrons in the form of David Sarnoff, chairman of NBC since its founding in 1937 (and of its parent company, the Radio Corporation of America, since 1930), and his son Robert W. Sarnoff, who became president of NBC in 1955. The elder Sarnoff had hired Samuel Chotzinoff in 1937, when Chotzinoff was a music critic for the *New York Post*, for the purpose of traveling to Italy to convince conductor Arturo Toscanini to return to the United States and take charge of the soon-to-be-formed NBC Symphony Orchestra. Sarnoff and his son owed much to Chotzinoff, and one suspects that their decision to support for so long an endeavor that "cost a lot of money" and "[did] not earn anything" stemmed more from loyalty than from a sense of altruism.[51] Chotzinoff died, at age seventy-four, on February 9, 1964. Three weeks earlier the NBC Opera Theatre had presented *Lucia di Lammermoor*; its only previous offering for the 1963–1964 season had been the perennially popular *Amahl*, and its only subsequent offering, on March 22, 1964, was the scheduled staged version of Bach's *St. Matthew Passion*. And that was the end of what remains "one of the most outstanding examples of support for worth-while cultural events by a commercial broadcasting network."[52]

Opera Boom

Writing in June 1945, shortly after Germany had surrendered to the Allies but when Japan still had a few weeks' worth of fight left in its collective soul, the music publishing executive Hans W. Heinsheimer, an Austrian-born Jew who had immigrated to the United States in 1938, hit the proverbial nail on the head when he observed that up to this time "the American composer, it is true, has not had much to say in the matter of opera in America." Heinsheimer suggested that "with the old European cradle of opera going down in flame and destruction," it would not be long before "the American creative genius [finds] itself ready to continue and to develop the traditions of the old world."[53]

Whether or not American opera composers in the postwar years continued and developed traditions of the old world remains open to debate. It seems incontrovertible, though, that opera in America fairly flourished throughout the long decade of the Fifties, and one could make a good case that most

American composers who engaged with opera during that period set out to explore territory that was at least in some respects new.

To be sure, the Fifties amounted to a boom time for opera of the sort that first caught the eye of American television cameras. Works that represented "the traditions of the old world" were delivered most spectacularly by New York's Metropolitan Opera, the San Francisco Opera, and, after 1954, the Lyric Opera in Chicago. But they were presented as well in smaller cities with long-established opera cultures, such as New Orleans and Cincinnati, and in cities that during the Fifties founded reputable companies devoted largely to the presentation of old-fashioned, European-style opera (for example, Louisville, Tulsa, Houston, Dallas, Kansas City, and Seattle). Featuring international stars and most often performances in languages other than English, these companies' repertoires were expensive to produce and perhaps difficult for the average American to fully comprehend. Still, enough people seemed to like the sound and sight of grand opera, and the glamour of it, to fill the seats on a regular basis, and the robust postwar economy generated enough money, both corporate and private, to pay the bills that could not possibly have been covered by revenues from ticket sales.

But the Fifties also generated opera of a different sort, opera that was not at all foreign but, rather, homegrown. Some of this was on a relatively small scale, perhaps influenced by the "new intimacy and power" demonstrated regularly on television by the NBC Opera Theatre,[54] perhaps just symptomatic of the same shifting currents in dramatic taste that prompted the NBC venture in the first place. Some of it, on the other hand, was as big as anything served up by the Met and its counterparts. And much of it, whether presented on a large scale or small, was in a very particular way distinctly American.

It was not simply the choice of American subject matter, or the use of librettos based on American literature, that gave an American flavor to this new body of work. The political weather of the postwar years included not just the dark clouds of McCarthyism but also the invigorating warmth of national pride. Whereas the former surely prompted the outspoken content of *Candide* and *The Crucible*, the latter arguably inspired "many politically-minded composers of the late 1940s and 1950s" to seek, in a less strident way, simply "to re-establish American values like independence, freedom, and tolerance," and "this made the 1950s a peak era of [American] historical opera."[55]

Operas based on American history, real or imagined, date back at least to James Hewitt's 1794 *Tammany; or, The Indian Chief,* and operas that dealt either with Native American lore or with America's immigrant culture were much in evidence in the years surrounding World War I. But the recognizable American quality of American opera that first manifested itself in the Fifties had little to do with subject matter. Nor did it have much to do with the fact that the scores of many of the postwar operas made reference to traditional American hymns or folk songs, or, to a lesser extent, to American-born jazz. That music should somehow *sound* "American," and thus be immediately recognized as patriotic in intent, was very much on the minds of many of the composers who during the late 1930s participated in the Composers' Forum-Laboratories sponsored by the Federal Music Project.[56] But in the Fifties, even with McCarthyism lurking everywhere, the need to demonstrate "musical nationalism" by quoting folk tunes and the like was not nearly so strong as it had been during the Great Depression.

During the Fifties, many American operas, whether their composers were native-born or immigrants, were indeed based on American topics. Already mentioned have been Weill's *Down in the Valley*, Copland's *The Tender Land*, Floyd's *Susannah*, and Ward's *The Crucible*. A longer, but hardly complete, list would include Virgil Thomson's *The Mother of Us All* (1947), Weill's *Street Scene* (1947), Marc Blitzstein's *Regina* (1949) and *Reuben, Reuben* (1955), Lukas Foss's *The Jumping Frog of Calaveras County* (1950), Douglas Moore's *Giants in the Earth* (1951) and *The Ballad of Baby Doe* (1956), Elie Siegmeister's *Darling Corie* (1952) and *The Mermaid in Lock 7* (1958), William Schuman's *The Mighty Casey* (1953), Menotti's *The Saint of Bleecker Street* (1954), and Norman Dello Joio's *Blood Moon* (1961). As had been the case with Gershwin's 1935 *Porgy and Bess,* most of these indeed allude to, or even quote, samples of American vernacular music. And thus all of these operas, some more memorably than others, qualify as being distinctly "American." But so do operas—the *Wuthering Heights* settings of Bernard Herrmann (1951) and Floyd (1958), for example, or Louis Gruenberg's *Antony and Cleopatra* (1955), or Samuel Barber's *Vanessa* (1957), or Hugo Weisgall's *Six Characters in Search of an Author* (1959)—in which one finds not a trace of Americana.

According to opera historian Elise K. Kirk, the "ubiquitous European spell" under which American opera had operated since the country's earliest days was finally broken by Thomson with his *The Mother of Us All.* This whimsical telling of the story of suffragette Susan B. Anthony has a libretto by Gertrude Stein that is not nearly so stylized or poetic as had been her contribution to Thomson's 1928 *Four Saints in Three Acts*, and its music, importantly, in terms of both melody and rhythm "closely follows the natural accents and inflections of American speech."[57] A "natural prosody" involving "typically American language" did not go unnoticed by critics and composers who wrote about the works under discussion when they were still fresh.[58] But while the handling of language might well be the key to it, the hallmarks of American opera in the Fifties surely include as well the "casual way in which characters often conduct themselves" and the same sense of "realism that was also infusing film and musical theatre at the time."[59]

Perhaps owing to the obvious fact that the United States had recently become the world's first superpower, or perhaps owing to the apparent fact that composers were aware that audiences might actually *want* to hear their music, the American-style opera that was born in the postwar years seems to exude confidence. "All these very American works—sectional, even factional, as they are—bear unmistakable primogeniture in their markings, and one doesn't mean the influence of Victor Herbert or Deems Taylor," observed Ethan Mordden. Their shared quality defies being put into words, yet Mordden tried: "Call it the conscience of the race, if such a word as race can be at all applied; or call it the familiarity of self, the knowing the palm of one's hand. Whatever it is, it *tells*, repeatedly, in terms instantly perceived or in a sly simplicity of music and word that evokes a cultural continent."[60]

* * *

Virgil Thomson's "spell-breaking" *The Mother of Us All* had its first performance not in an opera house or in a Broadway theater, but in an auditorium at New York's Columbia University; so did Gian Carlo Menotti's *The Medium* and Douglas Moore's *Giants in the Earth*. In 1947, the same year when *The Mother of Us All* supposedly gave birth to this new style of American opera, the University of California at Berkeley presented Roger Sessions's *The Trial of Lucullus*. Kurt Weill's *Down in the Valley* first went on the boards in 1948 at Indiana University. Leonard Bernstein's *Trouble in Tahiti* was premiered at Brandeis University in 1952, William Schuman's *The Mighty Casey* at the Hartt School of Music in 1953, and Carlisle Floyd's *Susannah* at Florida State University in 1954.

The same period that witnessed the establishment all across the country of small yet worthy opera companies devoted to the traditional repertoire also witnessed a flowering of opera-producing units in American colleges and universities. Along with those just mentioned, institutions of higher education that during the postwar years got into the business of presenting opera include the University of Southern California, the New England Conservatory of Music, the Mannes School of Music, the Carnegie Institute of Technology in Pittsburgh, Converse College (in Spartanburg, South Carolina), Baylor University, the Peabody Conservatory, Louisiana State University,

Hunter College, the Manhattan School of Music, Northwestern University, the University of California–Los Angeles, the University of Michigan, the University of Minnesota, the University of Washington, and the University of Illinois.

Often labeled "opera theaters" or "opera workshops," and often headed by opera-house veterans who had immigrated to the United States before or in the midst of World War II, these programs were parts of educational institutions, so they paid attention to the tried-and-true opera repertoire. But also because they belonged to educational institutions, they were relatively free of such worries as "high labour costs, lack of rehearsal time, and the need to please a mass audience."[61] Thus they could afford to experiment with new works and with older works well outside the canon. In this regard they were phenomenally productive. During the 1950s colleges and universities "facilitated the premieres of 233 new American works and American premieres of 114 foreign operas."[62] And the foreign operas served up by the college- or university-based opera workshops during the Fifties were almost always performed in English.

It is difficult to square the postwar fashion for opera in English, on campuses and on television, with the contemporaneous fashion, all around the country, for grand opera in its original languages. But these two streams of fashion did flow simultaneously, and they combined to form a torrent of operatic activity that "in its tempo, depth, and spirit [were] without precedent."[63] In 1951, when the opera boom of the Fifties had been in progress for just a few years, Hans Heinsheimer wrote: "The technical, financial, and artistic mechanics of such a sudden and, in its forcefulness and universality, unprecedented development are difficult, at this early stage, to analyze. The spirit behind it, its cultural significance, the intentions and the ultimate goal are simple and identical all over the country. But the ways and means of putting it all into effect are diversified and cannot be explained by any simple, general formula."[64]

Probably it is still too early to devise a formula that explains America's sudden fascination with opera. If one were to attempt such a formula, however, first on the list of ingredients would be the overall condition of the American economy, which provided the opera workshops and the regional opera companies alike with a climate favorable for expensive opera production. Also on the list would be the impetus of American corporations and foundations—perhaps out of a genuine desire to serve the public good, perhaps out of a hunger for the publicity and prestige that comes with well-displayed patronage—to support the arts in general and opera in particular. But how can one know, for sure, why the NBC network not only sponsored its on-screen Opera Theatre for fifteen years but also in 1956 launched a touring company that over the course of two seasons visited almost sixty different cities,[65] or why, really, between 1958 and 1960 the Ford Foundation sponsored the production of no fewer than eighteen American works at the New York City Opera?[66]

The list of ingredients would also include the vast amount of money that the U.S. government poured into institutions of higher learning during the postwar years—in the form of direct grants to the many schools that evolved from teachers' colleges into branch campuses of state universities, and in the form of credits to military veterans who had their higher education subsidized under the G.I. Bill of Rights. And the list of ingredients for a formula that explained America's postwar opera boom surely would include the idea, although hardly a provable fact, that, having helped defeat the European nation that for more than a hundred years had convincingly held up its music to be superior to that of all other countries, America in the Fifties had at long last gotten over its "cultural cringe."[67]

An "American Phenomenon"

Heinsheimer, in his 1945 account of opera in America, noted that the repertoire of American opera companies was "rather on the conservative side."[68] Almost four decades later, the executive director of the Metropolitan Opera's Central Opera Service described the postwar situation with the same adjective:

> As the forties gave way to the fifties, most opera companies continued their rather conservative bills of fare, since they played to an extremely conservative audience and were ruled by an equally conservative board. Due to their dependence upon ticket sales for part of their income, and upon the favor of private patrons who underwrote the deficit, the companies were reluctant to take chances with lesser-known or new operas. Contemporary works were considered highly suspect, and most opera managers who wanted to remain in their posts did not chance such experiments.[69]

The word "conservative" in these quotations applies to the activities of professional opera companies, which, with the notable exceptions of the New York City Opera and the Santa Fe Opera,[70] indeed preferred to invest their energies mostly into blue-chip stock. But the word applies as well to the music of the new American operas that had their premieres for the most part on television or on campuses.

In terms of its music, American opera in the Fifties was hardly adventurous. United by its emphasis on theatrical "realism" and a clear expression of idiomatic American language, it was also united by a harmonic/melodic idiom that admitted dissonance only when its dramas turned especially bitter. Perhaps American composers of opera truly believed that "modernist" music was simply "not compatible with the emotional expression necessary for convincing theater,"[71] or perhaps they merely "aimed," for careerist reasons, at "appealing to [an] audience through pleasing melodic music."[72] At any rate, it seems that as they accepted their commissions, the majority of them chose a musical path that in its own way was as tried and true as the one being taken by the managers of opera companies.

Reviewing the 1961 premiere of Robert Ward's *The Crucible*, Harold C. Schonberg noted that this new work and the New York City Opera's previous fresh offering, Douglas Moore's *The Wings of the Dove*, had "certain things in common, especially in [terms of] harmonic language." Both operas, he wrote, made use of a "completely non-dissonant language" that was "based on nineteenth-century procedures." And this, Schonberg suggested, was not the result of simple coincidence: "It is indicative of the current neo-romantic trend in composition. Ten years ago the chances are that a composer would have been laughed out of court had so 'old-fashioned' a work been presented. The diatonic idiom—that is, the nineteenth-century idiom based on the common triad—was passé, and no composer would have had the nerve to use it."[73] And he suggested, too, that "this particular revival" of comfortable-sounding, easy-to-grasp music was, perhaps uniquely, "an American phenomenon":

> Certainly none of the young opera composers in Europe would think of setting a libretto with the conventional harmonies that Mr. Ward has used. Generally speaking, European operatic composers, with the sole exception of Poulenc, are wedded to dodecaphony and its derivatives.
>
> But last night the audience heard an opera that, in philosophy and workmanship, could have been composed at the turn of the century or before.[74]

Regarded from a distance and heard against the background of twentieth-century "serious" music in general, American opera from the Fifties indeed comes across as conservative. But its arguably passé harmonies and old-fashioned melodies are really not that far from the musical language that dominated the concert hall during that period. Contrary to a mythology that seems to have arisen from music history textbooks that emphasize the innovative and downplay the norm, most concert-hall music produced in America during the Fifties was also "on the conservative side."

7

The Classical Music Mainstream

"Believe it or not," wrote Virgil Thomson in 1953, "among all of America's leisure activities, the most widely indulged . . . is the art of music." Thomson, who during the Fifties worked not just as a composer but also as the influential music critic for the *New York Herald Tribune*, cited a recent article in which the executive secretary of the American Symphony Orchestra League reported that "thirty million people in this country are 'actively interested in concert music.' This does not mean jazz or popular ditties, or hillbilly dance-bands, or shows and films employing music, or hymn singing, or wedding marches. It means the classical music of the last three centuries, including the one we live in. And thirty million people are one-fifth of our population."[1]

Thomson's column was aptly headlined "Bigger Than Baseball." Early in the column, he noted that whereas during the previous year ticket buyers had spent $40 million on baseball, patrons of classical music had spent $45 million. He went on to mention that "last year's sales of classical recordings totaled $60,000,000," and that the United States in 1953 boasted 80 opera companies, 150 periodicals dedicated to classical music, 750 classical music critics on the staffs of newspapers, 938 orchestras "all or in part professionally staffed," 15,000 school orchestras, and, in the schools, more than 20 million music students.[2] And he concluded with the fervor of a zealot:

> To occupy the young, to ennoble adulthood, to train the hand, elevate the mind, lift up the spirits, and at the same time make business boom—all these are what America expects out of music and, surprisingly enough, gets. No country before us, not Germany nor Austria nor Italy nor the England of the

Tudor times, ever quite so gleefully turned itself over to the tonal art. What will come of it all there is no way of knowing. But for this century at least, music is our hobby and our habit; and the chiefest, after breadwinning, among all our avowable preoccupations.[3]

This passion for what Thomson called "classical, or 'serious,' music" had been stirred even as World War II was in progress,[4] and by the end of the long decade of the Fifties it was still going strong. In 1962 New York Times music critic Harold C. Schonberg stated boldly: "We are assured that never before has there been such an interest in music in America. More people are attending concerts than ever before; more recordings are being purchased; cultural centers are popping up like crocuses in the spring."[5] The changed atmosphere had been apparent even just a few years after the war's end. For composers, this made the future seem very promising.

As early as March 1948 Aaron Copland, who, like Thomson, was not just an important composer during the Fifties but also an important commentator on the period's music, waxed enthusiastic over what he perceived to be a whole new world. "The generation of the 1940s," he wrote in a magazine article, "is being encouraged with prizes, commissions, fellowships, money grants, and, more often than not, performances of their works. Nowadays, in this country at any rate, a young composer with exceptional talent would have a hard time escaping detection."[6] Near the end of his piece on "The New School of American Composers," Copland presaged Thomson's later assessment with the remark that, at the moment, "serious music is thriving in the United States." With unrestrained optimism, Copland reminded readers that "our music schools and colleges are turning out composers in numbers unparalleled in our musical past," and he speculated that "if we can gauge the musical future of a nation by the healthy activity of its younger generation of composers, then America is likely to do well."[7] Copland envisioned a utopia that, depending on one's point of view, did or did not come to pass.

* * *

By the mid-1950s there were indeed numerous outlets that enabled American composers to put fresh compositions before the public. Among the orchestras that regularly programmed new works, the most prestigious were those in Boston, Philadelphia, New York, and Cleveland, led respectively by Charles Munch, Eugene Ormandy, Leonard Bernstein, and George Szell. Significant premieres took place as well in Pittsburgh under the baton of William Steinberg, in Seattle under Milton Katims, and in Dallas and Minneapolis under Antal Doráti. Remarkably, because in terms of annual budget it was not even a second-tier ensemble, the Louisville Orchestra and its founding conductor, Robert Whitney, launched a record label (First Edition Recordings) in 1947 dedicated exclusively to twentieth-century music, and in 1953 the orchestra was awarded a staggeringly large grant of five hundred thousand dollars from the Rockefeller Foundation for the purpose of commissioning new works. As noted in the previous chapter, in addition to the intense interest of the New York City Opera in American works, the postwar years also witnessed the blossoming of opera on television and of campus-based opera workshops, both of which not just showcased but thrived on the fresh efforts of American composers. The postwar years also witnessed countless premieres—made possible by grants from the federal government or, more often, from corporation-based foundations—of examples of American-authored chamber music. The result of all this, according to one eyewitness, was "the emergence of a public interested in hearing American works" and a climate for new music "incomparably more favorable" than had been experienced by American composers during the first half of the century.[8]

Yet for Copland several things were amiss. One of them had to do with the context in which music, especially orchestral music, was presented. Addressing the annual meeting of the American Symphony Orchestra League in 1956, Copland informed the group that their programs in general were "limited in scope, repetitious in content, and therefore unexciting," and that they tended to "stultify and mummify our musical public."[9] Furthermore, Copland argued, the programming of works by American composers amounted to mere tokenism. He cited figures gathered by the National Music Council, to the effect that in 1954 only 8 percent of the pieces offered by orchestras all around the country were by Americans, and most of these, he said, were familiar works authored by composers with familiar names. Copland complained, and he cautioned:

> These figures do not speak well for what is going on. Rather they indicate a shocking lack of live interest and civic pride in the accomplishments and future of our American music. The effect of all this on the developing composer is naturally very grave. A young composer simply cannot produce the best he is capable of in so unpromising an environment. In the last five years I can think of no single American composer under the age of thirty who has been nurtured or encouraged in the United States because of the efforts of one of our leading symphony orchestras. . . . Unless our symphonic organizations take on this responsibility, they are not entirely fulfilling their cultural task.

Worse still, they are obstructing the flowering of one of our most significant national assets, the gifted young composer.[10]

The other problem, as Copland eventually saw it, had to do with music itself, in particular the music being produced by the young American composers whom he believed were equipped with the most potential. In a 1959 postscript to the ebulliently optimistic magazine article he had penned eleven years earlier, Copland expressed disappointment at the apparent lack of sincerity in much of the music he had been hearing. "I detect in it no note of deep conviction," he wrote; the composers "seem to be exploring *possible* ways of writing music suggested to them by the example of composers abroad rather than creating out of their own experience and need a music that only they could write."[11] He also expressed political concerns. "The most striking tendency" discernible in "the ambitious compositions of our more adventurous composers," he complained, is

> the return, since 1950, to a preoccupation with the latest trends of European composition. This comes as a surprise, for, from the standpoint of their elders, it is a retrogression of a sort. It is retrogression because it places us in a provincial position *vis-à-vis* our European confreres. The older generation fought hard to free American composition from the dominance of European models because that struggle was basic to the establishment of an American music. The young composer of today, on the other hand, seems to be fighting hard to stay abreast of a fast-moving post–World War II European musical scene.[12]

Copland's use of the word "retrogression" is interesting, especially since a closely related word appears in Wilfred Mellers' 1964 assessment of what might be called America's postwar classical music mainstream.

In his *Music in a New Found Land*, after eight chapters that cover the history of American music since colonial days and emphasize the contributions of composers he considers to be genuinely individualistic, the British musicologist pointed out that, "with the exception of Copland," the composers he had thus far discussed in detail "are not those most frequently played in the States. There is a tiny audience for the music of the *avant-garde*; there is a slightly larger 'minority' audience for tough modern music that is not afraid of the nervous tensions of our urban lives; but there is a much larger middlebrow audience for a softer modern music that will offer us opportunities for nostalgia or self-dramatization."[13]

Even though they seem to be "slipping a little in the popularity-poll," Mellers noted, Tchaikovsky and Rachmaninoff remain the composers in which America's "middlebrow concert-going public finds its most direct satisfaction." Tchaikovsky and Rachmaninoff are composers of talent and genius, he granted, but he suggested that they are also "composers of adolescence, of arrested development." While admitting that "nothing . . . could be cosier than to regress to our memories of lost childhood and youth," Mellers nevertheless cautioned that "a large public's dedication to adolescence cannot be a sign of emotional health."[14]

Mellers reminded his readers that in the first chapter of his book he had explained that regression of this sort had been "a dominant theme both in [nineteenth-century] American literature and in the music of the American conservatives" who composed in the decades surrounding the start of the twentieth century.[15] And then he suggested that the best-known American composers of the Fifties explored precisely this same regressive "theme of adolescence," only "more immediately and more deeply."[16]

For Copland in 1959, "retrogression" was a politically charged negative concept that implied an abandonment of hard-won American musical independence from European influences. For Mellers in 1964, musical "regression" was a term that euphemistically described the vast bulk of new music that American audiences, throughout the Fifties, had been not just hearing but enjoying.

"Essentially Conservative"

The *New York Times*' Harold C. Schonberg did not think highly of Robert Ward's 1961 opera *The Crucible*, mostly because he felt the "noncommittal" score lacked "tension and drama" and was filled with "musical platitudes." Less by way of overt criticism than by way of reportage, Schonberg noted that *The Crucible*, with "a completely non-dissonant language" and a "nineteenth-century idiom based on the common triad," seemed "indicative of the current neo-romantic trend in [American] composition." Also by way of reportage, he perhaps begrudgingly added: "And, judging from the response at the end of the work, the audience loved it."[17]

Schonberg's opinion notwithstanding, music critics loved it, too. The *Saturday Review*'s Irving Kolodin commended Ward on his "overpowering conviction" and "his success in converting that conviction into musical meaning." In the *New York Journal-American*, Miles Kastendieck testified that Ward's music "reflects intelligent digestion and individual assertion"; in the *New York World-Telegram*, Louis Biancolli wrote that Ward had added "a third dimension" to Arthur Miller's play by supplying it with "a viable and thrusting score." Winthrop Sargeant, in the *New Yorker*, called the opera "an imposing work" that is "everywhere dignified and nowhere banal," and he noted that it is nonetheless "quite accessible to the average listener."[18]

Along with praise from most members of New York's musical press, Ward's *The Crucible* won an award from the New York Music Critics' Circle. More impressively, because both the jury and the scope of the award were not local but national, the opera won the 1962 Pulitzer Prize for Music. Like any other subjectively granted award, the Pulitzer Prize for Music cannot be regarded as certification of actual merit. Started in 1943, almost four decades after newspaper publisher Joseph Pulitzer first endowed the eponymous prizes for outstanding achievement in journalism and literature, and granted to "a distinguished musical composition of significant dimension by an American that has had its first performance in the United States during the [previous] year," the Pulitzer Prize for Music can, however, be regarded as a measure of the "official" esteem in which its winners are held. As such, the Pulitzer Prize from any period is a reliable gauge of the norms for excellence as set forth by that period's musical establishment.

During the long decade of the Fifties, the Pulitzer Prize for Music was awarded not just to Ward's *The Crucible* but to four other operas as well: Gian Carlo Menotti's *The Consul* in 1950, Douglas Moore's *Giants in the Earth* in 1951, Menotti's *The Saint of Bleecker Street* in 1955, and Samuel Barber's *Vanessa* in 1958. While World War II was still in progress, the prize went to William Schuman's *Secular Cantata No. 2: A Free Song* (in 1943), to Howard Hanson's Symphony No. 4 (in 1944), and to Copland's *Appalachian Spring* (in 1945). Along with the five operas, the postwar winners were Leo Sowerby's *The Canticle of the Sun* (1946), Charles Ives's Symphony No. 3 (1947), Walter Piston's Symphony No. 3 (1948), Virgil Thomson's score for the documentary film *Louisiana Story* (1949), Gail Kubick's *Symphony Concertante* (1952), Quincy Porter's Concerto for Two Pianos and Orchestra (1954), Ernst Toch's Symphony No. 3 (1956), Norman Dello Joio's ballet score *Meditations on Ecclesiastes* (1957), John La Montaine's Concerto for Piano and Orchestra (1959), Elliott Carter's String Quartet No. 2 (1960), Walter Piston's Symphony No. 7 (1961), and Samuel Barber's Piano Concerto No. 1 (1963).

With the notable exceptions of the Ives symphony and the Carter quartet,[19] all of these works fall squarely into the category of tonal music, and the same can be said for most other examples of American classical music written during the Fifties. Indeed, as Joseph N. Straus concluded after exhaustive research on prizes, reviews, concert programs, record label catalogs, and the music faculties of major universities during both the 1950s and the 1960s, "between half and two-thirds of composers, throughout the period and in all corners of the musical marketplace, wrote in a relatively conservative idiom, with a style that maintained strong ties to traditional tonality."[20]

That is not to say that the music of these composers consists—except when some "antique" source is being quoted—exclusively of chords that a first-year music student might easily describe, upon assignment, by means of simple Roman numerals. Typically, however, at any given moment within a work a certain tone occupies a central position around which all the other tones gravitate. For the most part, this music is notated not just with straightforward time signatures but also with unambiguous key signatures. More significant, the music *sounds* as though it is clearly in one key or another: if cleared of the dissonances that lend them such a wide variety of flavors and colorings, the music's harmonies can be shown to relate to one another in the same hierarchical, functional way that had governed Western music for more than three hundred years.

In a 1967 essay first published in *The American Record Guide*, composer Ned Rorem reflected happily on the role of the composer whose music fits the above description. To be sure, by 1967 there had been a radical shift in concert-hall aesthetics, and in this essay Rorem ruefully expressed the idea that composers of his ilk were being eclipsed by composers who espoused more fashionable trends. He proudly identified himself as a conservative, and he defined conservative composers as "those who persevered (shall we say logically?) according to European traditions set up in the 1600s."[21] Rorem went on to describe how the American style developed in the 1930s as a mixture of "sophisticated diatonic French economy soldered to local hymn tunes"; how it reached its "peak delineation during the war when isolation forced intervention"; and how, starting shortly after the war, the style "acquiesced, tail between its legs, to continental domination."[22] Perhaps wearing a chip on his shoulder, he noted that in spite of the attractions that in the 1950s and '60s led many of his contemporaries to change their tune, certain Americans were steadfast. They "kept their distance from global vogues," Rorem wrote, and "through pride and through habit they continued a national tradition."[23]

As global vogues gained ground in the increasingly turbulent '60s, it would indeed require strength of conviction for a conservative composer to hold to what fashionably up-to-date critics decried as old-fashioned ways. During the 1940s and '50s, however, it was fairly easy to go the traditional route, for the traditional route was the one with which audiences and performers were most comfortable. It was the route that most composers chose to take; it was the route that the leading music critics of the day most articulately supported.[24]

*   *   *

In the final installment of the Charles Eliot Norton lectures that he delivered at Harvard University during the 1951–1952 academic year, Aaron Copland described the mainstream style as a "musical vernacular," a kind of music "which, as a language, would cause no difficulties [for] listeners," a music through which a composer would be capable of "making a connection" with the life around him.[25] But not all composers strove toward that same goal. "Our serious composers have not been signally successful at making that kind of connection," Copland told his audience. "Oblivious to their surroundings, they live in constant communion with great works, which in turn seems to make it *de rigueur* for them to attempt to emulate the great works by writing one of their own on an equivalent plane." Surveying what he perceived as the entirety of "serious" musical activity in America, Copland complained: "Young composers are especially prone to overreaching themselves—to making the grand gesture by the writing of ambitious works, often in a crabbed style, that have no future whatever. It is unrealistic and a useless aping, generally of foreign models."[26]

It is a truism that from any musical period the percentage of works that might survive is very small, so Copland was right in suggesting that, even in the favorable environment of the Fifties, most of the music written by his contemporaries would have no future. On the other hand, his comments about young composers' tendencies form too harsh a criticism.

In the Fifties there were indeed composers who wrote "in a crabbed style" and "ape[d] . . . foreign models"; perhaps those judgments apply even to Copland, who flirted with the principles of twelve-tone serialism in his 1950 Piano Quartet and then fully embraced the method with his 1962 orchestral piece *Connotations*. But "oblivious" composers who had a real presence in the postwar concert world constituted a small minority. In fact, it was with an impressively large group of composers that in the postwar years Copland shared both attitude and overall aesthetic.

Not all of Copland's compatriots rode the bandwagon and produced works that were overtly "Americanist" in musical content or extra-musical subject matter. But most of them did, in their own ways, speak an American "musical vernacular," and most of them did strive to produce music that was, in the word that Winthrop Sargeant potently used to describe Robert Ward's *The Crucible*, "accessible." Whether abstract, programmatic, or theatrical, their music had in common a clarity of emotional content and communicative goals. Their harmonies made sense, their sonorities tended to be rich and colorful, their melodic and rhythmic materials were almost always of the sort that an audience, at least for the work's duration, could remember.

Variously and not at all inappropriately described as "nationalists," "classicists," and "romanticists,"[27] or as "neoclassicists" and "neoromantics,"[28] or as artists who chose to follow the "middle path,"[29] some of Copland's contemporaries were influential not just as composers but also as teachers and as players in the arts politics game. However much or little their work might be performed today, it remains that during World War II and the postwar years these mainstream composers fairly dominated the scene.

If it is necessary to have a sweeping generalization from a firsthand observer, an assessment more on the mark than Copland's can be had from Virgil Thomson, who wrote: "By the end of the 1940s American composers were numerous and fecund, but essentially conservative as viewed from postwar Europe."[30] The ranks of the "essentially conservative" composers certainly include Thomson himself, who, along with Copland, had been a firebrand expatriate in Paris during the 1920s before returning to the United States and, at least in of terms musical style, settling down. They include as well most of the above-mentioned Pulitzer Prize winners and all of the American composers mentioned in the previous chapter's account of operas performed by the NBC Opera Theatre. And they include Leonard Bernstein.

Copland, Thomson, and Bernstein form an interesting group, not just because their music is often performed nowadays but also because during the Fifties they were highly influential for reasons other than their composing activities. Bernstein was influential by virtue of his charismatic appearances on the television show *Omnibus* and, more significantly, his ascendancy in 1958 to the music directorship of the New York Philharmonic. Copland was influential because of his popular books—the 1952 *Music and Imagination*, the second edition (1957) of *What to Listen for in Music*, the 1960 collection of essays titled *Copland on Music*—and because throughout the Cold War period he was "one of the State Department's most dedicated composer-ambassadors."[31] Thomson was influential most overtly, at least until 1954, through his role as music critic for the *New York Herald Tribune*; covertly, he was greatly influential through his membership on the American National Theatre and Academy's Music Advisory Panel, a group that from 1954 until 1963 advised the State Department about which examples of American music should be presented overseas by government-funded performers.[32]

But Thomson and Copland were influential in yet another important way. At the twentieth century's midpoint these two middle-aged men, well established in their careers, gathered around them a group of still-emerging composers whom "they mentored and apprenticed" and with whom they "forged close personal and professional associations, shared knowledge and resources, and created a rich musical subculture."[33] Thomson, Copland, and their younger colleagues "performed and programmed" one another's work, and they "influenced each other personally, professionally, and aesthetically."[34] That the Thomson-Copland circle of archly conservative tonal composers even existed, writes Nadine Hubbs, "had everything to do with queerness."[35]

The Thomson-Copland Circle

After the *New York Times* published an article headlined "Composers' Closets Open for All to See" in June 1994, the newspaper was barraged with angry letters that argued that a composer's sexual preferences have nothing at all to do with a composer's music.[36] The complaining letter writers were doubtless correct in that the simple fact of being gay or straight has no more to do with the content of a composer's music than does the composer's DNA or the makeup of the composer's chromosomes. What the letter writers failed to note, but what K. Robert Schwarz implied throughout his article, is that the social context in which any composer works and the societal pressure *under* which a composer works very likely have quite a lot to do with the composer's output. Few musically knowledgeable persons today would suggest that the music that Dmitri Shostakovich wrote between 1936 and 1953 was not somehow influenced by the fact that during those years all Soviet artists functioned at the pleasure of dictator Joseph Stalin. By the same token, it makes sense to think that gay composers who worked during the Fifties were at least somehow affected by the fact that during this period homophobia in America was in "its most vigorous, potent phase."[37]

"Homophobia" is a troublesome word, for although literally it means a fear of homosexuals, and although in its first appearance in print (in 1969) it referred to a heterosexual male's fear of being taken for a homosexual,[38] in most usages it means only a strong dislike of, or a prejudice against, homosexuals. But fear and loathing often go hand in hand. On the surface, one can almost see an attempt at logic in a Senate subcommittee report from 1950, titled *Employment of Homosexuals and Other Sex Perverts in Government*, in which it was declared that

> homosexuals and other sex perverts are not proper persons to be employed in Government [primarily because] overt acts of sex perversion . . . constitute

a crime [and because] perverts are frequently victimized by blackmailers who threaten to expose their sexual deviance [but also because] the lack of emotional stability which is found in most sex perverts and the weakness of their moral fiber makes them susceptible to the blandishments of the foreign espionage agent.[39]

But with a document of this sort, who knows what motivations lurk between the lines?

* * *

Both Copland and Thomson had studied with Nadia Boulanger in the 1920s at the American Conservatory that the U.S. government, after World War I, established thirty miles south of Paris in the Louis XV wing of the Chateau de Fontainebleau. Copland remained deeply grateful for all that Boulanger had taught him, and he was hardly being mean-spirited when he wrote that "had she become a composer, she would of biological necessity have joined the automatically inferior ranks of the 'woman composer.'"[40] Virgil Thomson, who in 1921 began a long period of private study with Boulanger, likewise wholeheartedly sang her praise. In a 1962 magazine article headlined "Greatest Music Teacher" he offered keen insights into her "critical acumen" and her ability to get a student to "wrestle" his own "musical ideas into clarity and coherence," and he noted that by the time he first met her, "she had [already] renounced all worldly desire for personal fulfillment as a woman or as a composer, devoting herself solely to her remaining parent and to nurturing the musical young."[41]

Boulanger's commitment to "nurturing the musical young" perhaps had an influence on both Thomson and Copland as they gathered around themselves their coterie of gay-minded junior colleagues. The fact that Boulanger was French, however, had little to do with the penchant of all these composers for a French aesthetic: Boulanger's mission was to help composers find their own voices, and at least in her teaching she pledged allegiance to no particular style. Nor did the obvious fact that Thomson and Copland studied with Boulanger in France have anything seriously to do with the group's Francophile bent. To counter such an argument, all one has to do is point to Boulanger's many other American students whose music has nothing in common with that of the Thomson-Copland circle.[42]

Rather, the circle's "French connection," as Nadine Hubbs terms it, stems from a self-identification prompted as much by the Fifties' artistic politics as by its homophobic sexual politics. From the perspective both of "Englishness, which infused American cultural views generally," and of "German-ness, which was the basis of American serious music culture" in particular, "Frenchness was othered, effeminized, and sexualized," Hubbs writes.[43] The key elements of the Thomson-Copland circle's "definitional axis" included the polarities of "masculine/feminine, heterosexual/homosexual, complex/simple, atonal/tonal," and, importantly, "German/French." Along this axis, Hubbs contends, "gay modernists created identities [both] for themselves and [for] American music." Their efforts were by and large successful, but they were not always appreciated by "non-gay-identified colleagues and commentators [who] targeted [members of the Thomson-Copland circle, and others,] with homophobic censure and conspiracy theories."[44]

The "conspiracy theories" were ridiculous yet widespread, and they gained strength even as the repressive Fifties evolved into the supposedly free and easy Sixties. As late as 1966 *Time* magazine, playing on the words "homosexual" and "Comintern" (short for Communist International, the Soviet organization that from 1919 until 1943 ran the International Communist Party), would proclaim that "the arts are dominated by a kind of homosexual mafia—or 'Homintern,' as it has been called," and that in the spheres of "theater, dance and music . . . deviates are so widespread that they sometimes seem to be running a closed shop."[45] But the publicly expressed suspicion that the entirety of the American arts world was secretly controlled by closeted homosexuals dates back at least to 1950.[46] That homosexuals dominated the League of Composers—which fostered tonal music, in contrast to the various atonal styles championed by the New York chapter of the International Society for Contemporary Music (ISCM)—is an idea that likely dates back to the late 1930s.

If a "Homintern" indeed governed the League of Composers, as Bernstein biographers Humphrey Burton and Meryle Secrest suggested independently during the mid-1990s heyday of "outing,"[47] surely such a cabal lost its power when the League of Composers merged with the ISCM chapter in 1954. But by that time "essentially conservative" tonal music had become entrenched as the American norm, perhaps not in the individual minds of forward-looking critics and composers but certainly in the collective minds—and ears—of that apparently quite large portion of the general public that at least on occasion paid attention to "new" classical music when it was presented in the concert hall or, more often, via radio or television.

In private, Copland, to use the parlance of the time, was a "queer"—that is, a homosexual man who not only presented himself to the world as perfectly straight but who, to members of the gay community, also had the reputation of being aggressive in a "masculine" sort of way. Thomson, on the other hand, was famously a "pansy," or a "fairy," a homosexual who once out of the limelight reveled in "feminine" behavior and who in the bedroom preferred a submissive role. But in public Copland and Thomson were the very models of Fifties propriety, as were the younger members of their circle, and as were Samuel Barber and Gian Carlo Menotti, who met during their student days at the Curtis Institute of Music and who from 1943 until 1973 in effect lived the life of a married couple.[48]

Of all these, writes Howard Pollack, "it was Copland who more than anyone else opened up the doors for gay American composers." He did this "above all by his music, which . . . revealed that a homosexual could write music fully encompassing the American experience." He also did it "by directing concert venues [that were] free from the homophobia associated with the Composers' Guild and other new-music organizations; by championing homosexual composers and by functioning as an intermediary with patrons, music publishers, and musicians; [and] by serving as a role model in the conduct of his own life."[49]

Copland's serving as a good role model is especially important, for he did this in spite of being publicly identified in 1949 as one of the "dupes and fellow travelers" of the Communist Party and in 1950 being named by FBI agents as a suspected subversive. He did it in spite of having his *Lincoln Portrait* pulled at the last minute from the program for President Eisenhower's 1953 inauguration ceremonies and then having his music (along with that of Bernstein, Thomson, Roy Harris, Randall Thompson, Roger Sessions, and George Gershwin) officially banned from distribution to the almost two hundred overseas American libraries maintained by the State Department.[50] And he did it in spite of being subpoenaed in 1953 by Joseph McCarthy's Subcommittee on Investigations and then in 1955 being investigated by the FBI in the hopes of their finding evidence that Copland had perjured himself.[51]

Indeed, the calm dignity with which Copland endured all of this abuse, as well as vicious innuendoes from homophobic and anti-Semitic rivals,[52] made him a positive example not just for gay composers during the Fifties but for *all* American composers of that conflicted period.

Cold War Musical Weaponry

Although by the end of the 1950s Copland would be commonly known as both the "dean of American composers" and the "dean of American music," aside from a few semester-long guest lectureships (at Harvard and the State

University of New York at Buffalo) he never held an academic position. This was not the case for William Schuman and Howard Hanson, staunchly tonal composers who during the Fifties also ranked among the most powerful figures in American tertiary musical education. After teaching composition at Sarah Lawrence College for ten years, Schuman in 1945 was named president of a forty-year-old New York institution that would soon be known as the Julliard School of Music; he held that position until 1961, when he was named president of the new Lincoln Center for the Performing Arts. As early as 1924 Hanson was appointed director of the recently established Eastman School of Music in Rochester, New York, and he remained the school's chief administrator until his retirement forty years later.

Schuman and Hanson were the winners of the first two Pulitzer Prizes for Music (Schuman in 1943 for his *Secular Cantata No. 2: A Free Song*, Hanson in 1944 for his Symphony No. 4). By 1954 these two composers loomed so large on the American classical music landscape that it was natural that they, along with Virgil Thomson, would be appointed to the music advisory panel of a new initiative launched by Eisenhower and generously supported through the president's "emergency fund for international affairs."

Officially, the President's Special International Program for Cultural Presentations was set up in order to "contribute to the better understanding of the people of the world that must be the foundation for peace."[53] Unofficially, the program was an exercise in propaganda; although it involved dance and theater, its musical offerings were expected to be an especially useful "psychological tool that could counteract the stereotypical perception of Americans as 'bombastic, jingoistic, and totally devoted to the theories of force and power.'"[54] Indeed, for as long as the program lasted (from 1954 until 1963) the "secret weapon" of music was regularly awarded more than two-thirds of its approximately $2.5 million annual budget.[55]

The political agenda for the program's much-publicized overseas tours by jazz musicians has been discussed earlier in this book.[56] Tours by classical musicians, which at the time garnered not nearly so much attention yet consumed the larger share of the music budget, had more subtle goals whose realization was arguably less successful. The tours by Dizzy Gillespie, Louis Armstrong, and other African American jazz musicians were designed not just to entertain and thus win the hearts of audiences abroad; they were also designed to prove, for the sake of countering a long series of barbs from the Soviet Union that seemed uncomfortably on the mark after sensationalist press reports of white-on-black violence in 1954 and 1955, that America in fact was *not* a nation of brutal racists. Less dramatically, the tours by classical musicians were intended to show the rest of the world, especially the European world, that American "high art" was just as good as that of any other nation.

The government's ambitious plan for sending American artists abroad was put under the administrative care of the American National Theatre and Academy (ANTA), a New York–based not-for-profit organization that had been established in 1935, simultaneous with the New Deal's Federal Theater Project, for the sake of cultivating a "national theater" that was free of commercial considerations. Never very visible but equipped with a reputation for solid management and compliance with its mandate, ANTA was charged not just with disbursing the huge amounts of money the government was about to send its way but also with deciding which of the nation's many ensembles and solo performers were deserving of such largesse.

ANTA's first go at putting a representative of American culture on international display was a modest effort that involved José Limon and his nine-member modern dance troupe, sent off in November 1954 on a month-long tour comprising weeklong stints in the South American cities of Montevideo, Rio de Janeiro, Saõ Paulo, and Buenos Aires. Closely monitored by professional eyes and ears, the South American response to the Limon company's tour seemed to be everything that ANTA and its deep-pocketed sponsors had hoped for. Thus encouraged, in February 1955 ANTA made an announcement that fairly stunned America's classical music world.

The U.S. government would soon fund, ANTA announced, lengthy overseas tours by no less than three prestigious American orchestras. The first two of these would begin shortly, with the Philadelphia Orchestra and its esteemed music director, Eugene Ormandy, setting off in May 1955 on a tour that would have them performing in major cities in France, Belgium, Portugal, Spain, Italy, the Netherlands, Switzerland, Austria, West Germany, Sweden, and Finland, and the Symphony of the Air (formerly the NBC Symphony Orchestra) heading off at about the same time for a seven-week tour—under the batons of guest conductors Walter Hendl and Thor Johnson—to Japan, South Korea, Taiwan, Hong Kong, and the Philippines. In September 1955, ANTA also announced, the New York Philharmonic would embark upon a government-funded European tour that would start with six concerts at the Edinburgh Festival and then involve performances (led by either Dmitri Mitropoulos or Dino Cantelli) in the Netherlands, Belgium, Germany, France, Switzerland, Italy, Greece, and England.

Earlier in the year Robert C. Schnitzer, an actor who during the 1930s had served as deputy director of the Federal Theater Project and who in 1954 was appointed general manager of what had come to be known as simply the International Exchange Program (IEP), articulated the program's goals in a letter to the editor of the *New York Times*: "As the news columns have reported with more and more frequency, 'our enemies are making the utmost use of performing artists in their continuous campaign to win the good opinion of the rest of the world. It is our expectation that as this program expands America's best performers will be encouraged to contribute an important share to our side of the argument.'"[57] After the announcement of the three orchestral tours, the newspaper's chief music critic, Howard Taubman, responded with a comment that surely was music to Schnitzer's, and the government's, ears: "One becomes so inured to fine words being followed by no deeds that it comes as a delightful shock to note how rapidly the International Exchange Program has turned plans into action. In the few months since IEP decided to expand its activities, it has performed what amounts almost to a miracle."[58]

*   *   *

A year after declaring the new International Exchange Program to be nearly miraculous, Taubman raised a thorny issue. Responding to an announcement that the program's sponsorships for 1956 would include international tours by the New Orleans Philharmonic, the Los Angeles Philharmonic, the Robert Shaw Chorale, the Westminster Choir, the Boston Symphony Orchestra, and possibly the Symphony of the Air, the *Times* critic brought up the touchy subject of repertoire. "Regardless of where the Boston Symphony plays," Taubman wrote, "it should be mandatory that at least one American composition be on every program abroad. . . . The [American] pieces should not be trivial things chosen merely as lip-service to a principle. The American repertory is sufficiently extensive and representative to speak for us with some authority." Although Taubman was hardly in a position to give orders to representatives of the federal government, his statement nevertheless carried weight. Pointedly, he admonished: "It is ridiculous to spend hundreds of thousands of dollars to show off our accomplishment as performers and to give, at the same time, a contemptuous back of the hand to our creative achievements."[59] Taubman might have been clairvoyant, but it is more likely that he had heard through the grapevine that ANTA's music advisory panel had recently been considering an "American repertoire" policy and that this policy, by the time he wrote his article, was in effect official.

According to the minutes of the ANTA panel, it was Virgil Thomson who first suggested that the panel consider not just the performance abilities of ensembles that applied for IEP funding but also the "artistic quality" of whatever they intended to perform. Marked "please read carefully," the memo that

Thomson circulated to the panel in advance of its November 15, 1955, meeting proposed that *every* concert presented overseas by *every* ANTA-funded ensemble include one or more "representative American compositions of musical distinction."[60]

The proposal met with resistance. Read by Schnitzer at the same panel meeting was a memo from Julius Seebach, a consultant for the U.S. Information Agency that President Eisenhower had established in 1953 as an aboveboard organization that would seek to understand, for the sake of influencing, the populations of foreign countries. Based in Europe and imagining himself to have a finger on the cultural pulse of that entire continent, Seebach was of the opinion that American compositions "are just not good enough" and that "the European critics hold them in very low esteem."[61] Seebach argued that the advisory panel's "insisting on the performance of an American work on every program" would not enhance but would, rather, diminish "the United States' global reputation. . . . He believed the United States would be better served if musicians simply performed European canonical compositions to the highest level."[62]

But the panel—always made up of a dozen or so certifiable musical experts but invariably dominated by the triumvirate of Thomson, Hanson, and Schuman—prevailed. Beginning with the 1956 tours and extending through 1963, when the newly established Kennedy administration not only divested it of most of its power but also "undermined" its morale,[63] the panel indeed demanded that every program on every IEP-funded tour feature not simply a work that was American in origin but an American work of genuine substance. The panel never prescribed a list of acceptable repertoire, yet "it quickly became apparent that the panel would not approve any American classical work that they perceived to be 'light' or 'middlebrow.'" Applicants for IEP funding were asked to concentrate on "sonatas, symphonies, and song cycles, all of which were seen to demonstrate more effectively the full weight of America's contribution to classical music," and they were "repeatedly asked to do away with arrangements, folk songs, spirituals, and 'pops' repertoire."[64] Considering what had been happening lately with *Porgy and Bess*, it is interesting that applicants for IEP funds were also asked to do away with Gershwin.

An Aversion to Gershwin?

Even before the International Exchange Program had been established, the U.S. State Department in September 1952 funded a visit to Vienna and Berlin of a new production of George Gershwin's 1935 opera *Porgy and Bess*. The purpose of the production, clearly, was to make a profit for entrepreneurs Blevins Davis and Robert Breen, but the purpose of the short European tour, according to an anonymous newspaper reporter, was not only "to show central Europeans that the American theatre is vigorous and exciting" but also to demonstrate "that Negro players are not debased or oppressed, as the communist line says."[65] After a four-week run at the National Theatre in Washington, DC, the Davis/Breen production played for a week at the Vienna Volksoper and then for eleven performances at the second annual Berlin Cultural Festival. The opera was certainly "a first class cultural advertisement for the United States," wrote the *New York Times*' Jack Raymond, but it was only one offering among several of which he felt American citizens should be proud. As participants in what was "basically a propaganda measure," he suggested, "the singers, musicians and dancers who came here, sponsored with United States funds, were worth several divisions of troops in the cold war."[66]

After the performances in Vienna and Berlin, for which the press response was overwhelmingly positive, the Davis/Breen production of *Porgy and Bess* played for four months in London. Between March and November 1953 it ran for 305 performances at the Ziegfeld Theatre on Broadway, then it set out on a coast-to-coast American tour that lasted almost a year. Apparently aware that it had had a good thing on its hands when it sponsored the performances in Vienna and Berlin, late in 1954 the State Department—this time using IEP funds—sent *Porgy and Bess* first on an eleven-week tour of Mediterranean countries and the Middle East and then on a sixteen-week tour of Latin America.

By the summer of 1955 the Davis/Breen *Porgy and Bess* had become something of a blue-chip commodity in the cultural diplomacy market, so reporters for American newspapers took in stride the announcements that the Soviet Ministry of Culture had invited the production for a three-week stint in Moscow that would be followed by performances in Kiev, Leningrad, Bucharest, Budapest, Warsaw, Prague, and East Berlin. Judging from the size of the headlines, however, it struck the print media as rather big news that this time the U.S. government chose not to be involved. State Department officials were quoted as saying that while they indeed recognized *Porgy and Bess* as "one of the most effective cultural representations the United States could send abroad," their decision was brought about by a combination of "cost and political considerations."[67]

The political considerations apparently had to do with governmental nervousness in anticipation of the next meeting of "The Big Four" countries. The first-ever face-to-face meeting between the heads of state of England, France, the United States, and the Soviet Union had taken place in July 1955 in Geneva, and it constituted little more than a friendly conversation about how the four most militarily powerful nations might cooperate for the sake of easing Cold War tensions. The next meeting, scheduled to begin in Geneva on October 27 and involving only foreign ministers, promised to be more stressful, for the main topic on its agenda was the arms race. American officials had good reason to be nervous, for surely their intelligence agents had informed them that the Soviet Union planned to test, just a month after the October "Big Four" meeting, its first thermonuclear bomb.

Entertainment reporter Lewis Funke was referring to the largely inconsequential first "Big Four" meeting when early in October 1955 he remarked that, with invitations to *Porgy and Bess* coming from Moscow and then from the capital cities of several of the Soviet Union's satellite countries, "the spirit of Geneva" indeed "appeared to be operating in the arts." But at this moment relations between the United States and the Soviet Union were actually highly strained. This was hardly a secret, so Funke praised the "candor and caution" with which representatives of the State Department "frankly admitted that" *after* the upcoming "Big Four" meeting "the desirability of incurring the expense [of supporting *Porgy and Bess* on a tour behind the Iron Curtain] might be clearer." At the same time, he reminded his readers of the economic realities of the commercial theater, and he sympathized with producer Breen's concern that "waiting" for a government decision "would entail all sorts of complications, among these being the disbanding and reassembling of the company since originally its long international tour was to have ended after its current South American junket."[68]

So Breen accepted the invitation from the Soviet Union, and he scrambled to raise the money—by his estimate between $300,000 and $400,000—that would allow the tour to happen. Doubtless Breen was surprised to learn a month later that the Soviet Union had agreed to pay not just whatever fees were demanded by the production per se but also to "provide all housing and food for actors and stagehands without cost," and possibly to "pay the troupe's salaries . . . and furnish pocket money."[69]

One can only wonder about the motivations for this extraordinary largesse on the part of the Soviet Union. Perhaps the leaders of the USSR were indeed so genuinely intrigued by all that they had heard about this American "folk opera" that they were eager, at great expense to their governmental coffers, to share *Porgy and Bess* with their citizens. On the other hand, perhaps they saw the American government's sudden abandonment of the universally acclaimed Davis/Breen production as an opportunity for outplaying the United States at its own game. It had become widely known that the opera troupe's trip to Russia would mark "the first time since the 'cold war' began that cultural ambassadors of American goodwill have been permitted behind the Iron Curtain."[70] Perhaps it was hoped that a message of some sort would be read between the lines of news stories that reported how only the Soviet Union—and not the United States—was willing to invest heavily in this diplomatic effort.

In any case, the response to *Porgy and Bess* from operagoers first in Leningrad and then in Moscow was "overwhelmingly warm and sympathetic," and even the Soviet press—some of whose members "felt obliged to draw expected political conclusions" about "the corrosive effect of the capitalistic system" and the opera characters' "life filled with bitter need, great poverty and small joys"—was in general agreement that the opera "would help Russians to understand better the contemporary American artistic forms." "The spirit of Geneva may lie in tatters," wrote the Moscow correspondent for the *New York Times*, "but the pervasive Gershwin melodies that distinguish this opera have re-created here—at least temporarily—an emotional bond between Russians and Americans."[71]

As it happened, the *Porgy and Bess* production played behind the Iron Curtain only in East Berlin, Leningrad, Moscow, Warsaw, and Prague, and after that it had engagements in Amsterdam and The Hague. The troupe returned to New York on June 5, 1956; the press speculated about future travels to Australasia and a return to Europe, but these never came to pass. After what for all intents and purposes was the breakup of the company that came to be known as Everyman Opera, producer Robert Breen reflected optimistically on the show that over the course of four years had played, with or without government sponsorship, in eighty cities in twenty-nine different countries.

It is ironic, Breen wrote in an opinion piece for the *New York Times*, that it was "Communist activity abroad in the field of arts exchange" that "really awakened the official United States to the need for our involvement in such a program." And it is unfortunate, he continued, that in the United States "arts exchange is not as yet officially viewed . . . as being intrinsically desirable or necessary. It is used, as it were, in 'combat' as a tactical arm—fighting culture with culture—a new but not-so-secret weapon for use in various, ever-changing 'target areas.'" But cultural exchange with America's ideological enemies should most definitely continue, Breen argued. Responding to his own rhetorical question as to what sort of music America should send abroad, he suggested that "the only possible guiding factors" be "quality and comprehensibility." For Breen, this meant that the United States should "renounce self-consciousness regarding basic art rhythms only *we* have to offer."[72] What Breen meant by "rhythms only *we* have to offer," of course, was rhythms derived from jazz.

* * *

Although the decisions to fund jazz concerts overseas were indeed made by ANTA's music advisory panel, the genre was always a thorn in the panel's side. Jazz, the stronger members of the panel felt, was something so different from classical music that it should be handled separately, yet an advisory unit specifically devoted to jazz (and folk music) was not established until the mid-1960s. In November 1954, almost a year and a half before the IEP sent Dizzy Gillespie on the program's first jazz tour, a member of the panel cautioned that, after all, "Russian propaganda plays on [the idea of] jazz-crazy Americans."[73] In May 1955 an ANTA official reminded the panel that "we are known all over the world for jazz," and so with IEP tours "we are trying to indicate that we have other music."[74] In December of that year, just after the music advisory panel had formulated its "approved-repertoire-only" policy and just after the *Porgy and Bess* troupe arrived in Moscow, William Schuman told his fellow panelists that when touring American orchestras perform jazz-flavored works "some people feel that we are selling out on the more serious work."[75]

The ANTA panelists would indeed renounce their self-consciousness regarding the rhythms of jazz in classical music, and with it their aversion to Gershwin, but not until 1958. In the meantime, perhaps allowing "self-interest and cultural prejudices" on the part of certain members "to influence their decisions," the panel dutifully enforced the policy of its own making.[76] Under public pressure, the panel allowed the Cleveland Orchestra and the New York Philharmonic to include Gershwin's *An American in Paris* on their 1958 tours, and it allowed the New York Philharmonic to travel in 1959 with both *Rhapsody in Blue* and, if needed as an encore, a solo piano arrangement of "Summertime" from *Porgy and Bess*. Even with these concessions, though, there was remarkable consistency in the panel's dictates.

Until its overhaul by the new Kennedy administration in 1961, ANTA's advisory panel remained steadfast in its allegiance to what at least its three most dominant members—Howard Hanson, Virgil Thomson, and William Schuman—believed to be the best the United States had to offer in terms of homegrown classical music. Without exception, the works that the panel deemed acceptable for performance abroad were tonal in language, neoclassical or neo-romantic in attitude, and conventional in design.[77] Whether or not the individual items that made up the approved repertoire were truly representative of the cream of the nation's musical crop is debatable; it is indisputable, however, that the "essentially conservative" nature of this repertoire was indeed representative America's postwar classical music mainstream.

*   *   *

Anticipating the upcoming Brussels World's Fair, *New York Times* music critic Howard Taubman suggested in April 1958 that the six-month-long event "will be the place where the cold war, fought with the weapons of art and drama, music and dance, architecture, books and films, will reach a climax." Taubman noted that whereas "the United States has been a late starter in this campaign," "the Russian effort began the moment the war ended." He noted, too, the Russians' economic edge. According to "a shrewd calculation made two years ago," he wrote, the Soviet Union had spent "the equivalent of half a billion dollars" on the cultural Cold War, but the American investment that began in 1954 amounted only to "approximately $2,250,000" annually. For all that, there was reason to be optimistic, for "even as the contending giants compete for attention in probing the secrets of the atom and in conquests of outer space, even as they compete for goodwill with their largesse in under-privileged areas, they dare not forget the intangible things—the dreams and secret murmurings that speak from heart to heart more surely and swiftly than any guided missile."[78]

Taubman paints a rosy picture here, a picture in which the Cold War is not a war at all, or even a competition, but an international show-and-tell event in which everyone, especially the audience, is automatically a winner.[79] And perhaps that is indeed how the so-called cultural Cold War, when regarded from a distance, played out.

Yet during the Fifties there existed another international cultural "event" whose conclusion, at least for one observer, was not so pleasant. In his 1967 autobiography Virgil Thomson reflected on a music-related conflict "that went on throughout the Eisenhower decade." This was not an ideological conflict of the sort in which Thomson so vigorously participated from his powerful seat on the ANTA panel. Rather, it was a purely artistic conflict whose combatants in the aftermath of World War II *all* counted among the victorious "good guys."

It "was fought between Europe and America for world control over music's advanced positions," Thomson wrote, and it "was won by Europe." Bitterly, doubtless because he saw himself on the losing side, Thomson called it "the modern-music war."[80]

8

Modernists

When it comes to modernism in postwar America, the most influential European composers were the Frenchman Pierre Boulez, the Italians Luciano Berio and Luigi Nono, and the German Karlheinz Stockhausen. All of them were born between 1924 and 1928; as young men just entering adulthood, they had seen their homelands torn by the clash of Allied and Axis forces, and they had been personally shaken by the violence that nearly brought the whole of European civilization crashing down around them. All across continental Europe, museums, opera houses, and concert halls needed to be rebuilt. And so, it seemed to these young composers, did aesthetic values.

The Americans were slower to respond to the perceived need for a drastically new music than were the Europeans, and when their response did come it was not so blatantly confrontational. Although many of the American modernists doubtless had personal wartime experiences every bit as horrific as those of their European contemporaries, the heritage with which they had grown up was never so direly threatened as had been that of Europe. After all, the United States did not enter the war until 1941, a full three years after conflict had been raging openly in Europe, and except for island territories in the Pacific, American soil never hosted a battle or bombardment. Yet like their counterparts in Europe, American composers who came of age during the 1940s eventually did see the aftermath of World War II as a time for rebuilding, a time to sweep away artistic modes of the past and to construct in their place entirely new modes of expression and new systems of musical organization.

At least for some of America's postwar modernists, the preferred system of organization was serialism. But in a nation where most new music for the concert hall was "essentially conservative,"[1] this system—not at all a style, but rather a method for dealing in orderly fashion with all twelve pitches of the chromatic scale—came in for harsh criticism. Even before the war, Ernst Krenek, a Czech-Austrian composer of serialist persuasion who immigrated to the United States in 1938, wrote: "After the twelve-tone technique has been explained to the average man, he is likely to exclaim, 'But that is pure mathematics! Anyhow, I've always known that this kind of music is computed, not inspired.'"[2] In 1941, reporting for the journal *Modern Music* on the Philadelphia Orchestra's first American performance of Arnold Schoenberg's Violin Concerto, Henry Pleasants noted that although the music "does not seem to be derived from the basic elements of song," its "presumably related fragments" at least *appear* to be "organized in a possibly mathematical fashion."[3] In his 1942 book *This Modern Music: A Guide for the Bewildered Listener*, John Tasker Howard equated serial music with atonality in general and suggested that "whatever drawbacks [it] may possess generally result" not from "lack of craftsmanship" but from "an overscientific approach."[4]

Twelve-tone serialism had been invented by Schoenberg early in the 1920s. Whereas in Nazi Germany his modernist work had been branded as dangerously "degenerate" for a panoply of ideological reasons that had little to do with music per se, in the United States, although Schoenberg himself was accorded a fair amount of respect, his work was derided simply because listeners did not care for the way it sounded. The methods that led to this work, to the extent that they were understood by members of the general public, also came in for derision. Addressing an audience at the University of Chicago in 1946, Schoenberg focused on what he believed were the genuinely *expressive* qualities of compositions from his "later period," which he said were sometimes described as being produced "exclusively by the brain without the slightest participation of something like a human heart," and which have earned him "the title of constructionist, engineer, mathematician."[5]

Criticism along those same avenues appeared often in the popular press during the Fifties, although most often it was leveled at a perceived norm against which certain pieces seemed to stand as notable exceptions. Reviewing Roger Sessions's second piano sonata in 1947, for example, Virgil Thomson wrote that, quite unlike this particular "interesting" and "thoroughly sophisticated" work, most representatives of the serialist/modernist trend "pass for professors' music," with "the complexity and elaboration of their manner . . .

out of all proportion to the matter expressed."[6] Reviewing Milton Babbitt's Woodwind Quartet in 1953, Thomson contrasted this "strongly personal work" with so many other serial works that feature "a sterile academicism."[7] The *New York Times*' Howard Taubman, fairly open-minded when it came to new music, noted in 1955 that Wallingford Riegger's Symphony No. 3 is decidedly not just another "dry exercise" in serialism.[8] In 1958, while praising the twelve-tone classics of Schoenberg, Alban Berg, and Anton Webern, he acknowledged that many listeners find the idiom to be, by its very nature, "barren and futile."[9] Harold C. Schonberg, who in 1960 succeeded Taubman as the newspaper's chief music critic, was one of those listeners, and in various opinion pieces he described twelve-tone compositions as music governed by "the determination of [its] creators to aim for a degree of extreme complexity that loses touch with reality"; as music "that looks beautiful on paper" but that in the hearing is largely incomprehensible; and as music that is "greeted with a huge ho-hum not only by the public but also by the professionals."[10]

Reflecting from the perspective of 1967, Ned Rorem, always a staunchly tonal composer, regretted that so much of the postwar modernist music was devoid of self-expression. For thousands of years before World War II, he wrote, "the making of music was the making of romance insofar as romance means evasion of reality, or rather heightened reality, concentration of emotion as against logic, controlled fantasy of self-expression. . . . When the atomic age reared its ugly clouds, however, that rising generation which earlier would have been impelled toward art was deflected toward science," and the music of "the few young talents who inclined toward art" grew into "a demonstration of logic for its own sake."[11]

For Rorem, the serial music of the Fifties was music "made by brains and performed for brains—when it was performed at all." In fact, serial music and other forms of music representative of "high modernism" was performed quite a lot during the Fifties. But most of these "public auditions," as Rorem rightly notes, took place not in "urban concert halls" but on "subsidized campuses."[12]

Music in the Universities

The relationship between campus and composer in the Fifties was not at all the same as it had been previously; the shift resulted from several factors that, although seemingly unrelated, both stemmed directly from America's postwar circumstances. One of these factors was a side effect of the space race that transpired throughout the period and that, pointedly, in 1957 had the United States watching in chagrin as the Soviet Union launched the first-ever globe-orbiting satellite. America's involvement in the highly competitive space race triggered massive government investments into university-based research in all the "hard sciences." At least some of the benefits of this, albeit more in the form of prestige than actual money, spilled over onto "professors' music" that at least had the semblance of being grounded in quasi-scientific methodology.

Another factor was the burgeoning of tertiary education that began immediately after the war ended. Whereas on the eve of America's entry into World War II the number of students partaking of postsecondary education was slightly less than 1.5 million, in 1950 the number was almost 2.7 million, and by 1960 it had climbed to 3.6 million.[13] The institutions that catered to this postwar flood of students ranged from the newly invented junior college, or community college, to the prestigious "research university" that evolved during the Fifties from what earlier had been simply the main campus of a state university. Wherever these schools were located, and no matter how large or small their eventual fame, most of them had music departments. More students at more schools meant more work for instructors of music, many of whom were among the "staggering" number of European-born composers that in advance of and during World War II had immigrated to the United States,[14] and at least some of whom indeed produced the "foreign models" of "abstruse music" against which Aaron Copland so vehemently railed in his 1951–1952 lectures at Harvard.[15]

Before World War II, American higher education in music was of two basic types. On the one hand were the schools dedicated exclusively to the training of would-be professional performers; on the other hand, and with numbers of students that vastly exceeded those at the conservatories, were the music departments of universities and colleges. The craft of musical composition was indeed taught in the university/college music departments, but most often only in the most rudimentary of ways, and it was generally assumed that any young person who truly aspired to "be" a composer would follow the example of the instructors and hone his (rarely, her) skills in Europe. For the most part, music education in American universities and colleges before World War II focused not much at all on the making of music but, rather, on music's literature and on the "art" of listening to it. Even at prestigious schools such as Yale and Harvard, classes in music appreciation were not only endemic but also "notorious for their low demands."[16]

The situation started to change late in the 1930s, after an impressive cohort of musical scholars from Germany and Austria—*serious* scholars, with no patience for lightweight courses—fled the Third Reich and sooner or later found positions at major American universities. Perhaps it was just coincidence that most of the émigré musicologists specialized in the music of the Renaissance and that most of the émigré analysts specialized in the methods formulated in the 1910s and 1920s by Heinrich Schenker.[17] Coincidence or not, the convergence of these two areas of specialization had a profound effect on the way music would be treated in American universities. Together, these two concentrations—the one on the intricate counterpoint of European music from the fifteenth and sixteenth centuries, the other on the harmonic architecture and infrastructure of Germanic music from the "common practice" period—demonstrated to hitherto skeptical American university administrators that music was something not just to be "made" (by composers and performers) or "consumed" (by passive listeners); it was also something to be studied, with as much intellectual intensity as had been applied for decades to literature and painting. In particular, the work of the Schenkerian analysts demonstrated handily to university administrators that the great masterpieces of Western music need not be simply described, as had long been the wont of participants in what Virgil Thomson disdainfully called the "appreciation-racket";[18] the Schenkerians demonstrated that music could be—indeed, *should* be—explained.[19]

Early in the postwar years, after "the 'three P's' of prosperity, prestige, and popularity" had started to usher in the golden age of higher education in America,[20] administrators were open to considering the idea that the creation of serious music—so long as it was complex enough to warrant analytical scrutiny—might be a legitimate part of a university's agenda. For the mathematician-turned-composer who made it happen, however, realizing the change in thinking was still a struggle.

Electronic Music and Music Theory

Milton Babbitt nowadays is best known not for his exemplary compositions that make use of the twelve-tone method, or for his pioneering work in both the development and the utilization of the RCA Mark II electronic music synthesizer, or for his almost single-handed introduction of "music theory" into the university curriculum. Rather, he is best known for a 1958 magazine article titled "Who Cares If You Listen?"

Babbitt's original title was "The Composer as Specialist," and the thrust of the article was that the composition of any music that truly advances the art is a specialized, research-driven endeavor whose results have little to do with competition for success in the public arena. Arguing that universities ought to grant musical activity of this sort the same protective shelter they typically gave to pure research in the sciences, Babbitt made it clear that he was seeking not "to present a picture of virtuous music in a sinful world" but, rather, to illustrate the problems that "a special music" faced "in an alien and inapposite world." To that end, he suggested that the composer of "special music" would benefit hugely by retreating into a world of "private performance and electronic media, with its very real possibility of complete elimination of the public and social aspects of musical composition."[21]

Zeroing in on what he perceived to be the article's key idea, *High Fidelity* editor Roland Gelatt discarded Babbitt's prosaic original title and replaced it with the immeasurably more engaging title the essay now so famously bears. More than a quarter century after the article was published, Babbitt insisted that the title had been changed "without [his] knowledge, and, therefore, without [his] assent."[22] It seems more likely, though, that Babbitt was "willing to downgrade his original title to a mere journalistic lede" for the sake of getting his message out to a wide audience. As Brian Harker puts it: "With tenure now safely in hand, he spoke freely, giving vent no doubt to thoughts and feelings that had been building up for a long time."[23]

Tenure for Babbitt was at Princeton University, where in 1938 he was hired as an instructor in the small music section within the Department of Art and Archaeology and where nine years later his doctoral dissertation was turned down by its examining committee. Rejected but not dejected, Babbitt in 1948 once more took a teaching position at Princeton, again as a mere "instructor," because he did not hold a doctorate. Championed by his former composition teacher Roger Sessions, who after a sojourn at the University of California returned to Princeton to serve as chair of what by this time was a full-fledged music department, Babbitt was promoted in 1951 to the rank of assistant professor. In July 1956, still without a doctorate and with no significant publications to his credit, he was granted both tenure and the title of associate professor.

Babbitt had been writing music in the twelve-tone vein even before he set out on his long tenure track at Princeton, and by 1956 he had produced compositions that won official awards (his *Music for the Mass* took first prize in Columbia University's Joseph H. Bearns competition in 1942, for example, and in 1949 his *Composition for Four Instruments* belatedly garnered a New York Music Critics' Circle citation) as well as the occasional approbation of such mainstream-oriented music critics as Virgil Thomson and Howard Taubman. When his application for tenure at Princeton was being considered, however, Babbitt's most enduringly significant contributions to postwar musical modernism—his hands-on involvement with electronic music and his championing of music theory—had only just begun.

What eventually became known as the Columbia-Princeton Electronic Music Center, with Babbitt as director, did not open until 1959, but its origins date back ten years earlier, to work started by electronic engineers Herbert Belar and Harry F. Olson at the RCA laboratory in Princeton, New Jersey. Belar and Olson were trying to build a calculating machine that would analyze the characteristics of simple melodies and then generate melodies of its own that featured those same characteristics. Their research took a more productive turn late in 1950 when they realized that teaching a machine to produce tunes along the lines of Stephen Foster's was pointless and that engineers at the Bell Telephone Laboratories, also located in New Jersey, were at that time experimenting with the electronic synthesis of vocal sounds. The production of sound, rather than the production of music, was something indeed up the alley of the embryonic computers then being developed by companies such as Remington Rand and IBM. Now on the right track, by 1952 Belar and Olson had built prototypes, and in January 1956, at a New York meeting of the American Institute of Electrical Engineers, they gave a public demonstration of a self-contained device called the RCA Electronic Music Synthesizer.

The RCA synthesizer was very different from the homemade circuits that Louis and Bebe Barron were then using to create the vibrant electronic sonorities that would make up the score for the MGM science fiction film *Forbidden Planet*. It was different, too, from the instruments located in government-sponsored electronic music studios in such cities as Ottawa, Paris, Bonn, Cologne, and Milan. Like the synthesizers in the foreign studios, the RCA synthesizer produced sounds by means of oscillators and in effect colored those sounds by means of various filters and modulators. Whereas the sonic nuances of the foreign synthesizers needed to be controlled by hand, however, on the RCA synthesizer the instructions for the realization of those nuances were programmable.

Two American composers in particular expressed immediate interest in the RCA machine. One of them was Babbitt. The other, Vladimir Ussachevsky, was based at Columbia University, and with his colleague Otto Luening he had recently surveyed the facilities of electronic music studios both in America and abroad. Ussachevsky and Babbitt hoped, with realistic optimism, that their universities would purchase the RCA synthesizer. The device was hardly marketable, but RCA granted both Ussachevsky and Babbitt access to the working model that resided at RCA's Princeton laboratory.

Babbitt was closely involved in the development of a more powerful synthesizer that RCA dubbed the Mark II, and during the 1958–1959 academic year he worked with Ussachevsky on an application to the Rockefeller Foundation for funding for what they hoped would be a national center for experimentation in electronic music. The foundation responded, early in 1959, with a grant of $175,000 that would support the first five years of operation of a new facility called the Columbia-Princeton Electronic Music Center. Located on the Columbia campus, in upper Manhattan, the center housed both the retrospectively named Mark I original synthesizer and, as soon as it was finished, its much faster successor.[24]

In a 1985 interview Babbitt described the Mark II synthesizer as "a large, large, large machine" that "would look like a computer to most people" but "is not a computer," for "it has no capacity to compute" and "it has no memory."[25] He described, as well, how he interacted with the Mark II: "What I do is go to this large machine and to a keyboard, but not in the sense of a piano keyboard, in the sense of a typewriter keyboard. I code in my instructions for every aspect of my music, every single element and dimension of the musical event. I have to tell this dumb machine everything I want by way of the musical result—every aspect, every component of every sound, the pitch, the loudness, the timbre, the envelope, the shape of every single event."[26]

For Babbitt the Mark II was almost a dream come true, because it at last allowed him the total control over musical elements that he had been striving for since as early as 1947, when in his *Three Compositions for Piano* he anticipated the "integral" serialism that during the next decade his European contemporaries Pierre Boulez and Karlheinz Stockhausen would famously champion. He turned to the synthesizer, he recalled, "because my music demanded it." Speaking not just for himself but for many of the other American composers who late in the Fifties began to produce electronic music, he said: "[We] didn't turn to the electronic medium because [we] were grasping at straws. [We] knew precisely what [we] wanted to do, and [we] knew that the only way to do it precisely was by using this medium. It was a long, hard pull."[27]

* * *

Another "long, hard pull" whose efforts were led by Babbitt involved the establishment of so-called music theory as a legitimate academic discipline. Theories about how music "works" had been in existence since the time of the ancient Greeks. They loomed large in the third and fourth centuries A.D., when Christian philosophers such as Boethius not only speculated on the relationship of music to the cosmos as a whole but also extended to include the entire octave the correspondence of musical intervals to relatively simply ratios that their pagan counterpart Pythagoras had started hundreds of years earlier. They loomed large, too, during the later Medieval period and during the Renaissance, but especially large in the eighteenth century, when the French composer Jean-Philippe Rameau was earning a reputation as the "Isaac Newton of music" for his ideas about the "gravitational pull" of a tonic pitch upon all the other pitches in a major or minor scale,[28] and when organ builders all across Europe were struggling to adjust the tunings of their instruments to accommodate the growing desire of composers to write music that would sound more or less the same regardless of its pitch level. In the nineteenth century, after the mathematics of equal temperament had been confirmed, theoretical thinking about music was by and large limited to the ideas of A. B. Marx, who looked back on the piano sonatas of Beethoven and formulated the concept now commonly known as sonata form. Early in the twentieth century, thinking about how music worked—not all music, but at least the Germanic masterpieces that ranged from Bach to Brahms—reached a peak in the writings of Heinrich Schenker.

None of the German music analysts who specialized in Schenkerian theory and who immigrated to the United States before and during World War II settled at Princeton. Nevertheless, Schenkerian theory had long been in the air at Princeton. Roger Sessions, who had learned of Schenker's work when he was living in Europe in the late 1920s and early 1930s, brought Schenkerian theory with him when he joined the Princeton faculty in 1935, and he included Schenkerian analysis in the private lessons he gave to Babbitt. Indeed, Babbitt sought out Sessions as a teacher, three years before he began work on his master's degree at Princeton, not so much because he had heard Sessions's music as because he had read Sessions's 1935 article on Schenker in the journal *Modern Music*.[29]

Like his teacher, Babbitt was interested in composing archly modernist music that utilized the twelve-tone method, not old-fashioned tonal music of the sort on which Schenker's writing had focused. Babbitt was not drawn to Schenker because of the repertoire Schenker favored; rather, he was drawn to Schenker because Schenker's approach to that repertoire—in marked contrast to the approach taken for so many years by American participants in the "music appreciation racket"—was genuinely theoretical. With Schenker as a model, Babbitt sought to establish himself at Princeton not as a teacher of music theory but as a music theorist in his own right.

In a 1983 lecture at the University of Wisconsin, Babbitt recalled how in the Fifties "the idea of taking theory seriously" resulted in part from the Schenkerian ideas brought over by the German émigrés and also, perhaps in larger part, from the "greater interrelationship among the [academic] fields" that was characteristic of the expanded postwar American university. "The notion," Babbitt told his audience, was "almost totally new." When he began his academic career, "there was no such thing as a professional theorist at any university that I can think of." But "we have produced now," he said from the perspective of 1983, "at least two generations of professional theorists."[30]

Among the first generation of professional music theorists there were, of course, some who had been cultivated at Princeton. The best-known today is probably Edward T. Cone, who like Babbitt studied with Sessions and then joined the Princeton faculty. Also in the group would be Peter Westergaard and Godfrey Winham, both of whom were students at Princeton in the 1950s, and a later cohort that includes Benjamin Boretz, Michael Kassler, Arthur J. Komar, Joel Lester, and Robert P. Morgan. But professional music theorists were also cultivated at the City University of New York's Queens College (where Schenkerian theory had been taught, by Felix Salzer's student Saul Novack, since 1952), at Columbia (where Hans Weisse had introduced the ideas of Schenker as early as 1932), and—especially, but not starting until late in the Fifties—at Yale. Yale's prolific output of professional music theorists, in subsequent decades rivaled only by the output of Princeton, started with the appointment there in 1959 of the Columbia-trained Allen Forte.

Although Babbitt and Forte were the co-creators of the distinctly American discipline of music theory, Babbitt was easily the new discipline's most outspoken champion. Just ten years older than Forte, but by the start of the Fifties far more deeply embroiled in the politics of American academia than Forte would ever have to be, Babbitt realized early on that what a professor of music "needed in order to survive in the [postwar] university environment," what he needed in order to "attain intellectual respectability," was "rigorous theory."[31] And he realized that to be properly "theoretical," in a way that would satisfy administrators and other members of the university community, ideas about music needed to be not only thought but also written down.

Speaking as much for his fellow theorists as for his fellow composers of "advanced" music, Babbitt told his University of Wisconsin audience: "Back in the early fifties when we saw that we were in trouble, when we saw that we didn't have the appropriate audience . . . , we thought that perhaps we could appeal to our fellow intellectuals by impressing them with the seriousness of our words."[32] To that end, in 1957 Babbitt and his colleagues launched the *Journal of Music Theory* (based at Yale) and in 1962 *Perspectives of New Music* (based at Princeton). Older music of the sort that had so appealed to Schenker afforded the early contributors to these journals plenty of material with which to flex their intellectual muscles, and their heady articles indeed helped them secure positions within the university hierarchy.[33] But it was newer music, especially music involving twelve-tone methods or some other highly organized compositional system, on which these journals would thrive.

Resentments

The music theory journals that Babbitt helped found late in the Fifties won plenty of prestige for the authors of their articles and the composers about whose work some of these articles were written. They did not win, as Babbitt hoped they might, many friends for advanced music. "We thought we would attract [potential listeners] with our words about music and [that] this would eventually lead them to the sound of our music," he recalled. "Well of course our words went as unheeded as our music went unheard. But we learned a lesson. We discovered that what induces even more resentment than taking music seriously is taking talking about music seriously."[34]

The resentment of which Babbitt spoke ran deep. It did not come from fellow intellectuals, some of whom perhaps expressed an interest in modernist music for the same fashion-based reasons they expressed an interest in modernist visual art, but most of whom, to judge from the paucity of their comments, simply did not care one way or another about cutting-edge music. Nor did resentment come from university administrators and their minions, who personified the clichés about "judging books by their covers" and, when it came to research, "not being able to read but only able to count," and thus were favorably disposed (without ever having heard a single note of their music) toward whatever composers happened to be so much as mentioned in the prestigious-looking new journals. Rather, the resentment came from participants in the classical music mainstream.

To be sure, during the long decade of the Fifties articles on mainstream composers appeared often in newspapers and in journals such as *Musical Quarterly*. But these tended to be reviews or interviews, appreciative obituaries, or assessments of past accomplishments coupled with prognostications for the future. No one bothered to write explications of the infrastructural harmonic relationships in the new American operas that were performed on television or at the Met, or the rhythmic intricacies of the orchestral works that were regularly sent abroad, as "weapons in the Cold War," by the U.S. State Department. Detailed analyses of harmonies and rhythms in the music of Samuel Barber, Howard Hanson, Paul Creston, and other representatives of the Fifties mainstream have indeed been forthcoming, but only lately, and mostly in the form of dissertations by doctoral students in search of research topics. When this music was current, deep theoretical analyses would have seemed laughably beside the point, for this music was judged—by critics and, more importantly, by audiences—not by how it looked on paper but by how it sounded.

Despite a long-lived mythology that says otherwise, serialist composers, or modernists of any sort, were not at all in the majority during America's 1950s and '60s. They represented only a handful of the composers active during those years, and their representation in "jobs, grants, awards, publications, performances, recordings, and reviews" was "roughly in proportion to their numbers within the larger population of composers (around 15%)."[35] They did not dominate the scene, yet there was a *perception* that they did, and their falsely perceived sway (albeit often described in retrospect) has long been castigated just as bitterly as was the falsely perceived sway of the Thomson-Copland circle of gay composers.[36] Babbitt, for example, was said to have turned the activities of the League of Composers and the International Society for Contemporary Music into "a forum for uncompromising serialism," and Sessions was said to rule "from his throne at Princeton . . . over the fashions taught at countless university music departments."[37] The music championed by Babbitt and Sessions was called "doctrinaire," regarded by its adherents as "faith" and "gospel."[38] According to the myth, the serialists had an "incredible stranglehold" on postwar American music and bound it in "straightjackets";[39] according to legends still being told, they wielded "the greatest intimidating force in the small world of modern composition," and their "reign of terror pervaded the compositional world."[40]

The sources of this intense and long-lasting animosity toward modernist music are murky and doubtless many, but one suspects that the main reason for what Joseph N. Straus calls "the myth of serial tyranny" is the "provocative rhetoric" with which the leading serial composers regularly described themselves.[41] As expressed by Babbitt and his American colleagues, the suggestions of serialism as a possible path to the musical future rarely rang with the aggressiveness voiced early in the postwar period by Europeans such as René Leibowitz, who in his 1947/1949 book on Schoenberg wrote that serialism is "the *only* genuine and inevitable expression of the musical art of our time,"[42] or Pierre Boulez, who in a 1952 essay boldly declared that "any musician who has not experienced—I do not say understood, but truly experienced—the necessity of dodecaphonic music is useless."[43] Still, Babbitt's insistence on "scientific language [as] the sole, firmly required medium of the musical cognoscenti" must have been just as off-putting to American composers who preferred not to talk about music, but simply to make it.[44] For Babbitt, a complete engagement with *his* sort of music theory was absolutely necessary for any composer or critic who hoped "to attain that rarest of all states, that of the concerned and thoughtful musical citizen."[45]

"No one likes to be told that they are 'useless,'" Straus reminds us.[46] Likewise, no one likes to be told that his or her refusal to discuss music in terms of mathematical or scientific language makes them somehow ineligible for citizenship, or that as mere listeners they form "an irrelevant annoyance whose approval signals artistic failure."[47] Unless one were part of the relatively small group of composers whose academic careers depended upon their production of "professors' music," language that so smacked of superiority could only have been offensive.

Music and Politics

It was not just composers of Babbitt's sort, and their derisive critics, who combined imagery of mathematics and music into single thoughts. The Hungarian composer György Ligeti did so as well, although in a completely different context, likening mathematics to music only for the sake of arguing that both fields of human endeavor are so "pure" as to be above and beyond the reach of politics.

Ligeti offered the analogy in a spontaneous response to a discussion at Darmstadt that transpired in 1972, long after the Fifties had passed but when strong whiffs of musico-political thinking nonetheless hung in the air.[48] At a time when "it has become so fashionable to make an absolute demand for political commitment from composers," Ligeti said, "it is strange . . . that the same commitment is not expected from a mathematician." Mathematics, Ligeti told his audience, is actually "not a science in the same sense as physics or chemistry"; rather, it is "a type of language" that, like music, involves "a structure of thought."[49] A "situation of oppression" might indeed "give rise to a structure of thought," Ligeti said, but that structure of thought nevertheless "has a life of its own. For that reason . . . I think it's completely irrelevant to speak about the political progressivity or reactionary position of New Music. It is not progressive in a political sense nor is it regressive, just as mathematics is neither progressive nor regressive. It is of a region which lies elsewhere."[50]

And yet for decades commentators have been drawing music from that "region which lies elsewhere" into the mundane realm of politics. National anthems, military marches, and works with specifically evocative titles or texts—for example, Copland's *Fanfare for the Common Man* and *Lincoln Portrait*—have not sparked much debate, for such pieces obviously have political agendas. Plenty of debate, however, has been sparked by examples of "absolute" music whose political content, if it exists at all, has to be read into their abstract combinations of pitches and rhythms. It is perhaps an aspect of human nature that "political rhetoric seeps down into the nooks and crannies of individual consciousness, even of people who considered themselves to be apolitical."[51] But the "seeping down" of political rhetoric tends to happen most often when the music under discussion is regarded from a distance, as is the case with the large number of scholars who only in the last decade or so have opted to focus on American and European music during the Cold War.[52] When the music is close at hand, the rhetoric fairly boils to the surface. And the rhetoric is at its most intense when the commentators have something personal to gain, or to lose.

Hanns Eisler certainly had something to lose. The German composer, whose misadventures with the House Committee on Un-American Activities were noted earlier in this book, studied with Schoenberg in the early 1920s and was as much committed to the methods of twelve-tone serialism as were Schoenberg's better-known students Webern and Berg. In 1926, after pledging allegiance to communism, Eisler broke with Schoenberg because he believed that the very idea of serial music was elitist. "Modern music bores me, it doesn't interest me, some of it I even hate and despise," he wrote to his former teacher. "I want nothing to do with what is 'modern.' . . . Also, I understand nothing (except superficialities) of twelve-note technique and twelve-note music."[53] Eisler, of course, understood fully the workings of twelve-tone music, and he continued to employ the serial method in his "serious" works even as he produced anthems and marching songs for use by Germany's antifascist demonstrators. He continued, too, to maintain his faith in "modern" music. "Fascism, more organized and brutal than everything Napoleon III could imagine, cannot afford even the slightest dissonance in [its] artificial harmony," Eisler wrote in 1944; thus "everything fought for by the Nazis—enthusiasm for their imperialistic goals, devotion to their leader, conformity to their way of life—was challenged by the work of Schoenberg," and thus "modern music [in general] became the enemy of fascism."[54]

Arguably this was so, but it might have been more accurate for Eisler to write that Nazi-style fascism was the enemy of modern music, especially when that music was composed by Jews like himself and Schoenberg. At least one famous non-Jewish producer of serial music who sympathized with the "orderly" ideals of Nazism, however, wished aloud that someone would try "to convince the Hitler regime of the rightness of the twelve-tone system."[55]

The political implications of serialism's orderliness entered the conversation in the United States as well. Babbitt recalled that while he was an undergraduate at New York University in the mid-1930s he attended a discussion of new music sponsored by a group called the Jefferson School, and when the talk turned to Schoenberg

> the urgent, moot question was whether "twelve-tone music" was or was not "democratic." The initial vote was "yes," for wasn't each note in the "row" created free and equal? One note, one vote! But suddenly a querulous, dissenting voice was heard: Was it not the case that each twelve-note work was founded on an order of notes, and thus that each work was founded on a "new order"! The mere uttering of this ominous expression brought the symposium to a quiet, disquieting conclusion.[56]

Similarly, Ernst Krenek remembered that shortly after the United States became actively involved in World War II he was asked to serve as a peer reviewer for an article that had been submitted to the journal *Modern Music*. The never-published article, Krenek said, argued that the "12-tone technique was the purest expression of Fascist and Nazi philosophy" and that "Germany had deliberately sent twelve-tone composers to the United States [in order] to contaminate the [American] culture."[57]

Aaron Copland was not worried about contamination when in 1949 he wrote a highly negative review of René Leibowitz's book on Schoenberg. In that review Copland indeed complained that Leibowitz "grovels before tradition in a way that is most unsympathetic to the American mind,"[58] but it seems an exaggeration to suggest, as one scholar has, that this is evidence of "Copland's view that dodecaphony was 'un-American.'"[59] Copland's beef was not with the idea of serialism itself but with what he perceived to be Schoenberg's especially German form of serial music. Earlier in that year he had visited Paris and encountered the rigorously serial Piano Sonata No. 2 of Pierre Boulez, whose music he found to be refreshingly "independent of Germanic influence" and whom he extolled for having "demonstrated that the [twelve-tone] method could be retained without the German aesthetic."[60] It is hardly surprising, then, that when Copland himself engaged with serialism, in his 1950 Piano Quartet, he applied the "French touch" that throughout the Fifties characterized almost all the music of the Thomson-Copland circle.[61]

The timing of Copland's rapprochement with serialism is, at the very least, interesting. His public identification as a suspected communist sympathizer stemmed mostly from his participation in the three-day Cultural and Scientific Conference for World Peace held in March 1949 at New York's Waldorf Astoria hotel. An honored guest at that conference was Dmitri Shostakovich, sent as an ambassador by the Soviet Union precisely because his dramatically powerful yet always accessible tonal music by this time, albeit after several difficult encounters with the governors of Soviet art, fairly epitomized what Soviet authorities proudly called "socialist realism." The music that by this same time had made Copland internationally famous—in particular his scores for the American-themed ballets *Billy the Kid* (1938), *Rodeo* (1942), and *Appalachian Spring* (1944)—was likewise tonal and accessible, and the extra-musical themes of many of his works likewise attempted to address social issues in ways that were not abstract but more or less realistic.

If Copland had indeed since the war's end "considered twelve-tone composition to be foreign, bound up in a dying Germanic tradition, of limited expressive use, and ultimately un-American,"[62] perhaps in the wake of the World Peace conference he feared that his own music might somehow be thought to be un-American. Having been branded in 1949 a "dupe and fellow traveler," Copland might well have decided in 1950 that a sensible career move would be to adopt, whether he liked it or not, a musical methodology that Stalin's cultural monitors despised just as much as Hitler's had.

Hindsight tempts commentators to make near-definite statements about such iffy possibilities. "When one learns that Copland began sketching his Piano Quartet, the first of his twelve-tone compositions, in March 1950, the same month in which he was targeted by the American Legion," writes Richard Taruskin in his voluminous *Oxford History of Western Music*, "the coincidence of dates prompts the reflection that the composer may have been seeking refuge in the 'universal' (and politically safe) truth of numbers, rather than the particular (and politically risky) reality of a national or popular manner."[63] Copland's 1950 Piano Quartet is a legitimate step in the composer's "aesthetic evolution," writes Jennifer DeLapp-Berkitt in an article that stems from her exhaustive 1997 PhD dissertation, "yet the *timing* of his first conscious use of a twelve-tone technique, so close on the heels of the Peace Conference . . . , indicates that politics and Cold War rhetoric played a prominent role in Copland's decision to use a twelve-tone method."[64]

Perhaps it was indeed the case that twelve-tone music, at least in the minds of some, early in the 1950s morphed from "being 'un-American' to being 'anti-Stalinist' and therefore patriotic."[65] Perhaps Copland's adoption of serial methods in his Piano Quartet indeed represented not just "a technical advance" on the part of an individual composer but also, in a more general way, "a calculated retreat from explicit Americanism and from populism, both of which had paradoxically become politically suspect in the tense early years of the cold war."[66] Perhaps the Piano Quartet indeed "illustrates one poignant effect of the Cold War upon artists in the United States."[67]

On the other hand, perhaps it doesn't. Maybe Copland's flirtation with serialism in his Piano Quartet resulted only from his wanting, for the sake of a change, to try something new. Maybe Copland, as he told an interviewer, was attracted to serial methods because with them he was able "to hear chords that I wouldn't have heard otherwise."[68] Maybe, and most likely, Copland turned to twelve-tone techniques simply because by 1950 he felt that he had "run out of chords."[69]

*   *   *

New chords of the sort that Copland discovered in the course of writing his Piano Quartet did not figure much into the American music that the U.S. government used between 1954 and 1963, as part of its International Exchange Program, as Cold War "weaponry." As detailed in the previous chapter, the orchestral repertoire approved for overseas tours sponsored by the IEP was invariably representative of the tonal mainstream. The purpose of these tours, after all, was not just to demonstrate to the entire world the excellence of American ensembles but also, especially in Asian and Latin American countries whose postwar political stance was perhaps still undecided, to win friends for America and all it seemed to stand for. On much-publicized tours whose programs were designed first and foremost to be "friendly," and intended to garner loud applause as much on the home front as abroad, there was little place for aggressive modernist music.

There *was* a place for modernist music, however, on programs that the U.S. government supported covertly. On the surface, these events were sponsored by the Congress for Cultural Freedom, an international anticommunist organization that since its founding in 1950 supposedly functioned by means of private philanthropy but that in fact, as revealed in 1966 in a series of articles published in the *New York Times*,[70] was funded almost entirely by the American government's Central Intelligence Agency. It was important that the CIA's involvement with the Congress for Cultural Freedom be secret, for the congress's targeted audience—different from the targeted audiences of the IEP tours—was Western Europe's intelligentsia. In America in the early 1950s, when McCarthyism was not only very much in force but also supported by a sizeable number of American lawmakers, general awareness of the government's catering in any way to elitist Europeans would have caused an uproar. In postwar Europe, where left-leaning intellectuals were scornful of "what they saw as the U.S.'s shallow, business-dominated culture and its 'Coca-Colonization' of the rest of the world,"[71] and wary of any sort of governmental control over the arts, even a suspicion of the CIA's support of the Congress for Cultural Freedom would have led to a public relations disaster.

With this in mind, the Soviet-American composer/conductor Nicolas Nabokov, who during the congress's inaugural meeting in West Berlin had been "duly" elected secretary-general of the new organization,[72] carefully set up a main office in Paris and, eventually, offices in more than thirty other countries. Just as carefully, he recruited employees worldwide—most of whom were of the proper political mind-set yet had no knowledge of their relationship with the CIA[73]—to launch "intellectual" periodicals and to produce cultural events.[74] The cultural events included art exhibitions and poetry readings, but the most generously funded of them involved music.

Under Nabokov's direction, the Congress for Cultural Freedom sponsored four major events during the Fifties that either focused entirely on music or at least put music at the center of their audience's attention. These events were titled "The Works of the Twentieth Century" (Paris, April–May 1952), "The Music of the Twentieth Century" (Rome, April 1954), "Tradition and Change in Music" (Venice, September 1958), and "East-West Music Encounter" (Tokyo, April 1961). The first two of these have attracted the bulk of interest from scholars, primarily because of the way the congress's attitude toward modernist music so drastically shifted, apparently for political reasons, between one festival and the other.

The 1952 L'Œuvre du XXe Siècle in Paris was a lavish production that involved, along with art exhibitions and panels devoted to literature and philosophy, more than thirty musical events. Numerous critics were surprised that the repertoire was not nearly so up-to-date as they had been led to believe it would be. The secondary headline for Olin Downes's report in the *New York Times* summarized the general disappointment: "[The Paris Exposition] presented [a] vast variety of events, but it failed to explore [the] modern spirit beyond 'Sacre' and 'Wozzeck.'" Indeed, Downes wrote, the festival was "a lopsided affair," even "in respects old-fashioned, looking mainly at the past, and little at the present and future."[75]

From the point of view of a postwar modernist, the festival's only real glimpses toward the future occurred in chamber music concerts (most of which Downes admitted to having missed), in the form of Charles Ives's 1915 Sonata No. 2 ("Concord") for piano, Pierre Boulez's 1952 *Structures Ia* and Olivier Messiaen's 1943 *Visions de l'Amen*, both for two pianos, and Edgard

Varèse's 1931 *Ionisation*, for percussion ensemble. Along with Boulez's *Structures Ia*, the festival's only other twelve-tone piece was Luigi Dallapiccola's 1938–1941 *Canti di prigionia*, for chorus accompanied by percussion and pairs of pianos and harps. But Dallapiccola's deliberately lyrical *Canti* was far removed, in effect as well as in affect, from Boulez's brittle experiment in "integral" serialism. Unless they had carefully read the program notes, most listeners likely would have linked the *Canti* not with the atonal music of Boulez but with the ear-pleasing neoclassical, and for the most part tonal, repertoire that fairly dominated the festival.[76]

Even before the festival began, the negative critical buzz about its obvious conservatism reached the ears of the congress's CIA handlers. One can only wonder what sort of prodding led Herbert Read, the British poet and literary critic who had been involved with the congress since its inception, to say to the festival's board: "Let our next exhibition be, then, not a complacent look at the past, but a confident look into the future."[77]

Nabokov's agenda for L'Œuvre du XXe Siècle was to remind the intellectuals of Western Europe that "political freedom was a necessary precursor to individual freedom of expression," and thus the festival focused on "music that was possessed of a sense of closure capable of sustaining an ideological emphasis."[78] In contrast, his plan for the 1954 La Musica nel XX Secolo festival in Rome was not to celebrate the continuity of culture in non-totalitarian countries but, rather, to goad Soviet intellectuals by showcasing "the type of art most obviously uncongenial to totalitarian taste."[79]

Not all of the repertoire was confrontational, and certainly not all of the featured composers were of archly modernist persuasion.[80] But plenty of them were, enough so that the word could be spread—via the commentaries of the many open-minded music journalists who attended the festival at the congress's generous expense—that "art thrives on freedom" and that atonal modernism in general, and serialism in particular, had "come to typify a creative individualism and risk-taking that only the West could sanction."[81]

* * *

Political scientists still wonder about how effectively the Congress for Cultural Freedom's expensive propaganda message got through to the intellectuals of Western Europe or, more importantly, to the intellectuals and artists on the other side of the Iron Curtain. Historians concerned only with American music as it unfolded within the borders of America have little need to wonder, for the effects in the United States of La Musica nel XX Secolo were minimal.

The skyrocketing to international fame of Elliott Carter—never a serial-ist but always, after the century's midpoint, a composer whose hard-edged music was based on a rigorous ordering of pitches and intervals—surely had something to do with the much-praised Rome performance of his 1952 String Quartet No. 1.[82] Hardly skyrocketing but nonetheless on the rise, the careers of the American serialist composer Ben Weber and the sometimes serialists John Lessard and Lou Harrison were doubtless also aided by the inclusion of their music on the festival's programs.[83] It is worth noting that the failure of Copland's very tonal opera *The Tender Land* occurred almost simultaneously with the performance at the Rome festival of his quasi-serial Piano Quartet, and that after a seven-year hiatus Copland's next major effort would be his quite strictly serial 1962 *Connotations*. Whether the inclusion on the Rome program of his 1950 Piano Quartet helped or hindered Copland's already well-established international career, however, remains open to debate.

Beyond these more or less significant impacts on the careers of individual composers, the Congress for Cultural Freedom's dogged efforts in Europe had little to do with what was transpiring on the American classical music scene. At the very same time that the CIA secretly promoted modernism in Europe, the U.S. State Department all around the world very openly promoted the music of America's mainstream tonal composers. On the home front, many more paying customers heard—and likely enjoyed—the "friendly" music of the mainstreamers than the "advanced" music of the modernists. The music that was cleverly displayed in Rome because it was so "obviously uncongenial to totalitarian taste" was also, as Richard Taruskin reminds us, "uncongenial to 'free world' public taste."[84]

The mainstream of the 1950s might well have existed had the long decade of the Fifties never happened. It sprang from the past, its collective effort a continuation of what Virgil Thomson, reminiscing from the perspective of 1970, called a "commando unit" comprising himself, Copland, Roger Sessions, Roy Harris, and Walter Piston that had formed "during the mid-1930s" for the purpose of "penetrating one after another the reactionary strongholds" and was then succeeded by "the Barber-Menotti-Schuman generation" that "followed so closely, not exactly in our steps, but on our heels."[85]

The modernists, on the other hand, were very much products of the Fifties. Indeed, it is difficult to imagine that the modernists, especially the serialists among them, would have come as much to the fore as they did had it not been for the convergence of societal forces that were quite specific to this conflicted period in American history. The Cold War rhetoric that argued for "the righteousness of the twelve-tone method" certainly had something to do with

9

Mavericks

"Maverick" is a term as American as the Stars and Stripes, and some might be tempted to argue—although they would be exaggerating, probably for the sake of promoting a nationalist agenda—that the concept of the "maverick composer" is likewise unique to the United States. Most English-language dictionaries in their primary definitions of "maverick" describe a specimen of livestock that has not yet been branded and whose ownership thus remains open to question. It was not the eponymously unbranded animals owned by the nineteenth-century Texas legislator Samuel A. Maverick, however, that led the word "maverick" eventually to mean "an unorthodox or independent-minded person" or "one that resists adherence to a group."[1] Rather, it was Maverick himself who gave rise to this usage. He was by profession not a cattleman but a lawyer, and the fact that the herd he casually acquired in a poker game went unbranded had to do not at all with his independent-mindedness but only with his utter lack of interest in the actual business of ranching.

An important handful of American composers in the postwar years demonstrated a comparable lack of interest not in music but in the traditional "business" of music-making. As much as they could, they avoided the universities that supported so many of the modernists. They avoided, too, the opera companies and symphony orchestras that through commissions and performances supported so many of the mainstreamers. Occasionally they banded together in collectives whose members pursued similar goals and thus were mutually influential. But most of the time the maverick composers of the Fifties marched to the beats of very different drummers.

Some of them knew exactly how they wanted their music to sound. Like those of their modernist and mainstream contemporaries, their compositions resulted from deliberation followed by decision and then action. But often the maverick composers felt that existing resources were simply inadequate for their needs. As they deemed necessary for their work in general or for individual pieces, they invented new playing techniques, new methods of notation, new sounds, new tuning systems, new instruments. And they experimented—sometimes playfully, sometimes seriously—with the magnetic tape recorder that the Nazis invented and then gifted, with their surrender, to the rest of the world.

The most radical of the maverick composers challenged not just music's conventional resources but also its conventional definition. Up until the middle of the twentieth century, it might have been assumed that a musical "composition" was a prescribed set of instructions for sonic events that featured a relatively limited number of sonorities and were purposefully organized in order to make some sort of artistic point. In the postwar years, at least a few American mavericks were saying not only that music did not have to be written down and that *any* sounds could be considered musical but also that the organization of these sounds need not be purposeful at all, that certain aspects of a so-called composition could be left entirely to chance.

Different Drummers

Edgard Varèse was once known as the "high priest" of American musical modernism,[2] but in 1936, after a string of compositions that began with the boisterous *Amériques* for large orchestra and ended with the quiet *Density 21.5* for solo flute, he in effect went silent. What brought him out of his long funk was the gift of a professional-quality Ampex reel-to-reel tape deck. Experimenting in the privacy of his Greenwich Village home, Varèse started to realize sounds of the sort that two decades earlier he had only imagined. His masterpiece in the distinctly postwar genre of electronic music came in 1958 in the form of the eight-minute *Poème électronique*, which used three tracks of filtered sounds of bells, pianos, and human voices and which spun through three-dimensional space over an array of 150 loudspeakers installed in the interior of the Philips Electronics pavilion at the Brussels World's Fair.[3]

Before *Poème électronique*, however, there was *Déserts*, a work for twenty-piece ensemble that Varèse had started in 1950 but was not able to complete until 1954, because its relatively static instrumental passages so much *needed* to be disrupted by abrasive interludes of the sort that only a tape recorder could provide. *Déserts* was a meditation on "not only physical deserts of sand, sea, mountains, and snow" but also on those deserts "where man is alone in a world of mystery and essential isolation."[4] With its clangorous tape tracks made up of noise from wind and the sea, and garish industrial noise, *Déserts*, wrote one journalist after its Paris premiere, sounded like "music of the time of the H-bomb."[5]

* * *

Magnetic tape was essential to the brief career of maverick composers Louis and Bebe Barron.[6] The couple acquired their machine—"the same model Hitler had used to record his speeches"[7]—as a wedding present in 1948. Based in New York after university days in Minneapolis, the Barrons soon enough discovered the joys of recording ordinary sounds and then playing them at high or low speeds, or backward, or processed through homemade filters and reverberation units. More inventively, in 1952, after having assisted John Cage in his "Music for Magnetic Tape" project, the Barrons began experimenting with sounds of their own making.

Inspired by Norbert Wiener's postwar writings on "cybernetics," Louis Barron designed sound-producing circuits that, once activated by electricity, seemed to have lives of their own. Guided by "an aesthetic of composition based on the characteristics of their equipment,"[8] Bebe Barron dutifully recorded the resultant squeaks and sputters, and she discovered that these tiny noises, when very much slowed down, sometimes yielded extraordinarily rich sonorities. By 1955 the Barrons had accumulated enough material so that they were able to make an impression on MGM executive producer Dore Schary, who hired them to generate first sound effects and then eventually the full score for the studio's upcoming film *Forbidden Planet*.

Forbidden Planet remains a science fiction classic, in part because it features the first all-electronic score for a major Hollywood film, and perhaps in larger part because it offers a veritable trifecta of favorite Fifties themes: futuristic outer-space exploration, Freudian psychology, and a climactic scene that shows a thermonuclear weapon blowing an entire world to smithereens.

* * *

Harry Partch may or may not have been asked to contribute to MGM's 1956 *Forbidden Planet,*[9] but he was most definitely approached by the Paramount studio and invited to score a portion of *When Worlds Collide*, a 1951 sci-fi disaster film in which the Earth is destroyed not by nuclear holocaust but by the encroachment of a mysterious planet into its gravitational field.[10] Partch, however, would have nothing to do with Hollywood.

Raised by missionary parents in remote areas of Arizona and New Mexico, and almost entirely (albeit to a high degree) self-educated, Partch was the American maverick par excellence, a genuine "American aboriginal."[11] During the Great Depression he spent eight years as a vagabond, living hand-to-mouth while traveling by train around the country, and at the same time handcrafting musical instruments and working out the meticulous details of a tuning system that featured no fewer than forty-three pitches to the octave. Not surprisingly, in the 1930s Partch's compositions went largely unnoticed, yet by 1942 enough of his music had been heard—and apparently appreciated—by influential persons that his status began to change. In quick succession, he benefited from fellowships, performances in Carnegie Hall, residencies at universities, and the publication of a voluminous treatise he had started almost twenty years earlier.[12] By 1950 the former hobo had become "a cult darling."[13]

It is ironic that Partch was courted by universities, places where "specialized men . . . are determined at all costs to maintain their positions by keeping their specialties pure, undiluted, and therefore—as far as the world is concerned—sterile."[14] Yet Partch came to depend upon universities that were flush with postwar funding, especially the University of Illinois, for the support that allowed him to build increasingly complex new instruments and to present increasingly theatrical new works. Without generous academic subsidy of the sort that was unique to the Fifties, many of the works by which Partch remains known today simply never would have happened.

* * *

Lou Harrison also benefited from postwar largesse, but on a personal level he suffered terribly from all that World War II implied. He told an interviewer in 1996 that he "divides his life into B.B. ("'before bomb") and A.B. ("after bomb"),"[15] and the division can easily be heard in his music.

Before the bomb, Harrison evolved from an adventurous and eclectic West Coast composer into a fairly conventional participant in the New York classical music scene. After the bomb, Harrison had a nervous breakdown. This did not prevent him from conducting the premiere, in 1947, of Charles Ives's Pulitzer Prize–winning Symphony No. 3, or from applying for and receiving, in that same year, a grant from the American Academy of Arts and Letters. His productivity was sharply curtailed, however, and his recovery did not really begin until he returned to California in 1953. For the most part hunkered down in a mountain retreat near Santa Cruz, but always eager to take short-term teaching posts, and certainly willing to accept awards from such patrons as the Fromm, Rockefeller, and Guggenheim foundations, Harrison again became prolific. But his music from this point on rarely made use of conventional "Western" harmonies, and more often than not it featured tuning systems borrowed from various Asian countries. Harrison's strong attraction in the Fifties toward Asian music had little to do with the complex mathematical theories that had brought Harry Partch, decades earlier, to embrace the microtonal scales of these same cultures. Rather, Harrison was drawn to Asian music by the purity of its sound and the melodic possibilities of its exotic scales.

Given the opportunity, Harrison raged vociferously against the "nightmare of McCarthyism" and the sophisticated "tools of death" that seemed to be bringing humankind ever closer to extinction.[16] But likely it was with his own soft-spoken music that Harrison most effectively made his point.

Collectives

Before they had access to the sophisticated one-of-a-kind synthesizers developed in the late 1950s by RCA, Columbia University professors Otto Luening and Vladimir Ussachevsky explored electronic music the same way that Varèse and the Barrons did: they acquired reel-to-reel tape recorders and experimented, almost always not with sounds generated electrically or electronically, but—as the French composer Pierre Schaeffer had been doing since 1948 in the new genre he called *musique concrète*—with sounds recorded from the world around them. Despite their pedigrees and positions, in their work with tape recorders Luening and Ussachevsky were electronic music mavericks. But starting in 1956, with their access to the original Mark I synthesizer at the RCA Laboratories in Princeton, New Jersey, the two composers reverted into the academic modernists they had earlier been.

Toward the end of the Fifties, and well into the Sixties, almost all the electronic music activity on the East Coast of the United States took place in New York, at the Columbia-Princeton Electronic Music Center. At the same time, on the West Coast, electronic music activity took place for the most part at something called the San Francisco Tape Music Center, a collective founded by young musical mavericks—including Pauline Oliveros, Terry Riley, and Morton Subotnick—who had in common little more than the fact that they had participated in the Composers' Workshop concerts organized at the San Francisco Conservatory of Music by composition teacher Robert Erickson.[17]

In terms of both their technologies and their ideologies, and thus in terms of their outputs, these two centers of American electronic music could not have been more different. The programming required for the operation of the New York–based RCA Mark I and Mark II synthesizers depended at least in part on piano-like keyboards attuned to the familiar equal-tempered scale of twelve pitches to the octave, and thus most of the compositions that made use of these synthesizers held to that scale. On the other hand, the synthesizers used in San Francisco—prototypes of the modular synthesizers built by the young physicist Donald Buchla, who in the late 1950s both honed his craftsmanship and earned enough money to support himself by working on various NASA projects at the University of California–Berkeley[18]—were not attuned to any scale at all, and they were not programmed but, rather, controlled in "real time" by such interfaces as knobs and touch-sensitive plates. A more significant difference between the two centers, however, stemmed from how they were funded and organized.

Officially established in 1961 but in the works for several years before that, the San Francisco Tape Music Center had a "social agenda" that "distinguished [it]" not only from the Columbia-Princeton center but also "from the many other electronic music studios established during the same period," most of them—in Cologne, Paris, Tokyo, Milan, Utrecht, Toronto, and Warsaw, for example—sponsored by governments and connected with government-run broadcasting facilities.[19] In a report prepared in 1964 for the purposes of a grant application, Ramon Sender, one of the founders of the San Francisco Tape Music Center, articulated the philosophy that had driven the collective since its inception:

> There is a growing awareness on the part of young composers all over the country that they are not going to find the answers they are looking for in analysis and composition seminars of the academies. Some retreat from the "avant-garde" music environment, live marginally on the fringe of the community, or attempt to work isolated from musicians and concert groups. They have insulated themselves by this isolation from the sickness of culture, but too often also from their own creative potential.

To counter this regression, the Tape Music Center was intended to be "a community-sponsored composer's guild, which [offered] the young composer a place to work, to perform, to come into contact with others in his field, all away from an institutional environment. Each composer . . . through his contact with the Center [is] encouraged [not only] to fulfill his own musical needs and develop his own personal language . . . [but also] to involve himself in the musical life of the community-at-large."[20]

Until it received its sought-after grant from the Rockefeller Foundation, the San Francisco Tape Music Center's budget was minimal. And this, apparently, was all to the good. Had the West Coast composers been blessed with "all that institutional equipment" enjoyed by their East Coast counterparts, they might well have been "denied the stimulus of bohemian penury."[21] Put another way, whereas "New York's multi-million dollar installation flourished in the stern grip of academic and corporate control," "San Francisco's shoestring operation delighted in its freedom."[22]

*   *   *

The University of Michigan, in Ann Arbor, is one of numerous American universities whose faculties and student bodies expanded tremendously during the Fifties. Michigan's already well established School of Music thrived in the new economic environment, but it was the science departments that benefited the most not just from the government's generous funding for veterans of World War II and the Korean War but also from the government's vested interest in increasing high-level research. Some of the young maverick composers who started to band together in Ann Arbor around 1957 and who in 1960 mounted the first ONCE Festival of New Music were indeed graduate students in the School of Music, where they dutifully developed their skills in harmony and counterpoint and where their creative efforts were mentored, for the most part, by composition professor Ross Lee Finney. Others of them—no less musical in temperament, but perhaps more pragmatic in their career planning—were enrolled through the G.I. Bill in the University of Michigan's burgeoning departments of physics, mathematics, architecture, and speech pathology.

It might have been a 1958 visit to Ann Arbor by the German ultramodernist Karlheinz Stockhausen, who "urged young composers to assume responsibility for performances of their works rather than relying on institutional support,"[23] that first got the group thinking about a festival that would be entirely independent of university control. The catalyst might also have been the presence in Ann Arbor, replacing the on-leave Finney during the second semester of the 1960–1961 academic year, of Roberto Gerhard, a composition teacher from Spain who, "free of institutional entanglements," apparently "liberated the creative energies of those around him."[24]

In any case, the motley crew of young Ann Arbor composers—whose ranks included the likes of such eventually well-known mavericks as Robert Ashley, Gordon Mumma, and Roger Reynolds—launched a two-weekend festival in February 1961 that featured a combination of music representative of canonic modernists and their own stylistically diverse efforts. Over the course of the next four years the ONCE festival—so-called not because of some acronymic formulation but simply because it was originally intended to be a one-time-only event—rapidly gained not just nationwide but worldwide attention.

Like the San Francisco Tape Music Center, the ONCE group operated on a limited budget. That might have been one of the keys to its success, but another key was surely its members' unbridled ambition simply to get their own music heard. "Nurtured by mutual support and driven by youthful idealism," Leta A. Miller reminds us, "they refused to let financial or logistical barriers dampen their plans." Thanks in part to "the vision and stubborn persistence of its founders," but thanks also in part to the local participants' healthy need for attention, the ONCE group for a brief period "brought to Ann Arbor the leading edge of musical experimentation."[25]

*   *   *

The first "happening" that went by that name took place in the spring of 1959 on a New Jersey chicken farm owned by the sculptor George Segal, although historians of American culture often attribute the genre's origin to something instigated by John Cage and David Tudor at North Carolina's Black Mountain College in the summer of 1952. The term owes its official coinage to Rutgers University art professor Allan Kaprow, but there is good reason to link the idea with Cage, for by 1957 Cage was teaching classes in experimental musical composition at New York's New School for Social Research, and by this time the Black Mountain event had become the stuff of legend.

Described in "sometimes wildly different" ways by people who experienced it firsthand, or, more often, by those who simply paraphrased the recollections of others, what occurred in the dining hall at Black Mountain seems to have entailed the projection of various films and slides in the presence of freshly painted canvases by Robert Rauschenberg and Franz Kline, a lecture by Cage, readings from recent works by poets Charles Olson and M. C. Richards as they somehow perched on ladders, dancing of some sort by Merce Cunningham, the playing on an old phonograph of songs recorded by Edith Piaf, and live performances by pianist Tudor of various pieces composed by Cage.[26] The apparent madness was guided at least in part by method; although the participants were indeed free to do anything they liked, they needed to do it at specified locations and within "a series of time-brackets" whose starting and ending points were somehow determined in advance.[27]

Toward the end of a talk on experimental music that he presented before the Music Teachers National Association in Chicago in 1957, Cage posed a rhetorical question. After celebrating the liberation of sound and encouraging the gathered music educators to develop new ways of listening both in themselves and in their students, he asked: "Where do we go from here?" The immediate answer: "Towards theater. That art more than music resembles nature. We have eyes as well as ears, and it is our business while we are alive to use them."[28]

Cage's lecture was printed in the brochure included with the three-disc album on which Columbia Records producer George Avakian, working not with his company but independently, preserved the "25-Year Retrospective Concert of the Music of John Cage" that took place in New York's Town Hall on May 15, 1958. The ideas contained in the lecture of course figured into the seminars that Cage was leading at the New School for Social Research, and their gist—that not just new music but new art in general was moving increasingly "towards theater"—especially appealed to those members of the class who until this time had regarded themselves perhaps as artists but not as performers. The gist of Cage's ideas certainly appealed to Kaprow, who, likely as the result of Cage's teachings, evolved from a painter into a producer/scenarist of quasi-theatrical events. The gist appealed as well to the painter George Brecht and the poet Dick Higgins, both of whom after participating in Cage's seminars chose to re-identify themselves primarily as "musical" contributors to Kaprow's various happenings.

It was not until June 1963 that George Maciunas, a Lithuanian-born graphic designer and would-be gallery owner who had attended some of Cage's classes, officially applied the term "Fluxus" to what he optimistically envisioned as an international movement on the part of artists of all sorts who would "fuse the cadres of cultural, social & political revolutionaries into [a] united front and action" and "purge the world of bourgeois sickness, 'intellectual,' professional & commercialized culture."[29] In the years that led up to Maciunas's hot-aired manifesto, however, plenty of artists had participated musically in events of the sort that eventually would be Fluxus's deliberately outrageous norm.

Just as significant, a great many artists embellished Fluxus-like events with creative efforts that were at least obliquely musical. In his 1960 *Piano Piece for David Tudor #1*, for example, La Monte Young called for a bale of hay to be "fed" to an onstage piano; to perform his 1962 *String Quartet*, George Brecht asked the four members of a traditional quartet to come on stage, politely shake hands, and then leave; the entire "score" for Nam June Paik's 1962 *Danger Music for Dick Higgins* consisted of the instruction to "creep into the vagina of a living whale."[30]

Why the repeated references to music in the titles and texts of such arguably absurdist works? Perhaps it was because the standard formalities of musical performance provided the Fluxus/happening participants with a convenient structural link to the tradition they otherwise tried so hard to deny. Perhaps it was because music—unlike language, physical gesture, and imagery of any sort—is purely abstract and thus infinitely open to interpretation. Whatever the reasons, "there *is* a musical bias to Fluxwork. In the performance scores and directions realized in the Fluxus mode and context, musical referents and formats abound—parodistically, perhaps, yet undeniably."[31]

* * *

It was not until January 1964 that folksinger Bob Dylan released the LP whose title song reminded Americans that "the times, they are a-changin." But by then "the times" had for several years already been a-changin, in ways that both enabled and affected the output of the San Francisco Tape Music Center, the ONCE group, and, especially, the players on the Fluxus/happening stage.

On the one hand, toward the end of the 1950s the dark clouds had begun to part, and optimists looked forward to a sunnier future. In May 1957 the infamous senator Joseph McCarthy was literally dead and buried, and with him had gone most of the "ism" attached to his name. By October 1960, when Stanley Kubrick's film *Spartacus* opened in cinemas nationwide and in its credit sequence proudly declared that its screenwriter was Dalton Trumbo, the unofficial but always frighteningly real blacklist was for all intents and purposes a thing of the past. In June 1959 the U.S. Supreme Court contributed much to the idea of free speech by overturning an earlier ruling that had declared a film version of D. H. Lawrence's *Lady Chatterley's Lover* to be illegally obscene. In December of that same year, the U.S. Food and Drug Administration approved Enovid, a drug that had no other purpose other than to allow women to have sexual intercourse without conceiving.

On the other hand, toward the end of the 1950s the space race and the arms race were reaching maximum speed, and in both fields of competition the United States seemed to be lagging behind. By mid-summer 1958 Democrats as well as Republicans were peppering their rhetoric with the term "missile gap"—shorthand for the widely believed but patently untrue "fact" that the Soviet Union's stockpile of intercontinental ballistic missiles capable of delivering nuclear warheads was, or soon would be, vastly larger than America's. In September 1959, news of the Soviet Union's Lunik 2 missile successfully hitting the "bull's-eye"—a designated crater on the moon—sent shivers up the spines of Americans who wondered what might happen if the Soviets aimed their missiles at earthly targets. And throughout 1959 the military theorist Herman Kahn attracted thousands of awed listeners to public lectures in which he projected details of a possible thermonuclear holocaust. Like the title character of Peter George's 1963 novel *Dr. Strangelove; or, How I Learned to Stop Worrying and Love the Bomb*, Kahn sarcastically proposed a "doomsday machine" that would obliterate the Soviet Union in case the United States were taken by surprise; on a serious note, Kahn suggested that the impending nuclear war would not *really* mean the end of the world, because at least a few thousand Americans might survive if they heeded his advice on underground shelters, food storage, and protective clothing.[32]

There was much more room for self-expression in 1959 than there had been earlier in the anxious long decade of the Fifties. At the same time, there was more about which one might be inclined to express oneself, and about which to be fearful. And it was on the brink of "this twin precipice," "teetering on the edge of a new decade," facing both "the prospect of infinite possibilities" and the prospect of "instant annihilation,"[33] that collectives such as Fluxus, ONCE, and the San Francisco Tape Music Center came into existence.

A few of the participants had served in the military, but most of them were born during or shortly before World War II. They were still in elementary school when the Federal Civil Defense Administration began teaching children to "duck and cover" in case of an atom-bomb attack; they were likely to have still been teenagers when rock 'n' roll burst upon the scene in 1955; and possibly they were already thoughtful young adults when network television in 1957 showed members of the U.S. Army protecting African American schoolchildren from white racists in Arkansas. In any case, these men and women came of age at a time when "the assorted forms of repression—whether political or social or sexual—were simply too great for humans in an ostensibly open society to bear."[34] As evidenced by much of their music, they belonged to "a new generation of activists [that] had been raised in Cold War America."[35]

The New York School

If the composers of the New York school were activists, it was not in a political sense, or at least not in any sense that during the Fifties seemed overtly political. Their characteristic work will forever be tantalizingly cryptic. And thus to after-the-fact commentators with political agendas, the work of the

New York school—more than its contemporaneous representatives of twelve-tone serialism and the classical music mainstream, certainly, and more so even than the *quasi*-musical creations of the Fluxus participants—remains open to interpretation.

The New York school is so called not so much because of the fact that in the early 1950s its members all lived in New York but because of its members' association—for the most part personal, but to a certain extent aesthetic and ideological—with the diverse abstract expressionist painters whom art historians long after their heyday lumped into a unit they called the "New York school."[36] But whereas the 1969 exhibition at the Metropolitan Museum of Art that gave the group its name included the work of no fewer than forty-three painters and sculptors, the musical version of the New York school comprised just the charismatic John Cage and four like-minded colleagues. And whereas the work of the visual artists by the late 1950s was being "sent abroad by official agencies as evidence of America's coming of creative age" and by the mid-1970s had achieved "blue-chip status" in art markets world-wide,[37] the work of their musical counterparts was seldom anything more than a *succès d'estime.*

In Europe as well as in America, the music and ideas of the New York school were indeed highly influential, but only to a small handful of creative individuals who self-consciously positioned themselves on the cutting edges of various art forms. The members of the New York school indeed won awards from philanthropic organizations and recognition from forward-looking universities, but to America's music-loving general public of the Fifties they meant next to nothing, and they seem to have meant even less to the government that overtly promoted, through the auspices of the U.S. State Department, such tonal composers such as Samuel Barber and Howard Hanson and at the same time covertly promoted, through the auspices of the Congress for Cultural Freedom, such modernists as Ben Weber and Elliott Carter. To the press, the New York school composers were by and large attended to merely as novelties. Notwithstanding an occasional friendly review from junior writers on the staff of the *New York Times* and some coddling from *New York Herald Tribune* critic Virgil Thomson that might have resulted from his personal relationship with Cage,[38] their music was more often than not described, with great derision, as amounting to so much "hollow, sham, pretentious Greenwich Village exhibitionism" and belonging to the "beep-beep, ping-ping, boing-boing school."[39]

Along with Cage, the members of the New York school—who in fact seldom did anything that warranted their being collectively described as the "beep-beep" school—were the composers Earle Brown, Morton Feldman, and Christian Wolff, and the pianist David Tudor. Although Cage was older and better established than the others,[40] he was hardly old enough to be a father figure. Still, he served his colleagues importantly not so much as leader or teacher or ideologue, but rather as principal source of inspiration. "We didn't study with John, and we weren't influenced that much by John," Brown told an interviewer in 1995. "But John *gave us permission* to be ourselves, and to take a chance on our own instinctive artistic potential."[41] Cage felt that the permission-giving was entirely mutual; reflecting on the situation from the perspective of a dozen years later, he recalled that in the early 1950s "ideas just flew back and forth between us, and in a sense we gave each other permission for the new music we were discovering."[42]

The new music that Cage and company were discovering was a music that differed radically from the music of both the modernists and the representatives of the classical music mainstream. But in fundamental ways it differed as well from the music of all the American mavericks discussed above. The crucial difference between the New York school and almost everything else that was transpiring musically in the Fifties had to do with the concept of music's "authorship."

* * *

Like the modernists and the mainstreamers, maverick composers such as Edgard Varèse, Harry Partch, and Lou Harrison prided themselves in the details of their work. These composers had a huge investment, emotional as well as intellectual, in the way their music ultimately sounded. Even Louis and Bebe Barron, whose sonic materials for the most part consisted of whatever happened to result when they ran electricity through their cybernetic circuits, as a couple conceived musical "compositions" only after they had sifted through the raw or processed materials and then decided, quite deliberately, that this particular bit of sound should follow, or be combined with, this particular other bit of sound. Like Harrison, Partch, and Varèse, and like all the modernists and mainstreamers, and like all the composers and arrangers who throughout the Fifties contributed to film, Broadway, and the various genres of popular music, the Barrons maintained a tight control over not just their music's form but also its content.

The characteristic work of the New York school exhibits a great concern for form, but content was something that to these composers often seemed not to matter much at all. And this makes the compositions of the New York school intriguingly paradoxical. Our English verb "compose" derives from the Latin "*componere,*" which is based on the two roots "*com*" ("together") and "*ponere*" ("put"). By definition, it would seem, a composer is someone who "puts things together" precisely for the sake of "putting together" something called a composition. The composer need not be the creator of all the various elements that make up his composition; most poets or novelists "put together" words belonging to the common vocabulary, for example, and most composers of music "put together" pitches and durations and timbres that for millennia have been in the public domain. But the composer, by standard definition, is the person who deliberately and decisively performs the act of "putting together" whatever elements—whether commonplace or newly invented—that he or she has determined should be put together. In the characteristic work of the New York school, there is seldom a deliberate or decisive putting together of musical elements, and often the elements that simply *happen* to come together result not from determination on the composer's part, but from the whimsy of performers or from pure chance.

Cage used the adjective "indeterminate" to describe the "new music" that he and his colleagues were discovering in New York in the early 1950s. In the second of three lectures he delivered at Darmstadt in September 1958, he contrasted music that was indeterminate with respect to its composition with music that was indeterminate with respect to its performance. As an example of the former, he cited his own 1951 *Music of Changes*, an extended work for solo piano whose precise notation suggests that different performances "will resemble one another closely" but whose content was "determined" not by him, but by various chance operations.[43] As examples of the latter—works certain to vary widely from performance to performance yet whose overall forms were to an extent "determined" by their composers—he mentioned Earle Brown's 1952–1954 piece *4 Systems*, Morton Feldman's 1953 *Intersection 3*, and Christian Wolff's 1958 *Duo II for Pianists*.

The notation for Brown's *4 Systems*, Cage said, was "a drawing of rectangles of various lengths and widths in ink on a single cardboard having four equal divisions" that could be "read," "by one or several players," "right side up, upside down, sideways, up and down."[44] The notation for Feldman's *Intersection 3* was a series of boxes whose vertical dimensions indicate a range of pitch, whose horizontal dimensions indicate a span of time, and whose numerals indicate how many "sonic events" the solo pianist should iterate within the specified time limits.[45] Wolff's *Duo II*, Cage told his interested but not altogether friendly German audience, had no time limits whatsoever and "no fixed relation of the parts"; its instructions called simply for one pianist to start and the other to respond, after "noticing a particular sound or silence which is one of a gamut of cues," with "an action of his own determination" selected from a group of "given possibilities" and contained "within a given time bracket."[46]

In his Darmstadt lecture Cage did not mention, perhaps because its essence simply went without saying, a piece of his own that has long been held up as the epitome of indeterminate music. Since its premiere in August 1952, just a few weeks after the happening-like event at Black Mountain College that featured shadows and reflections playing on the shiny surfaces of Robert Rauschenberg's pure white paintings,[47] the piece has commonly but incorrectly been identified as *4′33″*, and it is often described, also incorrectly, as a work for solo pianist.

The performer involved in the premiere, held at the aptly named open-air Maverick Concert Hall near Woodstock, New York, was indeed a pianist who followed the still controversial Cage piece with Henry Cowell's *The Banshee* and prefaced it with compositions by Wolff, Feldman, Brown, and the French modernist Pierre Boulez.[48] And the pianist, David Tudor, indeed took precisely four minutes and thirty-three seconds to get through the piece. But during this time he did nothing other than close the keyboard's lid at the piece's start and then twice open and close the lid to indicate breaks between the piece's sections.[49]

These anecdotes easily give rise to the notion that in 1952 Cage concocted a piece for piano titled *4′33″*. In fact, though, the instructions for the piece call for *any* number of instrumentalists to do absolutely nothing for *any* amount of time, so long as that time is somehow determined in advance of the performance and, importantly, is divided into three discrete units. Late in his life Cage yielded to popular pressure and referred to the piece as "Four Thirty-Three." For decades after its premiere, however, he called it simply "the silent piece." But he reminded interviewers that the first performance was "full of accidental sounds" generated by nature or by members of the audience,[50] and he suggested that anyone who regarded the work as literally silent has missed the point.

Few people have actually heard Cage's "silent piece," but many sophisticates have heard *of* it, and at least some of them have celebrated it as a watershed event in American culture. But for certain appreciators of music, including patrons who since the early 1940s had been generous supporters of Cage's increasingly envelope-stretching efforts, the "silent piece" was and continues to be a slap in the face. Remembering the friends he lost because he dared to put a nonperformance on the performance stage, Cage regretted that "they thought [it] was a form of pulling the wool over their eyes."[51]

An Aesthetics of Indifference?

Cage maintained silence throughout the homophobic McCarthy era and the ensuing rapid escalation of the arms race. If it is true that "virtually every piece he made after 1950 was intended to further, one way or another, changes of mind and in society,"[52] then these efforts were so subtle as to go virtually unnoticed. Cage did speak out, and express himself in writing, on international relationships and domestic societal issues, but this was not until the late 1960s, when America found itself in the throes of both race-related violence and the Vietnam War. Tellingly, the dedication of his book *M: Writings, '67-'72* is "to us and all those who hate us, that the U.S.A. may become just another part of the world, no more, no less."[53] During the long decade of the Fifties, the closest Cage came to being outspoken about anything was during his January 1960 appearance on the *I've Got a Secret* television show. Asked by host Gary Moore if he could accept the idea that the studio audience might well snicker during his performance of *Water Walk*, Cage grinned and said: "Of course. I consider laughter preferable to tears."

Some European artists, aggressively active on the political front throughout the postwar years, accused the New York school in general of irresponsibly disengaging from "the historical moment."[54] Some American artists who were politically active not just during the turbulent Sixties, when protest was fashionable, but also during the waning years of the anxious Fifties, when protest of any sort required real courage, took offense in particular at Cage's supposedly feigned "goofy naiveté" and his "adherence to the messianic ideas of [Buckminster] Fuller, . . . with their total ignoring of worldwide struggles for liberation and the realities of imperialist politics."[55]

But most American artists, like most American journalists and most members of America's music-loving public, made no connection at all between politics and whatever shenanigans Cage and his colleagues were up to. In the early 1950s there was plenty about which an American artist of any sort might have been deeply concerned, but the members of the New York school, as Christian Wolff recalled, "simply paid no attention to it," for in America at that time "being a-political or keeping politically under cover was the norm."[56] At that time in Europe, of course, being apolitical was not at all the norm; upon learning that certain European critics were insistent that their work was laden with political messages, members of the New York school were, not surprisingly, flabbergasted.

Reflecting on a trip with Morton Feldman to Germany in 1957, and their meeting with the young but influential German critics Hans G. Helms and

Heinz-Klaus Metzger, Earle Brown told an interviewer that "what astonished me, and astonished Morty too, ultimately, was the fact that they read my action as political, you know, *America the Beautiful*, freedom for everybody, because of my *Folio* works, primarily, the graphic pieces, which are the most extreme, [and which] allow individuality, wild freedom!"[57] Of the same trip, Brown told another interviewer:

> [Cage, Feldman, and I] represented Nirvana to them, because we were anti-dictatorial and allowed freedom to people. . . . [But] I could not get it into Metzger's mind that I had not done things *politically*. . . . In his world, [my music] was a political statement. You've done away with the conductor, you've done away with everything authoritarian. [The Germans] were—and still are—so ingrained with political activism.
>
> When [Bruno] Maderna and I first conducted *Available Forms II* in Cologne, Helms wrote an introduction to the programme. He wrote, "It's like the Declaration of Independence! America the Beautiful! Everybody is free!" Well, everybody is *not* free in that piece. But he was so far to one side that he couldn't get it. Morty had the same problem. They thought his very quiet music was a statement against rock-and-roll, or something.[58]

The music of the New York school did not make statements, for or against, on rock 'n' roll, antiauthoritarianism, individuality, or freedom. This largely indeterminate music was not "about" anything, really, and it was most certainly not "about" the egos of its creators. Ironically, this made the lot of it—but especially the music of Cage—quite antithetical to the work of the abstract expressionist painters with whom the composers indeed associated and whose collective label eventually they shared.

*   *   *

At the time when Cage first came to know the painters of the New York school, when the painters had just begun their rise toward worldwide prominence, assessment of these artists' work both by the artists themselves and by disinterested critics focused sharply on the idea of individualism. Of course, decades of analysis by art historians have brought complex readings to the work of such diverse painters as Philip Guston, Franz Kline, Willem de Kooning, Robert Motherwell, Barnett Newman, Jackson Pollock, Mark Rothko, and Clyfford Still. But in the postwar years these artists as a group represented a "variant of modernism that became canonical in the United States during the cold war period," a variant—often attached to painters and writers but, curiously, almost never to composers—that depicted the artist either as "an isolated, autochthonic, angst-ridden male genius, alternating between bouts of melancholic depression and volcanic creativity" or as "a masculine solitary whose staunchly heterosexual libido drove his brush."[59]

It quickly enough came to the attention of the CIA that abstract expressionist paintings were generally thought of as representing "the unmediated self-expression of interiority or absolute truth" and that the painters themselves were celebrated in the popular press as "heroic artist-geniuses 'emptying their guts' on the canvas or transcending the self through aloof fields of color."[60] In combination with the way the paintings actually looked—in their obvious "abstractness" the polar opposite of the Soviet Union's aesthetic of social realism—the alleged feisty personalities of the various artists made abstract expressionism an ideal weapon in the cultural Cold War. In this respect the paintings had several important advantages over the modernist music that the CIA-backed Congress for Cultural Freedom showcased in its 1952 and 1954 European festivals: the paintings were physical objects able to be taken in with a single glance even by a layperson; the paintings were able to be reproduced cheaply in newspapers and magazines; and perhaps most significant, the paintings were not just works of art but also commodities, able to be sold to private collectors and to museums worldwide for ever-higher prices that in effect proved their value. At considerable expense, the CIA not only promoted the work of the abstract expressionists overseas but also enshrined it at home in the Museum of Modern Art.[61] Even before their fame and fortune, however, the painters of the New York school exhibited a wealth of "supersaturated individualism."[62] And this put both them and their collective public image "completely at odds with the cool, egoless passivity associated with Cage."[63]

The "loud and aggressively macho" social scene at the bars where the painters congregated did not suit Cage's personal style,[64] and he took a particular dislike to Jackson Pollock, who Cage said was "generally so drunk" as to be quite "an unpleasant person."[65] But Cage got along well enough with most of the other painters. Since its inception in 1949 he had been a regular participant in what began as something called Subjects of the Artist and then evolved into the Artists Club or, simply, "The Club," and on several occasions Cage was invited to address the group. In terms of the New York school of painting, the most important of Cage's talks, because it seemed to be "a critique of the overwrought emotionalism and heroic existentialist narcissism that characterized the abstract expressionist aesthetic,"[66] was his 1950 "Lecture on Nothing."

Quietly distancing himself from the painters who expressed themselves abstractly yet boldly via their canvases, Cage cast his "lecture" as a quasi-musical piece divided into forty-eight segments that each contain forty-eight "measures" of text and/or silence and whose reading, Cage noted in a preface to the published version, should feature "the rubato which one uses in everyday speech." The lecture's most oft-quoted phrase—"I have nothing to say and I am saying it"—does not occur until the sixteenth and seventeenth sets of measures. The lecture begins, potently, with: "I am here, and there is nothing to say."[67]

If the "dominant abstract expressionists in the group" indeed "recognized themselves as the bull's-eye in Cage's target,"[68] they did not register offense. And if Cage's soft-spoken "Lecture on Nothing" was indeed "an inflammatory jab aimed at the aesthetics of abstract expressionism,"[69] it failed to ignite much of a response. On two more occasions he was invited to address The Club, but its members had little use for his ideas about an art that was distinctly "not about the communication of ideas or the expression of . . . feelings" but was, rather, "an exploration of the 'silence' left by the stripping way of the authorial presence."[70] Invested very much in the authorship of their canvases, during the early 1950s the abstract expressionists ambitiously painted their way into the limelight. At the same time, Cage and his newfound younger colleagues, apparently with little desire or need for recognition, explored a new music whose indeterminate content literally had no author.

*　*　*

Cage's silence has been interpreted, in the last few decades, as a self-defensive retreat from the homophobia that throughout the Fifties troubled the New York visual art scene as much as it did American society in general.[71] Although Cage's opting to be an artist with "nothing to say" suggests a retreat, it is likely that the force that needed escaping was not so much sexual repression as the overall spirit of the times.

Homophobia, to be sure, was an issue. Just as mainstream and modernist composers grumbled that the Thomson-Copland circle exerted far more than its fair share of influence over performances, commissions, and prizes, so did abstract expressionist painters complain of "a 'homintern,' . . . a network of homosexual artists, dealers, and museum curators in league to promote the work of certain favorites at the expense of 'straight' artists."[72] Cage would not have wanted to be embroiled in any of this, and the same might be said for the gay artists with whom he most closely associated. Within the environs of the Artists Club it was hardly a secret that Cage, who in the mid-1940s had finally come to grips with his sexual ambivalence, by 1950 was involved with choreographer Merce Cunningham in a monogamous relationship that would last for the rest of his life.[73] Nor was it a secret that the painters Jasper Johns and Robert Rauschenberg, two of Cage's closest friends, were gay. Although "an anti-homosexual bias" likely percolated throughout the New York art scene, Cage, who "had a very peculiar reputation" and "was to some degree disturbing to a lot of people," was nevertheless generally "very well liked."[74] He was indeed opposed to "the overwrought emotionalism and heroic existentialist narcissism that characterized the abstract expressionist aesthetic,"[75] but by and large he was not opposed to the individual human beings who expressed that aesthetic.[76]

The concept of an "aesthetics of indifference"—attached most fixedly to Cage, Cunningham, and the proto-minimalist painters Johns and Rauschenberg, and to the French neo-Dada multimedia artist Marcel Duchamp—originated in a 1977 article by art critic Moira Roth. Although Roth was an outspoken feminist and thus presumably sensitive to gender-related issues, she linked these figures not because of their sexuality but because of their approach to creativity. It should be noted that this approach, which resulted in work "characterized by tones of neutrality, passivity, irony and, often, negation,"[77] was shared not just by Cage and his gay friends but also by the perfectly straight composers who along with Cage made up the musical version of the New York school. To an extent the approach was shared even by those overtly heterosexual abstract expressionist painters whose loud "ego noise," but not necessarily whose work, Cage found so annoying.[78]

Generalizing sweepingly just a few years after the exhibition that created an official label for the New York school, art critic Dore Ashton ventured that "the nearest thing to a definition" of the essence of the "school" would be "a summary of the philosophic preoccupations of the artists involved." After pondering these artists' diverse yet somehow related preoccupations, Ashton concluded that the so-called school was simply "a set of attitudes that generated works which reflected a set of attitudes."[79] And these attitudes, whether expressed by painters or musicians, had a distinctly postwar flavor.

For Christian Wolff, the work of the New York school composers in general was "a reaction of detachment from the massive tensions starting to be generated by re-emerging global conflict that was hard-line ideological and backed on both sides by the possibilities of nuclear destruction."[80] For art historian Serge Guilbaut, the work of the New York school painters was similarly detached. All too aware of tensions, internal as well as international, these painters "accepted the idea that modernity could no longer be expressed in the same terms as had been used by the two previous generations: not after the atom bomb."[81]

With paintings devoid of representation, the abstract expressionists were in a sense just as "silent" as the composers whose music was in large part indeterminate. Playing with oxymoron, Susan Sontag compared the painters' "loud" silence to silence of a calmer sort, and she noted that "while the clamorous style of proclaiming the rhetoric of silence may seem more passionate, its more subdued advocates (Cage, Johns) [were] saying something equally drastic."[82]

The drastic statements made in the 1950s as much by noisy painters as by quiet musicians can easily be interpreted as having to do only with art in its purest forms. After all, it was precisely at the time when both the painterly and the musical versions of the New York school were coalescing that we begin to witness the rise to power of "an institutionally and critically sanctioned modernist view of art, in which any discussion of the political [was] seen to be deeply irrelevant to considerations of the aesthetic value of works of art."[83] On the other hand, various statements from members of the New York school—precisely because of their defiantly apolitical silence—might be read, in the context of the Fifties, as being quite profoundly political.

To describe the work of Cage and others as representative of an "aesthetics of indifference," or as a "Buddhist-derived aesthetics of resignation,"[84] is perhaps to miss the point. Around 1950 there was indeed a deliberate withdrawal on Cage's part. But he was never a coward, and there is nothing "politically defeatist" about any of his postwar compositions or writings.[85] All things considered, what for Cage and many of his colleagues merely "*appears* to be an 'aesthetic of indifference' is in fact a new approach toward the social and political function of art."[86]

In his 1988 gloss on Moira Roth's still provocative 1977 "Aesthetics of Indifference" essay, Jonathan Katz suggested that the New York school—the composers as much as the painters—engaged in "a particular species of politics, one specifically calibrated to survive Cold War America."[87] He did not mean that their work was intended to endure, for the sake of posterity, well into a blissful future that artists of the 1950s could only have imagined. Rather, he meant that this by and large "silent" work was of a sort that enabled the artists, as human beings, to survive *in* Cold War America.

Epilogue

Seeking to encapsulate a period whose dynamic social forces were diverse and intertwined in immeasurably complex ways, historians have described America's postwar years as "the age of doubt" and "the age of abundance," as the "placid decade" and the "crucial decade," as the "proud decade" and the "decade of fear."[1] They were "The Fabulous Fifties," according to a 1972 article in *Newsweek* magazine, "the good old days," "a simple decade when hip was hep" and "good was boss."[2] For the sake of balance, though, the article quoted the socialist writer Michael Harrington to the effect that the Fifties had been "a moral disaster, an amusing waste of life."[3]

For the journalist I. F. Stone, who courageously slogged his way through the postwar years and had good reason to look warily over his shoulder every time he published a column dealing with what he thought was the truth about a matter at hand, the years under discussion here added up to "the haunted Fifties."[4] For the poet Robert Lowell, who wondered if he had squandered his manhood in feeble protest against first World War II and then what seemed to be a monolithic repressive government, they were "the tranquillized Fifties."[5] For television's fictional Archie Bunker, they were the days when "hair was short and skirts were long" and "Kate Smith really sung the song," when "fifty dollars paid the rent" and "freaks were in a circus tent."[6]

For younger baby boomers who since the 1980s have stood on the left or right side of the ideological divide, the once-upon-a-time Fifties continue to represent either "a low point for oppositional politics" or a period of "consensus worthy of celebration."[7] For an older boomer like me, the actually remembered Fifties were just my "normal" childhood, when I happily romped on the playground while wondering what would happen if those air-raid sirens ever sounded for real, when I proudly helped my dad navigate our way to yet another family vacation because I remembered the locations of all those "Evacuation Route" signs, when every Saturday I relished science fiction movies in an auditorium that doubled as a mustering point for Civil Defense emergencies, when at parties in the basements of new suburban homes I danced awkwardly to rock 'n' roll 45s while guiltily envying the bigger kids who sneaked off with girls—the ones wearing tight sweaters and what surely must have been padded bras—to make out in the bomb shelters.

In America the long decade of the Fifties was all of that. Even as it transpired, astute observers of human behavior noted the period's seemingly "opposite . . . trends" and its "shocking contradictions and tragic paradoxes."[8] And one suspects that it is precisely these paradoxes and contradictions—the national pride in America's wartime triumph versus a collective doubt about the nation's future directions, the placid comfort gained from postwar prosperity versus a pervading fear that all of this abundance could, in a nuclear flash, be gone—that gives the Fifties its special frisson.

* * *

Heralded loudly by the *Newsweek* article cited above and by a similar piece in *Life* magazine that celebrated "that sunnier time" of "The Nifty Fifties,"[9] the first wave of popular interest in the Fifties hit the shores of American culture early in the 1970s, and it was manifested most obviously in such films as *American Graffiti* (1973) and *Grease* (1978) and in such television programs as *Happy Days* (1974–1984) and *Sha Na Na* (1977–1981). The 1970s, to be sure, gave birth to serious dramatic films set in the Fifties,[10] but it was the feel-good efforts—animated by vintage rock 'n' roll music or by newly composed songs in the rock 'n' roll style[11]—that had the most enduring impact. These were highly successful commercial commodities that, especially for their baby boomer audiences, had the effect of triggering "memories" all warm and happy and nice.

Scholars of popular culture have pondered this first wave of enthusiasm for the Fifties, and they call attention to its timing. It does not take a mathematical wizard to observe that the 1970s were separated from the 1950s by the 1960s. But it takes a sociologically minded historian, perhaps even one with a political agenda, to explore the crucial ways in which the Seventies differed from the Sixties.

In the eyes of at least some such writers, the Seventies—the so-called Me Decade—amounted to a "slum of a decade" during which "a huge and infinitely variegated country changed suddenly, dramatically, and permanently" into a homogeneous nation characterized by "deplorable sensibilities and the general dumbing down of everything."[12] From a jaded point of view based in the twenty-first century, the Seventies might indeed seem to have been little more than "the sickly, neglected, disappointing stepsister to that brash, bruising blockbuster of a decade" we call the Sixties, just a "prolonged anticlimax" to the earlier period's "manic excitements."[13] From a more charitable point of view, perhaps the new era was a psychologically necessary counterbalance to "the massive identity dislocations" that so many Americans—older as well as younger—had experienced during the Sixties. As historian Fred Davis reminds us:

> Quite apart from such specific traumas as the Vietnam War, the assassinations of the brothers Kennedy and Martin Luther King, the ghetto riots, the student protests, the Civil Rights marches, the Kent State massacre, etc., millions upon millions of Americans experienced during [the Sixties] what is perhaps the most wide-ranging, sustained and profound assault on native belief concerning the "natural" and "proper" that has . . . ever been visited on a people over so short a span of time.[14]

Under constant pressure from the government and the apparently cooperative mass media, many Americans both young and old during the Fifties "exchanged real life for an *idea* of normal life," and it is largely this rose-colored "normative fantasy," not actual memories, that "survives in the nation's idea of the Fifties" as portrayed in the popular films and television shows from the 1970s.[15] People who indulged in this fantasy—those who enjoyed *Happy Days* when the show was new, who attended "Fifties parties" wearing poodle skirts and leather jackets, who consumed burgers and shakes in restaurants made up to look like '50s diners—thus experienced only a faux nostalgia. Like visitors to Disneyland's Main Street USA, they participated not in a simulation, or recreation, of an actual past, but rather in a "simulacrum," a fictionalized representation, of a past that never really existed.[16] For whatever reasons—palliative, or more likely just hedonistic—audiences enthusiastically took the bait of a marketing strategy that seems, in retrospect, to have been specifically designed to play on the needs of baby boomers.[17]

A faux nostalgia for "happy days" easily explains the interest in Fifties culture that was demonstrated in the 1970s. But what explains the second wave of interest, the much darker wave that hit with full force shortly after the start of the current century? This second wave was presaged by *Pleasantville* (1998), an ostensibly "light" romantic comedy but actually, or at least arguably, "a critique of 1950s McCarthyism and contemporary conservative nostalgia."[18] It is evidenced not just in numerous films and television programs since the Seventies but also in political rhetoric that had been voiced aplenty in the 1980s and early 1990s during the administrations of presidents Ronald Reagan and George H. W. Bush. Like *Back to the Future* (1985) and *Peggy Sue Got Married* (1986), Gary Ross's *Pleasantville* is an essay in science fiction that involves people from the present being transported into the Fifties. But whereas the "pasts" of *Back to the Future* and *Peggy Sue Got Married* are lively scenes more or less in keeping with the "normative fantasy" that had long been dished up by the popular media, the "past" of *Pleasantville* is a parody of one of that fantasy's principal modes of transmission.

In *Pleasantville* a pair of teenage siblings mysteriously migrate from their problem-filled real world of the late 1990s to the apparently problem-free make-believe world of a Fifties television show, a show set in a town where troubles simply do not exist, a town where "it never rains" and where "the basketball team never misses the hoop," where "there are no toilets or double beds," where "bodily fluids cannot be found."[19] Over the course of the film, the brother and sister in various ways introduce feelings-based complications into this "perfect" environment, and as they do so the town's black-and-white imagery little by little turns, literally, colorful. *Pleasantville* has a sugary Hollywood ending, with its main characters returned to their real present not older but certainly wiser, and thinking that they might have indeed gifted something to the denizens of their fictional past. Writer/director Ross claims that *Pleasantville* is for the most part "a wonderful metaphor [with which] to express what it means to come alive,"[20] and perhaps that is indeed how his film, to many of its viewers, is read. To more skeptical viewers, however, the bulk of *Pleasantville* is a creepy dystopia bleached of emotion, a nightmare vision that is played for laughs.

There is little to laugh at in such films as *A Beautiful Mind* (2001), *Far from Heaven* (2002), *Kinsey* (2004), *Capote* (2005), *Good Night, and Good Luck* (2005), *The Good Shepherd* (2006), *Hollywoodland* (2006), *Revolutionary Road* (2008), *Cadillac Records* (2008), *Shutter Island* (2010), and *On the Road* (2012). None of these is a "fantasy" film; indeed, most of them are based on real-life stories,[21] and their appeal to modern cinema audiences perhaps illustrates the bromide about truth often being stranger, or at least more dramatically compelling, than fiction. In any case, these recent films together paint a picture of the Fifties leavened hardly at all by the good-time rock 'n' roll music that seems to have been the key ingredient—the "tea-soaked madeleine of the masses," as David Shumway, alluding to Proust, puts it—in the Seventies' recipe for "evok[ing] the fiction of a common past."[22] Rather, these films together portray a Fifties made heavy not just by their themes of homophobia, unchecked consumerism, and Red Scare paranoia but also, and most pervasively, by their characters' essential loneliness.

*   *   *

We engage with history for many reasons. Just for the sake of keeping the record straight, for example, we seek to know what actually occurred in times past, and for the sake of perspective we want to know how events in the past—and all of their resulting artifacts—relate to events and artifacts from periods both earlier and later. But our quest for knowledge about our forebears is invariably mixed, I think, with a quest for knowledge about ourselves. By learning about where we came from we can perhaps get at least some idea about where we are today, and from that perhaps we can speculate about where we might be going.

Why is it that listeners at the dawn of the twenty-first century, with an unprecedented wealth of recorded material and a vast array of critical theories at their disposal, still gravitate toward the music of the Fifties? When it comes to discussion of "oldies but goodies," why do so many nominees, regardless of the genre under consideration, stem from this particular period in American musical history? What is it about American music from the postwar years, in general, that gives it—a half century after its creation—such an enduring resonance? What effect does an understanding of both the myths and the realities of the postwar period have on our modern perception of American music from the Fifties? What effect does empathy with denizens of the Fifties have on our grasp of their music, or of our own music?

One cannot help but notice that the start of the second wave of American films about the Fifties coincides with the infamous September 11, 2001, attack on the World Trade Center in New York. Whether or not Americans' renewed interest in the long-ago Fifties is somehow related to this horrific event is a question with which future historians can wrestle. For the moment, we can only observe that America in the twenty-first century is indeed clouded over by a great many concerns, at least some of them—worries that we might be attacked again, or infiltrated, by a mysterious foreign enemy; blustery talk from politicians and military strategists about "weapons of mass destruction" in the hands of rogue nations; intense surveillance of American citizens by their own government—directly related to 9/11. And we can only wonder if the reverberations from 9/11, echoing the reverberations from Hiroshima and Nagasaki, for Americans signaled yet another Age of Anxiety.

Notes

Prologue

1. David Halberstam, *The Fifties* (New York: Villard Books, 1993), 9.

2. The term "Cold War" was popularized by journalist Walter Lippmann, who in September 1947 used it as the heading for one of his "Today and Tomorrow" columns in the *New York Herald Tribune*. Later in that year a collection of Lippmann's columns was published under the title *The Cold War: A Study in U.S. Foreign Policy* (New York: Harper Brothers, 1947). Origin of the term is often attributed to financier and presidential advisor Bernard Baruch, who in April 1947 used it in a much-publicized debate regarding the proposed Truman Doctrine; in fact, the term was coined by novelist George Orwell in an October 1945 essay titled "You and the Atom Bomb."

3. Winston Churchill, quoted in McGeorge Bundy, *Danger and Survival: Choices about the Bomb in the First Fifty Years* (New York: Random House, 1988), 198.

4. Andrei Sakharov, *Memoirs*, trans. Richard Lourie (New York: Knopf, 1990), 99.

5. For a full account of the HUAC hearings and their effects on the entertainment industry, see Victor S. Navasky, *Naming Names* (New York: Penguin, 1980).

6. *The Adventures of Ozzie and Harriet* aired weekly on the ABC network from 1952 until 1966; *Leave It to Beaver* aired from 1957 until 1963 on CBS and then ABC.

7. Sloan Wilson, *The Man in the Gray Flannel Suit* (New York: Simon and Schuster, 1955), 3.

8. Lewis Mumford, *The City in History* (New York: Harcourt, Brace, and World, 1961), 486.

9. The marriage rate in 1945 was 12.2 per 1,000 citizens, and the divorce rate in the same year was 3.5 per 1,000 citizens. At 2.6 and 2.3 per 1,000 citizens, respectively, the divorce rates in 1950 and 1955 were the second and third highest since the National Center for Health Statistics began its tally in 1890.

10. David Riesman, Nathan Glazer, and Reuel Denney, *The Lonely Crowd: A Study of the Changing American Character* (New Haven, CT: Yale University Press, 1950; abridged ed., New York: Doubleday, 1953), 320.

11. Wini Breines, *Young, White, and Miserable: Growing Up Female in the Fifties* (Boston: Beacon Press, 1992), 99. Breines points out that sex researcher Alfred Kinsey saw American males' interest in female breasts as one of the things that distinguished them, sexually, from their European counterparts. See Alfred Kinsey, *Sexual Behavior in the Human Female* (Philadelphia: W. B. Saunders, 1953), 254–55.

12. Marjorie Rosen, *Popcorn Venus: Women, Movies, and the American Dream* (New York: Coward, McCann, and Geoghegan, 1973), 267.

13. Christopher Small, *Musicking: The Meanings of Performing and Listening* (Hanover, NH: Wesleyan University Press, 1998), 2; emphasis added.

14. The one channel was Channel 4, taken over by Milwaukee's WTMJ in July 1953. The last three of the four call letters stand for "*The Milwaukee Journal*," the newspaper that had been granted a television license as early as 1931 but that did not go on the air, with commercial programming, until 1947.

15. The Sputnik satellite was launched by the Soviet Union on October 4, 1957. It stayed in orbit for twenty-two days, and American observers were instructed to watch for its passing at dawn and twilight.

16. The first commercial stereo discs were released in November 1957 by Audio Fidelity Records. The press run of the company's stereo demonstration disc was limited, so it is likely that the recording I heard was one of those issued early in 1958 by Capitol or RCA.

17. McCarthy was officially "condemned," not "censured," by his fellow senators on December 2, 1954, but he remained in the Senate—and thus open to my uncle's criticism—for another two and a half years. Presley's debut on the *Ed Sullivan Show* took place on September 9, 1956.

18. Richard Taruskin, "Afterword: *Nicht blutbeflecht?*," *Journal of Musicology* 26, no. 2 (2009): 282. Taruskin's article is the last of nine featured in a pair of *Journal of Musicology* issues edited by Peter J. Schmelz and devoted to the music during the Cold War.

Chapter 1. The Pop Music Mainstream

1. For details, see James M. Manheim, "B-side Sentimentalizer: 'Tennessee Waltz' in the History of Popular Music," *Musical Quarterly* 76, no. 3 (1992): 354.

2. Donald Clarke, *The Rise and Fall of Popular Music* (New York: St. Martin's Griffin, 1995), 298.

3. The Weavers was made up of Ronnie Gilbert, Lee Hays, Fred Hellerman, and, most famously, Pete Seeger.

4. Charles Hamm, *Yesterdays: Popular Song in America* (New York: W. W. Norton, 1979), 386.

5. Ibid.

6. James Lincoln Collier, *Benny Goodman and the Swing Era* (New York: Oxford University Press, 1989), 320.

7. Clarke, *Rise and Fall*, 303.

8. Ibid.

9. This was "All or Nothing at All," a recording made in 1939 while Sinatra was still a rank-and-file singer with the Harry James band. The recording initially sold only eight thousand copies, but upon its rerelease it was the number one hit for two weeks. Much more successful had been the recording of "I'll Never Smile Again" that Sinatra made in 1940 with the Tommy Dorsey band. Beginning in July 1940, "I'll Never Smile Again" topped various *Billboard* charts for a total of twelve weeks, but in the charts the product was attributed not to Sinatra but to Dorsey.

10. Sinatra's recording of "Oh, What It Seemed to Be" reached the top of the *Billboard* chart in March 1946, and in September of that year Sinatra scored a number one hit with "Five Minutes More."

11. In 1943 Sinatra was the featured artist on the CBS network's *Songs by Sinatra* program; from 1943 to 1945 he co-starred on the same network's *Your Hit Parade* and then from 1947 to 1949 after the program shifted to NBC. In 1944 he was clearly the main attraction of CBS's *The Frank Sinatra Show* and *Frank Sinatra in Person*.

12. Sinatra's "What's This about Races?" appeared in the September 17, 1945, issue of *Scholastic*. It is reprinted in *Frank Sinatra and Popular Culture: Essays on an American Icon*, ed. Leonard Mustazza (Westport, CT: Praeger, 1998), 23–25.

13. The "skinny kid" description is attributed to Tommy Dorsey. James F. Smith, "Bobby Sox and Blue Suede Shoes: Frank Sinatra and Elvis Presley as Teen Idols," in Mustazza, *Frank Sinatra and Popular Culture*, 61. The "heartthrob" quote comes from Keir Keightley, review of *Sinatra! The Song Is You: A Singer's Art*, by Will Friedwald, *The Frank Sinatra Reader*, ed. Steven Petkov and Leonard Mustazza, and *Legend: Frank Sinatra and the American Dream*, ed. Ethlie Ann Vare, *American Music* 15, no. 1 (1997): 102. On the "maternal urge," see Arnold Shaw, "Sinatrauma: The Proclamation of a New Era," in Petkov and Mustazza, *Frank Sinatra Reader*, 27.

14. For details on the AFM's ban on recordings, see Scott DeVeaux, "Bebop and the Recording Industry: The 1942 AFM Recording Ban Reconsidered," *Journal of the American Musicological Society* 41, no. 1 (1988): 126–65.

15. Attributed to bandleader Alvino Rey. Cited in Clarke, *Rise and Fall*, 260–61.

16. For example, Glenn Miller's 1941 "Boogie Woogie Bugle Boy" and 1942 "Don't Sit Under the Apple Tree (With Anyone Else But Me)," Kay Kyser's 1943 "Praise the Lord and Pass the Ammunition," and Louis Jordan's 1944 "G.I. Jive."

17. For example, Kay Kyser's 1942 "(There'll Be Blue Birds Over) The White Cliffs of Dover" and Vaughan Monroe's 1943 "When the Lights Go On Again (All Over the World)." For an account of songs whose lyrics had to do with romantic couples separated by the circumstances of the war, see B. Lee Cooper, "From 'Love Letters' to 'Miss You': Popular Recordings, Epistolary Imagery, and Romance during War Time, 1941–1945," *Journal of American Culture* 19 (Winter 1996): 15–27.

18. The Les Brown band's recording of "Sentimental Journey" reached the number one position on May 26, 1945; it was displaced on July 28, 1945, by Johnny Mercer's "On the Atchison, Topeka, and the Santa Fe," which in turn was displaced on September 15 by Perry Como's recording of "Till the End of Time."

19. Dating from 1939, the song came to the attention of executives at Columbia Records in 1950 after it had been used in an off-Broadway play. The lyrics of "Come On-a My House" are by William Saroyan and the music is by Ross Bagdasarian. Saroyan was well-known as a playwright; Bagdasarian, his cousin, took the stage name David Seville in the late 1950s and achieved fame with novelty recordings featuring the pitch-shifted voices of Alvin and the Chipmunks.

20. Joanne Meyerowitz, "Sex, Gender, and the Cold War Language of Reform," in *Rethinking Cold War Culture*, ed. Peter J. Kuznick and James Gilbert (Washington, DC: Smithsonian Institution Press, 2001), 108.

21. Molly Haskell, *From Reverence to Rape: The Treatment of Women in the Movies* (New York: Penguin, 1974), 235; emphasis original.

22. Sara Davidson, introduction to Dan Wakefield's novel *Going All the Way* (New York: Dutton, 1989), viii; quoted in Breines, *Young, White, and Miserable*, 101.

23. Alan Brinkley, "The Illusion of Identity in Cold War Culture," in Kuznick and Gilbert, *Rethinking Cold War Culture*, 67.

24. Jack Gould, "Radio and Television," *New York Times*, December 3, 1951, 37.

25. Jack Gould, "Television in Review: Crazy Music," *New York Times*, December 16, 1953, 55.

26. Laurie Henshaw, review in *Melody Maker*, February 9, 1952; quoted in Charlie Gillett, *The Sound of the City: The Rise of Rock and Roll*, rev. ed. (1970; New York: Da Capo Press, 1996), 6.

27. Douglas T. Miller and Marion Nowak, *The Fifties: The Way We Really Were* (New York: Doubleday, 1977), 295.

28. E. J. Kahn Jr., *The Voice: The Story of an American Phenomenon—Frank Sinatra* (New York: Harper and Brothers, 1947). Kahn's book was based on a three-part profile that had appeared in the *New Yorker* magazine; the themes developed in the book had also been explored by Kahn in a lengthy article titled "What Will Sinatra Do Next?" that appeared in *Look* magazine on August 5, 1947.

29. Roger Gilbert, "The Swinger and the Loser: Sinatra, Masculinity, and Fifties Culture," in Mustazza, *Frank Sinatra and Popular Culture*, 41.

30. Keightley, review of *Sinatra!* 102.

31. Both Hudson and Hunter, ironically, were "closeted" homosexuals.

32. T. H. Adamowski, "Frank Sinatra: The Subject and His Music," *Journal of Popular Culture* 33, no. 4 (2000): 5. Adamowski explores the same idea in "Love in the Western World: Sinatra and the Conflict of Generations," in Mustazza, *Frank Sinatra and Popular Culture*, 26–37.

33. Adamowski, "Frank Sinatra," 5.

34. In film, Nunnally Johnson's 1956 *The Man in the Gray Flannel Suit* (based on Sloan Wilson's 1955 novel) stands out as an important exception. This poignant

film deals not with sexuality, however, but with the protagonist's concern over lack of meaningfulness in his professional life. Betty Friedan's nonfiction *The Feminine Mystique* deals eloquently with the sexual frustrations of Fifties women, but the book was not published until 1963.

35. In the mid-1950s singers Dean Martin and Sammy Davis Jr. certainly profited from playboy-style swagger, and later in the decade they would become members (with actor Peter Lawford and comedian Joey Bishop) of a Sinatra-led contingent that the media dubbed the "Rat Pack." For more on the double standard that involved behavioral allowances for men but not for women, see Breines, *Young, White, and Miserable*, 110–15.

36. Eric F. Goldman, *The Crucial Decade—and After: America, 1945–1960* (New York: Vintage, 1960), 263.

37. Elaine Tyler May, *Homeward Bound: American Families in the Cold War Era*, rev. ed. (1988; New York: Basic Books, 1999), xiv.

38. Ibid., 69–70.

39. Elaine Tyler May, "Explosive Issues: Sex, Women, and the Bomb," in *Recasting America: Culture and Politics in the Age of Cold War*, ed. Lary May (Chicago: University of Chicago Press, 1989), 166. The author has an identically titled chapter in her 1988 (rev. 1999) book *Homeward Bound*. While the essay in *Recasting America* and the chapter in *Homeward Bound* are similar in content and argument, the writing is substantially different.

40. Adamowski uses, and possibly introduces, the term "music noir" in his 2000 article, "Frank Sinatra: The Subject and His Music." Although the recordings under consideration are the same, the term does not appear in Adamowski's 1998 book chapter, "Love in the Western World."

41. Collier, *Benny Goodman*, 165.

42. The quoted phrase is from an advertisement for the Fred Astaire Dance Studios that appeared in the *New York Times* on February 17, 1952 (98), but four other advertisements on the same page make a comparable claim.

43. Gifford R. Adams, "Making Marriage Work: If You Don't Get Dates," *Ladies' Home Journal*, July 1955, 26; paraphrased in May, *Homeward Bound*, 105.

44. *New York Times*, March 7, 1954, M33.

45. Jerome Robbins, "From the Castle to the Creep," *New York Times*, March 21, 1954, M24.

46. Ray Anthony's numerous dance-oriented LPs for the Capitol label bore such titles as *Houseparty Hop, Campus Rumpus, Young Man with a Horn*, and *Arthur Murray Swing Foxtrots*. In 1952 Anthony reached the *Billboard* Top 100 chart, and spurred a short-lived dance craze, with a single titled "The Bunny Hop."

47. Breines, *Young, White, and Miserable*, 84–126. Among the studies she cites are Beth Bailey, *From Front Porch to Back Seat: Courtship in the Twentieth Century* (Baltimore: Johns Hopkins University Press, 1988); Elizabeth Douvan and Joseph Adelson, *The Adolescent Experience* (New York: John Wiley and Sons, 1966); Benita Eisler, *Private Lives: Men and Women of the Fifties* (New York: Franklin Watts, 1986);

Marty Jetzer, *The Dark Ages: Life in the United States, 1945–1960* (Boston: South End Press, 1982); and John Modell, *Into One's Own: From Youth to Adulthood in the United States, 1920–1975* (Berkeley: University of California Press, 1989).

48. In a section devoted to "learning to say no graciously," an advice book offers a list of fifteen techniques by which girls might stem the escalation of necking and petting. Judson and Mary Landis, *Building a Successful Marriage* (Englewood Cliffs, NJ: Prentice-Hall, 1953), 70–71; cited in Breines, *Young, White, and Miserable,* 238.

49. Breines, *Young, White, and Miserable,* 116.

50. For example, *Grease* (1978), *Carrie* (1976), *American Graffiti* (1973), *Back to the Future* (1985).

51. Among those mentioned by Breines are Alix Kates Shulman's 1972 *Memoirs of an Ex-Prom Queen,* Lisa Alther's 1975 *Kinflicks,* Ann River Siddons's 1976 *Heartbreak Hotel,* Kate Stimpson's 1979 *Class Notes,* Marge Piercy's 1982 *Braided Lives,* Joyce Johnson's 1983 *Minor Characters,* and Caryl Rivers's 1984 *Virgins.* The only autobiographical novel by a male author that Breines draws from is Dan Wakefield's 1970 *Going All the Way.*

52. Rebecca Leydon, "The Soft-Focus Sound: Reverb as a Gendered Attribute in Mid-Century Mood Music," *Perspectives of New Music* 39, no. 2 (2001): 105.

53. Ibid., 100.

54. Ibid., 104.

55. E. May, "Explosive Issues," 155.

56. Ibid., 167. The film's screenplay is by Terry Southern and director Kubrick; its plot is loosely based on the 1958 novel *Red Alert* (published in the United Kingdom as *Two Hours to Doom*) by Peter George.

57. Miller and Nowak, *The Fifties,* 293.

Chapter 2. Rock 'n' Roll

1. Bruce Tucker, "'Tell Tchaikovsky the News': Postmodernism, Popular Culture, and the Emergence of Rock 'n' Roll," *Black Music Research Journal* 9, no. 2 (1989): 272.

2. Nelson George, *The Death of Rhythm & Blues* (New York: E. P. Dutton, 1988), 67.

3. Bill Haley, *Haley News,* 1966; quoted in Gillett, *Sound of the City,* 24.

4. The original version of "Rocket 88," recorded by Jackie Brenston and the Delta Cats, was a number one rhythm-and-blues hit upon its release early in 1951. Jimmy Preston's less successful "Rock the Joint" dates from 1949.

5. Clarke, *Rise and Fall of Popular Music,* 382.

6. Ibid.

7. Peter Ford, "Rock Around the Clock and Me," http://www.peterford.com/ratc .html.

8. Hamm, *Yesterdays,* 391.

9. Langston Hughes, *The Big Sea* (New York: Knopf, 1940), 254. Hughes refers to "My Daddy Rocks Me (With One Steady Roll)," recorded in 1922 by Trixie Smith.

10. "Cherry Red" is the work of Pete Johnson and Big Joe Turner, the latter of whom, as noted above, was the vocalist in the first recording of "Shake, Rattle, and Roll."

11. First recorded by the Dominoes and featuring low-register vocals by the group's bass player, Bill Brown, "Sixty-Minute Man" is credited to William War and Rosa Marks.

12. In his biography of Freed, John A. Jackson points out that the 1934 United Artists film *Translatlantic Merry-Go-Round* features the Boswell Sisters, an all-white vocal trio, singing a swing-style song titled "Rock and Roll" and that the lyric of the 1937 mainstream pop song "Rock It for Me" asks, "Won't you satisfy my soul / With the rock and roll?" John A. Jackson, *Big Beat Heat: Alan Freed and the Early Years of Rock & Roll* (New York: Schirmer, 1991), 83.

13. Jackson, *Big Beat Heat*, 33–34.

14. John Buzzell, ed., *Mister Rock 'n' Roll: Alan Freed* (Los Angeles: National Rock 'n' Roll Archives, 1986), 64; quoted in Jackson, *Big Beat Heat*, 34.

15. Theodore Irwin, "Rock 'n' Roll 'n' Alan Freed," *Pageant*, July 1957; reprinted in Buzzell, *Mister Rock 'n' Roll*, 18; quoted in Jackson, *Big Beat Heat*, 34. Freed's claim can be challenged. Gillett notes that the growing number of white listeners among his radio audience was widely reported in *Billboard* magazine, and he suggests that it was in large part because of Freed's appeal to white teenagers that he was hired, in 1954, by New York's WINS. Gillett, *Sound of the City*, 13.

16. "Moondog" was a pseudonym/persona that Freed adopted to mark the shift in content from his mainstream programming to his rhythm-and-blues programming. In November 1954, four months after he moved to New York, Freed was debarred from using "Moondog" because since 1947 the appellation, according to a court ruling, had been the property of a blind street musician whose real name was Thomas Louis Hardin.

17. Valena Minor Williams, *Cleveland Call and Post*, n.d.; quoted in Jackson, *Big Beat Heat*, 3.

18. In fact, only about nine thousand tickets for the Moondog Coronation Ball had been sold in advance. The problem resulted when approximately twelve thousand people attempted to buy tickets, on the night of the show, for the remaining one thousand places.

19. The Moondog Balls presented in Cleveland in the summer of 1953, for example, featured Fats Domino, the Drifters, the Harptones, the Buddy Johnson Orchestra, Ella Johnson, the Moonglows, Red Prysock, Dakota Staton, and Big Joe Turner. The Moondog Holiday Ball presented in Akron in December 1953 featured Chuck Berry, Bo Diddley, Little Walter, the Moonglows, and Danny Overbea.

20. Payola, or the accepting of compensation in exchange for promoting certain musical products, became illegal on September 13, 1960, when amendments to that

effect were written into the Communications Act and the regulations of the Federal Communications Commission. Conducted by the House Subcommittee on Legislative Oversight, hearings on the so-called payola scandal began in November 1959, immediately after the subcommittee concluded its investigation of such "rigged" television quiz shows as *Twenty-One* and *The $64,000 Question*. In the course of the payola investigations, both Freed and Dick Clark, host of the *American Bandstand* television program, were called to testify; neither admitted any wrongdoing, but on November 22, 1959, Freed was fired from his job at radio station WABC, reportedly for his involvement with the scandal.

While the term "payola" did not come into common usage until the late 1950s, the practice of publishers paying surreptitiously for the promotion of certain songs was widespread not only in the early days of radio but also during the Tin Pan Alley era. For a detailed account of the 1959–1960 hearings and the history of payola, see R. H. Coase, "Payola in Radio and Television Broadcasting," *Journal of Law and Economics* 22, no. 2 (1979): 269–328.

21. *Variety*, February 25, 1953; quoted in Jackson, *Big Beat Heat*, 49.

22. Lawrence N. Redd makes the point that whereas most scholars today would argue that rock 'n' roll and rhythm-and-blues are musically distinct genres, in the second half of the 1950s the terms were for all intents and purposes synonymous. Lawrence N. Redd, "Rock! It's Still Rhythm and Blues," *Black Perspective in Music* 13, no. 1 (1985): 31.

23. Aided by their widespread distribution systems, in the mid-1950s Capitol, Columbia, Decca, and RCA pioneered the idea of selling records via suburban supermarkets. In 1956 supermarket revenues for the major labels totaled $14 million; a year later the figure had risen to $40 million. David P. Szatmary, *Rockin' in Time: A Social History of Rock-and-Roll*, 5th ed. (Upper Saddle River, NJ: Prentice-Hall, 2004), 25.

24. Other relatively successful mid-1950s white covers of songs first recorded by blacks—some of them not so much rock 'n' roll efforts as pop songs in the sentimental vein—were "Tweedle Dee" (originally recorded by LaVern Baker / covered by Georgia Gibbs), "Dance With Me, Henry" (Etta James / Georgia Gibbs), "You Send Me" (Sam Cooke / Teresa Brewer), "I Hear You Knocking" (Smiley Lewis / Gale Storm), "Sincerely" (the Moonglows / the McGuire Sisters), "Hearts of Stone" (the Charms / the Fontane Sisters), "Earth Angel" (the Penguins / the Crew Cuts), "Sh'Boom" (the Chords / the Crew Cuts), and "Why Do Fools Fall in Love?" (Frankie Lymon and the Teenagers / the Diamonds).

25. Gillett, *Sound of the City*, 38.

26. Buzzell, *Mister Rock 'n' Roll*, 30; quoted in Jackson, *Big Beat Heat*, 34.

27. Buzzell, *Mister Rock 'n' Roll*, 66, quoted in Jackson, *Big Beat Heat*, 77.

28. Gillett, *Sound of the City*, 14.

29. *Cleveland Press*, n.d., but probably 1954, since the article comments on Freed's recent departure from Cleveland; quoted in Linda Martin and Kerry Segrave, *Anti-Rock: The Opposition to Rock 'n' Roll* (New York: Da Capo Press, 1993), 98.

30. "White Council vs. Rock and Roll," *Newsweek*, April 23, 1956, 32.

31. Ibid.; "Leader of White Councils Lays Integration to Reds," *Washington Post and Times Herald*, June 16, 1956; quoted in Kevin J. H. Dettmar, *Is Rock Dead?* (New York: Routledge, 2006), 163.

32. Martin and Segrave, *Anti-Rock*, 42.

33. Malcolm Sargent, conductor of London's BBC Symphony Orchestra, in "Queen's Curiosity Aroused, Her Kingdom Much Upset by Rock 'n' Roll Film," *Variety*, September 26, 1956, 2.

34. Attributed to an anonymous Canadian minister, in "What You Don't Need to Know about Rock 'n' Roll," *Maclean's*, July 7, 1956, 51.

35. Bernard Travaille, quoted in "Baptist Pastor Sees Evil in Rock 'n' Roll," *Los Angeles Times*, September 2, 1956, F2.

36. "Rhythm and Rumble," *Washington Post and Times Herald*, June 6, 1956, 14.

37. Francis J. Braceland, director of the Institute of Living, in "Rock-and-roll Called Communicable Disease," *New York Times*, March 28, 1956, 3.

38. "Rose Raps BMI Songs as 'Junk,'" *Washington Post and Times Herald*, September 19, 1956, 36.

39. "Rock 'n' Roll Laid to B.M.I. Control," *New York Times*, September 18, 1956, 76.

40. Russell Sanjek, "The War on Rock," *DownBeat 17th Annual Yearbook / Music '72* (Chicago: Maher Publications, 1972), 63. The article in *Variety* appeared on page 1 of the November 11, 1959 issue.

41. For direct quotations from these and other recording artists, see Martin and Segrave, *Anti-Rock*, 43–45. The comments from jazz musicians Hinton and Taylor, Martin and Segrave note, were elicited by *DownBeat* magazine for a forum published in May 1956.

42. "A Disgrace to Music," *Music Journal* 19, no. 18 (1961); "Mel Torme Sez U.S. Disk Jockeys Off-Key," *Variety*, July 10, 1961; "Rock 'n' Roll Assaulted," *Instrumentalist* 13 (September 1958); all quoted in Martin and Segrave, *Anti-Rock*, 47, 45, and 46.

43. Frank Sinatra, quoted in "The Rock Is Solid," *Time*, November 3, 1957, 33, and in Gertrude Samuels, "Why They Rock 'n' Roll—And Should They?" *New York Times Magazine*, January 12, 1958, 19. Many sources that deal with the negative reception of rock 'n' roll suggest that the statement emerged during an interview conducted by the *New York Times* writer, but Samuels reports that the statement "was quoted in a Paris magazine recently."

44. The term "leer-ics" was introduced in "A Warning to the Music Business," *Variety*, February 23, 1955. Martin and Segrave, *Anti-Rock*, 9.

45. "Rock Around at Princeton," *Billboard*, May 28, 1955, 35.

46. "Cambridge Acts after Teen Riot," *Christian Science Monitor*, March 12, 1956, 2.

47. "Rock 'n' Roll Banned," *New York Times*, September 20, 1954, 29.

48. Martin and Segrave, *Anti-Rock*, 30–31.

49. "Rock 'n' Roll B.O. Dynamite," *Variety*, April 11, 1956, 60.

50. "Rocking and Rolling," *Newsweek*, June 18, 1956, 42.

51. Murray Schumach, "The Teen-age Gang—Who and Why," *New York Times*, September 2, 1956, M4.

52. Clare Booth Luce, quoted in J. Ronald Oakley, *God's Country: America in the Fifties* (New York: Dembner Books, 1986), 273.

53. Screenings in England were more provocative, resulting in disturbances in London, Manchester, and numerous other cities. For anecdotes on the trouble that followed screenings of *Rock Around the Clock* both in the United States and abroad, see Martin and Segrave, *Anti-Rock*, 32–36; Jackson, *Big Beat Heat*, 122–24; and Peter Wicke, *Rock Music: Culture, Aesthetics, and Sociology* (Cambridge, UK: Cambridge University Press, 1990), 58–59.

54. For more on the debate over the objectionable content of EC Comics and other publications, see Bradford W. Wright, *Comic Book Nation: The Transformation of Youth Culture in America* (Baltimore: Johns Hopkins University Press, 2001).

55. Dore Schary, in "Juvenile Delinquency (Motion Pictures): Hearings before the Committee to Investigate Juvenile Delinquency of the Committee on the Judiciary, United States Senate: June 15, 16, 17 and 18, 1955" (Washington, DC: U.S. Government Printing Office, 1956), 120.

56. William Revelli, in "Juvenile Delinquency: Hearings before the Committee to Investigate Juvenile Delinquency of the Committee on the Judiciary, United States Senate: December 7, 1955" (Washington, DC: U.S. Government Printing Office, 1956), 47.

57. James Gilbert, *A Cycle of Outrage: America's Reaction to the Juvenile Delinquent in the 1950s* (New York: Oxford University Press, 1986), 77–78.

58. Andrew Ross, *No Respect: Intellectuals and Popular Culture* (London: Routledge, 1989), 51.

59. Ibid. The dissenters, Ross writes, were Norman Mailer and C. Wright Mills.

60. Bernard Rosenberg, "Mass Culture in America," in *Mass Culture: The Popular Arts in America*, ed. Bernard Rosenberg and David Manning White (Glencoe, IL: Free Press, 1957), 3.

61. Ibid.

62. Randy Roberts, "Wild Delinquents and Misunderstood Rebels" (review of James Gilbert's *A Cycle of Outrage*), *Reviews in American History* 15, no. 2 (1987): 328; Dwight Macdonald, quoted in Gilbert, "Popular Culture," 146.

63. Roberts, "Wild Delinquents," 330.

64. In June 1957 a ban on rock 'n' roll was imposed by the communist-influenced, but not yet communist-led, government of Egypt. Cuba, although not officially a communist nation until the rebel forces led by Fidel Castro overthrew the dictatorship of Fulgencio Batista in January 1959, in February 1957 officially banned television programs that featured rock 'n' roll. Along with condemning the United States for its lack of attention to traditional musical culture, Dmitri T. Shepilov, a secretary of the Soviet Communist Party, bitterly decried the American popular music he encountered during a 1956 visit (as foreign minister) to the United States. "All this nervous and insane boogie woogie and rock 'n' roll are the wild orgies of cavemen," he told a

gathering of the Congress of Soviet Composers. "They are devoid of any elements of beauty and melody. They represent an uncontrolled release of base passions, a burst of the lowest feelings and sexual urges." Dmitri T. Shepilov, quoted in "Shepilov Assails Music of the U.S.," *New York Times*, April 4, 1957, 5.

65. Michael T. Bertrand, *Race, Rock, and Elvis* (Urbana: University of Illinois Press, 2005), 138–39.

66. Mitch Miller, "June, Moon, Swoon and Ko Ko Mo," *New York Times Magazine*, April 24, 1955, 69–70.

67. Mitch Miller, "The Man Who Makes the Stars," *Melody Maker*, November 30, 1957; quoted in Martin and Segrave, *Anti-Rock*, 46.

68. Ibid.

69. Samuels, "Why They Rock 'n' Roll," 16–17.

70. Pioneering studies in the behavior of adolescents were begun as early as 1941 by sociologist Hermann H. Remmers at Purdue University in Indiana. Remmers and his colleague Don Radler published the results of more than fifteen years' worth of surveys in *The American Teenager* (New York: Bobbs-Merrill, 1957). In "The Adolescent: His Characteristics and Development" (*Review of Educational Research* 30, no. 1 (1960): 13–22), Jacob T. Hunt lists ninety-eight scholarly books or articles having to do with the psychology of American teenagers.

71. Dick Clark and Richard Robinson, *Rock, Roll & Remember* (New York: Crowell, 1976), 67.

72. Steve Chapple and Reebee Garafalo, *Rock 'n' Roll Is Here to Pay: The History and Politics of the Music Industry* (Chicago: Nelson-Hall, 1977), 272.

73. Leerom Medovici, "Mapping the Rebel Image: Postmodernism and the Masculinist Politics of Rock in the U.S.A.," *Cultural Critique* 20 (Winter 1991–1992): 158.

74. Glenn C. Altschuler, *All Shook Up: How Rock 'n' Roll Changed America* (New York: Oxford University Press, 2003), 86; emphasis added.

75. B. Lee Cooper, *Images of American Society in Popular Music* (Chicago: Nelson-Hall, 1982), 113.

76. Martin Luther King Jr., speech delivered at the annual convention of the National Association of Television and Radio Announcers, Atlanta, Georgia, August 11, 1967.

Chapter 3. Jazz

1. The 1951 *Duck and Cover* film, made by Archer Productions for the Federal Civil Defense Administration, is available as a special feature on a digital videodisc titled *Atomic War Bride / This Is Not a Test* (ID1178SWDVD).

2. Norman Mailer, "The White Negro: Superficial Reflections on the Hipster," *Dissent* 4, no. 3 (1957): 276. The essay was anthologized in Mailer's *Advertisements for Myself* (New York: Putnam) and later in *Keeping Time: Readings in Jazz History*, ed. Robert Walser (New York: Oxford University Press, 1999).

3. While the term "white negro" is invariably associated with Mailer, it had been in use since early in the nineteenth century in the West Indies "to describe white men who [had] become submerged among their Negro servants and concubines." Gary T. Marx, "The White Negro and the Negro White," *Phylon* 28, no. 2 (1967): 169. For a source, Marx refers to A. C. Carmichael, *Domestic Manners in the West Indies* (London: Whittaker, Treacher & Co., 1833).

4. Steve Shoemaker, "Norman Mailer's 'White Negro': Historical Myth or Mythical History?" *Twentieth-Century Literature* 37, no. 3 (1991): 350.

5. Joseph Wenke, *Mailer's America* (Hanover, NH: University Press of New England, 1987), 71.

6. Mailer, introduction to "White Negro," in *Advertisements for Myself*, 298.

7. Mailer, "White Negro," 287.

8. Anatole Broyard, "Portrait of the Hipster," *Partisan Review* 15, no. 5 (1948): 721–27.

9. Mailer, "White Negro," 279.

10. Paul Fritz Laubenstein, "Jazz—Debit and Credit," *Musical Quarterly* 15, no. 4 (1929): 614.

11. Ibid., 617.

12. Ted Gioia, *The Imperfect Art: Reflections on Jazz and Modern Culture* (Oxford: Oxford University Press, 1988), 18.

13. See, for example, Ted Gioia, *The History of Jazz* (New York: Oxford University Press, 1997), and Scott DeVeaux, *The Birth of Bebop: A Social and Musical History* (Berkeley: University of California Press, 1997).

14. Ellington hosted annual concerts at Carnegie Hall between 1943 and 1952. On January 21, 1951, his band performed at the Metropolitan Opera House in a concert whose proceeds benefited the National Association for the Advancement of Colored People (NAACP).

15. For details on the music's southward migration, see DeVeaux, *Birth of Bebop*, 273–94.

16. Marshall Stearns, *The Story of Jazz* (New York: Oxford University Press, 1958), 155.

17. Bill Gottlieb, "Bebop Has Swing Stuff on the Run," *Washington Post*, September 28, 1947, L6.

18. Carter Harman, "Bop, Skee, Re or Be, 'It's Still Got to Swing,'" *New York Times*, December 5, 1948, X13.

19. Thomas Owens, "Bop," in the *New Grove Dictionary of American Music*, ed. H. Wiley Hitchcock and Stanley Sadie (London: Macmillan, 1986), 1: 260. The recording is of the song "Hotter Than That" (Okeh 8535).

20. "Ella Wants 'Dizzy' for Tour," *Chicago Defender*, August 31, 1946, 10; "Cootie Praises 'Dizzy's' Style," *Chicago Defender*, May 18, 1946, 10.

21. Display ad, *Los Angeles Times*, October 26, 1946, 4.

22. Display ad, *New York Times*, April 27, 1947, X2.

23. "Jazz Enters Curricula," *Los Angeles Times*, November 2, 1948, B1.

24. Leslie Lieber, "King of the Monkeys," *Los Angeles Times*, January 11, 1948, E10. The former name refers, of course, to the Cuban bandleader who through recordings and appearances in films helped spur America's interest in such Latin genres as the mambo, the conga, and the cha-cha.

25. Owens, "Bop."

26. J. W. W. [John Wesley Work], "Bop," in *The Harvard Dictionary of Music*, 2nd ed., ed. Willi Apel (Cambridge: Belknap Press of Harvard University Press, 1969), 101.

27. "Bop (bebop, rebop)," in J. A. Westrup and F. L. Harrison, rev. Conrad Wilson, *The New College Encyclopedia of Music* (New York: W. W. Norton, 1976), 79.

28. "Bebop," in Theodore Baker, *Pocket Manual of Musical Terms*, 5th ed., rev. Laura Kuhn (New York: Schirmer, 1995), 33.

29. "Radio and Television," *New York Times*, August 21, 1948, 26.

30. Display ad, *New York Times*, November 7, 1948, BR14. The book was published by Citadel Press.

31. Carter Harman, "Hot, Cool, and Gone," *New York Times*, July 31, 1949, BR18. The book was published by J. J. Robbins & Sons.

32. Will Davidson, "Recordially Yours," *Chicago Tribune*, January 19, 1947, C23. Davidson does not give the source of the Feather quotation.

33. Ibid.

34. Ibid. The four-disc Victor album under review is *New 52nd Street Jazz*.

35. Gottlieb, "Bebop Has Swing Stuff on the Run."

36. Harman, "Bop, Skee, Re or Be."

37. Ibid.

38. Of the artists just mentioned, all are African American except Herman, Kenton, Raeburn, McKinley, and Tormé.

39. For commentary on how jazz related not just to the civil rights movement in the United States but also to the African Independence movement, see Ingrid Monson, *Freedom Sounds: Civil Rights Call Out to Jazz and Africa* (Oxford: Oxford University Press, 2007). See LeRoi Jones, *Blues People: Negro Music in White America* (New York: HarperCollins, 1963), especially chapter 12, "The Modern Scene." In 1967 Jones took the African name Imamu Ameer Baraka, which he later shortened to Amiri Baraka.

40. Burton W. Peretti, "Caliban Reheard: New Voices on Jazz and American Consciousness," *Popular Music* 13, no. 2 (1994): 155–56.

41. For a blistering example of the black-oriented "reclamation" argument, see Kalamu ya Salaam (né Vallery Ferdinand III), "It Didn't Jes Grew: The Social and Aesthetic Significance of African American Music," *African American Review* 29, no. 2 (1995): 351–75. For expressions of the neo-Marxist argument, see Frank Kofsky, *Black Music, White Business: Illuminating the History and Political Economy of Jazz* (New York: Pathfinder, 1998). For pointed criticism of Kofsky's argument, see Peter J. Martin, "Black Music—White History?" *Race Relations Abstracts* 25, no. 2 (2000): 3–18.

42. Krin Gabbard, introduction to *Representing Jazz*, ed. Krin Gabbard (Durham, NC: Duke University Press, 1995), 2.

43. Eric Porter, "'Dizzy Atmosphere': The Challenge of Bebop," *American Music* 17, no. 4 (1999): 423.

44. Preston Whaley Jr., *Blows Like a Horn: Beat Writing, Jazz, Style, and Markets in the Transformation of U.S. Culture* (Cambridge: Harvard University Press, 2004), 27–28.

45. DeVeaux, *Birth of Bebop*, 6.

46. Ibid., 238.

47. Ibid.

48. Ibid.

49. Dwight D. Eisenhower, address to the U.S. Senate, July 27, 1954; quoted in Penny M. von Eschen, *Satchmo Blows Up the World: Jazz Ambassadors Play the Cold War* (Cambridge: Harvard University Press, 2004), 4. For more on the *Porgy and Bess* tour and subsequent tours sponsored by the U.S. State Department, see von Eschen, *Race against Empire: Black Americans and Anticolonialism, 1937–57* (Ithaca, NY: Cornell University Press, 1997).

50. Quoted in Monson, *Freedom Sounds*, 113.

51. Ibid., 114.

52. "Remote Lands to Hear Old Democracy Boogie," *New York Times*, November 18, 1955, 16.

53. "Dizzy to Rock India," *New York Times*, February 2, 1956, 19.

54. Dizzy Gillespie (with Al Fraser), *To Be or Not to Bop: Memoirs of Dizzy Gillespie* (New York: Da Capo Press, 1979), 417.

55. Scott Gac, "Jazz Strategy: Dizzy, Foreign Policy, and Government in 1956," *Americana: The Journal of American Popular Culture* 4, no. 1 (2005). Available online at http://www.americanpopularculture.com/journal/articles/spring_2005/gac.htm.

56. Ibid. See also Gillespie, *To Be or Not to Bop*, 414–16, and Alyn Shipton, *Groovin' High: The Life of Dizzy Gillespie* (New York: Oxford University Press, 1999), 280.

57. Quoted in Monson, *Freedom Sounds*, 114.

58. Burt Korall, "Jazz Speaks Many Tongues, Vaults National Barriers: Wider Jazz Market a By-Product of American Diplomacy Policy," *Billboard*, August 19, 1957, 1.

59. Quoted in Frances Stonor Saunders, *The Cultural Cold War: The CIA and the World of Arts and Letters* (New York: New Press, 1999), 256–57.

60. DeVeaux, *Birth of Bebop*, 238.

61. Ronald Radano, "Hot Fantasies: American Modernism and the Idea of Black Rhythm," in *Music and the Racial Imagination*, 459–80, ed. Ronald Radano and Philip V. Bohlman (Chicago: University of Chicago Press, 2000); Ronald Radano, *Lying Up a Nation: Race and Black Music* (Chicago: University of Chicago Press, 2003), 11–12.

62. Allen Ginsberg, "Howl," in *"Howl" and Other Poems* (San Francisco: City Lights, 1955), 9.

63. [John] Clellon Holmes, "This Is the Beat Generation," *New York Times Magazine*, November 16, 1952, SM10.

64. Ibid.

65. Kerouac's *Beat Generation* was discovered in a New Jersey warehouse in 2005. Its premiere performance—in the form of a staged reading by the Merrimack Repertory Theatre and the theater department of the University of Massachusetts–Lowell—took place in Lowell, Massachusetts, in October 2012.

66. Gene Feldman and Max Gartenberg, eds., *The Beat Generation and the Angry Young Men* (New York: Citadel Press, 1958).

67. Herb Caen, "Bagdad-by-the-Bay," *San Francisco Chronicle*, April 2, 1958; quoted in Tom Dalzell, *Flappers 2 Rappers: American Youth Slang* (Springfield, IL: Merriam-Webster, 1996), 91.

68. Ann Charters, *Kerouac* (San Francisco: Straight Arrow Press, 1973), 292–94.

69. Richard Rex, "The Origin of *Beatnik*," *American Speech* 50, no. 14 (1975): 330.

70. Joe Hyams, "Good-by to the Beatniks!" *Los Angeles Times*, September 28, 1958, TW33.

71. William Leonard, "In Chicago, We're Mostly Unbeat," *Chicago Sunday Tribune Magazine*, November 9, 1958, 8.

72. Kenneth Keniston, "Social Change and Youth in America," *Dædelus* 91, no. 1 (1962): 163.

73. Mel Van Elteren, "The Subculture of the Beats: A Sociological Revisit," *Journal of American Culture* 22, no. 3 (1999): 95.

74. Ray Carney, "Escape Velocity: Notes on Beat Film," in *Beat Culture and the New America: 1950–1965*, ed. Lisa Phillips (New York: Whitney Museum of American Art, 1995), 202.

75. Richard A. Schwartz, "Family, Gender, and Society in 1950s American Fiction of Nuclear Apocalypse: *Shadow on the Hearth*, *Tomorrow!*, *The Last Day*, and *Alas, Babylon*," *Journal of American Culture* 29, no. 4 (2006): 409. Schwartz's article is devoted primarily to '50s novels that represent dystopian or post-holocaust futures. An earlier review of the same literature, which similarly positions the contributions of the Beats within a broad context of fiction and poetry, is Ihab Hassan, "The Character of Post-War Fiction in America," *English Journal* 51, no. 1 (1962): 1–8.

76. Ginsberg, "America," in *"Howl" and Other Poems*, 39.

77. André Hodeir, *Jazz: Its Evolution and Essence*, trans. David Noakes (New York: Grove Press, 1956), 15. The book was originally titled *Hommes et problèmes du jazz* (Marseilles: Parenthèses, 1954).

78. Becker's 1949 MA thesis for the University of Chicago was titled "The Professional Dance Musician in Chicago." Summaries of his ethnographic research and conclusions were published as "The Professional Dance Musician and His Audience," *American Journal of Sociology* 57, no. 2 (1951) and "Some Contingencies of the Professional Dance Musician's Career," *Human Organization* 12 (Spring 1953), then expanded in chapters of his *Outsiders: Studies in the Sociology of Deviance* (New

York: Free Press, 1963). Becker persisted in using the term "dance musician," but it is clear that he was writing not about members of large swing bands that indeed accompanied dancing, but, rather, about members of small bebop-style combos whose music was intended less for dancing than for listening.

79. Along with Becker's, the more impressive sociological studies include William B. Cameron, "Sociological Notes on the Jam Session," *Social Forces* 33, no. 2 (1954): 177–82; and Alan P. Merriam and Raymond W. Mack, "The Jazz Community," *Social Forces* 38, no. 3 (1960): 211–22.

80. Gioia, *History of Jazz*, 201.

81. Jack Kerouac, *On the Road* (New York: Viking, 1957), 180.

82. Dick Hebdige, *Subculture: The Meaning of Style* (London: Methuen, 1979), 47.

83. Aaron H. Esman, "Jazz: A Study in Cultural Conflict," *American Imago* 8, no. 2 (1951): 221–25.

84. Norman M. Margolis, "A Theory on the Psychology of Jazz," *American Imago* 11, no. 3 (Fall 1954): 276.

85. Referring to rock 'n' roll's characteristic accented second and fourth beats, Berry's protagonist sings: "Just let me hear some of that / Rock and roll music / Any old way you choose it, / It's got a back beat, you can't lose it / Any old time you use it."

Chapter 4. Hollywood

1. Fred Vinson, quoted in "Secretary Vinson: In the 'Chaos' of Reconversion, He Stands Reassuringly for Goals the Country Wants," *Life*, July 23, 1945, 28. Vinson was director of the U.S. Office of War Mobilization and Reconversion.

2. Lary May, "Making the American Way: Moderne Theatres, Audiences, and the Film Industry, 1929–1945," *Prospects* 12 (October 1987): 92.

3. Ibid., 108–9.

4. Gerald Mast, *A Short History of the Movies* (New York: Pegasus, 1971), 272.

5. David O. Selznick, quoted in "Films 'Struggle,' Selznick Asserts," *New York Times*, March 31, 1949, 30. Selznick was addressing the annual convention of the National Board of Review of Motion Pictures.

6. Writing in 1971, Gerald Mast stated with confidence that 1946 was "the peak box-office year in movie history." Mast, *Short History*, 315. With the figures adjusted for inflation, Mast's statement still holds true.

7. "Movie Crisis Laid to Video Inroads and Dwindling of Foreign Market," *New York Times*, February 27, 1949, F1.

8. The House Committee on Un-American Activities was established in 1938 on an ad hoc basis and became a standing committee in 1945. In 1969 it was renamed the Internal Security Committee. HUAC was disbanded in 1975 and its duties were assigned to the House Judiciary Committee that had been in existence since 1813.

9. The "Hollywood Ten" comprised director Edward Dmytrik; screenwriter/director Herbert Biberman; screenwriter/producer Adrian Scott; and screenwriters Alvah Bes-

sie, Lester Cole, Ring Lardner Jr., John Howard Lawson, Albert Maltz, Samuel Ornitz, and Dalton Trumbo.

10. Among the more famous names on the blacklist were those of actors Eddie Albert, Orson Bean, Harry Belafonte, Irwin Corey, Dolores del Rio, José Ferrer, John Garfield, Lee Grant, Sam Jaffe, Burgess Meredith, Henry Morgan, Zero Mostel, Cliff Robertson, Paul Robeson, Edward G. Robinson, and Sam Wanamaker; directors Luis Buñuel and Charles Chaplin; writers Dashiel Hammett, Lillian Hellman, Langston Hughes, Arthur Miller, Dorothy Parker, Irwin Shaw, and Orson Welles; composers Elmer Bernstein, Marc Blitzstein, Aaron Copland, and Morton Gould; lyricist "Yip" Harburg; musicologist Alan Lomax; and folksinger Pete Seeger.

11. Irwin A. Conroe, quoted in Thomas M. Pryor, "Film Censorship Policy Defined," *New York Times*, February 10, 1946, 47. Since March 1945 Conroe had been acting director of the Motion Picture Division of the State Education Department of New York.

12. Samuel Goldwyn, quoted in "Sam Goldwyn Hits at Film Censorship," *Los Angeles Times*, September 15, 1949, A1.

13. Thomas M. Pryor, "Stritch Exhorts Theatre Owners—Cardinal Blames Economic Ills of Film Industry on Failure to Set Higher Standard," *New York Times*, September 26, 1948, 80.

14. Goldwyn, in "Sam Goldwyn Hits at Film Censorship."

15. Mike Conway, "A Guest in Our Living Room: The Television Newscaster before the Rise of the Dominant Anchor," *Journal of Broadcasting and Electronic Media* 51, no. 3 (2007): 464.

16. Samuel Goldwyn, "Hollywood in the Television Age," *New York Times*, February 13, 1949, SM15.

17. Peter Lev, *The Fifties: Transforming the Screen, 1950–1959* (Berkeley: University of California Press, 2003), 9. Lev's figures are drawn primarily from the FCC as reported by Christopher R. Sterling and Timothy R. Haight in *The Mass Media: Aspen Institute Guide to Communication Industry Trends* (New York: Praeger, 1978).

18. Gladwin Hill, "Hollywood Movie Men Facing Grim Problems," *New York Times*, February 22, 1948, E7; Gladwin Hill, "Hollywood Is Wary of TV," *New York Times*, April 24, 1949, XX18.

19. "TV's Impact a Puzzler," *Variety*, March 22, 1951, 1.

20. Samuel Goldwyn, quoted in "Goldwyn Decries Movie Censorship," *New York Times*, September 15, 1949, 34.

21. Thomas F. Brady, "Hollywood, 1947—Film Industry Not Sorry over Passing of Troubled Year Here and Abroad," *New York Times*, December 28, 1947, X5.

22. Thomas Schatz, *The Genius of the System: Hollywood Filmmaking in the Studio Era* (New York: Henry Holt, 1988), 411.

23. "Big Film Concerns Accused in U.S. Suit of Acting as Trust," *New York Times*, July 21, 1938, 1.

24. Ibid.

25. "Film Industry Given Setbacks by High Court," *Chicago Tribune*, May 4, 1948, 5.

26. "Supreme Court Upholds Government's Major Anti-Trust Charges against Film Distributors," *Wall Street Journal*, May 4, 1948, 3. For a detailed account of how the studio system worked, see Schatz, *Genius of the System, 159–481.*

27. Mast, *Short History*, 316.

28. Ibid., 316–17.

29. For differently worded yet wholly compatible lists of the musical conventions of the classical-style film, see, for example, Claudia Gorbman, *Unheard Melodies: Narrative Film Music* (Bloomington: Indiana University Press, 1987), 73–91, and Kathryn Kalinak, *Settling the Score: Music and the Classical Hollywood Film* (Madison: University of Wisconsin Press, 1992), 66–134.

30. Hill, "Hollywood Movie Men," E7.

31. Peter Biskind, *Seeing Is Believing: How Hollywood Taught Us to Stop Worrying and Love the Fifties* (New York: Henry Holt, 1983), 3–4.

32. Joyce A. Evans, *Celluloid Mushroom Clouds: Hollywood and the Atomic Bomb* (Boulder, CO: Westview Press, 1998), 75. Evans notes that between 1948 and 1962 approximately five hundred science fiction feature films and shorts were produced in the United States.

33. J. P. Telotte, *Science Fiction Film* (Cambridge, UK: Cambridge University Press, 2001), 96.

34. Susan Sontag, "The Imagination of Disaster," in *Against Interpretation and Other Essays* (New York: Farrar, Straus, and Giroux, 1966), 224.

35. Daniel Mainwaring's screenplay for Don Siegel's 1956 *Invasion of the Body Snatchers* is based on Jack Finney's *The Body Snatchers*, first published in serial fashion in the magazine *Collier's* in 1954 and then as a novel (New York: Dell) in 1955.

36. Carlos Clarens, *An Illustrated History of the Horror Film* (New York: Capricorn Books, 1967), 134; cited in Vivian Sobchack, *Screening Space: The American Science Fiction Film* (New York: Ungar, 1993), 123.

37. Thomas Doherty, *Teenagers and Teenpics: The Juvenilization of American Movies in the 1950s*, 2nd ed. (Philadelphia: Temple University Press, 2002), 161–62.

38. Biskind, *Seeing Is Believing*, 4.

39. Ibid.

40. Ibid.

41. Krin Gabbard, *Jammin' at the Margins: Jazz and the American Cinema* (Chicago: University of Chicago Press, 1996), 9.

42. Kalinak, *Settling the Score*, 167.

43. Gabbard, *Jammin' at the Margins*, 134.

44. Peter Townsend, *Jazz in American Culture* (Edinburgh, UK: Edinburgh University Press, 2000), 99.

45. Gabbard, *Jammin' at the Margins*, 79.

46. The postwar biopics that dealt with famous composers included *The Magic Bow* (1946), about Niccolò Paganini, and *Magic Fire* (1955), about Wagner. The "song" series ended, one hopes, with *Song of Norway* (1970), a film about Grieg.

47. These were *That Midnight Kiss* (1949), *The Toast of New Orleans* (1950), *Because You're Mine* (1952), *Serenade* (1956), and *For the First Time* (1959).

48. The notable exception, of course, is *The Glenn Miller Story*. The biopic celebrates the career of the bandleader (and, later, officer in the U.S. Army) who went missing in action when the plane on which he was flying apparently crashed into the English Channel in December 1944.

49. For attempts at definitions of the so-called film noir, see Raymond Border and Etienne Chaumeton, "Toward a Definition of *Film Noir*," in *Film Noir Reader*, ed. Alain Silver and James Ursini (New York: Limelight Editions, 1996), 17–26; Alexander Ballinger and Danny Graydon, *The Rough Guide to Film Noir* (London: Rough Guides, 2007), 4–5; and James Naremore, *More Than Night: Film Noir in Its Contexts*, 2nd ed. (Berkeley: University of California Press, 2008), 15–16.

50. *Hangover Square* was released in February 1945, so it is not really a postwar film. In a discussion of postwar film-music semiotics, however, its narrative is nonetheless noteworthy. In addition to being moved to murder whenever he hears ear-jarring noise, the high-minded composer is "corrupted" when a cabaret singer seduces him into writing songs for her.

51. Peter Kivy, *The Possessor and the Possessed: Handel, Mozart, Beethoven, and the Idea of Musical Genius* (New Haven, CT: Yale University Press, 2001), 21.

52. John C. Tibbetts, *Composers in the Movies* (New Haven, CT: Yale University Press, 2005), 9.

53. Ibid.

54. Heather Laing, *The Gendered Score: Music in 1940s Melodrama and the Woman's Film* (Aldershot, UK: Ashgate, 2007), 71.

55. Ibid., 99.

56. Elmer Bernstein, "What Ever Happened to Great Movie Music?," *High Fidelity*, July 1972, 58.

57. Ibid.; emphasis original.

58. Although the title song in *High Noon* is commonly known as "Do Not Forsake Me, Oh My Darlin'," officially it bears the title "The Ballad of High Noon." In the 1951 film the song is sung, off-camera, by Tex Ritter, and its popularization came with the 1952 commercial recording by Frankie Laine. In *The Man with the Golden Arm* the main title theme was performed by Shorty Rogers and His Giants; independent of the film, it was recorded by ensembles led by Les Elgart (1956), Billy May (1956), Richard Maltby (1956), Ray Anthony (1960), and Jet Harris (1962).

59. Gabbard, *Jammin' at the Margins*, 77.

60. Richard R. Ness, "A Lotta Night Music: The Sound of *Film Noir*," *Cinema Journal* 47, no. 2 (2008): 52.

61. Roger Hickman, "Wavering Sonorities and the Nascent Film Noir Musical Style," *Journal of Film Music* 2, nos. 2–4 (2009): 165–66.

62. Christopher Coady, "AfroModernist Subversion of Film Noir Conventions in John Lewis' Score to *Sait-on Jamais* (1957) and *Odds Against Tomorrow* (1959)," *Musicology Australia* 34, no. 1 (2012): 1.

63. J. D. Spiro, "Hollywood Resume: Producers and Petrillo Face the Music," *New York Times*, August 15, 1948, X3.

64. "Independents Band Together," *New York Times*, August 27, 1948, 12; "Indie Pix Want End to Deal on Contract Bands," *Billboard*, September 4, 1948, 17.

65. "5% Wage Rise Is Won by Movie Musicians," *New York Times*, January 28, 1954, 23.

66. "Musicians Guild Wins 14% Hike in Studio Pay," *Los Angeles Times*, August 28, 1958, B3.

67. Thomas Pryor, "Musicians Guild Wins Coast Vote," *New York Times*, July 13, 1958, 16.

68. Composers for the cited films are Malcolm Arnold (*The Bridge on the River Kwai*), Elmer Bernstein (*The Magnificent Seven*, *The Ten Commandments*), Mario Nascimbene (*The Vikings*), Alfred Newman (*The Robe*), Alex North (*Spartacus*), Miklós Rózsa (*Ben-Hur*, *King of Kings*, *Knights of the Round Table*, *El Cid*), Max Steiner (*The Searchers*), and Dimitri Tiomkin (*The Alamo*, *The Guns of Navarone*).

Chapter 5. Broadway

1. Lehman Engel's *The American Musical Theater: A Consideration* was published in 1967 by CBS Records and distributed, in a limited edition, by Macmillan. The more widely read revised edition, titled simply *The American Musical Theater* and published by Collier in 1975, includes in the chapter on "the contemporary musical" two shows—*Company* (1970) and *A Little Night Music* (1973)—with lyrics as well as music by Stephen Sondheim.

2. Engel, *American Musical Theater*, 40.

3. Ibid., 39.

4. Ibid.

5. Ibid., 40.

6. Lehman Engel and Howard Kissel, *Words with Music: Creating the Broadway Musical Libretto* (New York: Applause Books, 1971), 113.

7. Stacy Wolf, *A Problem Like Maria: Gender and Sexuality in the American Musical* (Ann Arbor: University of Michigan Press, 2002), 16.

8. William H. Chafe, "Social Change and the American Woman, 1940–1970," in *A History of Our Time: Readings on Postwar America*, ed. William H. Chafe and Harvard Sitkoff (New York: Oxford University Press, 1987), 208.

9. Maureen Honey, *Creating Rosie the Riveter: Class, Gender, and Propaganda during World War II* (Amherst: University of Massachusetts Press, 1984), 19.

10. Chafe, "Social Change," 210.

11. Ibid.

12. J. Edgar Hoover, "The Twin Enemies of Freedom: Crime and Communism," an address to the 28th Annual Convention of the National Council of Catholic Women, Chicago, November 9, 1956; quoted in E. May, *Homeward Bound*, 121.

13. John D. Durand, "Married Women in the Labor Force," *American Journal of Sociology* 52 (November 1946): 221.

14. "Books versus Babies," *Newsweek*, January 14, 1946, 79; quoted and paraphrased in E. May, *Homeward Bound*, 123.

15. Miller and Nowak, *The Fifties*, 153.

16. William H. Chafe, *The Paradox of Change: American Women in the 20th Century* (New York: Oxford University Press, 1992), 175.

17. Chafe, "Social Change," 211–12.

18. Ibid., 212.

19. E. May, "Explosive Issues," 166.

20. The quoted lyrics are from a same-titled song by Frank Churchill and Larry Morey that occurs two-thirds of the way through Walt Disney's 1937 animated feature film *Snow White and the Seven Dwarfs*; early in the film the character of Snow White, sorely in need of fulfillment via romance, sings a song titled "I'm Wishing (For the One I Love)."

21. The notable exception is "Broadway's most famous mother: *Gypsy*'s Mama Rose, described by reviewer Walter Kerr as 'the mastadon of all stage mothers.'" Stacy Wolf, *Changed for Good: A Feminist History of The Broadway Musical* (Oxford: Oxford University Press, 2011), 30.

22. George Gallup and Evan Hill, "The American Woman: Her Attitudes on Family, Sex, Religion and Society," *Saturday Evening Post*, December 22, 1962, 32. The comment by pollsters Gallup and Hill is quoted or paraphrased in, for example, Elizabeth Rose, *A Mother's Job: The History of Day Care, 1890–1960* (Oxford: Oxford University Press, 1998), 194; Alice Kessler-Harris, *Out to Work: A History of Wage-Earning Women in the United States* (Oxford: Oxford University Press, 1983), 301–2; and Rebecca Jo Plant, *Mom: The Transformation of Motherhood in Modern America* (Chicago: University of Chicago Press, 1983), 38.

23. It was not until 1967 that the U.S. Supreme Court declared antimiscegenation laws to be unconstitutional.

24. The details of America's various antimiscegenation laws are reported on the apparently well researched "Anti-miscegenation laws in the United States" Wikipedia page, available at http://en.wikipedia.org/wiki/Anti-miscegenation_laws_in_the_United_States.

25. Frances Negrón-Muntaner, "Feeling Pretty: *West Side Story* and Puerto Rican Identity Discourses," *Social Text* 18, no. 2 (2000): 92.

26. James A. Michener, *Tales of the South Pacific* (New York: Macmillan, 1949), 111–12.

27. James A. Michener, quoted in Hugh Fordin, *Getting to Know Him: A Biography of Oscar Hammerstein II* (New York: Da Capo Press, 1995), 270–71.

28. Andrea Most, "'You've Got to Be Carefully Taught': The Politics of Race in Rodgers and Hammerstein's *South Pacific*," *Theatre Journal* 52, no. 3 (2000): 308. The quoted material comes from an article in the *New York Herald Tribune*, March 2, 1953.

29. John Bush Jones, *Our Musicals, Ourselves: A Social History of the American Musical Theatre* (Lebanon, NH: University Press of England, 2003), 152.

30. Ibid., 152–53.

31. Stephen Citron, *The Wordsmiths: Oscar Hammerstein 2nd and Alan Jay Lerner* (New York: Oxford University Press, 1995), 193.

32. Philip D. Beidler, "*South Pacific* and American Remembering; or, 'Josh, We're Going to Buy That Son of a Bitch!'" *Journal of American Studies* 27, no. 2 (1993): 214.

33. Most, "'You've Got to Be Carefully Taught,'" 314.

34. Ibid., 317.

35. For more on the origins of *West Side Story*, see, for example, Joan Peyser, *Leonard Bernstein: A Biography* (New York: Beech Tree Press, 1987), 255–58, and Meryle Secrest, *Leonard Bernstein: A Life* (New York: Alfred A. Knopf, 1994), 211–13.

36. Negrón-Muntaner, "Feeling Pretty," 90.

37. Leonard Bernstein, quoted in Al Kasha and Joel Hirschhorn, *Notes on Broadway: Intimate Conversations with Broadway's Greatest Songwriters* (New York: Simon and Schuster, 1987), 15; emphasis original.

38. Wilfrid Mellers, "*West Side Story* Revisited," in *Approaches to the American Musical*, ed. Robert Lawson-Peebles (Exeter: University of Exeter Press, 1996), 134.

39. Denny Martin Flinn, *Musical! A Grand Tour* (New York: Schirmer, 1997), 254.

40. As Peter Biskind points out in the third chapter ("Pods and Blobs," 101–59) of his *Seeing Is Believing*, the vast majority of sci-fi invader films promote a right-wing agenda according to which the aliens, because they are in so many ways "different," simply *need* to be defeated. But sci-fi films from the Fifties also include left-wing efforts (for example, *The Day the Earth Stood Still* [1951], *It Came from Outer Space* [1953], and *This Island Earth* [1955]) that suggest that aliens, just because they appear to be different, are not necessarily hostile. These exceptions are so few, however, that they prove the rule.

41. Bruce A. McConachie, "The 'Oriental' Musicals of Rodgers and Hammerstein and the U.S. War in Southeast Asia," *Theatre Journal* 46, no. 3 (1994): 385.

42. The term "containment" was indeed popularized by its use in the 1947 "Sources of Soviet Conduct" article, but Kennan had used a variation of the word almost a year earlier in an address delivered to the U.S. State Department. Speaking in September 1946, he told his audience that his recommendations, if acted upon, "should enable us, if our policies are wise and non-provocative, to contain them [the Russians] both militarily and politically for a long time to come." George F. Kennan, *Memoirs: 1925–1950* (Boston: Little, Brown, 1967), 304.

43. "X" (aka George F. Kennan), "The Sources of Soviet Conduct," *Foreign Affairs* 25 (July 1947): 569.

44. Christina Klein, *Cold War Orientalism: Asia in the Middlebrow Imagination, 1945–1961* (Berkeley: University of California Press, 2003), 25–26.

45. Christina Klein, "Musicals and Modernization: Rodgers and Hammerstein's *The King and I*," in *Staging Growth: Modernization, Development, and the Global Cold War*, ed. David C. Engerman, Nils Gilman, Mark H. Haefele, and Michael E. Latham (Amherst: University of Massachusetts Press, 2003), 130.

46. Ibid., 132.

47. McConachie, "'Oriental' Musicals," 385–86.

48. Ibid., 396.

49. Ibid., 392.

50. Ibid., 397.

51. Most, "'You've Got to Be Carefully Taught,'" 312.

52. Marco Mariano, "Fear of a Nonwhite Planet: Clare Booth Luce, Race, and American Foreign Policy," *Prospects* 29 (2005): 374.

53. Thomas Borstelmann, *The Cold War and the Color Line: American Race Relations in the Global Arena* (Cambridge: Harvard University Press, 2001), 30.

54. Paul Filmer, Val Rimmer, and Dave Walsh, "*Oklahoma!*: Ideology and Politics in the Vernacular Tradition of the American Musical," *Popular Music* 18, no. 3 (1999): 383; David Walsh and Len Platt, *Musical Theater and American Culture* (Westport, CT: Praeger, 2003), 104.

55. Negrón-Muntaner, "Feeling Pretty," 93.

56. Wolf, *Problem Like Maria*, 31.

57. Wolf, *Changed for Good*, 31; emphasis added.

58. Wolf, *Problem Like Maria*, 31.

59. Thomas Patrick Doherty, *Cold War, Cool Medium: Television, McCarthyism, and American Culture* (New York: Columbia University Press, 2005), 128. Gavel-to-gavel telecasts of the so-called Army-McCarthy hearings, from April 22 through June 17, were aired by the ABC and DuMont networks.

60. Except for the obvious fact that it is based on characters and a plot created by Scottish playwright J. M. Barrie, the 1954 Broadway musical has almost nothing in common with the same-titled animated feature-length film that had been released by the Disney studio in February 1953.

61. *Allegro* opened in October 1947 and played for 315 performances.

62. *Me and Juliet* opened in May 1953 and played for 358 performances. Like the 1947 *Allegro*, *Me and Juliet* had a run long enough for it to be profitable. Only in relation to Rodgers and Hammerstein's fabulously successful other shows can *Me and Juliet*, like *Allegro*, be "classified as a failure." Frederick W. Nolan, *The Sound of Their Music: The Story of Rodgers and Hammerstein* (Milwaukee, WI: Applause Theatre & Cinema Books, 2002), 225.

63. Kim H. Kowalke, untitled review of nine books, *Journal of the American Musicological Society* 60, no. 3 (2007): 690.

64. James L. Baughman, *Same Time, Same Station: Creating American Television, 1948–1961* (Baltimore: Johns Hopkins University Press, 2007), 111.

65. Ibid. Baughman does not identify the NBC producer, but in an endnote (361–62n140) attached to his next sentence, which does not include a direct quotation, he refers to correspondence between Don Bishop and Ellis Moore and between Bob Daubenspeck and David Sarnoff.

66. The January 9, 1956, telecast, again part of the *Producers' Showcase* series, attracted a viewing audience of "more than 55,000,000." Val Adams, "N.B.C. Is Planning

'Peter Pan' Again," *New York Times*, November 4, 1957, 47. The December 8, 1960, telecast, aired simply as a "special," attracted "21 million viewers." Tim Allis, Victoria Balfour, and Doris Bacon, "Back from Legal Never-Never Land, Mary Martin's Magical *Peter Pan* Soars on the Airwaves Again," *People* 31, no. 12, March 27, 1989, 55. The 1960 videotaped performance was rebroadcast by NBC in 1963, 1966, 1973, 1989, and 1990.

67. A 1938 recording on the Musicraft label documents Marc Blitzstein's *The Cradle Will Rock*, albeit not with the original orchestrations but only with piano accompaniments. A 1939 recording (on the AEI label, produced not for commercial release but for distribution to radio outlets) documents Jerome Kern and Oscar Hammerstein II's *Very Warm for May*, but it does not include all of the show's songs.

68. Decca released a *Selections from George Gershwin's Folk Opera "Porgy and Bess"* album in conjunction with that show's 1942 Broadway revival and then followed up with original cast recordings of *Oklahoma!*, *Carmen Jones*, *Carousel*, and *Annie Get Your Gun*. Competing for a share of what promised to be a lucrative market, in 1946 Capitol produced an original cast recording of Harold Arlen and Johnny Mercer's *St. Louis Woman*, and the next year RCA Victor released a similar treatment of Lerner and Loewe's *Brigadoon*. Columbia's first entries into the arena involved the casts of the 1946 Broadway revival of Kern and Hammerstein's vintage *Show Boat* and the new 1947 *Finian's Rainbow* by Burton Lane and E. Y. Harburg.

69. In 1948 Columbia introduced the 33⅓ rpm disc in both 7-inch and 10-inch sizes, and only the latter was called "long play"; it was not until 1951 that Columbia introduced the "extended long play" 12-inch 33⅓ rpm disc, which accommodated approximately twenty minutes of music per side.

70. Beidler, "South Pacific," 217.

71. *Billboard*, "Singles Hit Makers Crash LP Charts Often, Fade Fast," September 7, 1953, 3; quoted in Keir Keightley, "Long Play: Adult-Oriented Popular Music and the Temporal Logics of the Post-War Sound Recording Industry in the USA," *Media, Culture & Society* 26, no. 3 (2004): 383.

72. Keightley, "Long Play," 383.

73. Geoffrey Block, "The Broadway Canon from *Show Boat* to *West Side Story* and the European Operatic Ideal," *Journal of Musicology* 11, no. 4 (1993): 532.

74. Ibid., 531.

75. Beidler, "South Pacific," 217.

76. Louis Scheeder, review of Ethan Mordden's *Coming Up Roses: The Broadway Musical of the 1950s*, *TDR: The Drama Review* 46, no. 1 (2002): 175.

Chapter 6. Opera

1. The pejorative phrase comes from "Red Visitors Cause Rumpus: Dupes and Fellow Travelers Dress Up Communist Fronts," *Life*, April 4, 1949, 42–43. The summary of the conference's noble goals, as stated by conference chair Harlow Shapely, comes

from Bertram D. Hulen, "U.S. to Admit Red Delegates; Scores Aims of Parley Here," *New York Times*, March 17, 1949, 1.

2. The June 22, 1950, special issue of *Counterattack* was titled "Red Channels: The Report of Communist Influence in Radio and Television." Although officially anonymous, "Red Channels" is commonly thought to be the work of various agents of the FBI. For a full account of "Red Channels" and its damaging effect on the American cultural industry, see Doherty, *Cold War, Cool Medium*.

3. Copland's *Lincoln Portrait* was removed from the program at the request of Fred E. Busbey, a Republican congressman from Illinois. McCarthy's interest in Copland had to do not with the composer's political sympathies per se but rather with the question of "who in the U.S. Information Agency had chosen Copland to represent the United States at functions abroad." Haynes Johnson, *The Age of Anxiety: McCarthyism to Terrorism* (New York: Harcourt, 2005), 300. Johnson offers a succinct account of Copland's dealings with McCarthy (298–304); some of his information comes from Copland's own accounts in Aaron Copland and Vivian Perlis, *Copland: Since 1943* (New York: St. Martin's Press, 1989), 181–200.

4. Barry Seldes, *Leonard Bernstein: The Political Life of an American Musician* (Berkeley: University of California Press, 2009), 74–76.

5. Elizabeth B. Crist, "Mutual Responses in the Midst of an Era: Aaron Copland's *The Tender Land* and Leonard Bernstein's *Candide*," *Journal of Musicology* 23, no. 4 (2006): 486.

6. The folk songs incorporated into *The Tender Land* are "Zion's Walls," "Cottage by the Sea," and "If You Want to Go a-Courting." As Crist notes, in the wake of the opera's first performances, at least three reviews (by Miles Kastendieck in the *New York Journal-American*, by Jay S. Harrison in the *New York Herald Tribune*, and by Harriett Johnson in the *New York Post*) used the term "homespun" to describe Copland's score. Crist, "Mutual Responses," 499.

7. Johns (1926–2001) wrote the libretto under the pen name Horace Everett.

8. Leonard Bernstein, "What Makes Opera Grand?" in *The Joy of Music* (New York: Simon and Schuster, 1959), 292. The chapter is based on the script for a program on NBC's *Omnibus* series that aired on March 23, 1958.

9. Erik Johns, in a letter to Copland apparently written shortly after the premiere. The undated letter is contained in the Aaron Copland Collection, Music Division, Library of Congress, and is quoted in Christopher W. Patton, "Discovering *The Tender Land*: A New Look at Aaron Copland's Opera," *American Music* 20, no. 3 (2007): 318.

10. The words come from an address that Copland delivered at the 1949 Cultural and Scientific Conference for World Peace, the text of which, unpublished at the time, is represented in a document titled "Effect of the Cold War on the Artist in the U.S.," which is included in *Aaron Copland: A Reader—Selected Writings, 1923–1972*, ed. Richard Kostelanetz (New York: Routledge, 2003). Specifically, the quoted words appear on page 129 of the Kostelanetz anthology.

11. Copland and Perlis, *Copland: Since 1943*, 202–3.

12. In the version of *The Tender Land* presented at the City Center, the grandfather makes little comment. After the two drifters are shown to be innocent, the only conclusive statement comes from a neighbor, who tries to rationalize the crowd's hostile behavior. "We was just overexcited," he says. "Dangerous thing, imagination can be."

13. Crist, "Mutual Responses," 504.

14. Murrow's crusade against McCarthy is depicted in George Clooney's 2005 film *Good Night, and Good Luck*.

15. Seldes, *Leonard Bernstein*, 77.

16. Ibid., 78. The information about Kennedy, Seldes writes, comes from Humphrey Burton, *Leonard Bernstein* (New York: Doubleday, 1994).

17. The questions were much debated in advance of *Candide*'s revival for a production by the New York City Opera in 1982. See John Rockwell, "Will *Candide* Survive in the Opera House?" *New York Times*, October 10, 1982, A1.

18. Crist, "Mutual Responses," 503–4, 506.

19. According to set designer Oliver Smith, at one rehearsal Hellman screamed at Guthrie: "You've sold out. You're just a whore." Burton, *Leonard Bernstein*, 260.

20. Klaus-Dieter Gross, "McCarthyism and American Opera," *Revue LISA* 2, no. 3 (2004): 176.

21. Bernstein, "Colloquy in Boston: *Candide* or *Omnibus*?" *New York Times*, November 18, 1956, 133.

22. Ibid.

23. Arthur Miller, *Timebends: A Life* (New York: Grove Press, 1973), 331; emphasis original.

24. Rachel Hutchins-Viroux, "Witch-hunts, Theocracies, and Hypocrisy: McCarthyism in Arthur Miller/Robert Ward's Opera *The Crucible* and Carlisle Floyd's *Susannah*," *Revue LISA* 6, no. 2 (2008): 146.

25. Robert Paul Kolt, *Robert Ward's* The Crucible: *Creating an American Musical Nationalism* (Lanham, MD: Scarecrow Press, 2008), 54–56.

26. Carlisle Floyd, "Recalling *Susannah*'s Beginnings," liner note essay for Virgin Classics 5 45039 2 (1994), 14.

27. Arthur Miller, "Why I Wrote *The Crucible*," *New Yorker*, October 21, 1996, 158.

28. Gross, "McCarthyism and American Opera," 166.

29. In her *The Cultural Cold War* Frances Stonor Saunders notes that Nabokov always denied being in the CIA's employ. But, she asks: "Could anyone seriously believe that Nabokov, in all those years, had never been told—or figured out for himself—that 'behind this stood the heavy guns of "the Virginian woods"'?" (395–96).

30. Ibid., 100.

31. Richard Taruskin, "Nabokov, Nicolas," in *The New Grove Dictionary of Opera*, ed. Stanley Sadie (London: Macmillan, 1992), 3: 543.

32. Gross, "McCarthyism and American Opera," 169.

33. Tammy L. Kernodle, "Arias, Communists, and Conspiracies: The History of Still's *Troubled Island*," *Musical Quarterly* 83, no. 4 (1999): 497–98.

34. Verna Arvey, in a September 23, 1950, letter to *Pittsburgh Courier* executive editor P. L. Prattis, quoted in Kernodle, "Arias, Communists, and Conspiracies," 500.

35. Gross, "McCarthyism and American Opera," 167. For more on Still's vociferous expressions of anticommunism, see Catherine Parsons Smith, "'Harlem Renaissance Man' Revisited: The Politics of Race and Class in Still's Later Career," in *William Grant Still: A Study in Contradictions*, ed. Catherine Parsons Smith, 182–212 (Berkeley: University of California Press, 2000).

36. For more on the history of televised opera in America, see, for example, Richard C. Burke, "Television in the Opera House," *Central States Speech Journal* 18, no. 3 (1967): 164–65; and Marcia J. Citron, *Opera on Screen* (New Haven, CT: Yale University Press).

37. Burke, "Television in the Opera House," 163.

38. Bosley Crowther, "Opera on the Screen: Telecast of Metropolitan Opening and Film 'Aida' Are Shown Here," *New York Times*, November 14, 1954, X1. The *Aida* mentioned in the headline and discussed in the review was the 1953 Italian full-color film directed by Clemente Fracassi. On screen the film featured Sophia Loren in the title role and Canadian actress Lois Maxwell as Amneris; their singing voices were dubbed, respectively, by Renata Tebaldi and Ebe Stignani.

39. The director of the 1948 telecast of Menotti's *The Medium* was Paul Nickell, who over the entire course of *Studio One*'s ten-year run directed 139 of its episodes.

40. Samuel Chotzinoff, quoted in "NBC Music Chief Sees New Approach," *Musical America,* February 1953, 23; emphasis added.

41. Brian G. Rose, *Television and the Performing Arts: A Handbook and Reference Guide to American Cultural Programming* (Westport, CT: Greenwood Press, 1986), 135.

42. *Down in the Valley*, described by the composer as a "folk opera," had been premiered at Indiana University in July 1948.

43. Quaintance Eaton, "Great Opera Houses: NBC TV," *Opera News*, February 8, 1964, 30.

44. "Menotti and Television," *Newsweek*, January 7, 1952, 37.

45. "Radio and Television Cited in Peabody Awards," *New York Times,* May 2, 1952, 27.

46. Olin Downes, "Menotti Opera, the First for TV, Has Its Premiere—Boy, 12, Is Star," *New York Times*, December 25, 1951, I1.

47. John Ardoin, "Opera and Television," *Opera Quarterly* 1, no. 1 (1983): 47. Ardoin was writing from the perspective of 1983, at which time the Public Broadcasting System's "Great Performances" series—whose opera presentations were, in Ardoin's opinion, highly sophisticated—had been in existence for nine years.

48. In summarizing the offerings of the NBC Opera Theatre, different scholars give different totals for both the number of performances and the number of works presented. This likely stems from the fact that several of the offerings were presented not as part of the NBC Opera Theatre's regular programming but as *Hallmark Hall of Fame* specials. In any case, the complete repertoire for the regular programs—

along with dates of telecasts, synopses of plots, and cast information—is available from the "The Classic TV Archive" at http://ctva.biz/US/MusicVariety/NBCOpera .htm.

49. Along with Weill's *Down in the Valley* and Menotti's *Amahl*, American works presented by the NBC Opera Theatre included Menotti's *Maria Golovin, Labyrinth*, and *The Saint of Bleecker Street*; Bernstein's *Trouble in Tahiti*; Bohuslav Martinů's *The Wedding*; Lukas Foss's *Griffelkin*; scenes from Vittorio Giannini's *The Taming of the Shrew*; Normon Dello Joio's *The Trial at Rouen*; Stanley Hollingsworth's *La Grande Bretèche*; and Leonard Kastle's *Deseret*.

50. Paul Henry Lang, "Review of *Fidelio*," *New York Herald Tribune*, November 9, 1959, 12.

51. Ibid.

52. Richard C. Burke, "The NBC Opera Theater," *Journal of Broadcasting* 10, no. 1 (1965): 13.

53. H. W. Heinsheimer, "Opera in America," *Tempo* 11 (June 1945): 9.

54. Elise K. Kirk, *American Opera* (Urbana: University of Illinois Press, 2001), 249.

55. Gross, "McCarthyism and American Opera," 171.

56. For an excellent account of the Composers' Forum-Laboratories and debates over music that in effect "bore the label, 'Made in America,'" see chapter 5, "The National Government and National Music," of Barbara L. Tischler's *An American Music: The Search for an American Musical Identity* (Oxford: Oxford University Press, 1986).

57. Elise K. Kirk, "United States of America," in *The New Grove Dictionary of Opera*, ed. Stanley Sadie (London: Macmillan, 1992), 4: 870.

58. Rachel Hutchins-Viroux, "The American Opera Boom of the 1950s and 1960s: History and Stylistic Analysis," *Revue LISA* 2, no. 3 (2004): 148. Along with quoting the writings of composers Floyd, Menotti, Moore, and Thomson, Hutchins-Viroux makes reference to such journalistic articles as "Opera Boom," *Time*, May 23, 1955, 62; Henry Cowell, "The Flavor of American Music," *Score*, June 1955, 5–6; and Deems Taylor, "What Is American Opera?" *Opera News* 25, no. 6 (1960): 9–10.

59. Ibid.; Elise K. Kirk, "American Opera: Innovation and Tradition," in *The Cambridge Companion to Twentieth-Century Opera*, ed. Mervyn Cooke (Cambridge: Cambridge University Press, 2005), 200.

60. Ethan Mordden, *Opera in the Twentieth Century: Sacred, Profane, Godot* (Oxford: Oxford University Press, 1978), 308–9; emphasis added.

61. Richard RePass, "Opera Workshops in the United States," *Tempo*, new series, 27 (Spring 1953): 11.

62. Maria F. Rich, "Opera USA—Perspective: The Popularization of Opera," *Opera Quarterly* 1, no. 2 (1983): 21.

63. H. W. Heinsheimer, "Opera in America Today," *Musical Quarterly* 37, no. 3 (1951): 321.

64. Ibid., 321–22.

65. Burke, "NBC Opera Theater," 17.

66. The works presented as part of the Ford Foundation's "American Series" in the 1958–1959 season were Moore's *The Ballad of Baby Doe*, Mark Bucci's *Tale for a Deaf Ear*, Bernstein's *Trouble in Tahiti*, Weill's *Lost in the Stars*, Giannini's *The Taming of the Shrew*, Menotti's *The Old Maid and the Thief* and *The Medium*, Robert Kurka's *The Good Soldier Schweik*, Floyd's *Susannah*, and Blitzstein's *Regina*. During the 1959–1960 season the "American Series" included Weill's *Street Scene*, Lee Hoiby's *The Scarf*, Moore's *The Devil and Daniel Webster*, Floyd's *Wuthering Heights*, Menotti's *Maria Golovin*, Ward's *He Who Gets Slapped*, Dello Joio's *The Triumph of St. Joan*, Hugo Weisgall's *Six Characters in Search of an Author*, and repeats of *The Ballad of Baby Doe*, *Regina*, *The Medium*, and *Susannah*.

67. The term "cultural cringe" originated in a 1950 essay by the Australian-born but Oxford-educated schoolmaster Arthur A. Phillips. Published in the Melbourne-based journal *Meanjin*, Phillips's "Cultural Cringe" essay harangued Australians on their mistaken habit of thinking that any of their homegrown cultural products must be, ipso facto, inferior to comparable products from Europe. The concept of "cultural cringe" easily relates to pre-nationalist and then nationalist musical activity not just in Australia but also in such other colonial nations as Canada, New Zealand, and the United States. "The Cultural Cringe," *Meanjin* 9, no. 4 (1950): 299–302.

68. Heinsheimer, "Opera in America," 8.

69. M. Rich, "Opera USA," 20.

70. Founded in 1943 and ceasing operations in 2013 due to bankruptcy, the New York City Opera presented no fewer than fourteen world premieres during the long decade of the Fifties. The operas were William Grant Still's *Troubled Island* (1949), David Tamkin's *The Dybbuk* (1951), Copland's *The Tender Land* (1954), Nevit Kodallı's *Van Gogh* (1957), Mark Bucci's *Tale for a Deaf Ear* (1958), Robert Kurka's *The Good Soldier Schweik* (1958), Weisgall's *Six Characters in Search of an Author* (1959), Dello Joio's *The Triumph of St. Joan* (1959), Ward's *He Who Gets Slapped* (1959), Moore's *The Wings of the Dove* (1961), Ward's *The Crucible* (1961), Abraham Ellstein's *The Golem* (1962), Floyd's *The Passion of Jonathan Wade* (1962), and Jerome Moross's *Gentlemen, Be Seated!* (1963).

Founded by conductor John Crosby in 1956, from its inception the Santa Fe Opera has had a policy of each season presenting—along with a handful of well-known and thus popular works—a revival of some obscure work from the past and the world or American premiere of a new work. The company's first two seasons featured the world premieres of Martin David Levy's *The Tower* (1957) and Carlisle Floyd's *Wuthering Heights* (1958); other more or less new works presented during the long decade of the Fifties were Blitzstein's *Regina* (1959), Stravinsky's *The Rake's Progress* (1960, 1961, and 1962), Moore's *The Ballad of Baby Doe* (1961), and Hindemith's *Neues vom Tage* (1961).

71. Hutchins-Veroux, "American Opera Boom," 153.

72. Ibid., 160.

73. Harold C. Schonberg, "Opera: Robert Ward's 'The Crucible': Work Based on Miller Play at City Center," *New York Times*, October 27, 1961, 25.

74. Ibid.

Chapter 7. The Classical Music Mainstream

1. Virgil Thomson, "Bigger Than Baseball," *New York Herald Tribune*, October 25, 1953; reprinted in Virgil Thomson, *Music Reviewed: 1940–1954* (New York: Random House, 1967), 384.

2. Ibid., 384–85.

3. Ibid., 388.

4. Ibid. For accounts of how classical music fared in America during the war years, see Joseph Horowitz, *Classical Music in America: A History* (New York: W. W. Norton, 2005), 433–74, and Annegret Fauser, *Sounds of War: Music in the United States during World War II* (Oxford: Oxford University Press, 2013), 224–71.

5. Harold C. Schonberg, "Where Are the Young Composers?" *New York Times*, January 14, 1962; reprinted in Harold C. Schonberg, *Facing the Music* (New York: Summit Books, 1981), 195.

6. Aaron Copland, "The New School of American Composers," *New York Times Magazine*, March 14, 1948; reprinted, with an interesting insertion of quotation marks around the word "school," as "The New 'School' of American Composers," in *Copland on Music* (New York: W. W. Norton, 1963), 165–66.

7. Ibid., 174.

8. Joseph Machlis, *Introduction to Contemporary Music* (New York: W. W. Norton, 1961), 451.

9. Aaron Copland, "The Dilemma of Our Symphony Orchestras" (originally an address delivered to the annual meeting of the American Symphony Orchestra League in Providence, Rhode Island, in June 1956, and first printed in *The Musical Courier*, November 1, 1956); reprinted in *Copland on Music*, 268.

10. Ibid., 270–71.

11. Aaron Copland, "1959: Postscript for the Generation of the Fifties," in *Copland on Music*, 177–78; emphasis original.

12. Ibid., 176; emphasis original.

13. Wilfrid Mellers, *Music in a New Found Land: Themes and Developments in the History of American Music* (New York: Alfred A. Knopf, 1964), 194; emphasis original. Along with Copland, whom Mellers describes as a "key figure in American music," albeit one characterized by "a severe limitation of range" (81), the composers that up to this point had been discussed in detail were, as grouped by chapter, Charles Ives; Carl Ruggles and Roy Harris; Elliott Carter; Wallingford Riegger and Roger Sessions; Charles Griffes, Henry Cowell, and Edgard Varèse; and Harry Partch, John Cage, and Morton Feldman.

14. Ibid., 194–95.

15. Ibid., 195. The literary figures Mellers cites early in his book include James Fenimore Cooper, Nathaniel Hawthorne, Emily Dickinson, Ralph Waldo Emerson, Mark Twain, and Herman Melville. The composers he labels "American conservatives" include John Knowles Paine, George Whitefield Chadwick, Arthur Foote, Horatio Parker, Edward MacDowell, and Henry Franklin Gilbert.

16. Ibid.

17. Harold C. Schonberg, "Opera: Robert Ward's 'The Crucible': Work Based on Miller Play at City Center," *New York Times*, October 27, 1961, 25.

18. All four of these reviews, and more, are quoted in Kolt, *Robert Ward's The Crucible*, 105–6.

19. The Ives symphony, composed for the most part in 1904 but not performed until 1946, remains famous for its jarring pre-postmodern clashes of musical materials in different tempos and various keys. The second quartet of Carter, who as a teenager was befriended by Ives and doubtless was influenced by the older composer's interest in musical multiplicities, is a jarring mélange of four independent musical "lines" that ultimately move toward the same goal. For more on Carter's String Quartet No. 2 and its confrontational relationship with America's musical mainstream, see James Wierzbicki, *Elliott Carter* (Urbana: University of Illinois Press, 2011), 50–74.

20. Joseph N. Straus, "The Myth of Serial 'Tyranny' in the 1950s and 1960s," *Musical Quarterly* 83, no. 3 (1999): 302.

21. Ned Rorem, "Where Is Our Music Going?" in *Music and People* (New York: George Braziller, 1968), 223.

22. Ibid., 223–24.

23. Ibid., 224.

24. These critics included Virgil Thomson, at the *New York Herald Tribune* from 1940 to 1954; Olin Downes, at the *New York Times* from 1924 to 1955; Howard Taubman, at the *New York Times* from 1955 to 1960; and Paul Hume, at the *Washington Post* from 1946 to 1982.

25. Aaron Copland, *Music and Imagination* (New York: New American Library, 1952), 115.

26. Ibid., 115–16.

27. These labels are used, for example, by Machlis in his 1961 *Introduction to Contemporary Music*.

28. These labels are used by John Tasker Howard in *Modern Music: A Popular Guide to Greater Musical Enjoyment* (New York: New American Library, 1957), 83–103.

29. Mellers, *Music in a New Found Land*, 205–6.

30. Virgil Thomson, *American Music since 1910* (New York: Holt, Rinehart, and Winston, 1970), 10.

31. Emily Abrams Ansari, "Aaron Copland and the Politics of Cultural Diplomacy," *Journal of the Society for American Music* 5, no. 3 (2011): 335.

32. Emily Abrams Ansari, "Shaping the Policies of Cold War Musical Diplomacy: An Epistemic Community of American Composers," *Diplomatic History* 36, no. 1 (2012): 41–43.

33. Nadine Hubbs, "Homophobia in Twentieth-Century Music: The Crucible of America's Sound," *Dædalus, the Journal of the American Academy of Arts & Sciences* 4 (Fall 2013): 47; Nadine Hubbs, "Bernstein, Homophobia, Historiography," *Women and Music: A Journal of Gender and Culture* 13 (2009): 33–34.

34. Ibid., 47.

35. Ibid., 46.

36. The article was K. Robert Schwarz, "Composers' Closets Open for All to See," *New York Times*, June 19, 1994, H2 and H24. Complaining letters to the editor, from Murray Rothstein, Gavin Borchert, Samuel Barber biographer Barbara B. Heyman, and Copland's cousin Rodney H. Clurman, were published on July 10 and 31, 1994.

37. Hubbs, "Bernstein, Homophobia, Historiography," 31.

38. The term was coined by American psychologist George Weinberg, in conversation and conference presentations, in 1966 or 1967; its first appearance in print was in the heterosexual-oriented pornographic magazine *Screw*, in the column "The Homosexual Citizen" co-authored by gay activists Jack Nichols and Lige Clarke. In his 1972 book *Society and the Healthy Homosexual*, Weinberg defined homophobia as both "the dread of being in close quarters with homosexuals" and as self-loathing on the part of homosexuals themselves. Gregory Herek, "Beyond 'Homophobia': Thinking about Sexual Prejudice and Stigma in the Twenty-first Century," *Sexuality Research and Social Policy* 1, no. 2 (2004): 6–8.

39. *Employment of Homosexuals and Other Sex Perverts in Government*, Senate Document No. 241, 81st Congress, second session (Washington, DC: U.S. Government Printing Office, 1950). The document is reprinted in Kathy Peiss, ed., *Major Problems in the History of Sexuality* (Boston: Houghton Mifflin, 2002), 376–79.

40. Aaron Copland, *Copland on Music* (New York: Doubleday, 1960), 84–85. Copland adjusted his language for the second edition of the book, published in 1963 by W. W. Norton. In the second edition the passage reads: "She was not herself a regularly practicing composer and in so far as she composed at all she must of necessity be listed in that unenviable category of the woman composer" (84–85).

41. Virgil Thomson, "Greatest Music Teacher," *New York Times Magazine*, February 4, 1962; reprinted as "Nadia Boulanger at 75," in *A Virgil Thomson Reader*, ed. John Rockwell (Boston: Houghton Mifflin, 1981), 389–93. The quoted passages are from *Virgil Thomson Reader*, 389, 391, and 392.

42. Drawing upon information contained in recent editions of *The New Grove Dictionary of Music and Musicians*, Bruce Brown and Lisa M. Cook have compiled a list of more than 130 American composers—as stylistically varied as Elliott Carter, Donald Erb, Hugo Friedhofer, and Philip Glass—who productively studied in France with Boulanger. The list, admittedly hardly complete, is available online at http://www.nadiaboulanger.org/nb/amstudents.html.

43. Nadine Hubbs, "A French Connection: Modernist Codes in the Musical Closet," *GLQ: A Journal of Lesbian and Gay Studies* 6, no. 3 (2000): 401.

44. Ibid., 398.

45. "The Homosexual in America," *Time*, January 21, 1966, 40–41.

46. In several of Hubbs's publications (*Queer Composition of America's Sound*, 159 and 238; "Bernstein, Homophobia, Historiography," 28) she makes reference to Michael S. Sherry's impressively long list of magazine and newspaper articles, dating

from 1950 to 1966, that deal with homosexuality in the arts world. See Sherry, *Gay Artists in Modern American Culture: An Imagined Conspiracy* (Chapel Hill: University of North Carolina Press, 2007), 27.

47. Burton, *Leonard Bernstein*, 45; and Secrest, *Leonard Bernstein*, 256–57.

48. For insights into the relationship between Barber and Menotti, see Peter Dickinson, *Samuel Barber Remembered: A Centenary Tribute* (Rochester, NY: University of Rochester Press, 2010), 55–72.

49. Howard Pollack, "The Dean of Gay American Composers," *American Music* 18, no. 1 (2000): 48–49.

50. Frederick Kuh, "Top American Composers' Works Barred at U.S. Libraries Abroad," *Chicago Sun-Times*, April 26, 1953; quoted in Howard Pollack, *Aaron Copland: The Life and Work of an Uncommon Man* (Urbana: University of Illinois Press, 2000), 454.

51. Pollack, *Aaron Copland*, 451–59.

52. Two of the most pointed of these, from Edgard Varèse and Lazare Saminsky, are quoted in Hubbs, *Queer Composition of America's Sound*, 156–57.

53. James C. Hagerty, press release, June 29, 1956.

54. Ansari, "Shaping the Policies," 41. The material that Ansari quotes is from a November 22, 1955, letter from Dwight D. Eisenhower to his brother Edgar.

55. Elmer B. Staats, memo to Dale O. Smith, September 19, 1955. The memo from the chief executive officer of the U.S. National Security Council to Brigadier General Smith, a member of Security Council's advisory board, is quoted by Ansari in "Shaping the Policies," 41.

56. See chapter 3 of the present text.

57. Robert C. Schnitzer, "Artists as Envoys: Their Contribution to International Goodwill," *New York Times*, January 1, 1955, 12.

58. Howard Taubman, "Orchestra Tours: Three American Ensembles Will Travel in Europe and Asia this Year," *New York Times*, February 27, 1955, X9.

59. Howard Taubman, "Making Friends: Two Orchestras Go Abroad This Year—They Should Play American Works," *New York Times*, January 22, 1956, 101.

60. Virgil Thomson, "Please Read Carefully," folder 1, box 100, in the Bureau for Educational and Cultural Affairs Historical Collection (hereafter, CU Collection) housed at the Special Collections section of the library at the University of Arkansas in Fayetteville; quoted by Ansari, "Shaping the Policies," 46.

61. Julius Seebach, memo, folder 1, box 100, CU Collection; quoted by Ansari, "Shaping the Policies," 51.

62. Ansari, "Shaping the Policies," 51.

63. Virgil Thomson, *Virgil Thomson* (New York: Alfred A. Knopf, 1966), 401.

64. Ansari, "Shaping the Policies," 46.

65. "President Attends New 'Porgy and Bess,'" *New York Times*, August 6, 1952, 17.

66. Jack Raymond, "U.S. Performers Hailed at Berlin Festival," *New York Times*, October 5, 1952, X7. Along with the sixty-five-member opera troupe, American

performers at the 1952 Berlin Cultural Festival included the New York City Center
Ballet, the U.S. Army Field Band, conductor Eugene Ormandy (leading the RIAS-
Symphonie Orchester), bass-baritone Kenneth Spencer, and soprano Astrid Varnay.
The RIAS (Rundfunk im amerikanischen Sektor) orchestra was established in 1946
by American occupation forces. In 1956 it was renamed the Radio-Symphonie-
Orchester Berlin, and since 1993 it has been known as the Deutsches Symphonie-
Orchester Berlin.

67. "U.S. Will Not Pay for 'Porgy' Visit," *New York Times*, September 28, 1955, 70.

68. Lewis Funke, "News and Gossip of the Rialto: 'Porgy and Bess' Loses Official
Support," *New York Times*, October 2, 1955, X1.

69. Welles Hangen, "Soviet to Finance 'Porgy' in Moscow: Will Pay Part of Expenses
for Troupe, Which Is Going Despite U.S. Opposition," *New York Times*, November
12, 1955, 24.

70. "Porgy and Bess" (editorial), *New York Times*, October 1, 1955, 18.

71. Welles Hangen, "'Porgy and Bess' in the U.S.S.R.," *New York Times*, January 15,
1956, X3.

72. Robert Breen, "Cultural Envoys: Some Thoughts on Our Arts-Exchange Plan,"
New York Times, August 5, 1956, X1; emphasis original.

73. Minutes of ANTA's music advisory policy, November 8, 1954, folder 1, box 100,
CU collection; quoted in Ansari, "Shaping the Policies," 45.

74. Minutes of ANTA's music advisory policy, November 3, 1955, folder 12, box 12,
CU collection; quoted in Monson, *Freedom Sounds*, 12.

75. Minutes of ANTA's music advisory policy, December 20, 1955, folder 1, box
100, CU collection; quoted in Ansari, "Shaping the Policies," 45.

76. Ansari, "Shaping the Policies," 46.

77. Along with the Gershwin pieces, the works approved for tours between 1956
and 1959 were Samuel Barber's *Adagio for Strings*, *Medea's Meditation and Dance of
Vengeance*, *Music for a Scene from Shelley*, *School for Scandal* overture, and *Second
Essay for Orchestra*; Leonard Bernstein's Symphony No. 1 ("Jeremiah") and Symphony
No. 2 ("The Age of Anxiety"); Aaron Copland's *Appalachian Spring*, *Quiet City*, *Symphonic Ode*, Symphony No. 3, and a suite from the *Billy the Kid* ballet; Paul Creston's
Chant for 1942, *Dance Overture*, Symphony No. 2, and Symphony No. 3; David Dia-
mond's *The World of Paul Klee*; Norman Dello Joio's *Triptych*; Isadore Freed's *Festi-
val Overture*; Howard Hanson's *Elegy in Memory of Serge Koussevitzky*; Roy Harris's
Symphony No. 3; Kent Kennan's *Night Soliloquy*; Peter Mennin's Symphony No. 3;
two "Interludes" from Gian Carlo Menotti's opera *The Island God*; Walter Piston's
Concerto for Orchestra and Symphony No. 6; William Schuman's Symphony No. 6
and *Symphony for Strings*; and Robert Turner's *Encounter*. For the Boston Symphony
Orchestra's 1956 European tour the ANTA panel approved Leroy Anderson's *Irish
Suite*, but only for the tour-opening concert in Dublin.

78. Howard Taubman, "Cold War on the Cultural Front," *New York Times*, April
13, 1958, SM12 and SM107–08.

79. Along with pop songs from Harry Belafonte, jazz numbers from Benny Goodman, and Leonard Bernstein's 1953 musical comedy *Wonderful Town*, America's musical offerings at the Brussels World's Fair consisted of two operas (Carlisle Floyd's *Susannah* and Gian Carlo Menotti's *Maria Golovin*), two orchestral works (William Schuman's *Credendum* and Samuel Barber's *Adagio for Strings*), and two ballet scores (Morton Gould's for choreographer Agnes de Mille's *Fall River Legend* and Bernstein's for choreographer Jerome Robbins's *Fancy Free*).

80. Thomson, *Virgil Thomson*, 419.

Chapter 8. Modernists

1. Thomson, *American Music since 1910*, 10.

2. Ernst Krenek, *Music: Here and Now*, trans. Barthold Fles (New York: W. W. Norton, 1939), 192.

3. Henry Pleasants, "Schoenberg, Shostakovitch, Stokowski," *Modern Music* 18, no. 2 (1941), 120–21.

4. John Tasker Howard, *This Modern Music: A Guide for the Bewildered Listener* (New York: Thomas Y. Cromwell, 1942), 98. In the second edition of the book (1957), titled *Modern Music: A Popular Guide to Greater Musical Enjoyment*, the quoted material appears on page 61.

5. Arnold Schoenberg, "Heart and Brain in Music," in *Style and Idea: Selected Writings of Arnold Schoenberg* (Berkeley: University of California Press, 1975), 69–71. The lecture, written in English, was delivered at the University of Chicago in May 1946.

6. Virgil Thomson, "New and Good," *New York Herald Tribune*, March 17, 1947; reprinted in Thomson, *Music Reviewed*, 211, and *Virgil Thomson Reader*, 298.

7. Thomson, "Rich Resources," *New York Herald Tribune*, November 23, 1953; reprinted in Thomson, *Music Reviewed*, 390–92.

8. Howard Taubman, "If One Had Time," *New York Times*, April 17, 1955, X9.

9. Howard Taubman, "In Time to Come?: Twelve-Tone Music Is Major Influence but Public Has Not Yet Accepted It," *New York Times*, March 23, 1958, X9.

10. Harold C. Schonberg, "An End in Itself," *New York Times*, March 26, 1961; "The Failures of Contemporary Composition—Again," *New York Times*, February 11, 1962; "Where Are the Young Composers?," *New York Times*, January 14, 1962; all reprinted in Schonberg, *Facing the Music*, in which the quoted material appears on pages 194, 200, and 197.

11. Ned Rorem, "Where Is Our Music Going?" in *Music and People* (New York: George Braziller, 1968), 219–20.

12. Ibid., 220.

13. John R. Thelin, *A History of American Higher Education* (Baltimore: Johns Hopkins University Press, 2004), 260–61.

14. Elliott Schwartz, "Directions in American Composition since the Second World War, Part I: 1945–1960," *Music Educators Journal* 61, no. 6 (1975): 31.

15. Copland, *Music and Imagination*, 116, 114.

16. Brian Harker, "Milton Babbitt Encounters Academia (and Vice Versa)," *American Music* 26, no. 3 (2008): 338–39.

17. The best-known of the musicologists included Willi Apel, Manfred Bukofzer, Hans T. David, Alfred Einstein, Karl Geiringer, Edward Lowinsky, Paul Nettl, Curt Sachs, Leo Schrade, and Emanuel Winternitz. The best-known of the analysts included Oswald Jonas, Ernst Oster, Felix Salzer, Hans Weisse, and Victor Zukerkandl.

18. Virgil Thomson, *The State of Music* (New York: Random House, 1939), 112–13.

19. Patrick McCreless, "Rethinking Contemporary Music Theory," in *Keeping Score: Music, Disciplinarity, Culture*, ed. David Schwarz, Anahid Kassabian, and Lawrence Siegel (Charlottesville: University Press of Virginia, 1997), 21.

20. Thelin, *History of American Higher Education*, 260.

21. Milton Babbitt, "Who Cares If You Listen?," *High Fidelity* 8, no. 2 (1958): 127. Under its original title, "The Composer as Specialist," the essay was first reprinted in *Music in the Western World: A History in Documents*, ed. Piero Weiss and Richard Taruskin (New York: Schirmer, 1984): 529–34.

22. Milton Babbitt, in "Milton Babbitt on Milton Babbitt," Anne Swartz and Milton Babbitt, *American Music* 3, no. 4 (1985): 471.

23. Harker, "Milton Babbitt Encounters Academia," 365.

24. For succinct accounts of the development of the RCA synthesizers, see Peter Manning, *Electronic & Computer Music* (Oxford: Oxford University Press, 1985), 97–114, and Thom Holmes, *Electronic and Experimental Music*, 3rd ed. (New York: Routledge, 2008), 142–57.

25. Babbitt, in Swartz and Babbitt, "Milton Babbitt on Milton Babbitt," 468.

26. Ibid.

27. Ibid., 468–69.

28. Thomas Christensen, *Rameau and Musical Thought in the Enlightenment* (Cambridge: Cambridge University Press, 1993), 7–15.

29. Sessions's article was "Heinrich Schenker's Contribution," *Modern Music* 12, no. 4 (1935): 170–78.

30. Milton Babbitt, "Professional Theorists and Their Influence," in *Words about Music*, ed. Stephen Dembski and Joseph N. Straus (Madison: University of Wisconsin Press, 1987), 121.

31. McCreless, "Rethinking Contemporary Music Theory," 21–22.

32. Babbitt, "The Unlikely Survival of Serious Music," in *Words about Music*, 174.

33. For details on the Schenker-based content of the early issues of the *Journal of Music Theory* and *Perspectives of New Music*, see David Carson Berry, "Schenkerian Theory in the United States: A Review of Its Establishment and a Survey of Current Research Topics," *Zeitschrift der Gesselschaft für Musiktheorie* 2, nos. 2–3 (2005): 109–11. For commentary on how articles in these journals affected the careers of their authors, see the section aptly headed "Music Theory as Power" in McCreless, "Rethinking Contemporary Music Theory," 32–41.

34. Babbitt, *Words about Music*, 174.

35. Joseph N. Straus, "A Revisionist History of Twelve-Tone Serialism in American Music," *Journal of the Society for American Music* 2, no. 2 (2008): 365. Straus dealt with the same topic almost a decade earlier in "The Myth of Serial 'Tyranny' in the 1950s and 1960s," *Musical Quarterly* 83, no. 3 (1999): 301–343. He summarizes his argument and offers further statistical data in *Twelve-Tone Music in America* (New York: Cambridge University Press, 2009).

36. For comment on this, see chapter 7 of the present text.

37. John Rockwell, *All American Music: Composition in the Late Twentieth Century* (New York: Alfred A. Knopf, 1983), 18; and Winthrop Sargeant, "Is Music Dead?" *New Yorker*, May 11, 1968; quoted in Straus, "Myth of Serial 'Tyranny,'" 311, 310.

38. Harold C. Schonberg, "The New Age Is Coming," *New York Times*, January 14, 1968; Donal Henahan, "And So We Bid Farewell to Atonality," *New York Times*, January 6, 1991; and David Denby, "The Trouble with Lenny," *New York Times*, August 17, 1998; quoted in Straus, "Myth of Serial 'Tyranny,'" 331, 306.

39. Harold C. Schonberg, "Are Reports of Its Death Greatly Exaggerated?" *New York Times*, September 29, 1968; and Donal Henahan, "Current Chronicle," *Musical Quarterly* 54, no. 1 (1968); quoted in Straus, "Myth of Serial 'Tyranny,'" 331, 332.

40. William Bolcom, "The End of the Mannerist Century," in *The Pleasure of Modernist Music: Listening, Meaning, Intention, Ideology*, ed. Arved Ashby (Rochester, NY: University of Rochester Press, 1996), 47; and Michael Broyles, *Mavericks and Other Traditions in American Music* (New Haven: Yale University Press, 2004), 171; quoted in Straus, "Revisionist History," 365.

41. Straus, "Myth of Serial 'Tyranny,'" 334.

42. René Leibowitz, *Schoenberg and His School*, trans. Dika Newlin (New York: Philosophical Library, 1949), x; emphasis added. Leibowitz's book was first published in 1947 as *Schönberg et son école: l'étape contemporaine du langage musical*. In the English-language version the subtitle, translated as "The Contemporary Stage of the Language of Music," appears on the title page but not on the cover.

43. Pierre Boulez, "Possibly . . . ," in *Stocktakings from an Apprenticeship*, ed. Paule Thévenin, trans. Stephen Walsh (New York: Oxford University Press), 113. The 1952 French version of the essay bears the title "Eventuellement . . . ."

44. Martin Brody, "'Music for the Masses': Milton Babbitt's Cold War Music Theory," *Musical Quarterly* 77, no. 2 (1993): 166.

45. Milton Babbitt, "The Structure and Function of Music Theory," in *Perspectives on Contemporary Music Theory*, ed. Benjamin Boretz and Edward T. Cone (New York: W. W. Norton, 1972), 21; originally published in *College Music Symposium* 5 (Fall 1965): 49–60.

46. Straus, "Myth of Serial 'Tyranny,'" 334.

47. Susan McClary, "Terminal Prestige: The Case of Avant-Garde Music Composition," in *Keeping Score: Music, Disciplinarity, Culture*, ed. David Schwarz, Anahid Kassabian, and Lawrence Siegel (Charlottesville: University Press of Virginia), 57.

48. The Internationale Ferienkurse für Neue Musik at Darmstadt, a small German city about fifteen miles south of Frankfurt, was established in 1946 as part of the American effort to rehabilitate German culture. Although the purpose of the Darmstadt program was simply to focus attention on developments in music that for the most part had been suppressed in Germany during the Third Reich, Darmstadt nevertheless quickly developed a reputation as "a summer camp dedicated to the exploration of electronic music and European serialism." Amy C. Beal, "Negotiating Cultural Allies: American Music in Darmstadt, 1946–1956," *Journal of the American Musicological Society* 53, no. 1 (2000): 105.

49. György Ligeti, "On Music and Politics," *Perspectives of New Music* 16, no. 2 (1978): 21. After Ligeti wrote up his 1972 remarks, they were published the next year in the German journal *Darmstädter Beiträge zue Neuen Musik*. The English translation is by Wes Blomster.

50. Ligeti, "On Music and Politics," 22.

51. Anne C. Shreffler, "Ideologies of Serialism: Stravinsky's *Threni* and the Congress for Cultural Freedom," in *Music and the Aesthetics of Modernity*, ed. Karol Berger and Anthony Newcomb (Cambridge: Harvard University Press, 2005), 219.

52. The American Musicological Society established a "Cold War and Music" study group in 2006. Journals that have published special editions devoted entirely to music during the Cold War include *Contemporary Music Review* 26, no. 1 (2007), *Journal of Musicology* 26, no. 1 (2009), and *Diplomatic History* 36, no. 1 (2012).

53. Undated letter from Eisler to Schoenberg, presumably written before March 10, 1926; quoted in Eberhardt Klemm, "'I Don't Give a Damn about This Spring': Hanns Eisler's Move to Berlin," in *Hanns Eisler: A Miscellany*, ed. David Blake (Luxembourg: Harwood Academic Publishers, 1995), 4. The article, which originally appeared in *Sinn und Form* 39, no. 3 (1987), is translated by Karin von Abrams.

54. Hanns Eisler, "Contemporary Music and Fascism," in *Musik und Politik Schriften*, ed. Günter Mayer (Leipzig: Deutscher Verlag für Musik, 1983), 490. The hitherto unpublished essay was written in English; the annotations by editor Günter Mayer suggest that the typescript was indeed intended for publication ("*wahrscheinlich für einen Vortrag*"), but there is no indication as to where Eisler hoped to publish the essay.

55. Anton Webern, quoted in Michael H. Kater, *The Twisted Muse: Musicians and Their Music in the Third Reich* (Oxford: Oxford University Press), 73. Kater, who does not give a source for the quotation, suggests that the statement dates from 1936 or 1937.

56. Milton Babbitt, "My Vienna Triangle at Washington Square Revisited and Dilated," in *Driven into Paradise: The Musical Migration from Nazi Germany to the United States*, ed. Reinhold Brinkman and Christoph Wolff (Berkeley: University of California Press, 1999), 34–35. In his 1991 "A Life of Learning" lecture, Babbitt embellished the anecdote. The idea that serial music is "fascistic [because] it imposed an 'order,' and [that] each work imposed 'a new order' upon the pitch classes," he said,

"compares in intellectual sophistication with that pronouncement of a celebrated French intellectual that language [itself] is fascistic, because it contains 'subjects,' 'subordinate clauses,' and the like." Babbitt, "A Life of Learning," in *The Collected Essays of Milton Babbitt*, edited by Stephen Peles, Stephen Dembski, Andrew Mead, and Joseph N. Straus (Princeton, NJ: Princeton University Press, 2003), 443.

57. Ernst Krenek, quoted and paraphrased in Harker, "Milton Babbitt Encounters Academia," 342, 372. The source of Krenek's comments is "America's Influence on Its Émigré Composers," *Perspectives of New Music* 8 (1970).

58. Aaron Copland, "The World of A-Tonality," *New York Times*, November 27, 1949, BR5.

59. Jennifer DeLapp-Birkett, "Aaron Copland and the Politics of Twelve-Tone Composition in the Early Cold War United States," *Journal of Musicological Research* 27 (2008): 55.

60. Ibid., 54; Copland and Perlis, *Copland: Since 1943*, 151.

61. See Hubbs, "French Connection," 389–412.

62. DeLapp-Birkett, "Aaron Copland and the Politics," 48.

63. Richard Taruskin, *The Oxford History of Western Music* (Oxford: Oxford University Press, 2010), 5: 109.

64. DeLapp-Birkett, "Aaron Copland and the Politics," 61; emphasis original.

65. Ibid., 59.

66. Taruskin, *Oxford History*, 5:105.

67. DeLapp-Birkett, "Aaron Copland and the Politics," 62.

68. Edward T. Cone, "Conversation with Aaron Copland," *Perspectives of New Music* 6, no. 2 (1968): 67.

69. Leonard Bernstein, "Aaron Copland: An Intimate Sketch," *High Fidelity* 20, no. 11 (1970): 55.

70. The link between the Congress for Cultural Freedom and the CIA was first revealed in "C.I.A. Operations: A Plot Scuttled; or, How Kennedy in '62 Undid Sugar Sabotage," *New York Times,* April 28, 1966, 28. The article was the third in a five-part exposé of covert and possibly illegal CIA operations worldwide.

71. Greg Barnhisel, "*Perspectives USA* and the Cultural Cold War: Modernism in Service of the State," *Modernism/modernity* 14, no. 4 (2007): 730.

72. For brief accounts of Nabokov's background, see Saunders, *Cultural Cold War*, 12–14, and Mark Carroll, *Music and Ideology in Cold War Europe* (Cambridge: Cambridge University Press, 2003), 28–30. For an assessment of Nabokov's entire career, see Ian Wellens, *Music on the Frontline: Nicolas Nabokov's Struggle against Communism and Middlebrow Culture* (Aldershot, UK: Ashgate, 2002). For Nabokov's own version of the story, see his autobiographical *Bagazh: Memoirs of a Russian Cosmopolitan* (New York: Atheneum, 1975).

73. "Officially" the only member of the Congress for Cultural Freedom who knew of the CIA's involvement was Michael Josselson, a CIA agent who on the surface served on the congress's steering committee. Peter Coleman, *The Liberal Conspiracy: The*

Congress for Cultural Freedom and the Struggle for the Mind of Postwar Europe (New York: Free Press, 1989), 220.

74. Among the journals or magazines that the Congress for Cultural Freedom launched, with funding from the CIA, were *Cuadernos* (in Latin America), *Encounter* (the UK), *Forum* (Austria), *Jiyu* (Japan), *Preuves* (France), *Quadrant* (Australia), *Quest* (India), *Science and Freedom* (Germany), *Soviet Survey* (Israel), and *Tempo Presente* (Italy). For details on the journals' content and operations, see Saunders, *Cultural Cold War*, 213–17.

75. Olin Downes, "Paris Exposition in Sum," *New York Times*, June 15, 1952, X7.

76. Along with the Ives sonata (and not counting music by such émigré composers as Hindemith, Martinů, and Stravinsky), the American works on the festival were Samuel Barber's Piano Sonata and *School for Scandal* overture, Aaron Copland's ballet *The Pied Piper* and *El salón Mexico*, Walter Piston's *Toccata*, William Schuman's Symphony No. 2, and Virgil Thomson's opera *Four Saints in Three Acts*.

77. Herbert Read, address to members of the governing board for L'Œuvre du XXe Siècle, April 1952 (in the American Committee for Cultural Freedom Papers, Tamiment Library, New York University); quoted in Saunders, *Cultural Cold War*, 221.

78. Carroll, *Music and Ideology*, 16.

79. Taruskin, *Oxford History*, 5:294.

80. In addition to modernist works by American composers Aaron Copland, Elliott Carter, Lou Harrison, John Lessard, and Ben Weber, La Musica nel XX Secolo included the very tonal *Three Pictures for Orchestra* (1949) of Virgil Thomson and the *Hermit Songs* (1952–1953) of Samuel Barber.

81. David Caute, *The Dancer Defects: The Struggles for Cultural Supremacy during the Cold War* (Oxford: Oxford University Press, 2003), 396; Carroll, *Music and Ideology*, 169. Of course, "the traditional assumption of 'free' Western serialism versus Soviet tonal 'control' has been revealed as a severe oversimplification, despite its powerful hold on the popular imagination at the time, a fact that should not be forgotten." Peter J. Schmelz, "Music in the Cold War," *Journal of Musicology* 26, no. 1 (2009): 8–9.

82. Completed in 1951, Carter's first string quartet was given its premiere by the Walden Quartet in New York in February 1953. A few months later the piece won first prize in a Belgian competition for string quartets, but since the competition was open only to works that had never been performed, Carter had to turn down the prize money. At the request of Nabokov, a close friend of Carter since the 1940s, the performance at the 1954 Rome festival was given by the Paris-based Parrenin Quartet. See Wierzbicki, *Elliott Carter*, 50–51, and Taruskin, *Oxford History*, 5:293–94.

83. Lessard, who happened to be in Rome on a Guggenheim Fellowship, was represented at the festival by his 1951 *Toccata for Harpsichord*. Weber, invited to participate in the festival's competition for young composers, was represented by his 1954 Violin Concerto, op. 41; Harrison, likewise invited to participate in the competition, was represented by his 1953 *Peace Piece Three*, for voice, harp, and strings.

84. Taruskin, *Oxford History*, 5: 294.

85. Thomson, *American Music since 1910*, 51, 66.

86. Alex Ross, *The Rest Is Noise: Listening to the Twentieth Century* (New York: Farrar, Straus, and Giroux, 2007), 401.

87. Anne C. Shreffler, "The Myth of Empirical Historiography: A Response to Joseph N. Straus," *Musical Quarterly* 84, no. 1 (2000): 23.

88. Thelin, *History of American Higher Education*, 263.

Chapter 9. Mavericks

1. "Maverick," *The Australian Oxford Dictionary* (Oxford: Oxford University Press, 1999); "Maverick," *The American Heritage Dictionary: Office Edition* (New York: Houghton Mifflin, 1994).

2. Lawrence Gilman, "The Philadelphia Orchestra Plays Varese's 'Hyperprism,' with Cheering Results, *New York Herald Tribune*, December 17, 1924; quoted in Carol Oja, *Making Music Modern: New York in the 1920s* (Oxford: Oxford University Press, 2000), 41.

3. Commissioned by the Philips Electronics company, the three-track *Poème électronique* was realized not in Varèse's still relatively primitive home studio but at Philips's state-of-the-art facility in Eindhoven, The Netherlands.

4. Edgard Varèse, quoted in Georges Charbonnier, *Entretiens avec Edgard Varèse: Suivis d'une étude de l'œuvre* (Paris: Éditions Pierre Belfond, 1970), 156; translation mine.

5. Nicole Hirsch, "'Désert,' oeuvre électrosymphonique, a été accueilli par des sifflets, des chants de coq et des aboiements au théâtre des Champs-Elysées," *France-Soir*, December 4, 1954; quoted in Olivia Mattis, "Varèse's Multimedia Conception of *Déserts*," *Musical Quarterly* 76, no. 4 (1992): 557. The two-track tape that figured into the 1954 premiere of *Déserts* was realized partly in Varèse's home studio and partly in Paris at Pierre Schaeffer's government-funded studio at Radiodiffusion-Télévision Française.

6. For details on the Barrons' career, see James Wierzbicki, *Louis and Bebe Barron's Forbidden Planet: A Film Score Guide* (Lanham, MD: Scarecrow Press, 2005), 4–16.

7. Bebe Barron, in *Incredibly Strange Music*, ed. Andrea Juno and V. Vale (San Francisco: V/Search, 1994), 194.

8. Barry Schrader, *Introduction to Electro-Acoustic Music* (Englewood Cliffs, NJ: Prentice-Hall, 1982), 78.

9. Louis Barron told an interviewer in 1986 that MGM producer Schary "wanted to bring in . . . Harry Partch" for that section of the film that involves music composed and recorded by the ancient "Krel" civilization that once inhabited the titular planet, but commentary to this effect appears nowhere in standard literature on Partch. Louis Barron, in Ted Greenwald, "The Self-Destructing Modules behind the Revolutionary 1956 Soundtrack of *Forbidden Planet*," *Keyboard* 12 (February 1986): 58.

10. For details on Partch's unsuccessful negotiations with Paramount, see Andrew Granade, "When Worlds Collide: Harry Partch's Encounters with Film Music," *Music and the Moving Image* 4, no. 1 (2011): 9–33. The composer assigned to *When Worlds Collide* was Leith Stevens, who had scored producer George Pal's 1950 *Destination Moon* and who would go on to score such other Fifties science fiction films as *The Atomic City* (1952), *The War of the Worlds* (1953), and *World Without End* (1956). According to Granade, it was in large part the idea of Stevens, whose medium was the conventional orchestra, that Partch be recruited for the sake of adding special touches to the *When Worlds Collide* project. "When Worlds Collide," 9–10.

11. Wilfred Mellers, "The Avant-garde in America," *Proceedings of the Royal Musical Association* 90, no. 1 (1963): 5.

12. The treatise was published, by the University of Wisconsin Press, in 1949 as *Genesis of a Music*; a second and much expanded edition was published by Da Capo Press in 1974.

13. Alan Rich, *American Pioneers: Ives to Cage and Beyond* (London: Phaidon Press, 1995), 203.

14. Harry Partch, "The University and the Creative Arts: Comment," *Arts in Society* 2, no. 3 (1963): 22. The short article is reprinted in full in Harry Partch, *Bitter Music: Collected Journals, Essays, Introductions, and Librettos*, ed. Thomas McGeary (Urbana: University of Illinois Press, 1991), 191–92.

15. David L. Brunner, "Cultural Diversity in the Choral Music of Louis Harrison," *Choral Journal* (May 1992): 20; quoted in Leta E. Miller and Frederic Lieberman, *Composing a World: Lou Harrison, Musical Wayfarer* (Urbana: University of Illinois Press, 1998), 177.

16. The quotations are from an informal talk that Harrison gave at the State University of New York–Buffalo in 1959 and from an address titled "Political Manifesto" that Harrison delivered in 1961 at the CIA-sponsored East-West Encounter conference in Tokyo; both quoted in Miller and Lieberman, *Composing a World*, 179, 181.

17. For details on the participants in the early Composers' Workshop concerts, see David Bernstein, *The San Francisco Tape Music Center: 1960s Counterculture and the Avant-Garde* (Berkeley: University of California Press, 2008), 9–11.

18. Trevor Pinch and Frank Trocco, *Analog Days: The Invention and Impact of the Moog Synthesizer* (Cambridge: Harvard University Press, 2002), 33–35.

19. D. Bernstein, *San Francisco Tape Music Center*, 19. For summaries of the electronic music studios established worldwide in the late 1950s, see, for example, Schrader, *Introduction to Electro-Acoustic Music*, 99–116; Manning, *Electronic & Computer Music*, 19–85; and Holmes, *Electronic and Experimental Music*, 64–75.

20. Ramon Sender, "The San Francisco Tape Music Center: A Report," unpublished manuscript (1964), 3–4; quoted in D. Bernstein, *San Francisco Tape Music Center*, 18–19. The manuscript is held in the archives of the Center for Contemporary Music at Mills College in Oakland, California, to which the San Francisco Tape Music Center relocated after receiving a grant from the Rockefeller Foundation in 1966.

21. John Rockwell, foreword to D. Bernstein, *San Francisco Tape Music Center*, ix.

22. A. Rich, *American Pioneers*, 211.

23. Leta A. Miller, "ONCE and Again: The Evolution of a Legendary Festival," liner note essay for *Music from the ONCE Festival: 1961–1966* (80567-2) (New York: New World Records, 2003), 28.

24. Mark Clague, "ONCE More: An Introduction," available at UMS Lobby, http://www.umslobby.org/index.php/2010/10/once-more-an-introduction-by-mark-clague-3576.

25. Miller, "ONCE and Again," 15.

26. Valerie Hellstein, "The Cage-iness of Abstract Expressionism," *American Art* 28, no. 1 (2014): 56.

27. Michael Nyman, *Experimental Music: Cage and Beyond*, 2nd ed. (Cambridge: Cambridge University Press, 1999), 72.

28. John Cage, "Experimental Music," in *Silence: Lectures and Writings* (Cambridge: M.I.T. Press, 1961), 12.

29. George Maciunas, "Fluxus Manifesto," 1963. Maciunas's one-page self-published manifesto is reproduced in, for example, Paul Wood, ed., *Varieties of Modernism* (New Haven, CT: Yale University Press, 2004), 309.

30. Hannah Higgins, "Border Crossings: Three Transnationalisms of Fluxus," in *Not the Other Avant-Garde: The Transnational Foundations of Avant-Garde Performance*, ed. James M. Harding and John Rouse (Ann Arbor: University of Michigan Press, 2006), 277.

31. Peter Frank, "Fluxus Music," in *Breaking the Sound Barrier: A Critical Anthology of the New Music*, ed. Gregory Battcock (New York: E. P. Dutton, 1981), 18; emphasis added; originally published in *Journal: Southern California Art Magazine* 22 (March–April 1979): 18–20.

32. Herman Kahn, *On Thermonuclear War* (Princeton, NJ: Princeton University Press, 1960), 140–48. For details on Kahn's colorful career, see Sharon Ghamri-Tabrizi, *The Worlds of Herman Kahn* (Cambridge: Harvard University Press, 2005).

33. Fred Kaplan, *1959: The Year Everything Changed* (Hoboken, NJ: John Wiley, 2009), 4.

34. Stephen J. Whitfield, "How the Fifties Became the Sixties," *Historically Speaking* (January–February 2008): 10.

35. Terry Anderson, "How the Fifties Became the Sixties: A Response," *Historically Speaking* (January–February 2008): 11.

36. The term seems to have originated with Henry Geldzahler, who used it in his catalog for the Metropolitan Museum of Art's 1969 exhibition "New York Painting and Sculpture: 1940–1970." Referring to, and arguing with, Geldzahler, art critic Harold Rosenberg sarcastically used the title "École de New York" for one of the essays in his 1972 *The De-Definition of Art* (New York: Macmillan). Apparently agreeing with Geldzahler, Dore Ashton published a book titled *The New York School: A Cultural Reckoning* (New York: Viking, 1973).

37. Max Kozloff, "American Painting during the Cold War," *Artforum* 11, no. 9 (1973): 51, 43.

38. In her exhaustive study of press coverage for the composers of the New York School, Suzanne Robinson notes that the relationship between Thomson and Cage "conformed to a model of homosexual patronage in which an older master shepherds a young ingénue." In the early 1950s, as Cage's music grew increasingly radical, "Thomson obstinately continued to defend Cage as a cause but remained strangely silent on the subject of individual works." Suzanne Robinson, "'A Ping, Qualified by a Thud': Music Criticism in Manhattan and the Case of Cage (1943–58)," *Journal of the Society for American Music* 1, no. 1 (2007): 83.

39. J. H., "Look, No Hands! And It's 'Music,'" *New York Times*, April 15, 1954, 34; Harold C. Schonberg, "'Advanced' Music Beeps and Plinks," *New York Times*, April 8, 1959, 43.

40. Cage was born in 1912; Brown, Feldman, and Tudor were all born in 1926; Wolff was born in 1934.

41. Earle Brown, in John Yaffé, "An Interview with Composer Earle Brown," *Contemporary Music Review* 26, nos. 3–4 (2007), 304; emphasis original.

42. John Cage, quoted in Calvin Tomkins, *The Bride and the Bachelors: Five Masters of the Avant-Garde* (New York: Viking, 1965), 108.

43. Cage, "Indeterminacy," in *Silence*, 36.

44. Ibid., 37–38.

45. Ibid., 36.

46. Ibid., 38.

47. For a description of these paintings and an account of how they directly inspired Cage's effort, see Calvin Tomkins, *Off the Wall: Robert Rauschenberg and the Art World of Our Time* (New York: Penguin Books, 1980), 70–75.

48. Cowell's 1925 *The Banshee*, a product of America's first wave of modernism, involves the scraping of the piano strings with a rubber wedge. The other compositions were Wolff's 1952 *For Piano* and 1951 *For Prepared Piano*, Feldman's 1952 *Extensions 3* and *Intermission 5*, Brown's 1951 *3 Pieces for Piano*, all of them in one way or another "indeterminate," and Boulez's 1946 Piano Sonata No. 1, a work whose content was to a large extent "determined" by the principles of twelve-note serialism.

49. The most detailed, and most carefully researched, account of the premiere is found in Kyle Gann, *No Such Thing as Silence: John Cage's 4'33"* (New Haven, CT: Yale University Press, 2010), 1–8.

50. John Cage, 1968 interview with John Kobler, quoted in *Conversing with Cage*, ed. Richard Kostelanetz (New York: Limelight Editions, 1988), 65.

51. John Cage, 1985 interview with Ellsworth Snyder, quoted in *Conversing with Cage*, 66; emphasis added.

52. William Brooks, "Music and Society," in *The Cambridge Companion to John Cage*, ed. David Nicholls (Cambridge: Cambridge University Press, 2002), 219.

53. John Cage, *M: Writings, '67-'72* (Middletown, CT: Wesleyan University Press, 1974), v. The dedication was penned in 1967. The first item in the collection, "Diary: How to Improve the World (You Will Only Make It Worse)," is rich with allusions to the American civil rights movement, the conflict in Southeast Asia, and strife in South Africa and the Middle East.

54. Luigi Nono, quoted in Michael Gorodecki, "Strands in 20th-Century Italian Music: Luigi Nono: A History of Belief," *Musical Times* 133, no. 1787 (1992): 10. The quotation is from Nono's "The Presence of History in Music Today," *Score* 27 (1960): 41–45; the article is a translation of an address that Nono gave at Darmstadt in the summer of 1959.

55. Yvonne Rainer, "Looking Myself in the Mouth," *October* 17 (Summer 1981): 67. Rainer was a dancer/choreographer whose early work, beginning around 1960, owed much to Cage's ideas of indeterminacy.

56. Christian Wolff, "Experimental Music around 1950 and Some Consequences and Causes (Socio-Political and Musical)," *American Music* 27, no. 4 (2009): 431.

57. Earle Brown, in Amy C. Beal, "An Interview with Earle Brown," *Contemporary Music Review* 26, nos. 3–4 (2007), 348.

58. Earle Brown, in Yaffé, "Interview with Composer Earle Brown," 305; emphasis original.

59. Caroline A. Jones, "Finishing School: John Cage and the Abstract Expressionist Ego," *Critical Inquiry* 19 (Summer 1993): 639.

60. Hellstein, "Cage-iness of Abstract Expressionism," 58.

61. Connections between the CIA and the Museum of Modern Art, whose board of directors included several wealthy New Yorkers who during World War II had served in the intelligence service, were first pointed out by Eva Cockroft in "Abstract Expressionism: Weapon of the Cold War," *Artforum* 12, no. 10 (1974): 39–41. For a full account of the CIA's involvement with the promotion of abstract expressionist painting, see chapter 16 ("Yanqui Doodles") of Saunders, *Cultural Cold War*, 252–78.

62. C. Jones, "Finishing School," 640.

63. Hellstein, "Cage-iness of Abstract Expressionism," 58.

64. Marjorie Perloff, "Watchman, Spy, and Dead Man: Jasper Johns, Frank O'Hara, John Cage and the 'Aesthetic of Indifference,'" *Modernism/modernity* 8, no. 2 (2001): 205.

65. John Cage, 1965 interview with Lars Gunnar Bodin et al., quoted in Kostelanetz, *Conversing with Cage*, 177.

66. David W. Bernstein, "John Cage and the 'Aesthetic of Indifference,'" in *The New York Schools of Music and Visual Arts*, ed. Steven Johnson (New York: Routledge, 2002), 121.

67. John Cage, "Lecture on Nothing," in *Silence*, 109.

68. C. Jones, "Finishing School," 643.

69. D. Bernstein, "John Cage and the 'Aesthetic of Indifference,'" 120.

70. Gavin Butt, "America and Its Discontents: Art and Politics 1945–1960," in *A Companion to Contemporary Art since 1945*, ed. Amelia Jones (Oxford: Blackwell, 2006), 26.

71. See, for example, Jonathan D. Katz, "John Cage's Queer Silence; or, How to Avoid Making Matters Worse," *GLQ* 5, no. 2 (1999): 231–52; Philip Gentry, chapter 5 ("The Cultural Politics of *4'33"*: Identity and Sexuality") of "The Age of Anxiety: Music, Politics and McCarthyism, 1948–1954," PhD dissertation, University of California–Los Angeles, 2008; and Rebecca Y. Kim, "In No Uncertain Musical Terms: The Cultural Politics of John Cage's Indeterminacy," PhD dissertation, Columbia University, 2008.

72. Tomkins, *Off the Wall*, 260.

73. Fearful of the laws against sodomy, Cage and Cunningham did not live together until 1971.

74. Morton Feldman, in *Morton Feldman Says: Selected Interviews and Lectures, 1964–1987*, ed. Chris Villars (London: Hyphen, 2006), 219–20.

75. D. Bernstein, "John Cage and the 'Aesthetic of Indifference,'" 121.

76. Debunking the idea that the homosexual Cage was in personal ways hostile to the mostly heterosexual abstract expressionists is the theme not only of Hellstein's "Cage-iness of Abstract Expressionism" and C. Jones's "Finishing School" but also of Douglas Kahn's "John Cage: Silence and Silencing," *Musical Quarterly* 81, no. 4 (1997): 556–98.

77. Moira Roth, "The Aesthetics of Indifference," in Moira Roth and Jonathan Katz, *Difference/Indifference: Musings on Postmodernism, Marcel Duchamp and John Cage* (Amsterdam: G + B Arts International, 1998), 35. Roth's essay first appeared in *Artforum* 16, no. 3 (November 1977): 46–53.

78. Kay Larson uses the phrase "ego noise" as the title of the sixth chapter (159–94) of her *Where the Heart Beats: John Cage, Zen Buddhism, and the Inner Life of Artists* (New York: Penguin, 2012).

79. Ashton, *New York School*, 3.

80. Wolff, "Experimental Music," 434.

81. Serge Guilbaut, *How New York Stole the Idea of Modern Art: Abstract Expressionism, Freedom, and the Cold War*, trans. Arthur Goldhammer (Chicago: University of Chicago Press, 1983), 196–97.

82. Susan Sontag, "The Aesthetics of Silence," in *Styles of Radical Will* (New York: Delta, 1969), 32.

83. Butt, "America and Its Discontents," 21.

84. Harold Rosenberg, *Artworks & Packages* (Chicago: University of Chicago Press, 1969), 132.

85. Mark Silverberg, *The New York School Poets and the Neo-Avant-Garde: Between Radical Art and Radical Chic* (Surrey, UK: Ashgate, 2013), 37.

86. D. Bernstein, "John Cage and the 'Aesthetic of Indifference,'" 128; emphasis added.

87. Jonathan Katz, "Identification," in Roth and Katz, *Difference/Indifference*, 51.

Epilogue

1. See William S. Graebner, *The Age of Doubt: American Thought and Culture in the 1940s* (Boston: G. K. Hall, 1991); Brink Lindsey, *The Age of Abundance: How Prosperity Transformed America's Politics and Culture* (New York: HarperCollins, 2007); Joseph Henry Satin, *The 1950s: America's "Placid" Decade* (New York: Houghton Mifflin, 1960); Goldman, *Crucial Decade and After*; John Patrick Diggins, *The Proud Decades: America in War and Peace, 1941–1960* (New York: W. W. Norton, 1989); and Sam Roberts, "A Decade of Fear," *New York Times Upfront: The Newsmagazine for Teens* 142, March 15, 2010, *Scholastic.com*, http://teacher.scholastic.com/scholasticnews/ indepth/upfront/features/index.asp?article=1031510_mccarthyism).

2. *Newsweek*, October 16, 1972, cover and 78.

3. Ibid., 78.

4. I. F. Stone, *The Haunted Fifties, 1953–1963: A Nonconformist History of Our Times* (Boston: Little, Brown, 1969).

5. Robert Lowell, "Memories of West Street and Lepke," in *Robert Lowell: Collected Poems*, ed. Frank Bidart and David Gewanter (New York: Farrar, Straus, and Giroux, 2003), 187. The poem dates from 1957.

6. Played by Carroll O'Connor, Archie Bunker was one of the main characters on the sitcom *All in the Family*, which aired on the CBS television network from 1971 until 1979. The quoted words are contained in the lyrics of the show's theme song, "Those Were the Days," by Lee Adams and Charles Strouse.

7. Martin Halliwell, *American Culture in the 1950s* (Edinburgh, UK: Edinburgh University Press, 2007), 3.

8. Norbert Wiener, *The Human Use of Human Beings: Cybernetics and Society* (New York: Da Capo Press, 1954), 112; Lewis Mumford, *Art and Technics* (New York: Oxford University Press, 1952), 3.

9. *Life*, June 16, 1972, 38.

10. These include *M*A*S*H* (1970), a "gallows humor" portrait of a Korean War medical unit; *The Last Picture Show* (1971), a melancholy story about a worn-out small Midwestern town in the early 1950s; *The Way We Were* (1973), a romance involving a couple whose left-leaning sympathies had been quite acceptable before World War II but became increasingly problematic in the postwar years; *Chinatown* (1974), a full-color "noir" film set in postwar Los Angeles; and *The Front* (1976), a tragicomedy that stars Woody Allen as a talentless writer who is hired to front for a blacklisted Hollywood scenarist.

11. Approximately half of the songs featured in *Grease* indeed date from the Fifties; the film's other songs, clearly intended to fit in with the film's fictional setting, were created afresh by Jim Jacobs and Warren Casey. The theme song for the television program *Happy Days*, which fairly wallows in the I-vi-IV-V chord progression endemic to rock 'n' roll songs of the late 1950s, was written especially for the show by Norman Gimbel and Charles Fox.

12. The quotations are from reviews—in *U.S. News & World Report*, the *National Review*, and the *Boston Sunday Globe*—excerpted as blurbs on the back cover of David Frum, *How We Got Here: The '70s, the Decade That Brought You Modern Life—For Better or Worse* (New York: Basic Books, 2000).

13. Bruce J. Schulman, *The Seventies: The Great Shift in American Culture, Society, and Politics* (New York: Simon and Schuster, 2002), 1. The first quotation belongs to Schulman; the second quotation is one that Schulman attributes only to "one journalist."

14. Fred Davis, "Nostalgia, Identity and the Current Nostalgia Wave," *Journal of Popular Culture* 11, no. 2 (1977): 421.

15. Daniel Marcus, *Happy Days and Wonder Years: The Fifties and the Sixties in Contemporary Cultural Politics* (New Brunswick, NJ: Rutgers University Press, 2004), 2. The first quotation, with emphasis added, is from Greil Marcus, *Double Trouble: Bill Clinton and Elvis Presley in a Land of No Alternatives* (New York: Henry Holt, 2000), 209.

16. The term "simulacrum" did not originate with the French philosopher Jean Baudrillard, but in the writings of thinkers in the so-called postmodern vein it is most often associated with him. Baudrillard's thoughts on Disneyland as "simulacrum" appear in many of his writings, most notably in *Simulacra and Simulation*, trans. Sheila Glaser (Ann Arbor: University of Michigan Press, 1994), and *America*, trans. Chris Turner (London: Verso, 1988). The original texts—*Simulacres et Simulation* and *Amérique*, respectively—date from 1981 and 1986.

17. For a statistics-rich analysis of how the Fifties-oriented marketing strategies of the 1970s played out, see Diane Furno-Lamude, "Baby Boomers' Susceptibility to Nostalgia," *Communication Reports* 7, no. 2 (1994): 130–35.

18. Robb McDaniel, "Pleasantville (Ross 1998)," *Film & History: An Interdisciplinary Journal of Film and Television Studies* 32, no. 1 (2002): 85.

19. Ibid., 86.

20. Gary Ross, in Amy Wallace, "Showing His True Colors," *Los Angeles Times*, September 20, 1998, http://articles.latimes.com/1998/sep/20/entertainment/ca-24474.

21. *A Beautiful Mind* tells the story of John Forbes Nash, a brilliant mathematician whose contributions to Cold War code-breaking were hampered by his severe schizophrenia. As their titles suggest, *Kinsey* and *Capote* are portraits of the pioneering sex researcher Alfred Kinsey and the writer Truman Capote, who at the biographical points on which the films focus were absorbed, respectively, in writing their reports on human sexuality (1948 and 1953) and the "non-fiction novel" *In Cold Blood* (1966). *Good Night, and Good Luck* centers on television journalist Edward R. Murrow's 1954 investigation of Senator Joseph McCarthy. *The Good Shepherd*, whose fictional main character is based on the real-life James Angleton, depicts the founding of the CIA. *Hollywoodland* deals with the investigation into the 1959 death of actor George Reeves. *Cadillac Records* concerns the founding of Chess Records and the creation of African American rock 'n' roll stars. *On the Road* is an adaptation of the

same-titled 1957 biographical novel by Beat writer Jack Kerouac. *Far from Heaven*, *Revolutionary Road*, and *Shutter Island* are entirely fictional. Whereas the first two are domestic romance-tragedies, *Shutter Island* is a murder mystery involving a U.S. marshal who perhaps had been involved in Cold War espionage. *Far from Heaven* features an original screenplay by director Todd Haynes; *Revolutionary Road* and *Shutter Island* are based on novels, respectively, by Richard Yates and Dennis Lehane.

22. David R. Shumway, "Rock 'n' Roll Sound Tracks and the Production of Nostalgia," *Cinema Journal* 38, no. 2 (1999): 40.

Bibliography

Adamowski, T. H. "Frank Sinatra: The Subject and His Music," *Journal of Popular Culture* 33, no. 4 (2000): 1–11.

———. "Love in the Western World: Sinatra and the Conflict of Generations." In Mustazza, *Frank Sinatra and Popular Culture*, 26–37.

Altschuler, Glenn C. *All Shook Up: How Rock 'n' Roll Changed America*. Oxford: Oxford University Press, 2003.

Anderson, Terry. "How the Fifties Became the Sixties: A Response." *Historically Speaking* (January–February 2008): 11–12.

Ansari, Emily Abrams. "Aaron Copland and the Politics of Cultural Diplomacy." *Journal of the Society for American Music* 5, no. 3 (2011): 335–64.

———. "Shaping the Policies of Cold War Musical Diplomacy: An Epistemic Community of American Composers." *Diplomatic History* 36, no. 1 (2012): 41–52.

Ardoin, John. "Opera and Television." *Opera Quarterly* 1, no. 1 (1983): 47–53.

Ashton, Dore. *The New York School: A Cultural Reckoning*. New York: Viking, 1973.

Auden, W. H. *The Age of Anxiety: A Baroque Eclogue*. Edited by Alan Jacobs. Princeton, NJ: Princeton University Press, 2011.

Babbitt, Milton. *The Collected Essays of Milton Babbitt*. Edited by Stephen Peles, Stephen Dembski, Andrew Mead, and Joseph N. Straus. Princeton, NJ: Princeton University Press, 2003.

———. "The Composer as Specialist." In *Music in the Western World: A History in Documents*, edited by Piero Weiss and Richard Taruskin, 529–34. New York: Schirmer, 1984.

———. "My Vienna Triangle at Washington Square Revisited and Dilated." In *Driven into Paradise: The Musical Migration from Nazi Germany to the United States*, edited by Reinhold Brinkman and Christoph Wolff, 33–53. Berkeley: University of California Press, 1999.

———. "The Structure and Function of Music Theory." In *Perspectives on Contemporary Music Theory*, edited by Benjamin Boretz and Edward T. Cone, 10–21. New York: W. W. Norton, 1972. Originally published in *College Music Symposium* 5 (Fall 1965): 49–60.

———. "Who Cares If You Listen?" *High Fidelity* 8, no. 2 (1958): 38–40, 126–27.

———. *Words about Music.* Edited by Stephen Dembski and Joseph N. Straus. Madison: University of Wisconsin Press, 1987.

Baker, Theodore. "Bebop." In *Pocket Manual of Musical Terms*, 5th ed. Revised by Laura Kuhn. New York: Schirmer, 1995.

Ballinger, Alexander, and Danny Graydon. *The Rough Guide to Film Noir.* London: Rough Guides, 2007.

Barnhisel, Greg. "*Perspectives USA* and the Cultural Cold War: Modernism in Service of the State." *Modernism/modernity* 14, no. 4 (2007): 729–54.

Baudrillard, Jean. *America.* Translated by Chris Turner. London: Verso, 1988.

———. *Simulacra and Simulation.* Translated by Sheila Glaser. Ann Arbor: University of Michigan Press, 1994.

Baughman, James L. *Same Time, Same Station: Creating American Television, 1948–1961.* Baltimore: Johns Hopkins University Press, 2007.

Beal, Amy C. "An Interview with Earle Brown." *Contemporary Music Review* 26, nos. 3–4 (2007): 341–56.

———. "Negotiating Cultural Allies: American Music in Darmstadt, 1946–1956." *Journal of the American Musicological Society* 53, no. 1 (2000): 105–39.

Becker, Howard S. *Outsiders: Studies in the Sociology of Deviance.* New York: Free Press, 1963.

———. "The Professional Dance Musician and His Audience." *American Journal of Sociology* 57, no. 2 (1951): 136–44.

———. "Some Contingencies of the Professional Dance Musician's Career." *Human Organization* 12 (Spring 1953): 22–26.

Beidler, Philip D. "*South Pacific* and American Remembering; or, 'Josh, We're Going to Buy This Son of a Bitch!'" *Journal of American Studies* 27, no. 2 (1993): 207–22.

Bernstein, David. "John Cage and the 'Aesthetic of Indifference.'" In *The New York Schools of Music and Visual Arts*, edited by Steven Johnson, 113–33. New York: Routledge, 2002.

———. *The San Francisco Tape Music Center: 1960s Counterculture and the Avant-Garde.* Berkeley: University of California Press, 2008.

Bernstein, Elmer. "What Ever Happened to Great Movie Music?" *High Fidelity* (July 1972): 55–58.

Bernstein, Leonard. "Aaron Copland: An Intimate Sketch." *High Fidelity* 20, no. 11 (1970): 53, 55, 63.

———. "What Makes Opera Grand?" In *The Joy of Music*, 278–316. New York: Simon and Schuster, 1959.

Berry, David Carson. "Schenkerian Theory in the United States: A Review of Its Establishment and a Survey of Current Research Topics." *Zeitschrift der Gesselschaft für Musiktheorie* 2, nos. 2–3 (2005): 101–37.

Bertrand, Michael T. *Race, Rock, and Elvis.* Urbana: University of Illinois Press, 2000.

Biskind, Peter. *Seeing Is Believing: How Hollywood Taught Us to Stop Worrying and Love the Fifties.* New York: Henry Holt, 1983.

Blake, David, ed. *Hanns Eisler: A Miscellany.* Luxembourg: Harwood Academic Publishers, 1995.

Block, Geoffrey. "The Broadway Canon from *Show Boat* to *West Side Story* and the European Operatic Ideal." *Journal of Musicology* 11, no. 4 (1993): 525–44.

Border, Raymond, and Etienne Chaumeton. "Toward a Definition of *Film Noir.*" In *Film Noir Reader*, edited by Alain Silver and James Ursini, 17–26. New York: Limelight Editions. 1996.

Borstelmann, Thomas. *The Cold War and the Color Line: American Race Relations in the Global Arena.* Cambridge: Harvard University Press, 2001.

Boulez, Pierre. "Possibly . . . ." In *Stocktakings from an Apprenticeship*, edited by Paule Thévenin; translated by Stephen Walsh, 111–40. New York: Oxford University Press, 1991.

Breines, Wini. *Young, White, and Miserable: Growing Up Female in the Fifties.* Boston: Beacon Press, 1992.

Brinkley, Alan. "The Illusion of Identity in Cold War Culture." In *Rethinking Cold War Culture*, edited by Peter J. Kuznick and James Gilbert, 61–73. Washington, DC: Smithsonian Institution Press, 2001.

Brody, Martin. "'Music for the Masses': Milton Babbitt's Cold War Music Theory." *Musical Quarterly* 77, no. 2 (1993): 161–92.

Brooks, William. "Music and Society." In *The Cambridge Companion to John Cage*, edited by David Nicholls, 214–26. Cambridge: Cambridge University Press, 2002.

Broyard, Anatole. "Portrait of the Hipster." *Partisan Review* 15, no. 5 (1948): 721–27.

Bundy, McGeorge. *Danger and Survival: Choices about the Bomb in the First Fifty Years.* New York: Random House, 1988.

Burke, Richard C. "The NBC Opera Theater." *Journal of Broadcasting* 10, no. 1 (1965): 13–23.

———. "Television in the Opera House." *Central States Speech Journal* 18, no. 3 (1967): 163–68.

Burton, Humphrey. *Leonard Bernstein.* New York: Doubleday, 1994.

Butt, Gavin. "America and Its Discontents: Art and Politics 1945–1960." In *A Companion to Contemporary Art since 1945*, edited by Amelia Jones, 19–36. Oxford: Blackwell, 2006.

Buzzell, John, ed. *Mister Rock 'n' Roll: Alan Freed.* Los Angeles: National Rock 'n' Roll Archives, 1986.

Cage, John. *M: Writings, '67–'72.* Middletown, CT: Wesleyan University Press, 1974.

———. *Silence: Lectures and Writings.* Cambridge: M.I.T. Press, 1961.

Cameron, William B. "Sociological Notes on the Jam Session." *Social Forces* 33, no. 2 (1954): 177–82.

Carney, Ray. "Escape Velocity: Notes on Beat Film." In *Beat Culture and the New America: 1950–1965*, edited by Lisa Phillips, 190–214. New York: Whitney Museum of American Art, 1995.

Carroll, Mark. *Music and Ideology in Cold War Europe*. New York: Cambridge University Press, 2003.

Caute, David. *The Dancer Defects: The Struggles for Cultural Supremacy during the Cold War*. Oxford: Oxford University Press, 2003.

Chafe, William H. *The Paradox of Change: American Women in the 20th Century*. New York: Oxford University Press, 1992.

———. "Social Change and the American Woman, 1940–1970." In Chafe and Sitkoff, *History of Our Time*, 207–15.

Chafe, William H., and Harvard Sitkoff, eds. *A History of Our Time: Readings on Postwar America*. New York: Oxford University Press, 1987.

Chapple, Steve, and Reebee Garafalo. *Rock 'n' Roll Is Here to Pay: The History and Politics of the Music Industry*. Chicago: Nelson-Hall, 1977.

Charbonnier, Georges. *Entretiens avec Edgard Varèse: Suivis d'une étude de l'œuvre*. Paris: Éditions Pierre Belfond, 1970.

Charters, Ann. *Kerouac*. San Francisco: Straight Arrow Press, 1973.

Christensen, Thomas. *Rameau and Musical Thought in the Enlightenment*. Cambridge: Cambridge University Press, 1993.

Citron, Marcia J. *Opera on Screen*. New Haven, CT: Yale University Press, 2000.

Citron, Stephen. *The Wordsmiths: Oscar Hammerstein 2nd and Alan Jay Lerner*. New York: Oxford University Press, 1995.

Clague, Mark. "ONCE More: An Introduction." *UMS Lobby*. http://www.umslobby .org/index.php/2010/10/once-more-an-introduction-by-mark-clague-3576.

Clarens, Carlos. *An Illustrated History of the Horror Film*. New York: Capricorn Books, 1967.

Clark, Dick, and Richard Robinson. *Rock, Roll & Remember*. New York: Crowell, 1976.

Clarke, Donald. *The Rise and Fall of Popular Music*. New York: St. Martin's Griffin, 1995.

Coady, Christopher. "AfroModernist Subversion of Film Noir Conventions in John Lewis' Score to *Sait-on Jamais* (1957) and *Odds Against Tomorrow* (1959)." *Musicology Australia* 34, no. 1 (2012): 1–31.

Coase, R. H. "Payola in Radio and Television Broadcasting." *Journal of Law and Economics* 22, no. 2 (1979): 269–328.

Cockroft, Eva. "Abstract Expressionism: Weapon of the Cold War." *Artforum* 12, no. 10 (1974): 39–41.

Coleman, Peter. *The Liberal Conspiracy: The Congress for Cultural Freedom and the Struggle for the Mind of Postwar Europe*. New York: Free Press, 1989.

Collier, James Lincoln. *Benny Goodman and the Swing Era*. New York: Oxford University Press, 1989.

Cone, Edward T. "Conversation with Aaron Copland." *Perspectives of New Music* 6, no. 2 (1968): 57–72. Reprinted in *Perspectives on American Composers*, edited by Benjamin Boretz and Edward T. Cone, 131–46. New York: W. W. Norton, 1971).

Conway, Mike. "A Guest in Our Living Room: The Television Newscaster before the Rise of the Dominant Anchor." *Journal of Broadcasting and Electronic Media* 51, no. 3 (2007): 457–78.

Cooper, Lee B. "From 'Love Letters' to 'Miss You': Popular Recordings, Epistolary Imagery, and Romance during War Time, 1941–1945." *Journal of American Culture* 19 (Winter 1996): 15–27.

———. *Images of American Society in Popular Music*. Chicago: Nelson-Hall, 1982.

Copland, Aaron. *Copland on Music*. 1960. New York: W. W. Norton, 1963.

———. *Music and Imagination*. New York: New American Library, 1952.

Copland, Aaron, and Vivian Perlis. *Copland: Since 1943*. New York: St. Martin's Press, 1989.

Crist, Elizabeth B. "Mutual Responses in the Midst of an Era: Aaron Copland's *The Tender Land* and Leonard Bernstein's *Candide*." *Journal of Musicology* 23, no. 4 (2006): 485–527.

Dalzell, Tom. *Flappers 2 Rappers: American Youth Slang*. Springfield, IL: Merriam-Webster, 1996.

Davis, Fred. "Nostalgia, Identity and the Current Nostalgia Wave." *Journal of Popular Culture* 11, no. 2 (1977): 414–24.

DeLapp-Birkett, Jennifer. "Aaron Copland and the Politics of Twelve-Tone Composition in the Early Cold War United States." *Journal of Musicological Research* 27 (2008): 31–62.

Dettmar, Kevin J. H. *Is Rock Dead?* New York: Routledge, 2006.

DeVeaux, Scott. "Bebop and the Recording Industry: The 1942 AFM Recording Ban Reconsidered." *Journal of the American Musicological Society* 41, no. 1 (1988): 126–65.

———. *The Birth of Bebop: A Social and Musical History*. Berkeley: University of California Press, 1997.

Dickinson, Peter. *Samuel Barber Remembered: A Centenary Tribute*. Rochester, NY: University of Rochester Press, 2010.

Diggins, John Patrick. *The Proud Decades: America in War and Peace, 1941–1960*. New York: W. W. Norton, 1989.

Doherty, Thomas Patrick. *Cold War, Cool Medium: Television, McCarthyism, and American Culture*. New York: Columbia University Press, 2005.

———. *Teenagers and Teenpics: The Juvenilization of American Movies in the 1950s*. 2nd ed. Philadelphia: Temple University Press, 2002.

Durand, John N. "Married Women in the Labor Force." *American Journal of Sociology* 52 (November 1946): 217–23.

Eaton, Quaintance. "Great Opera Houses: NBC TV." *Opera News*, February 8, 1964: 5, 30.

Eisler, Hanns. "Contemporary Music and Fascism." In *Hanns Eisler: Musik und Politik Schriften: 1924–1948*, edited by Günter Mayer, 489–93. Leipzig: Deutscher Verlag für Musik, 1983.

Engel, Lehman. *The American Musical Theater*. New York: Collier, 1975. Originally published as *The American Musical Theater: A Consideration* (New York: Macmillan, 1967).

———, and Howard Kissel. *Words with Music: Creating the Broadway Musical Libretto* (New York: Applause Books, 1971).

Esman, Aaron H. "Jazz—A Study in Cultural Conflict." *American Imago* 8, no. 2 (1951): 219–26.

Evans, Joyce A. *Celluloid Mushroom Clouds: Hollywood and the Atomic Bomb*. Boulder, CO: Westview Press, 1998.

Fauser, Annegret. *Sounds of War: Music in the United States during World War II*. Oxford: Oxford University Press, 2013.

Feldman, Gene, and Max Gartenberg, eds. *The Beat Generation and the Angry Young Men*. New York: Citadel Press, 1958.

Feldman, Morton. *Morton Feldman Says: Selected Interviews and Lectures, 1964–1987*. Edited by Chris Villars. London: Hyphen, 2006.

Filmer, Paul, Val Rimmer, and Dave Walsh. "*Oklahoma!*: Ideology and Politics in the Vernacular Tradition of the American Musical." *Popular Music* 18, no. 3 (1999): 381–95.

Flinn, Denny Martin. *Musical! A Grand Tour*. New York: Schirmer, 1997.

Floyd, Carlisle. "Recalling *Susannah*'s Beginnings." Liner note essay for *Susannah: A Musical Drama in Two Acts,* Virgin Classics 5 45039 2 (1994): 14–15.

Fordin, Hugh. *Getting to Know Him: A Biography of Oscar Hammerstein II*. New York: Da Capo Press, 1995.

Frank, Peter. "Fluxus Music." In *Breaking the Sound Barrier: A Critical Anthology of the New Music*, edited by Gregory Battcock, 13–19. New York: E. P. Dutton, 1981. Originally published in *Journal: Southern California Art Magazine* 22 (March–April 1979): 18–20.

Friedan, Betty. *The Feminine Mystique*. New York: Dell, 1963.

Frum, David. *How We Got Here: The '70s, the Decade That Brought You Modern Life—For Better or Worse*. New York: Basic Books, 2000.

Furno-Lamude, Diane. "Baby Boomers' Susceptibility to Nostalgia." *Communication Reports* 7, no. 2 (1994): 130–35.

Gabbard, Krin, ed. *Jammin' at the Margins: Jazz in the American Cinema*. Chicago: University of Chicago Press, 1996.

———. *Representing Jazz*. Durham, NC: Duke University Press, 1995.

Gac, Scott. "Jazz Strategy: Dizzy, Foreign Policy, and Government in 1956." *Americana: The Journal of American Popular Culture* 4, no. 1 (2005). http://www.americanpopularculture.com/journal/articles/spring_2005/gac.htm.

Gann, Kyle. *No Such Thing as Silence: John Cage's 4'33"*. New Haven, CT: Yale University Press, 2010.

George, Nelson. *The Death of Rhythm & Blues*. New York: E. P. Dutton, 1988.

Ghamri-Tabrizi, Sharon. *The Worlds of Herman Kahn*. Cambridge: Harvard University Press, 2005.

Gilbert, James B. *A Cycle of Outrage: America's Reaction to the Juvenile Delinquent in the 1950s*. New York: Oxford University Press, 1986.

Gilbert, Roger. "The Swinger and the Loser: Sinatra, Masculinity, and Fifties Culture." In Mustazza, *Frank Sinatra and Popular Culture*, 38–49.

Gillespie, Dizzy (with Al Fraser). *To Be or Not to Bop: Memoirs of Dizzy Gillespie*. New York: Da Capo Press, 1979.

Gillett, Charlie. *The Sound of the City: The Rise of Rock and Roll*. Rev. ed. New York: Da Capo Press, 1996. Originally published 1970.

Ginsberg, Allen. *"Howl" and Other Poems*. San Francisco: City Lights, 1955.

Gioia, Ted. *The History of Jazz*. New York: Oxford University Press, 1997.

———. *The Imperfect Art: Reflections on Jazz and Modern Culture*. New York: Oxford University Press, 1988.

Goldman, Eric F. *The Crucial Decade—and After: America, 1945–1960*. New York: Vintage, 1960.

Gorbman, Claudia. *Unheard Melodies: Narrative Film Music*. Bloomington: Indiana University Press, 1987.

Gorodecki, Michael. "Strands in 20th-Century Italian Music: Luigi Nono: A History of Belief." *Musical Times* 133, no. 1787 (1992): 10–14, 16–17.

Graebner, William S. *The Age of Doubt: American Thought and Culture in the 1940s*. Boston: G. K. Hall, 1991.

Granade, Andrew. "When Worlds Collide: Harry Partch's Encounters with Film Music." *Music and the Moving Image* 4, no. 1 (2011): 9–33.

Greenwald, Ted. "The Self-Destructing Modules behind the Revolutionary 1956 Soundtrack of *Forbidden Planet*." *Keyboard* 12 (February 1986): 54–60, 65.

Gross, Klaus-Dieter. "McCarthyism and American Opera." *Revue LISA* 2, no. 3 (2004): 164–87.

Guilbaut, Serge. *How New York Stole the Idea of Modern Art: Abstract Expressionism, Freedom, and the Cold War*. Translated by Arthur Goldhammer. Chicago: University of Chicago Press, 1983.

Halberstam, David. *The Fifties*. New York: Villard Books, 1993.

Halliwell, Martin. *American Culture in the 1950s*. Edinburgh, UK: Edinburgh University Press, 2007.

Hamm, Charles. *Yesterdays: Popular Song in America*. New York: W. W. Norton, 1979.

Harker, Brian. "Milton Babbitt Encounters Academia (and Vice Versa)." *American Music* 26, no. 3 (2008): 336–77.

Haskell, Molly. *From Reverence to Rape: The Treatment of Women in the Movies*. New York: Penguin Books, 1974.

Hassan, Ihab Hassan. "The Character of Post-War Fiction in America." *English Journal* 51, no. 1 (1962): 1–8.

Hebdige, Dick. *Subculture: The Meaning of Style*. London: Methuen, 1979.

Heinsheimer, H. W. "Opera in America." *Tempo* 11 (June 1945): 6–9.

———. "Opera in America Today." *Musical Quarterly* 37, no. 3 (1951): 315–29.

Hellstein, Valerie. "The Cage-iness of Abstract Expressionism." *American Art* 28, no. 1 (2014): 56–77.

Herek, Gregory. "Beyond 'Homophobia': Thinking about Sexual Prejudice and Stigma in the Twenty-first Century." *Sexuality Research and Social Policy* 1, no. 2 (2004): 6–24.

Hickman, Roger. "Wavering Sonorities and the Nascent Film Noir Musical Style." *Journal of Film Music* 2, nos. 2–4 (2009): 165–74.

Higgins, Hannah. "Border Crossings: Three Transnationalisms of Fluxus." In *Not the Other Avant-Garde: The Transnational Foundations of Avant-Garde Performance*, edited by James M. Harding and John Rouse, 265–85. Ann Arbor: University of Michigan Press, 2006.

Hodeir, André. *Jazz: Its Evolution and Essence.* Translated by David Noakes. New York: Grove Press, 1956. Originally published as *Hommes et problèmes du jazz* (Marseilles: Parenthèses, 1954).

Holmes, Thomas B. *Electronic and Experimental Music.* New York: Scribner's, 1985.

Honey, Maureen. *Creating Rosie the Riveter: Class, Gender, and Propaganda during World War II.* Amherst: University of Massachusetts Press, 1984.

Horowitz, Joseph. *Classical Music in America: A History.* New York: W. W. Norton, 2005.

Howard, John Tasker. *Modern Music: A Popular Guide to Greater Musical Enjoyment.* New York: New American Library, 1957.

———. *This Modern Music: A Guide for the Bewildered Listener.* New York: Thomas Y. Cromwell, 1942.

Hubbs, Nadine. "Bernstein, Homophobia, Historiography." *Women and Music: A Journal of Gender and Culture* 13 (2009): 24–42.

———. "A French Connection: Modernist Codes in the Musical Closet." *GLQ: A Journal of Lesbian and Gay Studies* 6, no. 3 (2000): 389–412.

———. "Homophobia in Twentieth-Century Music: The Crucible of America's Sound." *Dædalus, the Journal of the American Academy of Arts & Sciences* 4 (Fall 2013): 45–50.

———. *The Queer Composition of America's Sound: Gay Modernists, American Music, and National Identity.* Berkeley: University of California Press, 2004.

Hughes, Langston. *The Big Sea.* New York: Knopf, 1940.

Hunt, Jacob T. "The Adolescent: His Characteristics and Development." *Review of Educational Research* 30, no. 1 (1960): 13–22.

Hutchins-Viroux, Rachel. "The American Opera Boom of the 1950s and 1960s: History and Stylistic Analysis." *Revue LISA* 2, no. 3 (2004): 145–63.

———. "Witch-hunts, Theocracies, and Hypocrisy: McCarthyism in Arthur Miller/Robert Ward's Opera *The Crucible* and Carlisle Floyd's *Susannah*." *Revue LISA* 6, no. 2 (2008): 140–48.

Jackson, John A. *Big Beat Heat: Alan Freed and the Early Years of Rock & Roll*. New York: Schirmer, 1991.

Johnson, Haynes. *The Age of Anxiety: McCarthyism to Terrorism*. New York: Harcourt, 2005.

Jones, Amelia, ed. *A Companion to Contemporary Art since 1945*. Oxford: Blackwell, 2006.

Jones, Caroline A. "Finishing School: John Cage and the Abstract Expressionist Ego." *Critical Inquiry* 19, no. 4 (1993): 628–65.

Jones, John Bush. *Our Musicals, Ourselves: A Social History of the American Musical Theatre*. Lebanon, NH: University Press of England, 2003.

Jones, LeRoi (Amiri Baraka). *Blues People: Negro Music in White America*. New York: HarperCollins, 1963.

Juno, Andrea, and V. Vale, eds. *Incredibly Strange Music*. San Francisco: V/Search, 1994.

Kahn, Douglas. "John Cage: Silence and Silencing." *Musical Quarterly* 81, no. 4 (1997): 556–98.

Kahn, E. J., Jr. *The Voice: The Story of an American Phenomenon—Frank Sinatra*. New York: Harper and Brothers, 1947.

Kahn, Herman. *On Thermonuclear War*. Princeton, NJ: Princeton University Press, 1960.

Kalinak, Kathryn. *Settling the Score: Music and the Classical Hollywood Film*. Madison: University of Wisconsin Press, 1992.

Kaplan, Fred. *1959: The Year Everything Changed*. Hoboken, NJ: John Wiley, 2009.

Kasha, Al, and Joel Hirschhorn. *Notes on Broadway: Intimate Conversations with Broadway's Greatest Songwriters*. New York: Simon and Schuster, 1985.

Kater, Michael H. *The Twisted Muse: Musicians and Their Music in the Third Reich*. Oxford: Oxford University Press.

Katz, Jonathan. "Identification." In Roth and Katz, *Difference/Indifference*, 46–69.

———. "John Cage's Queer Silence; or, How to Avoid Making Matters Worse." *GLQ* 5, no. 2 (1999): 231–52.

———. "Long Play: Adult-Oriented Popular Music and the Temporal Logics of the Post-War Sound Recording Industry in the USA." *Media, Culture & Society* 26, no. 3 (2004): 375–91.

Keightley, Keir. Review of *Sinatra! The Song Is You: A Singer's Art*, by Will Friedwald, *The Frank Sinatra Reader*, ed. Steven Petkov and Leonard Mustazza, and *Legend: Frank Sinatra and the American Dream*, ed. Ethlie Ann Vare. *American Music* 15, no. 1 (1997): 101–10.

Keniston, Kenneth. "Social Change and Youth in America." *Dædelus* 91, no. 1 (1962): 145–71.

Kennan, George F., *Memoirs: 1925-1950*. Boston: Little, Brown, 1967.

———. (aka "X"). "The Sources of Soviet Conduct." *Foreign Affairs* 25 (July 1947): 566–82.

Kernodle, Tammy L. "Arias, Communists, and Conspiracies: The History of Still's *Troubled Island*." *Musical Quarterly* 83, no. 4 (1999): 487–508.

Kerouac, Jack. *On the Road*. New York: Viking, 1987.

Kessler-Harris, Alice. *Out to Work: A History of Wage-Earning Women in the United States*. Oxford: Oxford University Press, 1983.

Kinsey, Alfred. *Sexual Behavior in the Human Female*. Philadelphia: W. B. Saunders, 1953.

Kirk, Elise K. *American Opera*. Urbana: University of Illinois Press, 2001.

———. "American Opera: Innovation and Tradition." In *The Cambridge Companion to Twentieth-Century Opera*, edited by Mervyn Cooke, 197–208. Cambridge: Cambridge University Press, 2005.

———. "United States of America." In *The New Grove Dictionary of Opera*, edited by Stanley Sadie, 4: 867–73. London: Macmillan, 1992.

Kivy, Peter. *The Possessor and the Possessed: Handel, Mozart, Beethoven, and the Idea of Musical Genius*. New Haven, CT: Yale University Press, 2001.

Klein, Christina. *Cold War Orientalism: Asia in the Middlebrow Imagination, 1945–1961*. Berkeley: University of California Press, 2003.

———. "Musicals and Modernization: Rodgers and Hammerstein's *The King and I*." In *Staging Growth: Modernization, Development, and the Global Cold War*, edited by David C. Engerman, Nils Gilman, Mark H. Haefele, and Michael E. Latham, 129–62. Amherst: University of Massachusetts Press, 2003.

Kofsky, Frank. *Black Music, White Business: Illuminating the History and Political Economy of Jazz*. New York: Pathfinder, 1998.

Kolt, Robert Paul. *Robert Ward's* The Crucible: *Creating an American Musical Nationalism*. Lanham, MD: Scarecrow Press, 2008.

Kostelanetz, Richard, ed. *Aaron Copland: A Reader—Selected Writings, 1923–1972*. New York: Routledge, 2003.

———. *Conversing with Cage*. New York: Limelight Editions, 1988.

Kowalke, Kim H. Untitled review of nine books. *Journal of the American Musicological Society* 60, no. 3 (2007): 688–714.

Kozloff, Max. "American Painting during the Cold War." *Artforum* 11, no. 9 (1973): 43–54.

Krenek, Ernst. *Music: Here and Now*. Translated by Barthold Fles. New York: W. W. Norton, 1939.

Kuznick, Peter J., and James Gilbert, eds. *Rethinking Cold War Culture*. Washington, DC: Smithsonian Institution Press, 2001.

Laing, Heather. *The Gendered Score: Music in 1940s Melodrama and the Woman's Film*. Aldershot, UK: Ashgate, 2007.

Larson, Kay. *Where the Heart Beats: John Cage, Zen Buddhism, and the Inner Life of Artists*. New York: Penguin, 2012.

Laubenstein, Paul Fritz. "Jazz—Debit and Credit." *Musical Quarterly* 15, no. 4 (1929): 606–24.

Lawson-Peebles, Robert, ed. *Approaches to the American Musical*. Exeter, UK: University of Exeter Press, 1996.

Leibowitz, René. *Schoenberg and His School.* Translated by Dika Newlin. New York: Philosophical Library, 1949. Originally published as *Schönberg et son école: l'étape contemporaine du langage musical* (Paris: J. B. Janin, 1947).

Lev, Peter, ed. *The Fifties: Transforming the Screen, 1950–1959.* Berkeley: University of California Press, 2003.

Leydon, Rebecca. "The Soft-Focus Sound: Reverb as a Gendered Attribute in Mid-Century Mood Music." *Perspectives of New Music* 39, no. 2 (2001): 96–107.

Ligeti, György. "On Music and Politics." Translated by Wes Blomster. *Perspectives of New Music* 16, no. 2 (1978): 19–24. Originally published in *Darmstädter Beiträge zue Neuen Musik* 13 (1973): 42–46.

Lindsey, Brink. *The Age of Abundance: How Prosperity Transformed America's Politics and Culture.* New York: HarperCollins, 2007.

Lippman, Walter. *The Cold War: A Study in U.S. Foreign Policy.* New York: Harper Brothers, 1947.

Lowell, Robert. *Robert Lowell: Collected Poems.* Edited by Frank Bidart and David Gewanter. New York: Farrar, Straus, and Giroux, 2003.

Machlis, Joseph. *Introduction to Contemporary Music.* New York: W. W. Norton, 1961.

Mailer, Norman. "The White Negro: Superficial Reflections on the Hipster." *Dissent* 4, no. 3 (1957): 276–93.

Manheim, James M. "B-side Sentimentalizer: 'Tennessee Waltz' in the History of Popular Music." *Musical Quarterly* 76, no. 3 (1992): 337–54.

Manning, Peter. *Electronic & Computer Music.* Oxford: Clarendon Press, 1985.

Marcus, Daniel. *Happy Days and Wonder Years: The Fifties and the Sixties in Contemporary Cultural Politics.* New Brunswick, NJ: Rutgers University Press, 2004.

Marcus, Greil. *Double Trouble: Bill Clinton and Elvis Presley in a Land of No Alternatives.* New York: Henry Holt, 2000.

Margolis, Norman M. "A Theory on the Psychology of Jazz." *American Imago* 11, no. 3 (1954): 253–91.

Mariano, Marco. "Fear of a Nonwhite Planet: Clare Booth Luce, Race, and American Foreign Policy." *Prospects* 29 (2005): 373–94.

Martin, Peter J. "Black Music—White History?" *Race Relations Abstracts* 25, no. 2 (2000): 3–18.

Marx, Gary T. "The White Negro and the Negro White." *Phylon* 28, no. 2 (1967): 168–77.

Mattis, Olivia. "Varèse's Multimedia Conception of *Déserts.*" *Musical Quarterly* 76, no. 4 (1992): 557–83.

Martin, Linda, and Kerry Segrave. *Anti-Rock: The Opposition to Rock 'n' Roll.* New York: Da Capo Press, 1993.

Mast, Gerald. *A Short History of the Movies.* New York: Pegasus, 1971.

May, Elaine Tyler. "Explosive Issues: Sex, Women, and the Bomb." In *Recasting America: Culture and Politics in the Age of Cold War,* edited by Lary May, 155–70. Chicago: University of Chicago Press, 1989.

———. *Homeward Bound: American Families in the Cold War Era.* Rev. ed. New York: Basic Books, 1999. Originally published 1988.

May, Lary. "Making the American Way: Moderne Theatres, Audiences, and the Film Industry, 1929–1945." *Prospects* 12 (October 1987): 89–124.

———, ed. *Recasting America: Culture and Politics in the Age of Cold War*. Chicago: University of Chicago Press, 1989.

McClary, Susan. "Terminal Prestige: The Case of Avant-Garde Music Composition." In *Keeping Score: Music, Disciplinarity, Culture*, edited by David Schwarz, Anahid Kassabian, and Lawrence Siegel, 54–72. Charlottesville: University Press of Virginia.

McConachie, Bruce A. "The 'Oriental' Musicals of Rodgers and Hammerstein and the U.S. War in Southeast Asia." *Theatre Journal* 46, no. 3 (1994): 385–98.

McCreless, Patrick. "Rethinking Contemporary Music Theory." In *Keeping Score: Music, Disciplinarity, Culture*, edited by David Schwarz, Anahid Kassabian, and Lawrence Siegel, 13–53. Charlottesville: University Press of Virginia, 1997.

McDaniel, Robb. "*Pleasantville* (Ross 1998)." *Film & History: An Interdisciplinary Journal of Film and Television Studies* 32, no. 1 (2002): 85–86.

Medovici, Leerom. "Mapping the Rebel Image: Postmodernism and the Masculinist Politics of Rock in the U.S.A." *Cultural Critique* 20 (Winter 1991–92): 153–88.

Mellers, Wilfrid. "The Avant-garde in America." *Proceedings of the Royal Musical Association* 90, no. 1 (1963): 1–13.

———. *Music in a New Found Land: Themes and Developments in the History of American Music*. New York: Alfred A. Knopf, 1964.

———. "*West Side Story* Revisited." In *Approaches to the American Musical*, edited by Robert Lawson-Peebles, 127–36. Exeter, UK: University of Exeter Press, 1996.

Merriam, Alan P., and Raymond W. Mack. "The Jazz Community." *Social Forces* 38, no. 3 (1960): 211–22.

Meyerowitz, Joanne. "Sex, Gender, and the Cold War Language of Reform." In *Rethinking Cold War Culture*, edited by Peter J. Kuznick and James Gilbert, 108–23. Washington, DC: Smithsonian Institution Press, 2001.

Michener, James A. *Tales of the South Pacific*. New York: Macmillan, 1949.

Miller, Arthur. *Timebends: A Life*. New York: Grove Press, 1973.

———. "Why I Wrote *The Crucible*." *New Yorker*, October 21, 1996, 158–59.

Miller, Douglas T., and Marion Nowak. *The Fifties: The Way We Really Were*. Garden City, NY: Doubleday, 1977.

Miller, Leta A. "ONCE and Again: The Evolution of a Legendary Festival." Liner note essay for *Music from the ONCE Festival: 1961–1966* (80567-2). New York: New World Records, 2003.

Miller, Leta E., and Frederic Lieberman. *Composing a World: Lou Harrison, Musical Wayfarer*. Urbana: University of Illinois Press, 1998.

Monson, Ingrid. *Freedom Sounds: Civil Rights Call Out to Jazz and Africa*. Oxford: Oxford University Press, 2007.

Mordden, Ethan. *Coming Up Roses: The Broadway Musical in the 1950s*. New York: Oxford University Press, 2000.

———. *Opera in the Twentieth Century: Sacred, Profane, Godot*. Oxford: Oxford University Press, 1978.

Most, Andrea. "'You've Got to Be Carefully Taught': The Politics of Race in Rodgers and Hammerstein's *South Pacific.*" *Theatre Journal* 52, no. 3 (2000): 307–37.

Mumford, Lewis. *Art and Technics.* New York: Oxford University Press, 1952.

———. *The City in History.* New York: Harcourt, Brace, and World, 1961.

Mustazza, Leonard, ed. *Frank Sinatra and Popular Culture: Essays on an American Icon.* Westport, CT: Praeger, 1998.

Nabokov, Nicolas. *Bagazh: Memoirs of a Russian Cosmopolitan.* New York: Atheneum, 1975.

Naremore, James. *More Than Night: Film Noir in Its Contexts.* 2nd ed. Berkeley: University of California Press, 2008.

Navasky, Victor S. *Naming Names.* New York: Penguin, 1980.

Negrón-Muntaner, Frances. "Feeling Pretty: *West Side Story* and Puerto Rican Identity Discourses." *Social Text* 18, no. 2 (2000): 83–106.

Ness, Richard R. "A Lotta Night Music: The Sound of Film Noir." *Cinema Journal* 47, no. 2 (2008): 52–73.

Nicholls, David, ed. *The Cambridge Companion to John Cage.* Cambridge: Cambridge University Press, 2002.

Nolan, Frederick W. *The Sound of Their Music: The Story of Rodgers and Hammerstein.* Milwaukee, WI: Applause Theatre & Cinema Books, 2002.

Nyman, Michael. *Experimental Music: Cage and Beyond.*2nd ed. Cambridge: Cambridge University Press, 1999.

Oakley, J. Ronald. *God's Country: America in the Fifties.* New York: Dembner Books, 1986.

Oja, Carol. *Making Music Modern: New York in the 1920s.* Oxford: Oxford University Press, 2000.

Owens, Thomas. "Bop." In the *New Grove Dictionary of American Music*, edited by H. Wiley Hitchcock and Stanley Sadie, 1: 260–61. London: Macmillan, 1986.

Partch, Harry. *Bitter Music: Collected Journals, Essays, Introductions, and Librettos.* Edited by Thomas McGeary. Urbana: University of Illinois Press, 1991.

———. *Genesis of a Music*, 2nd ed. New York: Da Capo Press, 1974.

Patton, Christopher W. "Discovering *The Tender Land*: A New Look at Aaron Copland's Opera." *American Music* 20, no. 3 (2002): 317–40.

Peiss, Kathy, ed. *Major Problems in the History of Sexuality.* Boston: Houghton Mifflin, 2002.

Peretti, Burton W. "Caliban Reheard: New Voices on Jazz and American Consciousness." *Popular Music* 13, no. 2 (1994): 151–64.

Perloff, Marjorie. "Watchman, Spy, and Dead Man: Jasper Johns, Frank O'Hara, John Cage and the 'Aesthetic of Indifference.'" *Modernism/modernity* 8, no. 2 (2001): 197–223.

Peyser, Joan. *Leonard Bernstein: A Biography.* New York: Beech Tree Press, 1987.

Phillips, Arthur A. "The Cultural Cringe." *Meanjin* 9, no. 4 (1950): 299–302.

Phillips, Lisa, ed. *Beat Culture and the New America: 1950–1965.* New York: Whitney Museum of American Art, 1995.

Pinch, Trevor, and Frank Trocco. *Analog Days: The Invention and Impact of the Moog Synthesizer*. Cambridge: Harvard University Press, 2002.

Plant, Rebecca Jo. *Mom: The Transformation of Motherhood in Modern America*. Chicago: University of Chicago Press, 2010.

Pleasants, Henry. "Schoenberg, Shostakovitch, Stokowski." *Modern Music* 18, no. 2 (1941): 120–21.

Pollack, Howard. *Aaron Copland: The Life and Work of an Uncommon Man*. Urbana: University of Illinois Press, 2000.

——. "The Dean of Gay American Composers." *American Music* 18, no. 1 (2000): 39–49.

Porter, Eric. "'Dizzy Atmosphere': The Challenge of Bebop." *American Music* 17, no. 4 (1999): 422–46.

Radano, Ronald. "Hot Fantasies: American Modernism and the Idea of Black Rhythm." In *Music and the Racial Imagination*, edited by Ronald Radano and Philip V. Bohlman, 459–80. Chicago: University of Chicago Press, 2000.

——. *Lying Up a Nation: Race and Black Music*. Chicago: University of Chicago Press, 2003.

Rainer, Yvonne. "Looking Myself in the Mouth." *October* 17 (Summer 1981): 65–71.

Redd, Lawrence N. "Rock! It's Still Rhythm and Blues." *Black Perspective in Music* 13, no. 1 (1985): 31–47.

Remmers, Hermann H., and Don Radler. *The American Teenager*. New York: Bobbs-Merrill, 1957.

RePass, Richard. "Opera Workshops in the United States." *Tempo*, new series, 27 (Spring 1953): 10–18.

Rex, Richard. "The Origin of *Beatnik*." *American Speech* 50, no. 14 (1975): 329–31.

Rich, Alan. *American Pioneers: Ives to Cage and Beyond*. London: Phaidon Press, 1995.

Rich, Maria F. "Opera USA—Perspective: The Popularization of Opera." *Opera Quarterly* 1, no. 2 (1983): 19–27.

Riesman, David, Nathan Glazer, and Reuel Denney. *The Lonely Crowd: A Study of the Changing American Character*. New Haven, CT: Yale University Press, 1950.

Roberts, Randy. "Wild Delinquents and Misunderstood Rebels." *Reviews in American History* 15, no. 2 (1987): 327–31.

Robinson, Suzanne. "'A Ping, Qualified by a Thud': Music Criticism in Manhattan and the Case of Cage (1943–58)." *Journal of the Society for American Music* 1, no. 1 (2007): 79–139.

Rockwell, John. *All American Music: Composition in the Late Twentieth Century*. New York: Alfred A. Knopf, 1983.

Rorem, Ned. *Music and People*. New York: George Braziller, 1968.

Rose, Brian G. *Television and the Performing Arts: A Handbook and Reference Guide to American Cultural Programming*. Westport, CT: Greenwood Press, 1986.

Rose, Elizabeth. *A Mother's Job: The History of Day Care, 1890–1960*. Oxford: Oxford University Press, 1998.

Rosen, Marjorie. *Popcorn Venus: Women, Movies, and the American Dream*. New York: Coward, McCann, and Geoghegan, 1973.

Rosenberg, Bernard. "Mass Culture in America." In Rosenberg and White, *Mass Culture*, 3–12.

———, and David Manning White, eds. *Mass Culture: The Popular Arts in America*. Glencoe, IL: Free Press, 1957.

Rosenberg, Harold. *Artworks & Packages*. Chicago: University of Chicago Press, 1969.

———. *The De-Definition of Art*. New York: Macmillan, 1972.

Ross, Alex. *The Rest Is Noise: Listening to the Twentieth Century*. New York: Farrar, Straus, and Giroux, 2007.

Ross, Andrew. *No Respect: Intellectuals & Popular Culture*. London: Routledge, 1989.

Roth, Moira. "The Aesthetics of Indifference." In Roth and Katz, *Difference/Indifference*, 33–47.

Roth, Moira, and Jonathan Katz, eds. *Difference/Indifference: Musings on Postmodernism, Marcel Duchamp and John Cage*. Amsterdam: G + B Arts International, 1998.

Sakharov, Andrei. *Memoirs*. Translated by Richard Lourie. New York: Knopf, 1990.

Salaam, Kalamu ya. "It Didn't Jes Grew: The Social and Aesthetic Significance of African American Music." *African American Review* 29, no. 2 (1995): 351–75.

Sanjek, Russell. "The War on Rock." In *DownBeat 17th Annual Yearbook / Music '72*, 16–19, 62–66. Chicago: Maher Publications, 1972.

Satin, Joseph Henry. *The 1950s: America's "Placid" Decade*. New York: Houghton Mifflin, 1960.

Saunders, Frances Stonor. *The Cultural Cold War: The CIA and the World of Arts and Letters*. New York: New Press, 1999.

Schatz, Thomas. *The Genius of the System: Hollywood Filmmaking in the Studio Era*. New York: Henry Holt, 1988.

Scheeder, Louis. Review of Ethan Mordden's *Coming Up Roses: The Broadway Musical of the 1950s*. *TDR: The Drama Review* 46, no. 1 (2002): 174–77.

Schmelz, Peter J. "Music in the Cold War." *Journal of Musicology* 26, no. 1 (2009): 3–15.

Schoenberg, Arnold. "Heart and Brain in Music." In *Style and Idea: Selected Writings of Arnold Schoenberg*, edited by Leonard Stein, 53–76. Berkeley: University of California Press, 1975.

Schonberg, Harold C. *Facing the Music*. New York: Summit Books, 1981.

Schrader, Barry. *Introduction to Electro-Acoustic Music*. Englewood Cliffs, NJ: Prentice-Hall, 1982.

Schulman, Bruce J. *The Seventies: The Great Shift in American Culture, Society, and Politics*. New York: Simon and Schuster, 2002.

Schwartz, Elliott. "Directions in American Compostion since the Second World War, Part I: 1945–1960." *Music Educators Journal* 61, no. 6 (1975): 28–39.

Schwartz, Richard A. "Family, Gender, and Society in 1950s American Fiction of Nuclear Apocalypse: *Shadow on the Hearth*, *Tomorrow!*, *The Last Day*, and *Alas, Babylon*." *Journal of American Culture* 29, no. 4 (2006): 406–24.

Secrest, Meryle. *Leonard Bernstein: A Life*. New York: Vintage Books, 1995.

Seldes, Barry. *Leonard Bernstein: The Political Life of an American Musician*. Berkeley: University of California Press, 2009.

Sessions, Roger. "Heinrich Schenker's Contribution." *Modern Music* 12, no. 4 (1935): 170–78.

Shaw, Arnold. "Sinatrauma: The Proclamation of a New Era." In *The Frank Sinatra Reader*, edited by Steven Petkov and Leonard Mustazza, 18–30. New York: Oxford University Press, 1995.

Sherry, Michael S. *Gay Artists in Modern American Culture: An Imagined Conspiracy*. Chapel Hill: University of North Carolina Press, 2007.

Shipton, Alyn. *Groovin' High: The Life of Dizzy Gillespie*. New York: Oxford University Press, 1999.

Shoemaker, Steve. "Norman Mailer's 'White Negro': Historical Myth or Mythical History?" *Twentieth-Century Literature* 37, no. 3 (1991): 343–60.

Shreffler, Anne C. "Ideologies of Serialism: Stravinsky's *Threni* and the Congress for Cultural Freedom." In *Music and the Aesthetics of Modernity*, edited by Karol Berger and Anthony Newcomb, 217–45. Cambridge: Harvard University Press, 2005.

———. "The Myth of Empirical Historiography: A Response to Joseph N. Straus." *Musical Quarterly* 84, no. 1 (2000): 30–39.

Shumway, David R. "Rock 'n' Roll Sound Tracks and the Production of Nostalgia." *Cinema Journal* 38, no. 2 (1999): 36–51.

Silverberg, Mark. *The New York School Poets and the Neo-Avant-Garde: Between Radical Art and Radical Chic*. Surrey, UK: Ashgate, 2013.

Small, Chistopher. *Musicking: The Meanings of Performing and Listening*. Hanover, NH: Wesleyan University Press, 1998.

Smith, Catherine Parsons, ed. *William Grant Still: A Study in Contradictions*. Berkeley: University of California Press, 2000.

Smith, James F. "Bobby Sox and Blue Suede Shoes: Frank Sinatra and Elvis Presley as Teen Idols." In Mustazza, *Frank Sinatra and Popular Culture*, 50–68.

Sobchack, Vivian. *Screening Space: The American Science Fiction Film*. New York: Ungar, 1993.

Sontag, Susan. "The Aesthetics of Silence." In *Styles of Radical Will*, 3–34. New York: Delta, 1969.

———. "The Imagination of Disaster." In *Against Interpretation and Other Essays*, 209–225. New York: Farrar, Straus, and Giroux, 1966.

Stearns, Marshall. *The Story of Jazz*. New York: Oxford University Press, 1958.

Stone, I. F. *The Haunted Fifties, 1953–1963: A Nonconformist History of Our Times*. Boston: Little, Brown, 1969.

Straus, Joseph N. "The Myth of Serial 'Tyranny' in the 1950s and 1960s." *Musical Quarterly* 83, no. 3 (1999): 301–343.

———. "A Revisionist History of Twelve-Tone Serialism in American Music." *Journal of the Society for American Music* 2, no. 3 (2008): 355–95.

———. *Twelve-Tone Music in America*. New York: Cambridge University Press, 2009.

Swartz, Anne, and Milton Babbitt. "Milton Babbitt on Milton Babbitt." *American Music* 3, no. 4 (1985): 467–73.

Szatmary, David R. *Rockin' in Time; A Social History of Rock-and-Roll*. 5th ed. Upper Saddle River, NJ: Prentice-Hall, 2004.

Taruskin, Richard. "Afterword: *Nicht blutbeflecht?*" *Journal of Musicology* 26, no. 2 (2009): 274–84.

———. "Nabokov, Nicolas." In *The New Grove Dictionary of Opera*, edited by Stanley Sadie, 3: 543. London: Macmillan, 1992.

———. *The Oxford History of Western Music*. Oxford: Oxford University Press, 2010.

Telotte, J. P. *Science Fiction Film*. Cambridge, UK: Cambridge University Press, 2001.

Thelin, John R. *A History of American Higher Education*. Baltimore: Johns Hopkins University Press, 2004.

Thomson, Virgil. *American Music since 1910*. New York: Holt, Rinehart, and Winston, 1970.

———. *Music Reviewed: 1940–1954*. New York: Random House, 1967.

———. *The State of Music*. New York: Random House, 1939.

———. *Virgil Thomson*. New York: Alfred A. Knopf, 1966.

———. *A Virgil Thomson Reader*. Edited by John Rockwell. Boston: Houghton Mifflin, 1981.

Tibbetts, John C. *Composers in the Movies*. New Haven, CT: Yale University Press, 2005.

Tischler, Barbara L. *An American Music: The Search for an American Musical Identity*. Oxford: Oxford University Press, 1986.

Tomkins, Calvin. *The Bride and the Bachelors: Five Masters of the Avant-Garde*. New York: Viking, 1965.

———. *Off the Wall: Robert Rauschenberg and the Art World of Our Time*. New York: Penguin Books, 1980.

Townsend, Peter. *Jazz in American Culture*. Edinburgh, UK: Edinburgh University Press, 2000.

Tucker, Bruce. "'Tell Tchaikovsky the News': Postmodernism, Popular Culture, and the Emergence of Rock 'n' Roll." *Black Music Research Journal* 9, no. 2 (1989): 271–95.

Van Elteren, Mel. "The Subculture of the Beats: A Sociological Revisit." *Journal of American Culture* 22, no. 3 (1999): 71–99.

Von Eschen, Penny M. *Race against Empire: Black Americans and Anticolonialism, 1937–57*. Ithaca, NY: Cornell University Press, 1997.

———. *Satchmo Blows Up the World: Jazz Ambassadors Play the Cold War*. Cambridge: Harvard University Press, 2004.

Walser, Robert, ed. *Keeping Time: Readings in Jazz History*. New York: Oxford University Press, 1999.

Walsh, David, and Len Platt. *Musical Theater and American Culture*. Westport, CT: Praeger, 2003.

Weinberg, George. *Society and the Healthy Homosexual*. New York: St. Martin's Press, 1972.

Weiss, Piero, and Richard Taruskin, eds. *Music in the Western World: A History in Documents*. New York: Schirmer, 1984.

Wellens, Ian. *Music on the Frontline: Nicolas Nabokov's Struggle against Communism and Middlebrow Culture*. Aldershot, UK: Ashgate, 2002.

Wenke, Joseph. *Mailer's America*. Hanover, NH: University Press of New England, 1987.

Westrup, J. A., and F. L. Harrison. "Bop (bebop, rebop)." In *The New College Encyclopedia of Music*. Revised by Conrad Wilson. New York: W. W. Norton, 1976.

Whaley, Preston, Jr. *Blows Like a Horn: Beat Writing, Jazz, Style, and Markets in the Transformation of U.S. Culture*. Cambridge: Harvard University Press, 2004.

Whitfield, Stephen J. "How the Fifties Became the Sixties." *Historically Speaking* (January–February, 2008): 8–11.

Wicke, Peter. *Rock Music: Culture, Aesthetics, and Sociology*. Cambridge: Cambridge University Press, 1990. Originally published as *Rockmusik: zur Ästhetik und Soziologie eines Massenmediums* (Leipzig: Verlag Philipp Reclam, 1987).

Wiener, Norbert. *The Human Use of Human Beings: Cybernetics and Society*. New York: Da Capo Press, 1954.

Wierzbicki, James. *Elliott Carter*. Urbana: University of Illinois Press, 2011.

———. *Louis and Bebe Barron's* Forbidden Planet: *A Film Score Guide*. Lanham, MD: Scarecrow Press, 2005.

Wilson, Sloan. *The Man in the Gray Flannel Suit*. New York: Simon and Schuster, 1955.

Wolf, Stacy. *Changed for Good: A Feminist History of the Broadway Musical*. New York: Oxford University Press, 2011.

———. *A Problem Like Maria: Gender and Sexuality in the American Musical*. Ann Arbor: University of Michigan Press, 2002.

Wolff, Christian. "Experimental Music around 1950 and Some Consequences and Causes (Socio-Political and Musical)." *American Music* 27, no. 4 (2009): 424–40.

Wood, Paul Wood, ed. *Varieties of Modernism*. New Haven, CT: Yale University Press, 2004.

Work, John Wesley (J.W.W.) "Bop." In *The Harvard Dictionary of Music*, 2nd ed. Edited by Willi Apel. Cambridge: Belknap Press of Harvard University Press, 1969.

Wright, Bradford W. *Comic Book Nation: The Transformation of Youth Culture in America*. Baltimore: Johns Hopkins University Press, 2001.

Yaffé, John. "An Interview with Composer Earle Brown." *Contemporary Music Review* 26, nos. 3–4 (2007): 289–310.

Index

JAMES WIERZBICKI teaches musicology at the University of Sydney. His books include *Film Music: A History* and *Elliott Carter.*

The University of Illinois Press
is a founding member of the
Association of American University Presses.

University of Illinois Press
1325 South Oak Street
Champaign, IL 61820-6903
www.press.uillinois.edu